*Decisions about
the Teaching
of English*

Decisions about the Teaching of English

JOHN S. SIMMONS
Florida State University

ROBERT E. SHAFER
Arizona State University

GAIL B. WEST
Florida Technological University

Allyn and Bacon, Inc. Boston · London · Sydney

Library of Congress Cataloging in Publication Data

Simmons, John Stephen.
    Decisions about the teaching of English.

    Includes bibliographical references and index.
    1. English language—Study and teaching (Second-
ary) 2. English philology—Study and teaching
(Secondary) I. Shafer, Robert Eugene, date-
joint author. II. West, Gail B., date-
joint author. III. Title.
LB1631.S498   808'.007'12   75-25697

ISBN 0-205-04542-1

Contents

Preface   vii

Part I   What Is It All About?

CHAPTER 1   What We're Teaching and Its Familiar
             Shapes   3
CHAPTER 2   New Developments: Systems, Electives, and
             the Open Classroom   18
CHAPTER 3   On Knowing Those Who Learn in Your
             English Class   37

Part II   How Do We Deal with Imaginative Materials?

CHAPTER 4   Introducing Imaginative Literature   49
CHAPTER 5   Developing and Reinforcing the Study of
             Imaginative Literature   72

Part III   What Do We See in the Language We Use?

CHAPTER 6   A First Look at Elements of Our Language   109
CHAPTER 7   Pointing Out How Meaning Evolves   124

Part IV   *When and How Do We Compose in Communication?*

CHAPTER 8   Establishing Purposes for Communicating   181
CHAPTER 9   How to Put It Together   201
CHAPTER 10   Building Components of Communication   222

Part V   *How Do We Use Media in Communication?*

CHAPTER 11   Introducing Media Productions by Students   235
CHAPTER 12   Films: What They Are and How They Are
          Made   245

Part VI   *Where Is the Teacher in All of This?*

CHAPTER 13   Style: Strategy in Classroom Leadership   261
CHAPTER 14   Organizing What We Are to Teach   284

Index   305

Preface

As you prepare to teach English in secondary schools and take a look at what's happening in the field today, you may well come face to face with several major important decisions. Pursuant to those decisions we have tried to look both backward and forward. We have paid close attention to the arguments of those who would present English as it has been, and we have also heeded those who would junk all of what has been and would make the English of the future a totally new entity. The fundamental outlook to be found in this book should indicate that we see some merit in both points of view.

We can't buy the argument that this position represents a cop-out on our part. To us, the most compatible statement about teaching English to adolescents in the 1970s and following is one that would voice support for the practical, enduring aspects of traditional instruction but would also propose use of those innovative approaches that are not excessive, trivial, or faddish.

This book is directed primarily at those who have not yet taught English and who aspire to do so. It also can be helpful to those somewhat inexperienced teachers who feel the need for suggestions aimed at improving their early attempts at instruction. It may be of some value to those experienced teachers who feel themselves going "stale" in their efforts and who desire to review some innovative approaches.

As you look at several key dimensions of this field of study, you can't help but feel the need for serious decision making. In reviewing expression of attitudes on the study of the world of imagination, you will find those articulate spokesmen who would establish some careful, firmly set guidelines. Students who would approach this world should do so through the medium of silent reading. They should read from a distinctly prescriptive list of selections, and they should practice this reading along pretty narrow lines—major figures in literary scholarship usually refer to it as close text analysis or (if you really want to go academic) *explication du text*.

Another viewpoint, however, comes from those who feel that reading as a means of learning most anything is generally obsolete and, more particularly, those who are concerned with imaginative experience. For them, serious consideration of such experience will be most intensely significant, most familiar, and will have the most lasting impact when gained primarily, if not solely, through the nonprint media, preferably electronic. Beyond that, these spokesmen for the "forward" view of considering imaginative experiences would abolish the reading by adolescents of materials written in the past and would offer in their place those works completed since World War II, more preferably since the dawn of the Space Age, and most preferably since last week.

Look at current commentary on what to do about studying the vehicle for communication among English speaking people, and you will encounter more of the same feeling. Some would have adolescents study language in the abstract, as a system to be fully understood by the learner. Thus the committing to memory of rules, processes, and formulae become activities of great importance in coming to grips with the underlying structure of English. Along with this goes careful assignment of levels of preference in English usage. Certain patterns of choice in usage need to be comprehended by the learner, who then should be made aware in which situations each pattern applies.

Others perceive this vehicle as a human, vastly inconsistent thing. For them, studying it really means studying people. More precisely, they would have students look closely at the language of the immediate human environment, both as used by people in actual communication situations and as produced through the print and electronic media, which affects their daily lives. Concern with structures and principles, or with memorizing anything, are bad news to these folks, and most books about language, cherished by their opponents, would be quickly tossed out.

When you look at arguments on the issue of how to compose in communication, you must inevitably perceive the need for further decision making. There are those who are very concerned about the *form* of composed discourse, oral or (especially) written. They advocate establishing a definite set of rules for the presenting of a coherent statement, arguing that the *form* of discourse must be clearly understood by all parties if that *discourse* is to be understood. All else is chaos. They are confronted by those who feel that since you don't write writing (or speak speaking), the *content* of discourse is of primary importance. The latter group would have students concentrate on what they will write about and, more important, on finding out why they need to do it. Form is a matter of considerably less importance.

The above examples of decision making in English teaching really point to a basic, three-headed question about the whole matter that to us is crucial. We pose that teaching English is teaching *something to someone for some reason(s)*. The questions then come out: *what, to whom,* and *why?* The matters we have just brought up have most to do with *what,* but they are always asked in relation to *whom* and *why.* Therefore, let's examine these teaching conflicts a bit further.

You must decide, in starting at any level, which you will emphasize—the skills of communication or the teaching of a particular content; i.e., a package of information and ideas. If your preference is the latter, then you obviously need to decide which package is English (literary history, great ideas, the development of modern English, forms of discourse, and the like) and how you will mete out this lore. If you opt in favor of communication skills, you have an even more pressing set of choices: which skills you will *presume* your students to have, which you will *review*, and which you will need to build from scratch. Beneath the basic issue of content vs. skills, comes the series of subissues alluded to above. These are questions you must answer in order to state your objectives, plan your time, and select your materials. In this book we'll try to help you.

To assist you in making decisions about some specific aspects of your task, we have focused attention on six major topics on teaching English. We first present you with an overview of the total curriculum: where English is at in the final quarter of this century. Then, we turn to dealing with imaginative materials—which ones to consider teaching, when, and how. Next, we ask you to look at language as a commodity. We investigate what it is to young people and how that view can be refined and developed.

Having considered what our language *is*, we turn to a laying out of ideas as to how to produce it in composed form. We follow this by an introduction of means of developing ideas, information, and images through audiovisual means as well as through the printed word. We conclude with discussions of how you enter the world of English teaching as a person, how you extend your personality into the classroom as a leader, and how you manipulate the vast content of English to meet the needs of your students.

What we have described adds up to decisions to be made. That's the way we see it, and we will present our ideas in the light of this belief. We have no "cookbook" solutions to *prescribe* during the discussion that follows. Rather, we have some "if-then" propositions about teaching English. We offer them because in our teaching careers, we've tried hard to listen to the arguments that come from all sides of the spectrum. We ask you to recognize these arguments for what they are. Consider them in the light of your own background and interests, and plan your teaching in the light of the results of this deliberation. Going that route should make teaching English to adolescents a somewhat more reasonable and mutually satisfying task for you to handle.

JOHN S. SIMMONS
ROBERT E. SHAFER
GAIL B. WEST

Part I
What Is It All About?

Chapter 1

What We're Teaching and Its Familiar Shapes

INTRODUCTION

Let us begin with a proposition: the verb "teaching" takes a direct object. More accurately, it takes two: "what" and "whom." With that bit of traditional grammar, we want to state a premise to guide you through this book. Anyone who starts to teach a particular subject, such as English, to a group of human beings, must first decide *what* part or parts of that subject he will teach and *to whom* he will teach it. In the real world, the latter part of this statement is not accurate. In the overwhelming majority of schools the decision as to whom you will teach is in the hands of counselors and administrators; thus, the teacher must actually decide on what to do *in the light of* the students he is assigned to teach. These decisions, concerning what and to whom, call for a considerable amount of reflection, especially as they relate to the teaching of English. In considering the answers that others have proposed and in working out satisfactory answers for yourself, you will be developing a basic philosophy or rationale for the teaching of English, which is an *absolute necessity* if you are to be an effective teacher. We think that you should develop such a philosophy, and that is a primary goal that we, as authors, have attempted to help you reach through this book.

The fundamental question, "What is English?", is one that has been debated for a considerable length of time. There continues to be much disagreement about the answer, enough so that perhaps there will never be one universally satisfactory definition of English as a school subject. We offer you a number of proposals for a definition of English that have come to English teachers from various quarters. For one thing, there are a variety of ways of looking at the question of "what." We hope to help you develop some criteria for selecting what particular definition of English will best fit your own philosophy, and what kinds of choices you will have to make in order to bring that philosophy alive in any classroom in which you may find yourself. Certainly whatever you decide the "what" of English will be, will very much affect what you do with your students in the classroom. In addition, your assessment of the students you are to teach will very much affect what you do. These students represent the great diversity of adolescents who inhabit English classrooms in American schools today. In many ways they represent a decidedly different "youth culture" than the one you yourself passed through. They represent a great number of backgrounds, interests, expectations, and ability levels. Since English is a required subject for most of them, your view of it as a school subject and your assessment of your students' abilities, interests, and attitudes will very much affect what you will actually do as a teacher and what will happen to them as students.

There is general agreement that the study of English involves the manipulation of symbols. It follows that the development of students' abilities to deal creatively and effectively with symbols in all areas of communication is essential to the study of English.

Two other questions about English teaching are important for your consideration. These are concerned with the "why" and the "how."

WHY?

The "why" question deserves a close look early in the game, and from two perspectives. First, the questions "Why teach English at all?" and "What good is English?" are certainly not new to many American adolescents, who are plowing manfully through a multiyear wilderness of course offerings called English, Communication, Language Arts, or Humanities. While these questions relate closely to the one posed earlier, the need for a *rationale* has never been more prevalent than in the present era of "accountability" in English teaching, when English as a school subject is undergoing many changes. The questions of "what" and "why" are both very much related to the matter of basic aims and objectives for the English program. This subject of objectives is a particularly hot one at the moment, and will probably remain so throughout the 1970s. We do not choose either to defend or attack any one way of deciding on basic aims and objectives for English. Instead, we would like to share with you a number of different models for English, along with proposals for aims and objectives. At present, English is being very much affected by "behavioristic" psychology, as applied to the development of behavioral objectives and performance criteria. We do not intend to launch an all-out attack on behavioral objectives, nor do we feel that they represent a panacea for English teaching. We would like to present some ideas about the efficacy of behavioral objectives as they relate to English as a school subject, in order to help you better evaluate where "behaviorism" can be applied to the development of objectives for English, and also where other philosophies and psychologies can be applied. We would also like to show you how to write a behavioral objective in case anyone—your principal, for example—ever asks you to do so.

We hope that you will then be able to make your own judgments as to what areas of psychology apply effectively in developing an English program for the students in any of your classrooms. For the moment, let us divide objectives into: 1) *behavioral* objectives, which focus on what a student can do, which is measured by some sort of observation of his overt behavior after a particular unit of instruction, and 2) *humanistic* objectives, which can be stated more generally and which relate to the total role of the humanities in education, and which in most cases will allow him more of a choice in his own learning. Two basic questions for you to keep in mind and for which you will need to formulate answers in your own philosophy of English teaching, are the following: Can we erect common objectives for instruction in a class that contains widely different individuals? How can we tell when these objectives have been met by students? In other words, once we have decided there are legitimate reasons to teach the "what" of English, then we need to ask what kinds of outcomes we hope for after our students have learned it.

HOW?

Another basic question, that of "how," is essential in any book that purports to deal with methods of teaching. Unfortunately, it is not possible to consider matters relating to the "how" of teaching anything until the "what" and the "why" of the matter have been decided. Too often, we have seen students preparing to be teachers, and teachers who have been teaching for a number of years, become concerned only with the "how," neglecting the development of a basic philosophy of teaching the subject; if they had considered their philosophy of teaching more carefully in the first place, many of the "how" questions that plagued them would probably have been answered. *Such practical matters as how to organize and manage a classroom, how to develop interest in the subject, how to develop interest in a particular topic or unit, and how to deal with so-called "discipline problems" in English classrooms cannot be answered satisfactorily unless the "what" and the "why" have first been satisfactorily understood and decided.* Therefore, we hope that you will look carefully at the various definitions of English, and either choose the one that seems most appropriate to the students you are teaching, or develop one of your own that meets your own particular philosophy. Also, we hope that you will become familiar with a variety of ways to assess your students' interests, attitudes, and learning abilities, so that you will be able to decide how best to work with them. Only then will you be able to decide on the *manner* in which English will be taught in your classroom and what *methods* and *materials* you will use.

The decisions you make about the "how" of your teaching will be based on factors of style and method. In choosing a particular style, you will need to decide how you will present yourself to your students. In choosing a particular method, you will need to consider the appropriate way in which you will manipulate the various materials and activities, all of which—taken together—will represent your brand of English for that particular occasion.

WHAT IS ENGLISH?

Perhaps you have assumed that the answer to this question is an obvious one. You yourself have experienced the subject English from your very earliest days in school through a variety of undergraduate and graduate English classes. Many college and university students who have taken a variety of English courses consider English as made up largely of British and American literature, with some courses in writing and an occasional course in the study of the English language thrown in. Although some English departments are changing their English major requirements, the concept of English that many teachers carry from college and university studies into junior and senior high schools is a very different one from the English actually present in the schools. English as a subject of study in American schools has been and is being affected by a variety of social, philosophical, and historical factors that have been bringing sweeping changes over the past several decades. The history of the teaching of English is an interesting study in itself but there is neither time nor space here for considering it extensively. Suffice it to say that because of the forces affecting the school and its programs, you will probably find that English is different indeed from what it was when you were a student, or from what your study of it in a college or university English class or department may have led you to believe.

A variety of philosophical points of view exist about English in the schools. Some of these are presented here, not with the hope that you will be converted to any one of them but with the expectation that they will stimulate your thinking about English as a school subject as you develop your own philosophy of teaching.

ENGLISH AS A NON-SUBJECT

The first definition of English is a non-definition. Some authorities are proposing that English be abolished as a school subject altogether. Mary Beaneu has put it as follows:

> Let me utter the outrageous idea immediately: abolish English as a subject. There. It's out. And let me follow it with this addendum: replace it with *nothing*. Just let the poor, sick thing quietly slip into the night to find its dying place. And let it die.
>
> I predict no one will come to the funeral, either. Not even the English teachers. They'll be scurrying nervously for new certifications . . .
>
> English as a subject is dead. Ninety percent of our students killed it decades ago, but it has been denied interment by a tough band of necrophiliacs called English teachers. They have finally failed. They know now what their students knew decades ago . . .
>
> Right now, English is defined as whatever you do in an English class just as long as you can get away with it. And while it may sound liberating, it's more likely to be exasperating because if it leans toward social issues, a good history course can do it better. If it leans toward human relations, a good psychology course will be more appropriate. If movies, well, why not a film course? If contemporary culture, why not a course in sociology? And if TV is your bag, why not an elective in the mass media?
>
> But English? What's that? Try calling it "attention to basics," and you'll be turned off quicker than a leaky faucet in a desert.
>
> It's just no use. Pack it in . . .
>
> The teacher is so lineal! The student so allatonce! So involved! A blast of music will do for them all they need, all anyone needs. Soul food, not words. What is this thing called sequence of ideas? This is no age of ideas; this is the age of Aquarius![1]

The writer of the above comment may have been serious or semi-serious in her intent. She may have been calling for changes in English as a subject in response to various kinds of developments outside the English classroom, e.g., the influence of TV on adolescents, or she may have been disillusioned by the effects of behavioral objectives and other manifestations of systems approaches currently being applied to English in the schools. She may actually believe that English should be abandoned as a school subject. If this is her real position, we take violent exception. Why? We simply don't believe that English should be abandoned. English may well be more important today than it was when it first appeared in the school curriculum in the early days of the nineteenth

---

[1] Mary H. Beaneu, "Delete English Courses from the Curriculum," *English Journal* 59, No. 6 (Sept. 1970): 798–799. Copyright 1970 by National Council of Teachers of English, Champaign, Ill.

century. Everything in this book from now on will be an attempt to demonstrate a variety of ways in which the teaching of English can be improved. English needs improvement, not abandonment. We will discuss a number of proposals for improving English that have been recommended to English teachers from various sources. All of these proposals have their own built-in value systems, which in most cases are easily recognizable. We hope you will consider them carefully and develop your own philosophy of teaching English and your own views about the nature of English as a school subject. Here are some of our views:

1. Growth in language power involves growth in the ability to understand oneself and others and to develop integration of self.
2. Growth in language contributes directly to the development of both intellect and feeling in all human beings.
3. Growth in language contributes directly to the ability to make evaluations of human events and to affect social change.
4. Growth in language power involves growth in symbolic awareness that allows an individual to participate in art, music, literature, film, and all other areas of human symbolic experience.
5. Through language we develop a system of values as well as the ability to test our values against those of others, and to anticipate the consequences of holding a certain set of values.
6. Language lies at the heart of man's experience as a human being and, to a considerable extent, determines his humanity. Learning the uses of language, then, should be at the heart of the curriculum.

If these or any other reasons for keeping English in the school program are to be realized, then English teachers need specific, practical ways to develop the potentials for symbolic awareness and growth that lie within each student. That is precisely our reason for writing this book.

There are many ways to teach English and many models of English as a school subject. Which model is the best one and which are the best ways to teach? Here are several models of English. How and what you will teach if you subscribe to a particular model, you will probably be able to determine once you have examined all the models—but just to make sure you know how we feel, we make some comments about each model as we go along. We hope you will make up your own mind, develop your own model, your own philosophy, and your own ways to help students learn. That's our goal. That's what we really believe will get you "hooked" on teaching. Here's the first model:

The Tripod

In 1958, representatives of the National Council of Teachers of English, the Modern Language Association of America, the American Studies Association, and the College English Association gathered together and, after a series of conferences, published "The Basic Issues in the Teaching of English." The key word in these basic issues was "sequential." The conference proposed thirty-five issues to the profession as questions with the "only vested interest . . . the development of an increasingly higher degree of literacy in young American citizens." The first issue presented was "What is English?" The words that appear over and over again in the statement of issues proposing an answer to the "what" of English are the words "sequential" and "cumulative." The complete text of Basic Issue Number Two is typical:

> *Can basic programs in English be devised that are sequential and cumulative from the kindergarten through the graduate school?* Can agreement be reached upon a body of knowledge and a set of skills as standard at certain points in the curriculum, making due allowances for flexibility of planning, individual differences, and patterns of growth? This issue seems crucial to this entire document and to any serious approach to the problem. Unless we can find an answer to it, we must resign ourselves to an unhappy future in which the present curricular disorder persists and the whole liberal discipline of English continues to disintegrate and lose its character . . .[2]

Stone's hypothesis created considerable interest among English teachers throughout the country, and perhaps the Basic Issues Conference and his proposal for English that grew out of it might have been just one more event in a series of many interesting ones on the educational scene of the 1950s, if it had not happened at a time when a national survey of the teaching of English was undertaken and published by the National Council of Teachers of English. This national survey dealt with both the inadequacies of English programs, including teacher preparation, and the lack of basic research into teacher preparation in such areas as literary scholarship, linguistic study, and rhetoric, and also "the lack of basic research into the problems of English teaching." The document stressed the "complex incremental nature of the subject" and called for the "sound articulation of English programs." English as a school subject was defined as a large problem area, subject to certain unfortunate pressures:

> The ultimate result of all these pressures—the great heterogeneity of pupils, the increasing complexity of our society, the development of modern media communication, the proliferation of responsibilities of the English teacher—is that English is in danger of losing still more of its central focus.[3]

More than did any other single piece of evidence concerning the teaching of English, this national survey influenced the Congress of the United States to support a massive effort into research and curriculum development in the teaching of English throughout most of the 1960s. More than $7,700,000 were

---

[2] "The Basic Issues in the Teaching of English," George Winchester Stone (editor), *Publication of the Modern Language Association* (Sept. 1959): 7.

[3] *Ibid.*

spent in developing more than twenty English curriculum centers located in colleges and universities throughout the country. Additional federal funds were spent on summer and year-round institutes for the "retraining" of English teachers during the 1960s. A variety of conferences on research in English and the teaching of English were also held. From these conferences and these curriculum centers came further refinements of the tripod model for English programs.[4]

The unprecedented input of federal funds gave rise to considerable ferment in the field of English teaching. Old arguments that had gone on in teachers' rooms began anew as teachers attended summer institutes and returned with new knowledge of rhetoric and linguistics, literary criticism, and methods of teaching. Research problems long since discarded for lack of funds to investigate them began to be discussed once again in conferences devoted to the teaching of English.[5] There was much discussion of the tripod or tri-component curriculum of literature, language, and composition as a viable answer to the "what" of English. The Commission on the English Curriculum of the National Council of Teachers of English, under the direction of Alexander Frazier, attempted to delineate some of the questions arising in the minds of many English teachers about the efficacy of the newly proposed model. Their publication, *Ends and Issues—1965–1966*, contains a summary of many of the points being debated at that time concerning the model.[6] In a preface to the statement, Alexander Frazier, chairman of the Commission on the English Curriculum at the time, wrote as follows:

> . . . we are witnessing throughout education the rebirth of the concept of mastery. For more than a generation, we have acted on the assumption that not everybody can learn what we teach, at least not the first time around. New developments in associationist psychology coupled with a new zeal for analyzing more minutely what should be learned are offering us materials and techniques of teaching that assume failure-free learning for all. Simultaneously, we have an equally stimulating revival of interest in the discovery method of learning, tied in with a conception of organizing the curriculum not in bits and pieces but in larger wholes around basic ideas that compose the structure of a discipline.[7]

In 1968, the Commission on the English Curriculum published a *Summary Progress Report of the English Curriculum Study and Demonstration Centers*,

---

[4] "The National Interest and the Teaching of English," National Council of Teachers of English (Champaign, Ill., 1961), p. 26.

[5] An extensive discussion of the relationship between the Basic Issues Conference and the application of the sequential and cumulative model to English curriculum centers can be found in Robert E. Shafer, "The Attempt to Make English a Discipline," *The High School Journal* 52, No. 7 (April 1969): 336–351.

[6] *Research Design in the Teaching of English: Proceedings of the San Francisco Conference*, National Council of Teachers of English (Champaign, Ill., 1964).

[7] *Ends and Issues—1965–1966*, Commission on the English Curriculum, National Council of Teachers of English (Champaign, Ill., 1966).

revealing progress of the work of various federally funded projects.[8]   The report demonstrated that the "what" of English had been perceived as "sequential and cumulative" by a number of the national curriculum demonstration and study centers.   Although the "tripod model" was initially an extremely popular one among the curriculum centers and among some university teachers, and (as was shown by a further study of the Commission on the English Curriculum) although it influenced a number of local school districts, it was by no means the only model either produced by the national centers or proposed from other sources, nor has its popularity persisted.[9]

In some cases the tripod has persisted in modified form, e.g., in some schools students take composition for one semester, literature for another, and language for still another.   English elective or selective programs all usually contain special courses in these areas.   But the basic problem with the tripod as a model for English seems to be its rigid structure.   The idea of setting up small increments of subject matter to be learned in sequence seems to place too many restrictions on the involvement of students in their own learning and in the selection of texts, media of instruction, and appropriate content.   As one English teacher stated after hearing about the tripod model for the first time, "I never saw a 'sequential, incremental' child."

LANGUAGE AS THE "WHAT" OF ENGLISH

The scientific study of language, known as *linguistics,* made great strides in its development throughout the twentieth century and many American linguists in the 1930s—and increasingly in the 1940s, 1950s, and 1960s—began to devote their energies to the teaching of English in the schools.   It was perhaps to be expected that their work would greatly influence the work of the various curriculum study centers and demonstration centers in English as well as local school curriculum projects.   One of the curriculum study centers (located at the University of Minnesota) proposed that the "what" of English should be almost exclusively centered in the study of the English language.   Linguists may well have proposed that the study of language have a much more central place in the English curriculum than previously, partly in response to the development of the tripod model wherein language was proposed as only one of three components of the subject.   In looking at the relationships between the three components, many linguists felt that the centrality of language was obvious.

---

[8] *Summary Progress Report of the English Curriculum Study and Demonstration Centers,* National Council of Teachers of English (Champaign, Ill., 1968).

[9] *English Curriculum Development Projects; A Representative Collection,* Commission on the English Curriculum, National Council of Teachers of English (Champaign, Ill., 1968).

Since both composition and its end product, literary expression, involve manipulation of the symbols of language, it seemed to some linguists that the study of *style* should be central to the English program. English, they argued, should concern itself with the understanding, manipulation, and appreciation of language. Reading, writing, and literature should be viewed as functions of the development of language power in human beings and should be given a central position in the English program beginning with the earliest years of schooling. At first, it appeared that the linguists were recommending the study of the end products of their own research as a specific subject matter. Indeed, a number of the curriculum centers following the tripod model set up specific units of study, e.g., transformational grammar, American dialects, and semantics.

As more attention began to be focused by linguists and psychologists on the ways in which human beings acquire language in the first place, it became clear that what was most important for language teaching were the implications of their research into language acquisition—*not* the new terminology they used in transformational grammar, nor even the perennial question of which of the new grammars were best to teach in school or when grammar was best taught.

The implications of recent research into language acquisition have changed the older concept of a language model as a viable focus for English. The change, which is fully explored and extended in Section III of this book, is to a languaging model for English.

THE LANGUAGING MODEL

What we have learned from the linguists studying the acquisition of articulate language in human beings is that articulate language makes its appearance in most human beings after a phase of spontaneous vocalization (common to children of all cultures between six and eleven months). After the age of two years, children begin to use short complete sentences followed gradually by grammatical structures. One especially significant finding seems to indicate that the child not only imitates adults but, even during this early period, brings to bear his own world of experience, his own meanings, and his own interpretation of what he sees and hears to the process of acquiring symbols to represent his own meanings. The child then actually participates creatively in the learning of his own language. Research further indicates that a genuine communication situation must exist in order for a child to learn. That is, the child must participate actively in the act of communication. He cannot be merely a passive listener.

Usually the child's first adult language models are the parents, especially the mother. It is here that the adult-child dialogue which will ultimately result in the learning of articulate language begins. Andrew Wilkinson of the University of Birmingham has stated that "the most fundamental fact in language development seems to be the nature of the adult-child dialogue" and notes further that "when language development is poor it is because there has been either no language teaching going on, or the wrong sort; when it is good there has been the right sort."[10]

Although much of the research in language acquisition has centered on the language learning of preschool children, some research points clearly to what many classroom teachers have known for many years simply by observing the growth of their own students in language power—competence in syntactics and semantics extends throughout the years of schooling. Since one develops language competence in all its various forms by being in situations that call for language, what we as teachers do is a crucial matter. Since a major means of developing cognition *within limits* seems to be through the development of language power, the languaging model—that is, what actually happens in the adult-child dialogue—is very important. Once again, research findings to date seem to show that language develops when teachers extend the language of the child in ways such as the following:

1. Requesting further information
2. Requesting further accuracy
3. Requesting explanations and explorations of feelings
4. Requesting explanations of processes and relationships

Extensive developments of these and other aspects of the languaging model are to be found in Parts II and III of this book, especially in those chapters dealing with language, media, and the composition process.

THE LITERARY EXPERIENCE AS MODEL

One of the persisting models for the "what" of English is the study of literature. Few other aspects of the English curriculum have received as much discussion over the past three decades as the teaching of literature—both as to its relevance for students in our times and as to various ways it may be taught successfully if taught at all. The majority of the courses you have taken in your English major undoubtedly have been in literature, and if you are a typical English major you undoubtedly like to read. Your own interests may make you singularly unprepared for the reactions of many of your students when you first attempt to persuade them that there is some value in reading literature. In his NCTE distinguished lecture of 1967, J. N. Hook paraphrased a scene from Dickens's *Christmas Carol* in which Scrooge's nephew comes to the office to invite him to Christmas dinner and Scrooge proceeds to attack the whole idea of Christmas

---

[10] Andrew Wilkinson, *The Foundations of Language* (New York: Oxford University Press, 1971), p. 104.

on the grounds of practicality and usefulness. In Hook's parody, Scrooge is a "most recalcitrant student" and his nephew is a "kindly teacher" of *literature* or *reading*:

"Happy reading, student!" cried a cheerful voice.

It was the voice of the teacher, who came upon him so quickly that this was the first intimation he had of his approach.

"Bah!" said the student. "Humbug!"

"Reading and literature a humbug, student! You don't mean that, I'm sure."

"I do," said the student. "Literature! What right have you to gloat about literature? What has literature ever done for you? You're poor enough."

"Come, then," said the teacher gayly. "What right have you to condemn it? Are you so rich without it?"

"Bah! Humbug!"

"Don't be cross, student."

"What else can I be, when I live in such a world of fools as this? Literature! What's with this literature stuff? What's literature to you but a lot of hard work; something that you waste your time reading and get not an hour richer; something that you have to pass tests on and have every question in 'em through a whole nine months of school turned dead against you? If I could have my way, every idiot who goes about with 'Literature' on his lips should be reduced to the size of a worm and allowed to bury himself forever inside of a book. He should!"

"Student," pleaded the teacher.

"Teacher," returned the student, "keep literature in your own way, and let me keep it in mine."

"Keep it!" repeated the teacher. "But you don't keep it."

"Let me leave it alone, then. Much good may it do you! Much good it's ever done you!"

"There are many things from which I might have derived good, by which I have not profited, I dare say," said the teacher, "literature among them. But I am sure I have always thought of literature when I have time to read or meditate, as a good thing; a pleasant, informative, often helpful thing; the only thing I know of, in the years of a man's life, that shows men and women opening their shut-up hearts freely, that reveals them for what they are as fellow-passengers in life's journey and not another race bound on other journeys. Literature is a human and humane thing. It is not meter and vocabulary study and tests. It is man speaking as man; it is man thinking; it is man feeling. And therefore, student, though it has never put a scrap of gold or silver in my pocket, I believe it *has* done me good, and *will* do me good; and I say, God bless it."[11]

A dialogue such as this between teacher and student has taken place and will probably continue to take place in many English classrooms, yours included. Although there is much evidence that the teacher's last statement to the student is a commonly accepted rationale for the "what" of English as being literature-centered, it is clear that although recognizing the centrality of literature, many

---

[11] J. N. Hook, "So What Good is English?" in *The Shape of English*, National Council of Teachers of English (Champaign, Ill., 1967), pp. 23–24.

English teachers continue to debate the specific reasons for its being included in the English program. Although few people would deny literature a place in the "what" of English, many would propose that literature in the modern school program should be central because of the contributions it can make to the development of the student's imagination.

In her preface to the first edition of *Literature as Exploration,* written in the 1930s, Louise M. Rosenblatt urged that teachers avoid a concern with literature as a social document or a moral tract and that they avoid a purely aesthetic point of view toward it. She urged teachers of literature to concentrate on the totality of the experience of the reader with the book:

> Since the varied powers of literature cannot be confined within a single phrase, the title of this book should be understood as a metaphor, not as a limiting definition. The word *exploration* is designed to suggest primarily that the experience of literature, far from being for the reader a passive process of absorption, is a form of intense personal activity. The reader counts for at least as much as the book or poem itself; he responds to some of its aspects and not others; he finds it refreshing and stimulating, or barren and unrewarding. Through books, the reader may explore his own nature, become aware of potentialities for thought and feeling within himself, acquire clearer perspective, develop aims and a sense of direction. He may explore the outer world, other personalities, other ways of life. Liberated from the insularity of time and space, he may range through the wide gamut of social and temperamental alternatives that men have created or imagined.[12]

Benjamin DeMott also speaks of the "right course for English studies or humanities" as one that "prizes the poem and the play as windows opening on a livingness that would otherwise be unseen and dead to the human eye . . ." and offers a proposal that the direct involvement of students in literary works transforms them in a kind of awakening of themselves. "Is it not a fact," he asks, "that whatever serves the interests of that consciousness—the interest of a man's awareness of the immediacy of himself—also serves the highest interests of the highest art as well?"[13]

In marshalling the evidence for the imaginative impact of literature as central to the "what" of English, Dwight Burton noted that:

> Experience with literature enables the reader to build a level of imaginative living which is very real in itself and which lies somewhere between dead-level literalness and hallucination. Even in so-called escape reading, for example, one comes to terms with experience at the same time that he is escaping from it.[14]

---

[12] Louise M. Rosenblatt, *Literature as Exploration,* rev. ed. (New York: Noble and Noble Publishers, Inc., 1968), p. x.

[13] Benjamin DeMott, *Supergrow: Essays and Reports on Imagination in America* (New York: E. P. Dutton and Co., 1969), pp. 154–155.

[14] Dwight L. Burton, "The Centrality of Literature in the English Curriculum," in *The Range of English,* National Council of Teachers of English (Champaign, Ill., 1968), p. 63.

It seems clear that although there are differences in points of view among teachers as to how to best evoke responses of students to literature, there is considerable agreement about the need to develop those responses. A growing consensus of teachers supports the development of response rather than the communication of facts about literature, or the development of a comprehensive knowledge of literary classics among students. The importance of a knowledge of literary classics, however, continues to persist among many teachers, both in high schools and colleges:

A Literary Canon

"Sometimes," remarked one of the English professors, "I have the uneasy feeling that the only thing holding our culture together is the *Tale of Two Cities* . . ."

. . . one of the most important aims of a general education in literature should be to provide all capable students with a common literary background. This background is an invaluable part of our cultural inheritance, and a familiarity with it should be expected of anybody who deserves to be called educated.[15]

Although many English teachers hold this view or something like it, we might speculate as to how opposing views of the literature-centered English program should exist in many schools. There is no doubt as to the existence of a rich literary heritage. Probably most of your English major has consisted of a study of that heritage. It is not uncommon for many student teachers to enter classrooms thinking that most of their students feel essentially as they do about literary classics that they have read and enjoyed both as children and adults. Considerable research shows that a large majority of children do *not* like the literature that they are asked to read in school—in many elementary schools, children are kept so busy with basic readers that they have little time to enjoy good children's books. Therefore, many of these youngsters have not developed a taste for reading when they move into junior and senior high school. You may well have had the experience of finding out that in a "typical" class of seventh or eighth grade students there are many boys and girls who have never in their lives read a book nor do they have any intention of doing so. All of these young people have heard of the classics but their acquaintance with them may be mostly through *Classic Comics*. It may be of more than passing interest to note how the "classics" came into American education. In the first years of this century, almost no English literature was "taught" in secondary schools and it was the prevailing view among most of the public that reading was learned in the elementary schools.

The introduction of literature into secondary schools was almost a coincidence. A century ago many young men came from academies to the universities of the East to prepare for careers in medicine, law, and the ministry. In many

---

[15] Albert R. Kitzhaber, Robert M. Gorrell, and Paul Roberts, *Education for College* (New York: The Ronald Press Co., 1961), pp. 64–65.

cases they did not write well, so, in addition to entrance examinations in mathematics, natural philosophy, and languages, the committees on entrance decided to add the task of writing an essay. Applicants were given a topic on which to produce a certain amount of writing in a specified time. A potential student might be asked to write about the various dilemmas of Hamlet. Those who had never read *Hamlet* complained that they might be subject to failure because they had not read *Hamlet* and not because of their inability to write. The entrance boards agreed to set up, a year or so in advance, a list of the three or four books on which essay questions would be based. These lists grew and, as might have been anticipated, were adopted into the high school literature curriculum. Thus "the classics" were born and, as tradition grew, the list of books grew. They were seen primarily as works to be studied in order to pass an examination. The study of literature as an end in itself or the reading of literature for the enrichment and stimulation of the imagination lost out in most English classrooms because teachers felt strongly that they had to prepare students to answer questions on specific books and authors.

Since the writing of the essay came ultimately to be replaced by an examination section containing specific questions, the teachers' feelings were justified. However, in recent years literature questions on specific books have disappeared from the College Board Examinations, although they still exist in some statewide tests. With the growing developments in statewide and national assessment and testing, we may be in for a resurgence of this type of literature test.

You can expect the influence of "the classics" to remain strong as a justification for the prevailing view of the centrality of literature as a model for the "what" of English. New views of English dealing with both organization and substance are concerned with the development of imagination through literature, music, art, film, and the other humanities. The development of imagination can take place with science fiction, multiethnic literature, regional literature, indeed any literature as well as "the classics." With the increasing diversification of literature programs in phase-elective and selective English programs, the role of "the classics" as the backbone of the literature program is changing. Part II of this book explores the various directions of that change.

Chapter 2

New Developments: Systems, Electives, and the Open Classroom

NEW ALTERNATIVES FOR ENGLISH

In many cases we English teachers have tended to view our students as taking only English and have tended to view our subject as being the most central in their school experience. Many of us have gone even further than this and tended to view the school as the central force in shaping society rather than as a reflection of it. In any case, few of us have ever viewed the school as an unnecessary institution in our society. In addition to the article "Let's Abolish English," cited earlier, an exploration of the basic purpose of English in the school and the place of the school in our society was proposed in the mid-1960s by Charles Weingartner. He noted that the basic purposes for including English as a subject in school have not been examined critically in the light of changes in contemporary society:

> The adequacy of such an emotional base must be judged from student response. To date, such a mode of judgment is rare. The rarity with which such student response is included in determining the *what* and *how* of English is in no small measure a result of the fact that teachers of English are largely uninformed about:
> 1. the psychology of learning,
> 2. the psychology of communication,

3. the significance of scientific knowledge about language, and
4. the significance of cultural changes consequent to technological change.[1]

In *Future Shock*, Alvin Toffler accents the need for us to capture control of the accelerative thrusts that are changing our society and to create an education whose prime objective is to increase the individual's ability to cope with a continuously accelerating rate of societal change. Toffler proposes that the school should be primarily oriented around helping students to learn how to anticipate the future and to generate a variety of alternative images of the future concerned with the kinds of jobs, professions, locations, and human relationships that will be produced by our developing technology. He notes that:

> We must create a "Council of the Future" in every school and community: Teams of men and women devoted to probing the future in the interests of the present. By projecting "assumed futures," by defining coherent educational responses to them, by opening these alternatives to active public debate, such councils—similar in some ways to the "prognostic cells" advocated by Robert Jungk of the Technische Hochschule in Berlin—could have a powerful impact on education.[2]

We might consider the possibilities of the "Council of the Future" in proposing changes for the English program, if we were to organize them in the way that Toffler suggests. There are several models that are being proposed. The extent to which any of these models will allow students to become creatively involved in determining their own future in schools and to have a say in what they are studying remains to be seen.

SYSTEMS AND SYSTEMS APPROACHES IN ENGLISH

The choice is not between leaving an instructional system and not having one. "Every curriculum is an instructional system."[3] The basic reader, for example, with its extensive teacher handbook, may be considered one of the most highly sophisticated materials for teachers and students ever developed by commercial textbook firms. But today, highly sophisticated systems of institutional management, which have originated in the world of business and have functioned successfully in military and industrial organizations, are being applied to education.

---

[1] Charles Weingartner, "English for What?" in *English and the Disadvantaged*, ed. Edward R. Fagan (Scranton, Pa.: International Textbook Company, 1967), pp. 9–19.

[2] Alvin Toffler, *Future Shock* (New York: Bantam Books, 1970), p. 404.

[3] James Hoetker, with Robert Fichtenau and Helen L. K. Farr, *Systems, Systems Approaches, and the Teacher*, National Council of Teachers of English (Champaign, Ill., 1972), p. 2.

The systems approach in education has come about because of the interests of both teachers and the general public in ensuring that the general goals and specific objectives proposed for schools are actually being met. Taxpayers' groups and citizens' groups have expressed considerable interest in making sure that educators are *accountable* for the fulfillment of their general functions in society. When applications of various forms of institutional management systems affect teachers and students, the system becomes an accountability system. That is what is happening in education today, and it will affect you and your teaching. Proposals for the various ways in which accountability is to be achieved in schools are subjects of intense discussion and debate, and are having their effect both on the organization of schools and on curriculum development in school subjects such as English.

The systems approach is a product of several forces, one of these having to do with the development of management procedures in industry and defense. Such procedures are concerned with the development of strategic planning by which the overall goals of the organization are made clear, and the particular goals of each subunit are made very specific. A time schedule is made out wherein the plans for meeting the various goals and objectives are designed on a week-by-week and a month-by-month basis during the year. Evaluations and appraisals are made periodically as to the attainment of progress toward both the general goals and the specific objectives. Every subunit of the organization as well as those responsible for the total organization are accountable for reaching the various goals and objectives that have been established. If it becomes clear that any subunit or any part of the organization is failing to achieve its specified goals for a particular time period, resources from other parts of the total organization are brought to bear on these units in an attempt both to discover the reasons for failures and to devise practical plans for overcoming them. In industry and defense much success has been achieved with the application of the "systems" model in such areas as clarifying general goals, developing specific objectives, designing plans, dividing and subdividing the organizational chart with both long-range goals and various subgoals specified along a particular time-line. Difficulties are diagnosed and a redesigned plan made (with subsequent appraisal and further revisions of the total system) if it appears to be needed.

Applying the systems approach to any type of organization makes the total system, as well as its various parts, accountable for reaching various goals. Although there is a long history of attempts to apply techniques from management in business, industry, and defense to education, both the refinement of these techniques and the interest of the public in accountability have led national, state, and local educational groups to view the "systems" model as a viable one for all future educational planning.

As various groups concerned with the accreditation of schools and the development of educational programs in various subject fields have become influenced by the systems approach, they have discovered that one important aspect of its application is the development of behavioral objectives. In a recent book on applying systems approaches to education, Vernon S. Gerlach and Donald P. Ely spend one chapter describing the systems approach and nine chapters writing behavioral objectives "that are representative of those commonly dealt with in elementary and secondary schools." As they point out concerning the application of systems approaches to education:

> Writing objectives is the initial stage of this approach. For the purposes of our analysis, we assume that the content of learning has been specified, since objectives cannot be adequately stated apart from content. In fact, these two are so closely related in the teaching-learning process that they must be treated together.
>
> The only useful objectives are those that describe the ultimate actions, skills, or products of the learner. Objectives such as these are called *behavioral* objectives. ... Since the statement of objectives is so fundamental to our approach, we demonstrate how to use a specific classification scheme that will help teachers to select or write them precisely.[4]

Discussions of the development of behavioral objectives have pervaded educational literature over the past five years. The Bureau of Research in the United States Office of Education committed a substantial share of its budget to the commissioning of taxonomies in seventeen large, cooperating school systems. At the time of this writing, every school system and individual school in California is charged with framing, in behavioral terms, the outcomes of its courses, with the development of criterion measures and statewide testing as justification for state support of local schools.[5]

Experts in the field of English curriculum development differ in their concerns about the writing of behavioral objectives in English and the ultimate effect of the application of behavioral objectives to English programs. At the present time many teachers and curriculum specialists in English differ as to whether behavioral objectives should even be connected with "behaviorism"— the psychological system that "offers a rival structure and logic to other psychological systems such as Freudianism, Gestalt theory, field psychology, the psychology of person constructs, or Rogerian psychology."[6] Purves further proposes a differentiation between the psychological system of "behaviorism" and the actual identification of behaviors in the learner which he argues that every teacher makes. "Teachers want to change behavior," he argues, "otherwise they would not teach." Purves differentiates "behaviors," "behaviorism,"

---

[4] Vernon S. Gerlach and Donald P. Ely, *Teaching and Media: A Systematic Approach* (Englewood Cliffs, N.J.: Prentice-Hall, Inc., 1971), p. 39.

[5] Maxwell H. Goldberg, *Cybernation Systems and the Teaching of English: The Dilemma of Control,* unpublished manuscript (University Park, Pa.: Center for Continuing Liberal Education, Pennsylvania State University, 1971), p. 88.

[6] Alan C. Purves, "Of Behaviors, Objectives, and English," *English Journal* 59, No. 6 (Sept. 1970): 793.

and "behavioral objectives" from each other, claiming that "behavioral objectives deal in input, process, and output, in conditions and observable behaviors, and in criteria." "Behavioral objectives," he states, "constitute a way of looking at the educational process and of applying a number of logics or pseudologics to it simultaneously."[7] Most specialists advocating the systems approach feel that there is an intimate connection between "behaviors," "behavioral objectives," and the psychological system of behaviorism. In their previously mentioned book, Gerlach and Ely define the nature of learning in essentially behavioristic terms as follows:

> What is learning? To begin with, learning must somehow be related to behavior. Behavior refers to any observable act.
> ... *Behavior is an observable act or an observable product which is a result of an act or acts.*[8]

In the face of such evidence, it seems evident that the distinction which Purves attempts to set up between behaviors, behaviorism, and behavioral objectives is not as clear-cut as he would like it to be, since when teachers are asked to write behavioral objectives they are asked to consider the overt behavior of the learner as manifested through instruction in some sort of behavioral outcome. Richard W. Burns gives some specific definitions and examples of terminal behavioral objectives of the sort that English teachers are being asked to write today. If you are in a school or school system that requires you to write behavioral objectives, we suggest you follow these guidelines to the extent possible:

> Terminal behavioral objectives are relatively specific statements of learning outcomes expressed from the learner's point-of-view and telling what the learner is to *do* at the end of instruction.
> Examples of terminal behavioral objectives:
> 1. The learner is to identify the twelve cranial nerves so that he can, when given a diagram, label each nerve correctly.
> 2. The learner is to know the names of the fifty states so that he can list them (from memory) in any order.
> 3. The learner is to develop skill in typing so that he can copy a "rough" of a business letter of approximately 300 words, in proper style, within six minutes, and with no more than three errors.
> 4. The learner is to develop an understanding of social problems and conceptualize solutions so that he can:
>   a. Define in writing a problem he has personally observed
>   b. Describe in writing the problem above in terms of interpersonal relationships
>   c. Outline the steps of a plan for solving that problem.

---

[7] *Ibid.*
[8] Gerlach and Ely, *op. cit.,* p. 43.

Terminal behavioral objectives are:

1. Specific rather than broad
2. Always expressed from the learner's point of view
3. Statements which include a description of the behaviors of the learner or what he is able to do as a result of or at the end of instruction.[9]

Teachers in all fields of the humanities such as art, literature, and music attempting to follow instructions like these to develop terminal behavioral objectives are presented with a number of difficulties.

We want you to be aware of the difficulties in writing behavioral objectives for English. Terminal behavioral objectives are clearly designed to describe learning outcomes in terms of specific overt behavior. The problem of writing such descriptions comes home dramatically to the teacher who simply wants his students to appreciate the beauty of a symphony, a painting, or a poem. A teacher must ask himself such questions as the following:

1. What overt behavior will a student be engaging in when he is appreciating?
2. If his head is down on his desk and his eyes are closed, could he nevertheless be appreciating a symphony or a poem being read orally?

Perhaps you agree that he could. How, then, can the teacher tell if the instruction has been successful? The problems become obvious immediately and result in considerable frustration among teachers of English, art, music, and other areas of the humanities as they struggle to write terminal behavioral objectives. Although no one would argue the value of thinking through overall goals of writing objectives, the problem of describing "behavior" that represents thought and feeling occurring inside an individual, in language requiring descriptions of "overt behavior," has not yet been solved.

One of the most pervasive arguments raised against the writing of terminal behavioral objectives is the fact that long-range humanistic objectives of education have not been adequately defined or agreed upon. Since there have been no agreements on long-range objectives, argue the critics, how can agreements be reached on short-range goals? Hans Guth proposes three important humanistic goals for the teaching of English that he feels are not susceptible to the specifics required in developing terminal behavioral objectives and therefore are incompatible with them:

... first, *imagination*, the area of extending feeling and thinking on the part of the student; second, *power*, the ability to use language, for a purpose—the power of words, the power of language as a medium; third, *understanding*, the ability to relate a piece of poetry to your own experience, to relate one piece of

---

[9] Richard W. Burns, *New Approaches to Behavioral Objectives* (Dubuque, Iowa: Wm. C. Brown Publishers, 1972), pp. 5–6.

poetry to another and talk about a common theme or something of that sort. I call these humanistic goals, because they all have to do with the basic goals of humanistic education, which are to develop more fully and to bring out more fully whatever human potential there is in the student.[10]

What would be a logical point of view for you to take on the matter of accountability in English teaching in view of the expectations of the public, your students' expectations, and your own obligations to your students to do a good job in teaching English? It seems wise for you to remember a number of points that are especially important in considering this question. First of all, most of us who have backgrounds in literature and the other arts are wont to believe that the interaction between literary art and human beings will change human beings dramatically as individuals and will ultimately result in an enriched life. Most teachers of English have believed this for a long time. Hence, our instruction has not promoted enrichment of the lives of a great many students.

After the period of intensive federal support to curriculum development in English during the 1960s, dissatisfaction continued with the school English program. Officials of the United States Office of Education and those especially concerned with the measurement and assessment of education began, in the 1970s, to demand more immediate feedback on the results or outcomes of education. As noted above, institutional management models of teaching and learning are being used to develop systems approaches in education. There is little question that you will be subjected to some aspects of systems approaches in your own teaching. We recommend that you study the movement carefully and determine your own point of view.

In the course of developing your own philosophy of teaching English, you should decide which objectives are most important to you and your students. Then you will need to consider which objectives can be stated in behavioral terms and which cannot. However, you must not attempt to meet the issue of "accountability" with an entirely negative stance, since it is clear that as a professional person you *are* accountable to your students, your colleagues, and your community. Of course, students are also accountable for being active learners, which is important in considering the learning process used in your class; in addition, their parents are accountable for supplying their home learning environment, and your colleagues are accountable for developing appropriate learning programs. Your administrators are accountable for developing a school atmosphere in which you and your colleagues can carry on the teaching and learning processes that will afford your students the maximum opportunity to develop their full potentials. This is the kind of accountability that most of the parents and citizens of your community are ultimately after. The Commission of the English Curriculum of the National Council of Teachers of English,

---

[10] Hans P. Guth, "The Monkey on the Bicycle: Behavioral Objectives and the Teaching of English," *English Journal* 59, No. 6 (Sept. 1970): 792.

after an examination of the issue of accountability, issued a position statement in which they advised all teachers of English that:

> ... a broad perspective on goals must be maintained at this time. The present very real and complex problems of adequate measurement and reasonable bases for holding teachers accountable for instruction hold a threat to the discipline of English, the threat of a narrowly defined, "Measurable" curriculum and the spectre of teachers defensively limiting themselves to the superficial aspects of literacy in language and literature.
>
> ... The Commission also observes that any narrow system of accountability which is predicated upon a single psychology of learning may impinge on freedom to teach and learn and may stifle the diversity of approach and style that must mark education in a democratic society.
>
> ... The Commission maintains that some results of learning English, particularly those that lie in the affective domain, such as heightened sensitivity to literary works, are not amenable to definitive measurement. Most particularly, they cannot be adequately measured at or near the time of instruction. The results desired from such instruction are subtle and often private and may not be measured except by a discerning teacher over a period of time. Or the real results may not be manifest until long after the student has left the school. The Commission therefore rejects the notion that if any real changes have been brought about by teaching, they can be identified and quantified objectively and immediately. Such a notion rests on major unestablished assumptions about the powers of the "objective" human observer and upon naive perception of what human learning is, particularly human learning built upon and through the medium of language.[11]

You will encounter continuing efforts to clarify how accountability in English is to be achieved under any system. You will need to give your attention to the concern for ways to continue the humanistic goals and objectives for English teaching in the face of strong forces proposing the application of systems approaches and terminal behavioral objectives, which seem to conflict with humanistic goals. You will need to evaluate carefully the extent of these conflicts. The Commission on the English Curriculum of the National Council of Teachers of English has recently published *Accountability and the Teaching of English*, which will be a valuable resource for you in studying this important subject—one that has deep value implications for all teachers and, indeed, for all of society.

ELECTIVES AND SELECTIVES

At present, the most drastic change in English is in the English electives program. Although it developed as a result of all the forces mentioned earlier, as well as

---

[11] "Accountability and the Teacher of English," *Junior Membership Newsletter* 11, No. 1, National Council of Teachers of English (Champaign, Ill., Jan. 1972), pp. 1, 6.

through a variety of similar experimental programs, the APEX (Appropriate Placement for Excellence) program of Trenton, Michigan, is perhaps the best known. There, the English faculty took note of the problems facing English in the 1970s and with the assistance of some intensive research and development, facilitated by a $200,000 federal grant, made a complete change in the organization, structure, and substance of their English program. Donald F. Weise, department chairman at Trenton, has noted that the program grew from an analysis his staff made of the problems facing students in English in their school, which they believed stemmed from the overall effects of grading and tracking within the educational process. These problems, he feels, are typical of those faced by many junior and senior high school English teachers:

1. Lack of success with slow learners.
2. Restricted opportunities for fast learners.
3. Difficulties with the individualizing of instruction.
4. Poor results with composition instruction.
5. Haphazard teaching of reading skills.
6. Instruction gaps, especially in nonprint communications media.
7. Teacher insecurity about what should be taught.
8. Redundancy of instruction.
9. General student apathy.[12]

After the development of the APEX program by the consultants and staff at Trenton, Weise and his staff decided that they would put into operation a nongraded, phase-elective English program. The APEX curriculum employed the following guidelines:

Nongrading is the eliminating of grade levels and tracks as devices for grouping students and defining courses. It is accomplished by dropping grade and track distinctions and allowing students, regardless of their age, to select from any of the learning experiences in the program. Practically speaking, it means that in a great many of the courses offered, it is possible to find freshmen, sophomores, juniors, or seniors, all of whom have the common learning bond, not of age, but of similar interest in the course, similar abilities, and similar needs.

Electing is the allowing of students to freely select their own courses. In this curriculum, there are no required courses or prerequisites. Students are permitted to pick any courses that they feel best meet their individual interests, needs, and abilities. To assist them in making wise choices, extensive assistance is provided by English staff advisors and school counselors, who function as information-givers, constructive critics, and facilitators rather than as dictators of what *should* be taken.

Phasing is the describing of courses, in a general way, by assigning to them a number from one to five to indicate their degree of difficulty. This concept is useful

---

[12] Donald F. Weise, "Nongrading, Electing, and Phasing: Basics of Revolution for Relevance," *English Journal* 59, No. 1 (Jan. 1970): 123. Copyright 1970 by National Council of Teachers of English, Champaign, Ill.

in that it allows one to describe elective courses more readily for guidance purposes. Phasing, in this program, describes courses only and is not used to describe students. The Phase levels are defined in the following fashion:

Phase 1 courses are designed for students who find reading, writing, speaking, and thinking quite difficult and have serious problems with basic skills.

Phase 2 courses have been created for students who do not have serious difficulty with basic skills, but need to refine them, and can do so best by learning at a somewhat slower pace.

Phase 3 courses are particularly for those who have a fair command of the basic language skills and would like to advance beyond them but do so at a moderate rather than accelerated pace.

Phase 4 courses are for students who learn fairly rapidly and are in good command of the basic skills.

Phase 5 courses offer a challenge to advanced students who have excellent control of basic skills and are looking for stimulating and self-motivated academic learning experiences.

A nongraded phase-elective curriculum, then, is one that offers to students a wide variety of courses, grouped for guidance purposes in levels of difficulty which may be freely elected by students of any age on the basis of their own individual interests, needs, and abilities.

Currently the following courses are offered to the students at our school:

Course Number	Course Title	Phase Level
111	Fundamental English	1
112	Vocational English	1
121	Basic Reading Skills	1–2
124	Ideas and Ideals	1–2
151	Seminar in New Dimensions	1–5
152	Independent Study	1–5
221	Film Explorations	2
222	Literary Explorations	2
232	Contemporary Humanities	2–3
235	Basic Communications	2–3
251	Individualized Reading	2–5
254	Theater Arts	2–5
331	Introductory Composition	3
333	Modern Literature	3–4
341	Reading Techniques	3–4
342	Mythology	3–4
343	Nobel Prize Authors	3–4
344	Contemporary Reading	3–4
346	Public Speaking	3–4
351	Discussion and Debate	3–5
352	Forensics	3–5
353	Journalism	3–5
356	Advanced Theater Arts	3–5

357	Filmmaking	3–5
358	Art of the Motion Picture	3–5
359	Nature of Man	3–5
441	Modern American Literature	4
443	American Heritage	4
444	Modern World Literature	4
452	Humanities	4–5
453	Creative Writing	4–5
454	Seminar in Ideas	4–5
455	Journalistic Writing	4–5
456	Advanced Composition	4–5
457	Language and Human Behavior	4–5
458	Poetry Seminar	4–5
459	Literature of the East	4–5
551	Great Books	5
553	Shakespeare Seminar	5
554	Research Seminar	5
556	Advanced Reading Techniques	5
557	Advanced Seminar in Ideas	5

Courses can be added or dropped from the list depending on the needs of the students. Many courses are multi-phased (e.g., 2–5), which means that a range of learning experiences is provided in the course. Each of the courses, regardless of content, has built into it learning experiences in what we feel are the basic language skills: reading, writing, speaking, thinking, and listening. Because this is so, it is not absolutely critical what combination of courses the student takes, since regardless of the selections he chooses, he will be helped, in the manner most suitable, to grow in each of the basic skills.[13]

Further, Mr. Weise and his English teachers felt that certain new priorities needed to be established in the teaching of English and that a set of concepts in English that provided for nongrading, phasing, electing, and individualizing was essential in bringing the students into a sharing process to bring out the best in both student and teacher alike.

The English "elective" and "selective" programs have now become a major organizing curriculum pattern for English throughout the country. There are undoubtedly many reasons for this, one of which is the way in which students from the "counterculture" have been involved in developing elective and selective programs and have participated *with English teachers* in developing programs they feel are much more significant for them than the traditional English programs. This point is emphasized by Andreas Lehner, who notes that in English elective and selective programs, responsibility for learning is transferred from teachers, who have traditionally been in control, to students, who consciously have a share in developing their own programs. Lehner feels that there is great significance in actually involving students in developing their

---

[13] *Ibid.*, pp. 124–125.

own programs. He points out that although we have voiced the fact that we feel student involvement is important, we have not really given students an opportunity to be involved in creating their own programs or making any choices about what they take. Most significantly, Lehner notes that when students share in the development of areas of study in the phase-elective English programs "they are thereby obliged to take an active role in shaping the events of their school day, just as they will, we hope, participate in shaping the events of the community as adults."[14] We feel that this sharing of responsibility for the development of an English program within a single school is one of the most unique aspects of the elective program and certainly one of its most important contributions. We are beginning to accumulate a literature of the development of the phase-elective programs and various evaluations of the results. Jack E. Smith, Jr., of Hickory Township High School in Sharon, Pennsylvania, describes the development of a nongraded elective program of study in a serious attempt to show what worked and what didn't work during the first year of its operation. He carefully followed the way in which the English elective program was developed in the total curriculum of the school. Here are some of his observations:

1. During the first week of school in September fewer students than ever before requested schedule changes. The fact that they had chosen their classes in English seemed to be the reason.
2. By the end of the first twelve-week term we learned that sophomores can compete successfully with juniors and seniors in some courses, but not in others. In courses concerning the acquisition of information and the practice of basic skills, sophomores competed without handicap. But courses requiring students to engage in mature intellectual debate were too much for sophomores to handle when upperclassmen were present.
3. Slow learners and emotionally immature learners could not cope with their freedom to pick and choose. Until we hire more teachers for these people, we have assigned them to conventional long courses that meet with one teacher for a whole school year.
4. Our main problem at the present time is lack of enough English teachers. We should offer courses in remedial reading, mythology, linguistics, and humanities . . .[15]

Undoubtedly the most comprehensive evaluation of an English elective program to date was done over a five-year period of the Project APEX program. This evaluation was conducted with the assistance of a federal grant involving outside consultants and a carefully developed research design. Beginning in 1968, students in Project APEX were matched with two high schools of

---

[14] Andreas P. Lehner, "The Laissez-faire Curriculum in the Democratic School," *English Journal* 59, No. 6 (Sept. 1970): 803–810.
[15] Jack E. Smith, Jr., "180 Days: Observations of an Elective Year," *English Journal* 60, No. 2 (Feb. 1971): 230, 235.

nearly the same size located in communities of approximately the same socio-economic makeup in suburban Detroit. Each of the control schools used traditional English programs and continued to do so throughout the course of the five-year evaluation study. Some of the key conclusions of the evaluation were:

> No great differences in achievement, as measured by standardized tests and essay tests, appear among the various school populations. Literary taste as defined by the conditions and materials of the poetry tests is essentially the same from one group to another. While some differences in attitudes toward traditional aspects of English study (literature, writing, grammar, and mechanics) appear, the main differences among the school populations appear in their attitudes toward the actual activities in their English classes. Questionnaire results reveal that the attitudes of Trenton students are far more positive than those of students in the control schools. They feel that the APEX classes have introduced them to new ideas, have made them more aware of current social problems, have helped to make them more tolerant of other points of view, and, in some cases, have given them greater empathy with their fellow human beings. Thus, it appears that Trenton students have learned a good many things which cannot be measured by traditional tests of achievement.[16]

Although it seems clear that many of the evaluations of the phase-elective program in English are positive, particularly to the extent that they concern the students' attitudes toward English, it would be surprising if all students or English teachers agreed on the efficacy of this program as it exists at present. Many teachers and parents continue to have mixed feelings about English electives. The movement is by now widespread, however, and it would be likely for any English teacher applying for a first-year or new position to be asked by a principal or English department chairman, "What elective are you able to teach?" or "What kind of elective would you have an interest in developing?" There are, nevertheless, many schools where elective programs have not been developed or where for a variety of reasons they are not being developed as quickly as in some of the ones we have mentioned.

Opposition to the elective program is undoubtedly based on a variety of feelings that many English teachers have about 1) the necessity for any change in English at all; 2) the proper direction of change in English programs, and 3) the guarantee that in making changes in English, we do not throw away many of the traditional values residing in the study of language, literature, and composition that have been an established part of English programs throughout the past. John K. Crabbe, for example, sees the English elective programs as a "national stampede" that has become "the current palliative to student and teacher boredom.[17] Crabbe likens the development of the English elective

---

[16] George Hillocks, Jr., *An Evaluation of Project APEX: A Nongraded Phase-Elective English Program*, Trenton Public Schools (Trenton, Mich., 1971), pp. 119–120.

[17] John K. Crabbe, "Those Infernal Electives," *English Journal* 59, No. 7 (Oct. 1970): 990.

program to developments in flexible scheduling, team-teaching to large lecture sections of high school students, and fears that our high schools in adopting elective programs will adopt many of the bad practices currently to be seen in large lecture classes in many colleges and universities. Crabbe also is concerned that the teaching of writing in the elective program will somehow get lost, a concern also voiced by a number of other high school and college teachers, since many teachers apparently see in the elective program the possibility of teachers taking an "ego trip" and teaching their favorite literature course. He is also concerned about what will happen in scheduling electives for students who have difficulty making choices, and questions how a sequence of writing skills can be developed throughout an elective program.[18] These are excellent questions and will need to become a part of future evaluations of elective programs. In any case, the elective program is likely to be with us for some time, so it would be well for you to make a study of the kinds of elective programs that are in effect in any school in which you may be planning to teach.

A number of elective programs currently being developed are using techniques of placing evaluation and development together. An example of English electives in which students and teachers have participated in their development is seen in the work of Mary Carroll Fox of Carl Hayden High School in Phoenix, Arizona. Working from expressions of student need and interest, she has developed an elective called the *College Survival Kit*. The objectives, outline, and description of the course, along with suggestions for student activity, are as follows:

    I. The advertisement used to attract students to choose this elective:

How strong is *your* English vocabulary—the backbone of your power of expression? Do you have a supply of words broad enough to express your thoughts with exactness and variety? Do you generally know the meaning of the words you read and hear in daily life? Do you know the correct spelling of words you use?

Can you read fast and still remember what you have read? Can you listen to a lecture and remember what is important? Do you know how to study? If you are planning to continue your education after high school these skills are especially important.

Do you want to improve your power of expression, your vocabulary, spelling, punctuation? Do you want to learn valuable skills which will help you succeed in college? In this course you will become acquainted with the science of our language and learn to apply its concepts to add power to your speech, composition writing, and reading comprehension. You will learn those valuable skills which will help you succeed in college: efficient study methods, test-taking techniques, and proficiency in reading, writing, and listening.

---

[18] *Ibid.*, p. 993.

II. Objectives

The student will accomplish the following:

1. identify the relationship between the spoken and written forms of of language: spelling, pronunciation, punctuation
2. differentiate and identify various parts of words: affixes, roots, syllables, inflections
3. construct and identify the basic patterns of English sentences
4. distinguish and identify the subject-predicate relationship
5. develop reading power through vocabulary growth
6. improve reading comprehension and retain what is read
7. increase ability to read critically
8. increase rate of reading, and learn skimming and scanning techniques
9. develop effective study techniques including listening, questioning, note-taking, use of reference materials, organizing, and summarizing skills
10. apply reading, writing, usage, and study skills to subject matter areas.

III. Course Outline

Reading and Study Skills Quarter

Weeks 1–2	Speed reading techniques (students were taught skills of phrase reading and practiced with pacers, controlled readers, and timed readings).
Week 3	OARWET (a planned study approach). They then applied this to their textbooks for other classes.
Week 4	Reading for main ideas and details. Standardized reading comprehension tests were taken for practice.
Weeks 5–6	Listening skills, note-taking, outlining, and summarizing.
Week 7	Skimming and scanning; vocabulary development (students studied vocabulary throughout the quarter, but affixes-roots were stressed here).
Weeks 8–9	Test-taking (following directions, hints for essay, objective, and standardized tests). Critical reading (included logical fallacies).

Grammar-Writing Skills Quarter

Weeks 1–3	Introduction to development of English language; work on pronunciation and spelling.
Weeks 4–7	Study of grammar, sentence structure, punctuation. Work on "trial-run" college entrance and scholarship tests.
Weeks 8–10	Composition writing. Students spent Fridays throughout the quarter working on a required research paper.

IV. Books and Materials

Text: *Vitalized English*, by Mary Didas.
This book includes chapters on vocabulary, pronunciation, spelling, grammar, composition, and sample standardized verbal tests.

Materials
for Reading
Skills:
SRA pacers, Psycho-techniques Tachomatic 500, Listen and Read tapes, timed readings.

Reading-Study Games

1. Vocabulary Bingo

Preparation: Prepare three different sets of Bingo cards (on ditto) using vocabulary words studied or prefixes and roots.

Steps: Each student has a Bingo card. Teacher calls out definition. Students put a marker in the correct square. When a student has Bingo, he has his card checked and is given ten points. Highest scorer wins. For fun, the teacher might provide popcorn for students to use as markers!

2. Vocabulary Concentration

Preparation: Using index cards prepare several sets, using vocabulary words and definitions on separate cards.

Steps: Class divides into groups of four. The pack of cards is put face down on desk. Each student is allowed to turn up two cards. If they match (word with definition), he keeps the trick. If not, he puts the cards face down again and next player takes a turn. (Game continues as the TV Concentration game.)

3. Skimming Games

Newspaper Skimming Practice

Preparation: Teacher makes up ten questions from newspaper articles, using as many different sections of the newspaper as possible. Each student must have a copy of the newspaper.

Steps: Each student is handed the list of ten questions. He must skim the paper to find the answers. First one finished with correct answers is winner.

Newspaper Mix-up

Preparation: Teacher cuts up a newspaper page, using about nine headlines and the first three paragraphs of the articles under these headlines. Each paragraph is cut separately. The cut up page is then put into an envelope. There must be enough cut up pages for as many groups of three as there are in the class.

Steps: Each team must arrange the paragraphs and headlines on its desk. (The second and third paragraphs in each article may be in reverse order.) The first team finished correctly wins.

Skimming-Memory Game

Preparation: Prepare a transparency of about fifty words spread out on the page. Half of these words should be of one category like food, birds, etc.

Steps: The class can look at the words for thirty seconds. Then each team must write down as many of the words of the one category as they can remember. The team with the most correct words wins.

Surveying the Textbook Game
Preparation: Prepare a list of questions from different parts of the textbook (use Table of Contents, Glossary, Index, Chapter titles, subtitles, etc.).
Steps: Team completing the list first wins.[19]

Much more could be said about the possibilities and problems of elective programs. It seems clear, however, that the junior and senior high school English programs of the future will contain electives like World Literature, Paperback Power, Literature and the Supernatural, Creative Writing, and a variety of others. Undoubtedly, this means that a variety of changes will have to take place in English departments and in teacher preparation programs. Many English departments, such as the one at Michigan State University, are already leading the way with a variety of choices in areas of emphasis in language, media, reading, and literature. As teacher preparation in English grows more diverse, and as English programs are planned to meet the individual needs of students, we might well ask: What are to be the guiding principles of the English programs of the future? Will the elective program lead to chaos and confusion as some are predicting, or will it ultimately become "systematized" and "structured" by advocates of the Planned Program and Budgeting System (PPBS) and other systems approaches? We feel that, with its emphasis on sharing and on flexibility and diversity in planning within a single school, it holds great promise for English.

FREE SCHOOLS AND OPEN CLASSROOMS

Books like Everett Riemer's *School Is Dead* and Ivan Illich's *Deschooling Society* contain indictments of the system and propose sweeping changes in the form schooling should take in our society. Some of these proposed changes are clearly reactions to the ways schools have been run, and some of them are reactions to systems approaches currently applied to education. Some of the impetus for alternative organizations of schools and classrooms has come from the influence of other systems of education, chiefly the developments within the British primary schools. At the same time that Americans were learning about the developments within these schools during the 1960s, American students were demanding a more extensive opportunity to share in their own learning. When they are given an opportunity to express themselves (as discussed in the next chapter), young people state that *they feel* that much of what

[19] Mary Carroll Fox, "College Survival Kit," Carl Hayden High School (Phoenix, Ariz., 1972), mimeographed.

they are expected to learn is 1) not organized very well, 2) not helpful in giving them the tools they need for thinking and learning, and 3) not helpful enough in enabling them to develop opportunities and materials to inquire, discuss, and probe issues and questions meaningful to them. They state further that schools should be organized more informally and related more directly to outside life. Others want more individual contacts with teachers, smaller classes, and smaller schools.

Almost all of these features of schooling are to be found in the best British primary schools. Although the British primary schools in no sense display a uniformity of practice, American observers have noted some "broad qualities and concerns" that do distinguish them from more traditional schools on both sides of the Atlantic:

1. Informal British schools are distinguished by the degree to which they have become "de-institutionalized." Children move relatively freely about such schools, in classrooms and corridors alive with color and things of all sorts. Old chairs, rugs and carpets, ovens and animals, all give a warm, human, non-school (in the traditional sense) atmosphere to the building.
2. Teachers seem to accept a fuller, broader interpretation of the idea of "individualization." Children are seen as unique or different in terms of their total growth patterns as human beings rather than in a narrow, skill development sense.
3. Teachers in informal schools place far more value on detailed observation of a child's work over a long period of time as a primary evaluative source than they do on more formal testing procedures.
4. Teachers (and headmasters or principals) play a far more active role in making day-to-day curricular decisions of all kinds than do their counterparts in more formal schools. If, in fact, teachers are more attuned to children and their needs and interests in such schools, city- or district-wide "programs" or curricula make little sense, and the individual teacher becomes a dynamic curricular agent.
5. Teachers in such schools seem to accept fully the notion (so much the essence of Piaget) that children's learning proceeds from the concrete to the abstract, and that premature abstraction is one of the great weaknesses of the traditional school. Thus the emphasis on concrete materials, and encounters with real people and places whenever possible.[20]

Open education and informal schooling are influencing the teaching of English. In 1966, British, Canadian, and American teachers of English met formally in an Anglo-American seminar at Dartmouth College to discuss mutual concerns. In general, many of the British were dismayed by the American tripod model for English (the systems model had not yet appeared) and reacted strongly against structured curricula of any sort and opted for a more informal,

---

[20] Vincent Rogers, "Open Schools on the British Model," *Educational Leadership* 25, No. 5, Association for Supervision and Curriculum Development (Feb. 1972): 402.

personal schooling in the mother tongue. John Dixon, in *Growth Through English*, one report of that conference, notes the

> fatal inattention to the processes involved in such everyday activities as talking and thinking things over, writing a diary or a letter home, even enjoying a TV play.[21]

Dixon writes extensively about his model for the "what" of English, which he calls "language and personal growth" and which he feels is essential for the development of true language power in young people in both elementary and secondary schools.

The emphasis, stemming considerably from the "processes involved in everyday activities," has meant that many English classrooms on both sides of the Atlantic have begun to experiment with various forms of a more open, more realistic type of schooling. The English elective program described earlier may be considered a part of this movement. Some of this experimentation is taking place inside public school systems. Indeed, whole states like North Dakota and North Carolina are attempting to transplant entire British primary school practices into their public schools. The Parkway School in Philadelphia and the Morgan School in Washington have attempted informal, open education within the public school framework at the secondary level. Although there are those who would argue that viable models for education cannot be developed within the public school system, recent reports of experiments in St. Paul, Louisville, New York City, and a variety of other public school systems would seem to belie their fears.[22] A National Consortium on Educational Alternatives has been formed and much experimentation is under way. Open education in English classes is growing and should be considered a healthy movement. The healthy features lie in its focus on changing the nature of the school from within. Open education is giving new impetus to an old idea in education— that teachers and students working together can change the system for the better.

---

[21] John Dixon, *Growth Through English*, National Association for the Teaching of English (Reading, England, 1967), pp. 2–3.

[22] Firmim L. Alexander, "Integration Through Alternatives: The St. Paul Learning Centers Program," *Changing Schools*, Educational Alternatives Project, Indiana University (Bloomington, Sept. 1972), pp. 2–10.

Chapter 3

On Knowing Those Who Learn in Your English Class

New movements like open education are bringing teachers of English together. In July 1971, over 500 teachers of English from Great Britain, Canada, and the United States met on the campus of York University in York, England, to compare their hopes and expectations. After two weeks of intensive discussions, the teachers prepared a statement concerning their own responsibilities for teaching English in the three countries. Part of the statement reads as follows:

> We look for the opportunity to enquire further into such matters as the following:
>
> the advantages of leaving the ultimate responsibility for his own learning in the hands of the student, and seeing our task as ensuring his commitment to it.
>
> The full implications of the non-authoritarian teacher role we are committed to: how it relates to methods of control, school organization, and the form of the curriculum.
>
> The re-defining of our subject in the light of the language needs of all children and their probable needs in a kind of society that may emerge in part as a result of the successful teaching of our subject as re-defined.[1]

Whether the teaching of English will affect the future in the ways projected by the teachers at York, or whether the work of English teachers can or will

---

[1] James Britton, "The York International Conference 1971," *English in Education* 6, No. 1 (Spring 1972): 5.

bring about fundamental changes in our society—or any changes at all—remains to be seen. We tend to agree with the teachers at York that such changes will occur. We hope that you will have a part in shaping them. In order to ensure constructive changes in schools, you will need to know your students very well. How do you get to know your students?

During the course of your preparation as a teacher you were probably asked to take some courses in child psychology or educational psychology. These courses attempted to give you a basic groundwork in such areas as human development, including the various theories of learning and the application of psychological principles to the teaching of your subject. It has been our experience that teachers rarely know enough about human development, including language development. Rarely are applications made to teaching and learning of any specific subject matter. It is our position that understanding the nature of human development, particularly language development, as well as understanding the various theories of learning and their possible applications to English, are essential as you develop your philosophy of teaching English. We say "essential," since it will help you to understand and accept—insofar as one human being *can* understand another—the student who presents himself to you in your classroom. There is a great deal of evidence, mostly from empirical observation of teachers' behavior and also from research, which indicates that teachers' attitudes toward students as a result of courses in educational psychology and child development do not actually develop in the manner intended.

Why is this true? Probably because of the way many courses in human development, child psychology, and learning theory are taught, since it is impossible in most college and university programs to bring prospective teachers into direct contact with children at different stages of behavioral development. If you had this kind of opportunity, you might well come to some of the same conclusions that psychologists reached after years of study and research. Furthermore, the knowledge in this field has been developing rapidly and much of the research is only now being made available to teachers. Researchers in human development have been asking the following kinds of questions for the past several decades:

1. What are the causative factors of a particular child's behavior at a particular time?
2. What causative factors predominate in the determination of the growth and behavior of any one individual child?
3. In what ways do children develop language ability? How can the development of language be facilitated by experiences that are planned in home and school?

The facts of human development indicate that you can expect to find great variations in language development among children entering school, and you can expect these variations to increase as students grow older. This means that the students in your English class will very likely exhibit wide ranges of talent, energy, aspiration, intelligence, and creativity. Their social and cultural backgrounds will also have a great deal to do with their development and ability in language. Nevertheless, for many teachers, the shock of experiencing this type of variation in achievement and motivation is something that requires hard work to overcome. Since almost all of our children attend school throughout adolescence, this variation in language ability persists and in fact increases with age. Our educational system, as you know, is designed to keep all students in school and not to select the most talented or creative for special training—as some other educational systems do. All of our suggestions are designed to help you develop your own philosophy as a teacher of English, and to help you make up your own mind as to what you think about it.

Regardless of their college experiences, many teachers tend to teach as they were taught, demonstrating that their own education has at least as great an effect on them as the reading of any theories or the hearing of any lectures. They explain the behavior of their students from a common sense view of human behavior rather than from any coherent theory they may have learned in teacher preparation courses. This common sense psychology, or *naive psychology*, is based on a system of tacit assumptions that we all have about human behavior, in which all children learn to some extent as they grow up.

This concerns the whole matter of *naive psychology*. The psychologist Fritz Heider devoted a lifetime to formulating the important principles of this naive or common sense psychology, and described them in his book *The Psychology of Interpersonal Relations* (1958).[2] According to Heider's description of *naive psychology*, children are primarily ignorant adults, whose behavior is not governed by laws markedly different from those governing adults. They simply lack much of the knowledge necessary for sensible action. Thus, education is a process of giving them knowledge, either through experience or through verbal instruction. Although there are many theories of child development, we still do not know nearly as much as we would like to about the ways in which children grow. Specialists in child development are attempting to find out a great deal more. Although we cannot attempt a comprehensive review of the major theories of child development here, suffice it to say that most experts agree on the fact that as a child grows, he develops a "second level of functioning" which is "conceptual, symbolic, or cognitively mediated."[3] Most theories seem to substantiate what many teachers in schools have noted, essentially, that the individuals in our classrooms differ so greatly that we need to be constantly on the alert in order to find new ways to motivate them. Their world of experience has given them a variety of different attitudes and interests, which we as teachers need to discover and use. Your discovery of the particular

---

[2] Fritz Heider, *The Psychology of Interpersonal Relations* (New York: John Wiley, 1958).

[3] Alfred L. Baldwin, *Theories of Child Development* (New York: John Wiley, 1968), pp. 598–599.

interests and attitudes that affect the development of your students will be especially important in affecting your plans for them. Since English is a subject not ordinarily liked by many students, it is crucial that you give as much attention as you can to finding out what your students are like. The above comments on the characteristics of human language development also indicate that as teachers we undoubtedly need to be much more diagnostic than we have been before. We can expect that since students are passing through the various stages of development individually, they will be at different points at different times. Therefore, whatever we can do to find out where a specific student is at a particular point in development will aid us immeasurably in helping him through a particular stage. For example, before a student can gain some understanding of symbolic action in a short story, he will need to be able to understand the sequence of events in it. Many times you may be tempted to assume that he can answer questions about symbols, unless you have taken steps to find out that he simply does not have sufficient reading maturity to do so.

Rousseau denied the theory of learning implicit in *naive psychology* when he said, "Look at the child and see what he's like. He is not a miniature adult, and your efforts will go to waste if you begin where you, the teacher, stand instead of at the point which the child has reached." If you have not already begun to observe individual students closely, and have not worked with them in a tutorial situation or in small groups, you should undoubtedly begin to do so as soon as possible, noting carefully their individual styles and rates of learning, the effect of their social and cultural background on their learning, and the kinds of knowledge you can gain from simply getting acquainted with them; all of this will be helpful to you in knowing where they are in their own development. There is still another way to learn about young people, in addition to studying the works of those who have studied them intensively: this is by listening to what they say.

WHAT YOUNG PEOPLE ARE SAYING

More than a decade ago, Edgar Z. Friedenberg wrote of the cultural forces at work in human development. He noted

> ... there is more to it than sexual maturation. It is also—and primarily—a social process, whose fundamental task is clear and stable self-identification.
>
> This process may be frustrated and emptied of meaning in a society which, like our own, is hostile to clarity and vividness. Our culture impedes the clear definition of any faithful self-image—indeed, of any clear image whatsoever. We do not break images; there are few iconoclasts among us. Instead, we blur and soften them. The resulting pliability gives life in our society its familiar

plastic texture. It also makes adolescence more difficult, more dangerous, and more troublesome to the adolescent and to society itself. And it makes adolescence rarer. Fewer youngsters really dare to go through with it; they merely undergo puberty and simulate maturity.[4]

Such a statement was made at a time when many were calling adolescents and young adults "the silent majority," urging them to speak out on political and social issues. Although one might argue that adolescence indeed has "vanished" in Friedenberg's sense, few would argue that something else has taken its place. Theodore Roszak proposes that we have the development of a counterculture in many of our adolescent young. Oriental mysticism, psychedelic drugs, and communitarian experiments are all part of this counterculture that is also identifiable in the changes in appearances of clothing many young people have affected in all stages of adolescence and young adulthood. In many individuals passing through these stages, these phenomena comprise "a cultural constellation that radically diverges from the values and assumptions that have been in the mainstream of our society at least since the Scientific Revolution of the seventeenth century."[5]

Roszak cites the development of this "counterculture" as a direct reaction to the "technocracy" that he notes is a "social form in which an industrial society reaches the peak of its organizational integration. It is the ideal men usually have in mind when they speak of modernizing, up-dating, rationalizing, planning."[6] He notes that a growing group of dissenting and alienated young rebel against the consumer society either by direct action or by "dropping out." He asks, "Why should it be the young who rise most noticeably in protest against the expansion of the technocracy?"

He proposes that many of the young acting as a "counterculture" believe they have the opportunity to change the nature of the technological and scientific world, which they believe has become corrupted, and proposes that the scientists, bureaucrats, and technocrats have become "a new regime of bad magicians . . . for ruling political and economic elites to begin buying up the experts and using them for their own purposes."[7] Roszak proposes that the growing "counterculture" of youth has no choice but to rebel under such circumstances. He proposes that what the more hip Bohemian youth are up to, in the development of a pop music that knits together an age group between thirteen and thirty, is to become prophets of a new and rising generation, one of dissent and revolution. Dissent and revolution are evident in the lyrics of the songs as well as in their style and sound of performance. But one who focuses on such external and symbolic elements of the "counterculture" will miss its true essence. That

---

[4] Edgar Z. Friedenberg, *The Vanishing Adolescent* (Boston: Beacon Press, 1959), p. 2.

[5] Theodore Roszak, *The Making of a Counterculture* (Garden City, N.Y.: Anchor Books, 1968), p. xii.

[6] *Ibid.*, p. 5.

[7] *Ibid.*, p. 263.

true essence, Roszak claims, is the thrust toward true "participative democracy." He sees the "counterculture" as groping toward a new kind of society.

One way to examine Roszak's hypothesis is to listen to what young people are saying. Listen to the ones you know personally in your community and your school. Read what they write. Do you read, or have you read, any "underground" newspapers or magazines? These, perhaps more than any other medium except underground student film and rock music, represent the "counterculture." We recommend such papers as the *Berkeley Barb*, the *East Village Other*, the *Los Angeles* and *New York Free Presses*, and in London the *International Times Peace News* and *Oz* as representative of "counterculture" expressions and concerns. Underground papers and free presses have also been developed by high school students. John Birmingham, editor of a collection of writing from high school underground papers, called *Our Time Is Now*, admits the existence of a "counterculture" in Roszak's terms, but distinguishes between the college revolutionaries and the movement developing in high schools. Although many lump the two groups together, college revolutionaries have played only a small part in the growth of the high school revolution. Birmingham estimates that only about five percent of high school students are actively involved in the underground movement, but he feels that the five percent represent a national movement of significance. In editing his underground paper in Hackensack, New Jersey, High School, called *Smuff*, he and other students who developed the paper ultimately made contact with other underground newspapers, many of which had developed because of censorship problems with the administrations of their various high schools. After talking with a number of these students, he concluded:

> ... What that interview told me clearly was that the high school underground movement was on a larger scale than I'd ever imagined. I realized that we were just in the first stages in my school. The high school students in the New York City underground talked about a movement that had had time to develop, a movement that had already been involved in riots as well as in producing underground papers. One of the most meaningful lessons I learned was that where it had had a chance to develop, the underground was dealing with issues that are more directly concerned with the schools than censorship. Student power, of course, was a big issue. The students simply wanted more control over the school of which they were a part—as we did. I also understood that the underground movement was, or should be, deeply concerned with cultural revolution. As Robby Newton said, "Something about this youth culture is revolutionary." The culture was an essential part of the movement and, therefore, the movement should protect the culture. Youth culture was to be valued by the young and was worth fighting for. This should be one of our major aims. Also, through the underground press and any other "tools" we had, we should educate our fellow students about how and where the schools had failed us.[8]

---

[8] John Birmingham, ed., *Our Time Is Now* (New York: Bantam Books, 1970), pp. 19–20.

Although Birmingham argues that the expressions of the high school underground presses reveal something different about the high school "counterculture" than the university "counterculture," it would seem that the two movements are closely related, if not indeed the same thing. As Birmingham summarizes the goals of the student underground movement in high schools, he stresses the idea of "participative democracy," which to Roszak represents the heart of the whole "counterculture" movement. He later describes an "independent study course" developed and planned by students that became part of the Hackensack High School curriculum. He projects that underground student film festivals will become part of the movement, as will draft counseling and the development of political participation as well as much more concentrated concern with alternative schools, open classrooms, and political education.

Much of the outrage that exists in the collections of writings from high school students indicates considerable dissatisfaction with school, with both the organization and content of the curriculum, with the grading system, with the "generation gap," and with the inability of high school students to communicate satisfactorily with teachers, parents, and adults, with their attempts to find (like Studs Lonigan) a "place in the world they never made." The poignant and insightful expressions of young people in our high schools as written in these publications show the seriousness with which they view the institution of the school as it functions in their society. As a teacher you will be a part of that institution, and will therefore need to consider carefully what your point of view will be on the matters of concern expressed in these publications. We have long known from the studies of adolescents in other cultures that the time between preadolescence and adulthood is a perilous time in growth for many young people. Our technological society has created even sharper distinctions between generations. As teachers, we see that careful consideration of the stages of human growth is essential if we are to continue to develop humanistic goals of education, concerned with the nurturing of self-directed, autonomous human beings.

Implied in the idea of stages of growth is the sense that an individual is a different person at different stages of his life. Studies of child development indicate that we may well be moving toward a better understanding of the stages of growth and development of human beings. Heider, in his *naive psychology*, identified childhood as a situation of dependence. Other students of child development have substantiated his view. Children require others for the satisfaction of their basic needs, and in many cases the needs are shaped externally. Ultimately, children require others to tell them who and what they are. They receive their names from others, and are born into a culture that possesses a collection of values and beliefs concerning the nature of childhood. The school constitutes another external force of dependence for the child. There the content, rewards, and aims of education are determined externally, without reference to the individuals being educated. It is clear to the child immediately that adults are determining what he should learn, what the purposes of learning are, and what kinds of rewards he will receive. What the student free presses seem to say most clearly is that we have extended the patterns of dependence appropriate for the developmental stage of childhood into adolescence to an extent far beyond that needed, and that we are now receiving dramatic notice from the young people themselves that we need a basic change in our social, political, and educational institutions.

As Friedenberg indicated earlier, adolescence begins with the discovery, "I am alive: I am a person and an individual achieving self-definition." Such a realization comes suddenly in the midst of a situation in which a child is still dependent on his family for economic support and still finds himself in a school situation set up for dependency, when the primary thrust of his life is exploration —including exploration of self—moving toward the discovery of autonomy and a new identity. This new identity *must* be self-determined. It is not accidental, then, that young people of high school age begin to combine periods of dependency and introspection with an outward-moving exploration of alternative modes of living. What the youth of the counterculture are apparently telling us through their underground presses, and in a variety of other ways, is that the opportunities we have given them for exploration of alternative modes of life are not adequate. This is of vital concern to us as teachers, particularly as English teachers, since one of the ways in which we may explore alternative modes of life is vicariously through literature. The current generation of young people is a much lonelier one than ever before, in that they are not only alienated from themselves but estranged from others and from such traditions as religious beliefs and practices, such as the Puritan ethic and many of the subsystems of society that they confront in their development—including the school. It is an anachronism that many who feel alone and who seek alternative forms of life have not discovered reading.

Many of the young people who inhabit our schools and who form the "counterculture" are disappointed with the way we have organized the schools. It seems apparent that their needs for self-development and self-definition should include, more than ever before, specific ways for them to express their feelings in school and to develop more intimate cooperative relationships and communication. The growing interest in folk rock, drugs, and T-groups is based in part on their needs to learn how to feel like children again and to communicate emotionally with each other and to recover a sense of integration or wholeness. Particularly in adolescence, when so much growth is determined by the quality of interpersonal relationships, particularly with peers, we need to change our schools into places where adolescents can have encounters that center on the development of values for selfhood and personal survival. English classes will then hopefully be places where students can learn to reflect upon their experiences and where they can integrate the development of cognitive skills, human values, and social ideals. Once you begin to assess, understand, and value the "who" inside *each* of your students, you will begin to find ways to live with them inside the school and to work with them to make the English classroom a human place in which to learn.

As you begin to observe your students, read what they write and find other ways to assess them—you will be struck by their differences. For many years, teachers have accepted the idea that there are almost infinite variations in the capacities of children to learn. Psychologists have examined various causes for failure in school, running the gamut from heredity to motivation, knowledge of standard English, socioeconomic class, and the effects of teachers' attitudes toward learning. Some educators have been working for many years to establish *uniform conditions* for learning, with the assumption that schools could then better accommodate this infinite variation among students. Each student, they feel, would be using this equal opportunity to develop his or her potential. As we have come to understand more of human development and learning, a new conclusion has emerged that may drastically change our view of the possibilities we can provide for human beings to learn in our society and within various social subsystems, including the school. Recent research indicates that students differ more markedly in the rates at which they can learn than in their basic capacity to learn.[9] The quest for the development of new English programs, using a variety of new techniques and new media to help promote the development of young people, is a necessary one. This is a many-sided quest, a quest in which you should join as a teacher of English—that of using what you already know and will ultimately find out about the development of those human beings who inhabit your classrooms. You will never be able to know too much about their language, their unique identities, or their "secret places." You will need to know much about them to begin a quest with them for new alternatives in schools and in English as a school subject. In the following sections we will propose some further alternatives of our own that we value in English teaching. We hope these will be valuable to you. But it seems clear from all we know that you must find your own way in becoming a teacher; that way will be closely related to your basic values as a human being, your creative powers, and perhaps most important of all—your genuine desire.

---

[9] Benjamin S. Bloom, "Innocence in Education," *School Review* 80, No. 3 (University of Chicago Press, May 1972): 337.

Part II

How Do We Deal with Imaginative Materials?

Chapter 4

Introducing Imaginative Literature

A BROAD OVERVIEW

In describing earlier some of the conflicting aims in teaching literature, we noted the importance of developing your own philosophy, especially concerning the "what" of literature and the matters of "to whom" and "why." "Why" grows out of your view of "what" the literary experience is and "whom" you see as an audience for your work. How you use the suggested methods and techniques should grow out of your view of "what," "to whom," and "why." Our purpose is to give you some basic, practical suggestions that will enable you to bring your students together with books, films, and other media so that experience with literature can become a meaningful part of their lives. Included are suggestions for *readiness* and *reinforcement* activities for early adolescents, as well as *preteaching*, *reading*, and *response* activities for older adolescents. In addition to your own philosophy of teaching literature, you will be functioning within a particular school and within a particular English department, both of which may impose their own special constraints upon you and upon the execution and development of your philosophy.

These constraints may influence the organization of the literature program in your school and may influence the kinds of materials you can use with your students. You may need to reconcile your own philosophy with that of others in your school and in your department. You will find that in addition to *readiness* and *reinforcement* and to *preteaching*, *reading,* and *response*, we tend to favor certain points of view and approaches in the teaching of literature such as the value of teaching the reading of literature, the use of student interest to individualize the teaching of literature, the thematic approach, the phase-elective program, and experimentation with the various uses of media. We do so because of the success of these approaches in our own teaching and in that of teachers we know and respect, and because research tends to support these particular strategies. We urge you to experiment with our proposals and to develop new ones of your own.

Although we mentioned research, there has been precious little research concerned with the teaching of literature. There have been significant proposals for research and some equally significant theoretical statements. One valuable theoretical construct concerned with the growth of literary appreciation is that of the identification of stages of growth in the development of appreciation of literature. Influenced perhaps by Piaget's work in describing the factors involved in human intellectual and emotional growth, Early proposes that readers pass through three stages on their way to achieving conscious delight in literature.[1] She theorizes that readers pass through reading for *unconscious delight*, wherein the reader knows what he likes but is unable to give reasons for it. In order to progress to the stage of *self-conscious delight*, the reader begins to analyze what he reads and his reactions to it. She posits that the reader, after reaching the stage of *conscious delight*, must "be willing to struggle for the artist's meaning even through barriers of time and distance."[2]

She further proposes that if the reader is willing, he can ultimately reach the stage of conscious delight, wherein he will know why he responds to literature with delight, choosing what he reads with discrimination and relying on his own value of a work. At this point, according to Early, the reader has reached the highest level of literary appreciation. Jerry Walker agrees with Early that "our aim as teachers of literature must be to make the reading of literature a delightful experience for our students..." and disagrees with Early that delight occurs in stages. He proposes instead that:

> ... we must accept whatever appreciation a student has to offer, which means that we have to turn our attention from levels to kinds of appreciation. Essentially, there are two kinds: the one which comes from feeling and the one which comes from knowing. The former is the *ooh* experience and the latter is the *aah* experience. Love at first sight is an *ooh* experience; a Platonic relationship is an *aah* experience.[3]

Most teachers would agree with Early and Walker that the cultivation of delight is one of the most important aims in the teaching of literature, whether

---

[1] Margaret Early, "Stages of Growth in Literary Appreciation," *English Journal* 49 (March 1960): 161–167.

[2] *Ibid.*, p. 165.

[3] Jerry L. Walker, "Fostering Literary Appreciation in Junior High School," *English Journal* 55 (Dec. 1966): 1157.

it occurs in stages or not. You will find the task of cultivating delight a challenging one with either early adolescents or late adolescents in whatever kind of school and literature program you work.

THE YOUNGER ONES

As we begin to examine viable approaches that you can use in teaching literature to early adolescents, let us take a look at two potential problems: *you* and *them*. The teacher's background, interests, and understanding of his students is invariably a potent factor in shaping the kind of instruction that will go on in the middle school/junior high school classroom, as well as in determining its relative effectiveness.

Perhaps you are a prospective *or* first-year teacher. What has been your involvement in literature for the past four or five years? Chances are that you've been a *literature major* during your college years rather than (strictly speaking) an *English* major. Chances are, also, that you weren't forced into this decision. You chose it because you like to read and study literature. You enjoy looking at impressive styles, searching for possible meaning, admiring great philosophical truths you sense to be present, and analyzing man in the plights afforded him by various authors. Reading to you isn't a chore; it is an enjoyable pursuit, one from which you never shrink.

You are probably *good* in literature study. You can approach selections written in a variety of genres, from several eras, and by a host of different authors and deal with their symbolized meanings as well as with their complex styles. You can read through these materials with increasing facility and are able to draw inferences and make judgments on them quite independently. Not only that, you have learned to express those inferences and judgments, especially in writing. After a few initial frustrations in sophomore year with the writing of long, scholarly, technically correct papers, you became an old hand at cranking out a coherent piece of prose in reaction to some literary work you'd read.

During this period of growing interest and ability, you may have become, at least to some extent, enamored of literary scholarship. You admire the "Great Books" you have read and enjoyed so much. You are impressed by the smooth critical prose, the brilliant deductions, the far-reaching generalizations and their relation to the human situation. During your reading, you may well have begun to formulate some distinct impressions of the value of literature and literary study of its essential place in the background of the enlightened and liberally educated man.

Another thing about you: there's a distinct possibility that you come from a middle-class background. Maybe you don't passionately espouse William

H. Whyte's Protestant Ethic, but you are quite convinced that there are certain advantages in going to school, working hard at your studies, avoiding penalties for not doing your assigned work, getting good grades, and demonstrating your awareness of ideas and information.

How were you taught during your student years, and how did you go about succeeding in your work? You were usually taught by the lecture-recitation approach. *The Professor* came in with his well-prepared notes, picked up where he left off, and socked it to you for the full period. You sat quietly, took complete notes, asked few questions, accepted his stated inferences and judgments. Then you took a break and headed for another course and another lecture. At appropriate intervals you went to your room or to the library, did your readings, took your notes, and put them together with the lectures. When the time came for the midterm, the term paper, or the final exam, you put a lot of trust in your class notes and in the required work.

While the above description may not fit all people, it probably fits most of us. Prospective teachers need to do some careful introspection before they begin to teach literature to early adolescents. First and foremost, they should be aware of what an imposing number of analyses demonstrate: that we frequently teach the way we were taught. While no one is going to castigate imitation categorically, there are several implications in any such attempts at teaching literature, and these deserve careful review.

With *you* as the basis, then, let's look for a moment at *them* (your students) as prospective readers of literature, also keeping in mind the "to whom" factor discussed earlier.

First of all, in teaching literature to early adolescents, you aren't teaching college literature majors, or even prospective majors. Most of them have *no* background in the study of literature, and they do *not* come to you burning with the desire to learn the great truths from and about the Great Books. If you teach at the fifth or sixth (for middle school) or seventh (for junior high) grade level, you will almost invariably be the *first* literature major who has taught them. Moreover, studies on the certication status of secondary school English teachers indicate that you may be the first bona fide English (that is to say, literature) major who has taught them English, since across the nation three out of five such teachers do *not* have this type of undergraduate background.

One of the first things you must do, then, is to attempt to reconcile your background and motivation with that of your students. Somewhere along the line, someone or something turned you on to the interest, enjoyment, and value of reading serious literary works. (Usually, it was *someone*.) Genuine incentive must be provided for your students—and this holds true for older ones as well. Such incentive does not come in the form of grades, quantitative reading requirements, penalties for lack of productive effort, or other factors. So long as you remember that student motivation in an English class is generally different from yours, you have a good chance of starting off on the right foot.

One of your basic concerns in literature study is your students' relative reading skills. Teenagers who can't read obviously can't read literature. Considering the complex of reading skills involved in the careful, analytic reading of literature, some types of assignments may be presuming too much— such as the barefaced instruction, "Read and explain the real (deeper, author's, etc.) meaning in ————." Critical reaction represents a level of reading ability that must be carefully developed and that depends on some basic skills for its operation.

Word attack skill is another ability that is often presumed when a teacher assigns a literary selection. When a reader encounters a word that is either difficult or unfamiliar to him, he needs to know what to *do* so that the word in question will help him better understand the passage in which it occurs. He needs to have a *variety* of word attack skills at his fingertips, and to be prepared to use another method if the first one doesn't work. The student's success at finding meanings, then, depends both on the skills he has assimilated and on his willingness to try other methods when needed.

In Charles Dickens's *A Christmas Carol*, a work familiar to a large number of early adolescents, Scrooge is described vividly in the final pages as a man deliriously happy to be alive. Dickens pictures his behavior thus:

> "I don't know what to do!" cried Scrooge, laughing and crying in the same breath, and making a perfect Laocoön of himself with his stockings. "I am as light as a feather, I am as happy as an angel, I am as merry as a schoolboy! I am as giddy as a drunken man! A merry Christmas to everybody!"

If the author's picture is to be clearly perceived, it is important for the reader to know *who* Laocoön is and *how* he is being used in this instance. Without describing the process of problem-solving here, this is a clear example of the need for finding meaning in metaphor, a word attack skill basic to the study of not only literature but of all printed discourse. If you can't figure out the answer to the two questions just posed, then this writer has used a counterproductive device: he has *confused* when he hoped to *clarify*.

BUILDING READINESS

While this is not a book on the teaching of reading, it is important to know something about basic reading skills: what they are, where they probably exist in the literary selections students may read, and how to help students work on them, both in isolation and in context. Practice in various approaches toward recognition, work in both the structure and purpose aspects of basic comprehension, the building of appropriate informational and conceptual backgrounds, the use of references, the adjustment of rate to purpose, and the *sustaining* of understanding of unifying ideas—these are some of the more important reading skills that can be profitably *reviewed* and *applied* in preparing early adolescents to read imaginative literature. The fact that these students have been exposed to a good deal of reading instruction in earlier grades is no guarantee that they are efficient readers at the grade level they presently occupy, nor does it mean that they can apply these basic skills to the often highly special contexts of imaginative literature.

All this means that before assigning the independent silent reading of literature, a teacher would do well to work on the prerequisite reading skills. Much suitable instructional material has been published, and some of it is listed in the appendix. In working with students on basic reading skills, however, you should remember that *attitude* may well be a major factor. When we talked earlier about the need for a reader's being *willing* to try subsequent word attack skills when initial ones failed, we were touching on a vital issue. In many cases, you will be dealing not just with poor readers, but with students who have been poor readers for a long time, students who have endured several years of failure in a basic intellectual activity. Therefore you may have to "sell' the need for working on these skills before you begin any actual activity. Much of the success in the teaching of literature may hinge on a teacher's being able and willing to diagnose reading problems, to prepare students for needed instruction, and to execute this instruction. We hope that the "to whom" aspect will be of aid in dealing with this problem.

Beyond ability in teaching basic reading skills, literature teachers should be adept at introducing students to critical reading, especially in regard to drawing inferences and making judgments. Again, a good deal of worthwhile material is available. Hayakawa's discussion of reports, inferences, and judgments in *Language in Thought and Action* can be of real value, as can Booth's *The Rhetoric of Fiction* and Ciardi's *How Does a Poem Mean?*, even though none of these works devotes itself directly to the problems of teaching critical reading. Some further references are also listed in the appendix. It is important to remember that critical reading skills are not easy to master and are built only on a foundation of sound basic ability, especially ability in comprehension. Whatever you do, don't ask your students what *might be meant* in a literary work until you are reasonably sure that they know *what* is going on in the work, *who* is in it, *when* and *where* things are occurring, and in *what order*. Some of the suggestions about asking questions of students, described in Part VI, may help you in this area.

Since most teachers want their students to do more than *just read* literary selections, some attention needs to be paid to eliciting reactions from them. A study made over twenty years ago by Walter Loban concluded, among other things, that students often don't know what to say about the works they read. More recently, James Britton raised the contention that *saying nothing* about a literary selection may not necessarily mean that the student did not understand the work or that it had no impact on him. On the contrary, Britton claims, there may be a powerful reaction going on; we just can't perceive it because the reader is either unable or unwilling to express his response. In any case, the structuring of situations in which early adolescents will be able and comfortable in expressing their responses—*any* responses—to what they have read needs careful attention. Some of the suggestions made in Part IV (on the composition process) could be helpful here, as well as the discussion on method in Part VI teaching (on style). In any event, several things may hamper the early adolescent in his honest, independent response to selections he has read. Here are a few of them:

1. Emphasis on the factual aspects of the work—right-or-wrong questions on the concrete elements of a work *as ends in themselves*. This approach tends to emphasize isolated aspects of a work rather than its total meaning.
2. The assigning and grading of written answers to comprehension and interpretation questions—much groundwork of various kinds, with stress on oral classroom interaction (described in both Part IV and Part VI), should precede any "book report" or "essay question" assignment. To make such assignments without preparing students for them, is really testing something you haven't taught.
3. Teachers' pronouncements on what works "really mean"—let's face it: most students, early in their education, learn to be pragmatists. They sense that if they say what *you* say, they'll do well in a given response situation. The more you inflict your inferences and judgments on them, the more they may conform in their responses and stop making *their own* inferences and judgments.
4. Lack of cooperative investigation of what we *know* in the work. While facts and details aren't an end in themselves, they are a means to an end, and as such should be understood by the students through the classroom interaction strategies that you devise and introduce. What a selection *means* has a lot to do with *what happens* in it, and these happenings should be clear to all your students before any more complex thinking is demanded. Such a simple matter as who is speaking in the work, to whom, and under what circumstances— these are all fundamentally important in arriving at deeper understandings, and should not be overlooked.
5. Lack of allowance for personal involvement—Archibald MacLeish has said that the good teacher of literature has "one foot in the text and one in reality." It is important that you give your students every opportunity to express what their reading means *to them*. While this matter will be covered shortly in some detail, responses will be better developed when students can express ways in which things they have just read relate to their world; you should therefore be wary of denying them this opportunity.
6. Lack of variety in the patterns of response—some responses can be written, some oral. Some can be made on an individual basis, some by groups. Some questions may come from the students, some from you. Monotony, as represented by a "read the story; answer the questions in the study guide" approach can go a long way toward frustrating enthusiastic responses from

readers of all ages (see the article by John S. Simmons in *Journal of Reading*, Oct. 1968).

7. Insensitivity to affective causes of failure to respond—before they can be asked to offer their insights or opinions on various aspects of literary works, students need to be made as comfortable as possible with their peers and with the teacher. If an atmosphere of repression, skepticism, or intolerance is present in the classroom, many students may feel too intimidated to express their feelings. They will generally clam up, and will offer only standard clichés when called upon. By creating a positive, accepting, enthusiastic atmosphere for responses from all students, the teacher can help immeasurably in the growth of a stimulating and thriving classroom.

Students who are not guided in structuring responses, who are not motivated to respond to what they read, or who are frustrated in their attempts to express what *they* perceive and feel may tune themselves out completely to the literature they read. They may plagiarize, overgeneralize, or resort to clichés ("the work was interesting," "the characters were lifelike," "I couldn't put it down"). Or they may just clam up. In any case, ability and desire to respond to what has been read cannot be *presumed;* they must be developed carefully and instituted tactfully if we are ever to know *any* of the things that happen to our students through their reading.

Early adolescents come to the study of literature with another important characteristic: that of relatively limited experience. Literature is about *life;* thus when one reads literature, he must be able to relate it in some way to life situations in order for it to be meaningful. Without a fund of personal experience, it is difficult for a reader of literature to empathize with the human situations he finds therein. As so many American novelists of this century have suggested, the adolescent is in *the process of becoming;* he has not yet arrived at adulthood nor has he participated in many of the climactic, far-reaching decisions common to people who marry, raise families, become involved in the world of work, joust for political power, face death in war, or what have you. While this statement is probably obvious, it does point out the need for careful selection of literary materials for the early adolescent reader. Works based on adult situations and life styles may well confuse him, escape him entirely, or turn him off. He may well have some indirect involvement in such situations, as in the viewing of movies and television dramas, but his actual participation in many matters described in literature will probably be severely limited, making many works of literature fully *irrelevant.* The teacher who wishes to demonstrate dramatically the parallels between experience as recorded in literature and as occurring in real life needs to consider two main courses of action. He must either choose works that are within the emotional range of his readers, or he must provide related activities that will build necessary awarenesses in his students. Using both strategies will probably be the most effective way of making literature meaningful to them.

We have already discussed the fact that many novels are within the emotional range of adolescent students, so selecting them is not as hard as providing activities that will build necessary awarenesses. It is in this area that the humanists have provided the most help. For example, in George Isaac Brown's *Human Teaching for Learning: An Introduction to Confluent Education*, several unit and lesson outlines are provided that illustrate how you go about not only developing skills but also eliciting "felt knowledge," that is, awarenesses. Two general objectives repeated over and over in the English units in this book are: to gain further understanding of human beings and to see ourselves in the lives of others. Though these general objectives are not new in English classrooms and though they are not stated in behavioral skill-oriented terms, the means by which they are attained are new and are humanistically student-centered. Another book that gives many illustrations of how to develop awarenesses is *Will the Real Teacher Please Stand Up?*, by Greer and Rubinstein.

Those critics who have cast aspersions on humanistic approaches have done so, we feel, because they have not seen how these exercises can be translated into meaningful ways of building awarenesses that can be directly related to the classroom, especially the English classroom in which the study of literature is based almost entirely on the way an artist has expressed his message about human relations.

Although students are constantly interacting with other humans in a variety of roles and situations, many may not have stopped to analyze or even attempt to express the complex web of emotions, motivations, and reactions in which they are involved daily. Therefore, it is important that they be allowed to express their feelings, to learn how to express them, in order for them to experience how difficult expression really is. Perhaps they will not immediately "appreciate" how an artist does this through poetry, drama, or prose, but they might develop awarenesses of how difficult it is to express honest feelings to someone else in any form through some of the humanistic exercises described in the books mentioned.

Another way to develop awareness is to get the students involved in what it is like to be a writer—a writer of science fiction or biography, for example. Though this might be classified as creative writing and really should appear in the composition section, research has shown that students write better when they are writing *about* something, and literature study often is the vehicle to write something about. That is, how do writers *do* writing? Where do they get their ideas? They do *not* get them from some English teacher assigning something in a classroom about something unrelated to their interest and experience. Most of the people who make a living by writing have had a great deal of living experience, both actual and vicarious, and, of course, most of them write about what they like, know, have done, or have fantasized about. Hemingway drove ambulances, attended bullfights, fished near Pamplona, Spain, and off the shores of Cuba, knew soldiers, experienced war, talked and drank with interesting people. All of his novels and stories are fictionalized versions of what he did or thought he did. James Joyce was Irish, Catholic, and a Dubliner —he wrote about Irish, Catholic Dubliners. But most kids, you say, have not done such exciting things or met such exotic people. However, S. E. Hinton was just a kid writing about what she knew when she wrote *The Outsiders*, and the anonymous writer of *Go Ask Alice* wrote about what she knew and had experienced. This means that even junior high school students can write about what they know if they take the time to observe, think about it, and try to express it. Or, they can find out about things they are interested in and become "experts."

For example, most adolescent readers seem to be interested in science fiction. Isaac Asimov, Robert Heinlein, Andre Norton, Jules Verne, and Ray Bradbury consistently rank as favorite authors, but probably few students feel they can write science fiction because it seems to require a scientific background (like that of Asimov or Crichton) in order to come up with plausible yet fantastic material. Yet, plausible, fantastic information is available to anyone who wants to search for it. Most science fiction starts with fact, then goes one step beyond and asks, "What if . . . ?"

Suppose you have developed a unit or a phase-elective course on science fiction. It would seem appropriate that one of the assignments would be for the students to try to write their own science fiction stories. Part of your study might well entail the analysis of how much science fiction is based on fact or phenomena, where the writer got his idea, and how he went beyond the known, scientific information. This could provide the basis for the students' own fantastic renditions.

One such phenomenon is the "Bermuda triangle"—a triangular area that includes part of the east coast of Florida, the Atlantic Ocean, and Bermuda, in which ships, planes, and even squadrons of planes, have been mysteriously lost. The triangle might be a magnetic field, but whatever it is, it causes instruments and humans to lose orientation so that people suddenly, strangely vanish with no trace, nothing to witness what happened to them. Navy and other government documents describe some of the strange losses that have occurred in this area. In preparation for writing their stories, students could do intensive research on this phenomenon—finding what has happened, when, and to whom. (What better way to teach research skills than in preparation for creative writing?) After doing their research, the students translate their information into a fictional story about a particular plane or ship that became lost in this area, relating from a particular character's point of view what "actually" happened, what he experienced, what he saw, what he felt. No one knows what really did occur, and this "step beyond fact" makes for the fantasy of science fiction. This is only one example of scores of strange physical phenomena in the world in which students could become actively engaged. This type of writing experience not only provides the opportunity for research, but also helps students to become aware of what a science fiction writer does in order to create his exciting stories.

A reader's background is closely related to his experience, but this creates another kind of problem in the teaching of literature. While *experience* is what actually happens to a person firsthand—with its intense impact on him— background is what the individual accumulates through a variety of secondhand sources such as reading, listening, and viewing. Since input of this nature is not usually as intense, it may not be as meaningful as actual experience. However, a person needs background from a variety of sources in order for much of what he reads to make any sense to him. One of the major reasons for introducing units on mythology, folklore, legendry, and biblical narrative in the middle school-junior high years is that they help to build such background. A knowledge of history, current affairs, sociology, and other topics should also aid the student in understanding the literary works he reads. This background, it must be realized, doesn't automatically ooze through a reader's pores. It must be accumulated by either direct or indirect means, and many well-intentioned teachers become sorely frustrated when they *presume* some things are in their students' backgrounds that, in fact, aren't.

To be more specific, let's take a quick look at "Musée des Beaux Arts," a well-known poem by the twentieth century poet W. H. Auden.

Musée des Beaux Arts

About suffering they were never wrong,
The Old Masters: how well they understood
Its human position; how it takes place
While someone else is eating or opening a window or just
    walking dully along;
How, when the aged are reverently, passionately waiting
For the miraculous birth, there always must be
Children who did not specially want it to happen, skating
On a pond at the edge of the wood:
They never forgot
That even the dreadful martyrdom must run its course
Anyhow in a corner, some untidy spot
Where the dogs go on with their doggy life and the torturer's
    horse
Scratches its innocent behind on a tree.
In Brueghel's Icarus, *for instance: how everything turns away*
Quite leisurely from the disaster; the ploughman may
Have heard the splash, the forsaken cry,
But for him it was not an important failure; the sun shone
As it had to on the white legs disappearing into the green
Water; the expensive delicate ship that must have seen
Something amazing, a boy falling out of the sky,
Had somewhere to get to and sailed calmly on.[4]

W. H. AUDEN

Notice the need for background on the part of the reader right from the start. He has to know who the "Old Masters" were right away. (They must be capitalized for a reason.) Then, a few lines later, he must have some handle

---

on "the miraculous birth" (which one?) in order for the next couple of lines to make sense. This would also apply to the "dreadful martyrdom" that follows shortly. If the reader puts the latter two images together, he *may* visualize the birth and death of Christ, which will help in giving some concreteness to the abstract concept of suffering. In any event, he needs background in order for the allusions to make sense.

The most critical need for background, however, can be found in the *Icarus* allusion. The image of Icarus falling into the sea, as Brueghel portrays it, is essential if one is to comprehend how Auden perceives and illustrates suffering. The reader needs more than a glossary-type meaning: he needs to be able to recall the story of Icarus mentally, so that he can see the context in which his fall took place. That background must be *built* somehow, and it can be built effectively through the presentation of units such as mythology, folklore, legendry, and biblical narrative (*all* of which contain some pretty exciting, suspenseful stuff). The use of nonprint media to reinforce silent reading should also be considered.

Early adolescents need classroom assistance in the building of a background of human experiences. Willie Loman (in the play *Death of a Salesman*), in trying to explain his situation in the hotel room to his son Biff, says, "When you're older, you'll understand these things." The fact is, however, that Biff *isn't* older—nor are the early adolescents who have not experienced or developed enough background, or felt the pressing need to generalize to any appreciable degree. For these reasons the teacher who would promote the literature-life relationship among his young students had better go slowly and carefully.

Let's go back to Auden's poem one more time to identify a matter closely related both to background and experience. We mentioned metaphor previously in reference to Laocoön. The fact is that the whole matter of suffering is an *abstract*. Laocoön was a man. You could draw him, watch him in action, running down from the temple or being killed by the serpents, or you could touch his statue. Not so with suffering, or with any other abstract concepts with which teachers may wish to deal. The ability to identify and express meanings (note the plural) of abstract terms is a much overlooked skill. Involved here is the ability to conceptualize, to manipulate symbols, to perceive relationships among entities—all quite intellectually demanding tasks. If students haven't been given exercises in the simplest forms of abstract meaning, it will be difficult for them to deal with abstract concepts or propositions that they encounter in literary works. Suffering isn't always as simple as the loss of an arm. It is often hard to visualize, to describe, or to put into concrete, mutually intelligible terms. Therefore, when abstract concepts are dealt with, the literature teacher should be certain that the necessary background and thinking processes have been developed. The units in Perceiving Relationships in the Cognitive Processes Curriculum (grades seven through nine), developed by the Florida State University Project English Curriculum Center, offer some excellent *readiness* activities in learning to perceive the abstract.

Closely related to the factors of experience and background is that of interest. Among early adolescents, distinct patterns of interest can be discerned. Unquestionably, the interests of a reader are vital in any attempt to involve him actively in the reading and study of literature. It may be worthwhile to remind teachers that boys' interests, especially in reading, are much more *limited* than those of girls. Boys are also less tolerant of the materials they read, are more critical of assigned readings, and tend to give up more quickly. Both sexes, however, exhibit low interest in topics such as didacticism, moral-religious themes, community life, and literary form—to mention only a few. Interest, however, can be *built* in the classroom, and Norvell, in both of his well-known summaries on adolescent reading interest, insists that teacher enthusiasm is an important factor at all levels. An important question, raised earlier, is how involved will teenagers become in literary works that focus wholly or largely on adult situations. While a teacher's enthusiasm can do much to promote these works, he should have some background in popular literature for adolescents at the middle school-junior high level. Most well-written works on the teen-age situation focus on one meaningful factor: the *process of becoming.* The concept of initiation into adulthood can be found in literary works of all genres, from various eras, and on all levels of subtlety. Teachers would do well to keep abreast of books that portray the adolescent situation. They can provide an effective mirror through which early adolescents can view themselves while taking their initial look at literary selections.

Also related to the interest factor is that of *choice.* We suggest that teachers vary their assignments from all-class to group to individualized reading. Whenever possible, give your students some choice in kinds of responses to the works they read, especially in the case of all-class reading of a given selection. Naturally, the building of reading lists related to various themes and topics, as well as lists found in a variety of readily available professional publications, will aid greatly in the individualizing process. It is probably safe to say that the days of a rigidly prescribed reading list for all secondary school students, including the familiar *Silas Marner, Ivanhoe, Great Expectations, Tale of Two Cities,* and *Macbeth* standbys, have passed, and that there is a widespread movement toward more individualized choice in literary selections, with emphasis on literary realism, contemporary works, multiethnic materials, and science fiction. We applaud this movement and encourage teachers to make more works available, to make choices easier, to relax taboos, and tolerate individual tastes. Teachers should be eternally vigilant against overemphasis on forced choices and values in literature assignments, especially when antithetical to the interests of the students.

Before leaving the matter of reading interests, we'd like to remind you of the unique spot in which you find yourself when you introduce literature to early adolescents. When (and *if*) you attempt to move your students from the *reading* to the *study* of literature, you are doing something that is probably unique in the curriculum. During their earlier years in school, most kids probably perceived literature as a "fun" or a "change of pace" activity. They *studied* math, they *studied* spelling, they *worked on* science. But literature was typically not a commodity to be studied. It was read aloud to them. They acted it, they sang it. They dealt with it at a leisurely pace. This was their *modus operandi* with literature.

Then along *you* come. You introduce the notion that literature is also a commodity to be studied. It deals with serious matters, which need to be considered seriously. It has a history. It is manifested in a variety of describable genres. It has a unique way of expressing things symbolically. It can be complex because it is about life, which can in turn be complex. It may require close, analytic, *critical* reading, and this takes effort and intensive analysis. These are some of the things you ask kids to do when you ask them to begin the *study* of literature. They take something that *used to be fun* and work hard at it. "But," you may say almost as an afterthought, "I'd still like you to enjoy it!" Thus, literature really has a singular role in a school curriculum. It can be approached in either of the ways described. There can be, as Margaret Early states, both unconscious and self-conscious appreciation to be gained from the same reading assignment. The reconciling of the two ways of dealing with literature—as a form of enjoyment and as a task—is one of your most crucial jobs, especially when *introducing* literature to younger students.

Differences between your own social background and that of your students may cause other kinds of problems in introducing literature study. There are many students in secondary schools today who just don't want to be there. If there are any aspects of the curriculum that do interest them, they are of a concrete, applicable nature. These students may participate in certain physical education activities, they may work hard in the automotive shop or the cosmetology lab, or they may just tune education out. Their perspective of the past and present probably comes largely through television viewing and the piles of sensation magazines readily available in virtually every drugstore or newsstand. They have difficulty in perceiving the value of reading serious works slowly (hard work), in relating these works to reality as they understand it (intellectually demanding), and in expressing these perceptions orally or in writing (a time-consuming, often clumsy task). A teacher of these youngsters needs to get off the "academic kick" fast. His first move should be an appraisal of himself as a purveyor of literature and a search for ways in which reading can be meaningfully related to their world. The saturation and permissive approaches described in some detail in Fader and McNeil's *Hooked on Books* are worth investigating before a teacher attempts to introduce literature to these students.

One more characteristic of your students should be mentioned before further suggestions for teaching can be made. It is important to keep in mind the relative attention spans of your students. The task of concentrating on independent, silent, purposeful reading is a demanding one for all people. For some, especially for those who are relatively immature and unmotivated, it can be an overwhelming one. They find it nearly impossible to stay with a literary work for long periods of time when so many potential distractions exist. To help with the attention span problem, here are some suggestions:

1. Use many short, high-interest selections at the outset.
2. Provide breaks in the reading, at which time discussion can take place.
3. Assign in-class reading so that you can observe students in the act of concentration.
4. Interchange silent with oral reading of the same or related works.
5. Establish clear, simple, concrete goals at the outset of reading assignments, and state them in nontechnical language.
6. Provide nonprinted aids to supplement the text—bulletin boards, slide-tape presentations, filmstrips, records can all help.
7. Keep the room as free from distractions as possible during independent, silent reading.
8. Make yourself available for conference with your students on what they are reading silently.
9. *Reward* completion of assigned reading tasks, especially with erstwhile reluctant students.
10. Make alternate and supplementary materials available whenever possible.

Limited attention span is a major problem with anyone who doesn't read well or doesn't like to read. That's one of the big reasons why he has reading problems. As a diagnostician, you should plan in-class silent reading periods early in the year in order to make an assessment of the varying degrees with which your students can concentrate.

Two kinds of classroom activity seem to us to have great potential value in leading early adolescents into the study of imaginative literature. They can be labelled as *readiness* and *reinforcement* activities, and their main purpose is to provide an adequate context in which the independent silent reading of a literary work can be undertaken more easily and meaningfully. The use of short thematic units (two to three weeks), typically based on concrete topics ("The Village," "Man Among Enemies," "Far Away Places," and the like) is better than more abstract ways of providing such a context. In this approach, the theme is introduced first; it is illustrated and discussed with the class, *and then* works related in various ways to the theme can be introduced. The use of nonreading activities—media presentations, improvised dramatic activities, analyses of language similar to that used in the works to be studied, divergent questions (described in Section VI), the writing of hypothetical prologues and epilogues to selections—all these can help provide a clearer context for reading.

Specifically, readiness activities are those that are utilized before independent silent reading takes place. They may relate to needed reading skills. They may involve consideration of experience correlative to that in the work. They may include a look at language characteristic of that used. The main intention of readiness work is to maneuver the student into a position where he can more easily cope with the style, content, and relevance of a work he is asked to read.

WORKING ON REINFORCEMENT

Reinforcement has to do with what happens in class once the independent, silent reading of a work is completed. It can take the form of reactions (either oral or written), and can be by individual or group, formal or informal. It can involve readers assuming the roles of characters in the work. It can involve the use of nonprinted media to illustrate the total work, excerpts from it, or a selection to be composed or contracted. In the reading of longer works (novels, biographies, plays) reinforcement can be utilized during the reading as well as at the conclusion. An example of this is the "Progressive Exercise," in which the teacher has the student read up to a certain predetermined juncture, usually a climactic moment, in the work. Then the student asks himself three questions and answers them orally or (preferably) in writing. They are:

1. What has happened to this point?
2. What effect has the action had on the people involved?
3. What do you think will happen next?

By using this technique, the reader soon realizes how his insight into the work can grow as he reads further. He can check back, after subsequent reading, to see how valid his earlier predictions were. This activity can keep the younger reader on the track, it can help him sustain his understanding of the work, and hopefully it can increase his attention span.

A teacher should always be alert to the possibilities for including both readiness and reinforcement activities with early adolescent readers. For example, here is a teaching activity one of us used recently with a group of seventh graders.

This activity revolved around the reading of and reaction to Shirley Jackson's well-known short story "The Lottery," which has proved to be a highly popular selection among junior high students in six schools during the Florida State University Curriculum Study Center experiment and among countless students everywhere in past years. The seventh-graders introduced to this treatment were of "modest" ability, a mean reading level of 3.6 years on the Gates-McGinitie Reading Survey.

With the awareness of the students' relative immaturity and lack of reading ability, the teacher developed two kinds of readiness activities: *word attack* and *experiential.* The word attack exercises were of two kinds: using context clues and finding meaning in metaphor. Sections on these two skills in the text *Success in Reading, Book One* (Silver Burdett) were used as a guide, but much of the introduction was done orally. Sentences such as "He laughed. He jumped. He shouted. He had never been so happy. He was simply *buoyant*" were put on the board, and the clues to the meaning of the hard words were identified. Then the teacher passed out some further context clue sentences, which the students worked on at their desks. The sentences contained increasingly harder words and fewer clues:

> The morning of June 27th was clear and sunny, with the fresh warmth of a full-summer day; the flowers were blossoming *profusely* and the grass was richly green.
>
> School was recently over for the summer, and the feeling of liberty sat uneasily on most of them; they tended to gather together quietly for a while before they broke into *boisterous* play, and their talk was still of the classroom and the teacher, of books and reprimands.
>
> The lottery was conducted—as were the square dances, the teen-age club, the Halloween program—by Mr. Summers, who had time and energy to devote to *civic* activities.
>
> There was a story that the present box had been made with some pieces of the box that had *preceded* it, the one that had been constructed when the first people settled down to make a village here. Every year, after the lottery, Mr. Summers began talking again about a new box, but every year the subject was allowed to fade off without anything's being done.
>
> There was the proper swearing-in of Mr. Summers by the postmaster, as the official of the lottery; at one time, some people remembered, there had been a recital of some sort, performed by the official of the lottery, a *perfunctory*, tuneless chant that had been rattled off duly each year; some people believed that the official of the lottery used to stand just so when he said or sang it, others believed that he was supposed to walk among the people, but years and years ago this part of the *ritual* had been allowed to lapse.
>
> She hesitated for a minute, looking around *defiantly*, and then set her lips and went up to the box. She snatched a paper out and held it behind her.[5]

If you have read the story, you will recognize these passages as being from "The Lottery."

After the context work had been completed, the teacher put a sentence such as this on the board: "I really fell for that used-car salesman's line." Through discussion the students demonstrated their awareness of the *metaphoric* nature of this statement and the difference between the literal and the intended meaning of it. Following the discussion, material was passed out to them containing metaphoric expressions composed by the teacher, and they worked through the problem-solving process of identifying the intended meanings:

1. "The rest of the year, the Box was put away, sometimes one place, sometimes another; it had spent one year in Mr. Grave's barn and another year

---

[5] Reprinted with the permission of Farrar, Straus & Giroux, Inc. from "The Lottery" by Shirley Jackson. Copyright 1948, 1949 by Shirley Jackson. "The Lottery" originally appeared in *The New Yorker*.

underfoot in the post office, and sometimes it was set on a shelf in the Martin grocery and left there."

2. "There was the proper swearing-in of Mr. Summers by the postmaster, as the official of the lottery; at one time, some people remembered, there had been a recital of some sort, performed by the official of the lottery, a perfunctory, tuneless chant that had been rattled off duly each year."
3. "Mrs. Hutchinson craned her neck to see through the crowd and found her husband and children standing near the front."
4. "Horace's not but sixteen yet," Mrs. Dunbar said regretfully. "Guess I gotta fill in for the old man this year."
5. "A sudden hush fell over the crowd."
6. "Nancy and Bill, Jr., opened theirs at the same time, and both beamed, and laughed, turning around to the crowd and holding their slips of paper above their heads."

Once more, the sentences were taken from the text that the students would eventually read.

After the work on these two word attack skills had been completed (these two skills are often needed in the reading of literature), the teacher put this question on the board and asked the students to think about it:

"Suppose you lived in a place where they had a custom which could hurt people badly. The people in that place had been doing it for years, but you thought it was wrong. What would you do?"

This question was the focus of a good deal of animated discussion and constitutes a means of providing a second kind of readiness—that of an experiential nature. The students had a chance to think about, visualize, and discuss a hypothetical experience that was *correlative* with that which they would find in "The Lottery." They dealt with a human problem and proposed their solutions, comparing these solutions with those of other class members. Among other things, the text provided them with the problem and a solution played out in dramatic terms.

At the conclusion of this discussion, the teacher passed out copies of the story and gave the students the entire period to read it silently, encouraging them to finish, reread, or review the story after class. At the next class meeting, he played a record of Shirley Jackson reading the story. (If the record isn't available, the teacher could read it himself and make a tape or cassette of the reading.) During the playing of the record, the students could follow along in the text or not, as they wished. While there are definite advantages to the relating of language expressed orally to its appearance in print, this attempt to follow the oral reading in the text can be confusing to some students, especially those with reading disabilities. For this reason, the choice was left to the students.

The playing of the recording was the first of a series of *reinforcement* activities conducted by the teacher. Impressions gained through silent reading were broadened and intensified through the use of Miss Jackson's adept oral interpretation. Following this, the teacher tacked a large drawing on the board, a drawing of an incident. The drawing (the first of five to be exhibited) was done by a senior high art student who, at the teacher's request, identified for himself five striking visual images in the story as *he* perceived them and then drew his impression of them. (Maybe you could do this yourself; the author-teacher in this case is decidedly *unrenowned* as an artist!) The students were then asked if the drawing represented a scene from the story they had just read. They agreed that it did, and then the teacher asked them to *find the words* that represented *to them* the drawing they were viewing. Here are two examples:

As a reinforcement activity, drawings (including paintings, photographs, cartoons, and slides) have three potentially valuable uses:

1. They provide an opportunity for the students to relate the *verbal* to the visual. Most of today's adolescents are highly oriented to visual media.
2. They get the student to examine the text for evidence, a habit badly needed in the qualifying of generalizations. The students had to find the *exact* words representing the drawing, which served as an introductory exercise in reading to analyze.
3. The students were asked to compare *their* visual impression, gained from looking at the words, to another person's, who had also read them, thus introducing the reading of material for inferences. This shows the students that the same words can often create different *impressions* from reader to reader.

Each of the five drawings was shown in its turn, and the students searched the text for the verbal representation of each one. When this was

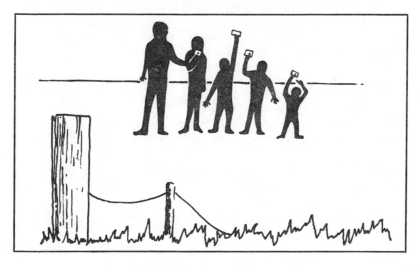

completed, the teacher replaced all five on the board *but out of the order in which they occurred in the story*. The students were then asked to rearrange them in the order in which they had actually occurred. This exercise relates to one of the great, overlooked problems in reading comprehension: reading to identify order or establish sequence. If a student can't identify the chronological events in a selection as they occur, he will obviously have trouble identifying *cause-and-effect* relationships, which are so vital in understanding what literature is all about. Thus the establishment of sequence is an important reading reinforcement exercise and needs, we feel, to be stressed heavily.

When the pictures had been taken down, the teacher passed out this exercise to the students:

DIRECTIONS: PUT THE FOLLOWING EVENTS IN THE ORDER IN WHICH THEY ACTUALLY OCCUR IN THE STORY

1. Mrs. Hutchinson arrives at the square.
2. Five slips of paper are returned to the black box.
3. All the villagers open their slips of paper.
4. The villagers begin to throw the stones.
5. The townspeople, first the children, then the elders, gather in the town square.
6. The first men come forward to draw slips of paper from the box.
7. Mr. Summers arrives with the black wooden box.

In this exercise, the students were asked to establish proper sequence of events as seen in print. The movement in the sequence exercise was, again, *from visual to verbal*, thus capitalizing on early adolescents' potential *strength* in perception.

Following this comprehension reinforcement, the teacher divided the class into four groups of unequal numbers and passed out this set of activities:

ROLE PLAYING ACTIVITIES—"THE LOTTERY"

1. Assume that we have a young person who lives in the town, another young person from a town that has dropped the Lottery, and that they confront Old Man Warner about the advisability of continuing the custom.
2. Let us assume Mr. Summers has become less henpecked and suddenly takes on a more rebellious nature. What would he say to his wife and a group of village residents?
3. Assume that a group of five townsfolk got together to discuss the stoning of Tessie Hutchinson after the event had taken place. Recreate the way their conversation might have run.
4. Recreate the discussions that might have taken place between Mr. Hutchinson and his children in the privacy of their home after the stoning of Tessie.

Each of the four situations was discussed briefly, and then each group was given a situation to act out via an improvised drama.* While the teacher

---

*For a detailed discussion of this classroom activity, see pp. 294–298.

in this case allowed the groups an entire period to prepare their presentations (and he spent that period working with each group as time allowed), the amount of time spent in preparation is really up to you. We point out, however, that this was a purely *oral* activity with no written scripts at all. Each group then gave its presentation, and the rest of the class was asked to react to it.

In a role playing activity, the students are asked to *react critically* to a work they have just read but are asked to do so via *involvement* and *use of imagination* rather than by some quasi-scholarly, written "book report" device. Needless to say, this activity should not be *graded*, nor should it be in the other activities previously described. If a teacher prefers to use writing exercises as reinforcement, here are some exercises that can be used. Note the degree to which they also require various degrees of involvement and use of imagination, asking the student to relate the work to life as he perceives it—this is, after all, one of the things literature is all about.

ORAL OR WRITTEN STATEMENTS—"THE LOTTERY"

1. Change the handling of the story to the way it might appear in a TV serial.
2. Suppose you were a person of your age living in the town and that you opposed this custom. What arguments would you use with your parents? With your peers?
3. Do you think this story could have taken place in 1971? Why, or why not?
4. What might happen if all the children of the village lined up together and opposed their parents on continuing the lottery?
5. (For urban students.) Would the lottery be a likely custom in a city of this size? Why, or why not?

The use of readiness and reinforcement activities, then, can aid the early adolescent in developing a meaningful context for works he reads. If his limitations and needs are seriously considered by the teacher, and if contexts for his reading are carefully established, the transition we ask him to make from reading to the study of literature may not be so difficult after all.

Chapter 5

Developing and Reinforcing the Study of Imaginative Literature

PROBLEMS WITH OLDER KIDS

Much of what we have said about matters of concern in teaching literature to early adolescents also applies directly to those more mature students in senior high school. This can represent an initial problem for you in the classroom. It comes as a great shock to many inexperienced teachers, for example, that numbers of senior high students, especially boys, are inefficient readers. The fact is that these youngsters have had a few more years to "practice" their ineptness and to beome more aware of their plight than have their younger counterparts. Many of these older students also have relatively limited experiences, inadequate backgrounds for some literary works, difficulty in dealing with abstract concepts, pronounced and often nonacademic interests, widely varied socioeconomic backgrounds, and short attention spans. Moreover, if they have been turned off by initial forays into the study of literature, they may be very difficult to rehabilitate. Their inevitably increasing pragmatism about school in general and its relation to their lives may lead them to become adept "con artists" in literary study or to tell the teacher to go to hell with his reading-and-response demands.

One problem a teacher of older adolescents faces more intensively in literature study than probably any other area is that of range of reading abilities and tastes. Some students in your classes will be quite advanced in reading ability and will have very mature, sophisticated tastes. In the same classroom will be students who are badly disabled readers and whose taste does not go beyond the comic book, "poisonous passion" (complete with seminude, buxom blonde on the cover) offerings of the drugstore spindle. Thus plenty of non-reading readiness work needs to be done with senior high students, both in terms of identifying conditions present and in providing correlative experiences to upcoming reading assignments. A good bit of investigation should be done in the early days of class before any full-blown literature unit is introduced. Teacher-led or student-led activities such as discussions on contemporary issues, speech essays, films, slide-tape presentations, visual poems, collages, and the like (described in Section V) are good beginnings. A teacher who uses these readiness approaches will probably learn a great deal about what students are and are not interested in, the nature and extent of their responses to serious issues, their ability to see *their* involvement as an aspect of human experience, and will come to realize much about the background and prejudice they bring to issues of human value. In order to gain these insights a teacher has to be highly enthusiastic during the readiness period, but must refrain from dominating discussions or inflicting *his* set of values on his students.

Improvised drama also poses a problem at this level. While role playing activities may work with middle school and junior high students, many of the more blasé senior high types may consider them silly and back off entirely. For this reason, you should look around carefully during the investigation period and try to pick out those who like to act. Then try an improvised dramatic exercise early in the year and reward the participants vigorously. If entered into in the proper spirit, improvised drama can be of inestimable value, both as readiness and as reinforcement.

More than anything else, you need to provide for a variety of approaches to the study of literature with your older students, in terms of the preteaching, reading, and response phases. Try to avoid such stereotyped approaches as:

1. Read Chapters one–three of *Tale of Two Cities* on Monday. We'll discuss them on Tuesday. Chapters four–six on Wednesday, discussion on Thursday —and, of course, thirty spelling words takes care of Friday.
2. Read about the author's life in the anthology. Then read the story and answer the study questions that follow. There will be a test next Friday.
3. Here is a reading list—of the Classics. Your first book report is due September 30th, the second on October 25th, and the third on November 20th. Now, let's get on with our diagramming of participial phrases.

VARIOUS APPROACHES

The kinds of variety we recommend are explained in some detail in the method discussion of Part VI. Relating literary concern to the increasingly mature, serious outlook of the majority of senior high students is a most important goal. Monotony in such study can largely frustrate this goal. Beyond this, senior high students, because they are closer to adulthood, should be given not more of the same, but more. By "more of the same" we mean assigning 250 pages instead of 100, *because the students are older*, or asking for 500 to 800 words in a paper rather than 100 to 200. By "more" we mean that students should be able to approach their reading from a variety of directions and should participate both in choice of works to be read and in kinds of responses to be rendered; i.e., "more" means variety of classroom strategies. Obviously, in terms of choices of selections, the mores of the community remain a potent factor. Don't forget that censorship is still a major issue in this country and that the Bill of Rights may not be as all-encompassing as it once was. As Postman and Weingartner would probably say, you must learn to act well your part in the Soft Revolution. Naturally, though, student participation in choosing materials to be read and discussed can't help but increase enthusiasm for the task.[1]

When it comes to choosing the packages (units) for literature teaching, several factors need to be considered. The growing, popular trend toward elective programs solves much of the problem of packaging. When we encounter semester-long components such as "Black Literature," "Science Fiction," or "The Romantic Spirit," we almost immediately have a pretty good insight into what is going to be taught.

Chronological organization, a time-honored approach, has some obvious drawbacks. It is *not* too popular with adolescent classes. The era-by-era approach typically features a group of old standby selections, and becomes rather mundane and monotonous unless taught by a distinctly dynamic individual. A more serious problem lies in the level of language of works typically taught early in the year. Particularly in British and American literature surveys, this language is the type *most remote* from the understandings and experiences of the students who must wade through it. Thus there is a danger that some of the reading that is predictably the most difficult must be done early in the year and possibly without adequate readiness.

---

[1] The issue of censorship in the teaching of literature is a serious and ongoing problem. It involves the attitudes and values of school boards, religious leaders, citizens' organizations, political pressure groups, sometimes even the police! There is not space in this chapter to discuss the matter adequately, but you should be aware that several prominent national organizations have brought this matter before the American public. Some publications on this topic include:

1. NCTE, *The Students' Right to Read* (Urbana, Ill., 1974).
2. Lee Burress, "How Censorship Affects the School," Wisconsin Council of Teachers of English, Special Bulletin # 8 (Oct. 1963).
3. John P. Frank and Robert F. Hogan, "Obscenity, the Language and the English Teacher," NCTE (1966).
4. Arizona English Bulletin, "Censorship and the English Teacher," Arizona State University (Feb. 1969).
5. American Library Association, "The Library Bill of Rights," rev. ed. (Chicago, 1971).
6. Dan Gacy, *Freedom and Communications*, 2nd ed. (University of Illinois Press, 1965). Remember the discussion of elective programs in Chapter Two.

Perhaps the most significant drawback to the chronological approach lies in the lack of relevance to contemporary areas of concern exemplified by so many works read during the opening weeks of the year. *Beowulf* probably comes in September, when the students are potentially fresh and ready for some interesting reading. The modern British writers get treated in May or early June (if at all), when large numbers of students have already tuned out of the school scene. Thus much material with involvement potential doesn't have the impact it might have if it were taught at a different time of the year and in different contexts. One can hardly argue with the *organization* potential of chronology; it's obvious and relatively easy to relate. It is not, however, an ideal approach in the light of reading difficulties and factors of relevance.

The *genre approach* is another popular one, and one that is being widely used in phase-elective programs. It must be remembered, however, that very few students are vitally interested in the study of form *per se*, and when a teacher attempts to sustain this approach over an entire year, interest levels can become dangerously low. You should also remember that aspects of literary form are inevitably *abstract*, and when taught in fine detail, can become quite esoteric. This approach also gives rise to some fairly arid assignments, such as writing plot summaries of novels and sleuthing through lines of poems for stressed and unstressed syllables, intricate rhyme schemes, and what have you. When some variety is added to the straight genre approach, things may perk up. Such units as "The Tragic Hero in Modern Drama," "Short Stories of Urban America," or "Lyrical Poetry of the Black Slave" may provide added interest and relevance. In such units, genres can be made more specific and can be combined with themes, modes, or geography areas, thus offering even broader consideration.

The approach to organizing literature study for older adolescents that seems to *us* to have the most potential appeal is the *thematic* one. Here is some rationale for thematic teaching:

1. Literature is important chiefly in that it reveals things about human experience.
2. In order for students, particularly younger ones, to understand meaning in literature, the experience described must be within the realm of their comprehension.
3. The closer the relationships the teacher can establish between that which has been presented in literature and that which has been experienced by the students, the better chance there is of giving emphatic meaning to the selections studied. Conversely, the work that describes experiences remote from that of the readers may cause difficulties in perception of meaning equal to those caused by complexity of structure.

With these precepts in mind, teachers using the thematic approach should begin with a theme of general and continuing significance. This they should do at the outset of instruction, before any works are read. They should raise some issue in human experience that men have concerned themselves with through the ages, that is still of concern today, that hopefully holds some interest for all members of the class, and that is capable of being understood, in varying degrees of depth, by all members of the class. The teacher's premises should be that: 1) it *is* of general interest, 2) all students have *some* notions concerning it, and 3) further knowledge about it, through reading and study, should be a worthwhile venture.

Once such a theme has been raised and discussed, it would logically follow that one of the best ways to learn *more* about it would be through the reading of one or more relevant literary selections. The student then reads these selections with one major purpose in mind (though the teacher may have others, particularly the uniqueness of its *structure*). This purpose is to find meaning in the work and then relate it to the theme introduced at the outset of the unit.

When properly used, the thematic approach can help to solve the vexing problem of differences in ability and can build on interests previously established. More importantly, it can assist the student to think independently and critically about his task of extrapolating inferred meaning from the works he reads. Fully aware that these works have been chosen because of their relevance, he is then faced with the necessity of ascertaining, by comparison or contrast, ways in which the central issue in the work pertains to the idea already discussed. Thus the literary selection can be seen in the light of past considerations, and is no longer remote from the student's interests and understanding. His search for related ideas becomes more meaningful; less remote and sterile. Furthermore, it will be easier for him to compare works by different writers and in different *genres* when it has been clearly established that the selections relate, in some manner, to a common theme. The more the younger reader pursues this means of study, the more he can relate past experience and discussion to present reading, and the more aware he will become of some of the great abstract concepts in the human situation.

Thematic teaching has had its ups and downs over the years, but with today's youth and their cries for relevance, what could be more appropriate than using literature study as a vehicle for exploring some of the serious concerns of their time? With the alarming drug problem among American teenagers, the much heralded "youth culture," problems of repression and revolt on high school as well as college campuses, the question of teen-age civil rights, and the stance young men should take toward military service, the search for self-identity is a theme that should be of real significance in today's senior high school English classrooms.

The self-identity theme is crucial to adolescents and can be developed in several ways. There is plenty of literary material around which to develop it. There are many other themes, however, that can also be developed into literature-centered units of great potential appeal to large numbers of senior high students. Here are a few:

1. *Alienation:* the whole problem of people tuning out of society and attempting to find "their own thing" is one that has been treated in literature virtually since the beginning of writing.

2. *The Black Experience: The Deferred Dream:* a very popular theme with high school students as well as young teachers. It draws on literary selections from all genres, has great potential for modern reinforcement, and contains works from both white and black authors.

3. *Appearance vs. Reality:* young people today are engaged in a vigorous search for what really is happening to them and to their society. The whole problem of credibility can be treated here, and the universality of the theme can be clearly indicated by contrasting works of early times with recent ones.

4. *Literature and War:* a natural for today, particularly when combined with the "fall of the hero" notion given so much attention in today's literature. There is no end of material for development of such a unit, all the way from *The Iliad* to today's newspaper.

5. *The "God is Dead" Concern:* maybe a "hot potato" in some communities, this could be a unit in which students investigate the nature and meaning of spiritual belief and skepticism. Once again, there should be no problem in finding materials from all eras and of all genres. Some natural situations for *written* responses are presented in this unit.

6. *Individualism vs. Conformity:* the conflict between these two human needs has been spelled out in a great deal of literature. It can be related to the "Search for Utopia" concern and can thus bring in such still-popular works as *Brave New World, Erewhon, 1984, Lost Horizon,* and *The Adding Machine,* as well as some contemporary material.

7. *Man and Nature:* a theme that has been used by teachers for a long time, it becomes even more pertinent today because of deep concern shown by adolescents about the ecology of their world. Romantic and naturalistic perspectives can easily be developed within such a unit.

8. *The Generation Gap:* there is much literature portraying this perennial but currently heated controversy. Within such a unit, a good deal of discrimination in literary excellence must be employed, since there are many works, especially novels written for teen-agers, in which this matter is very clumsily handled.

9. *The World of the Future:* some excellent contrasts can be made between fiction and nonfiction as well as between philosophical speculations in the literature of today with that of the past. There is plenty of opportunity for science fiction here, as well as a good deal of fiction study relating early films with those produced recently.

10. *Initiation:* closely related to self-identity, this theme has to do with the adolescent's entry into the adult world, with a substantial concern about the dialectic of pleasurable and painful dimensions of his experience. There is a great fund of highly popular literature to develop such a theme, going back to the Twain era and moving through major American writers of the 1920s (Anderson, Fitzgerald, Hemingway, Faulkner, *et al.*) down to the present day. Those who wish to treat the Salinger, Knowles, Nabokov, Bellow, Kerouac, McCullers, and Roth outlooks could find this theme highly adaptable. The junior novels, many of which focus on the theme, also offer plenty of *range* in levels of difficulty for individualized activities.

These are only a few of the virtually limitless number of interesting and significant themes for older adolescents, and for which a great fund of material is readily available. Student suggestions for the study of particular works within these frameworks is a very real possibility. If you are curious about the framing of this kind of instructional unit, take a look at the Scholastic Literature Units, developed as complete packaged thematic units, which go back to 1958 and are still quite popular today (bear in mind, though, that they are aimed more at an early adolescent audience). Some of the newer ones such as "Prejudice" and "Who Am I?" treat themes of contemporary significance. If nothing else, these materials can provide a model for a highly structured thematic unit.

Throughout our description of the thematic approach, we frequently alluded to the use of media, especially film, as a desirable activity. Whether employed within the thematic context or simply as a separate activity, the relating of film to literature is something we encourage you to try with your students. There are large numbers of excellent full-length, commercially prepared films, directly related to major literary works, which can be rented inexpensively and conveniently. While these longer films relate most typically to long fiction and biography, the rise during recent years of the short, artistic film allows teachers to use many films in the teaching of short fiction, poetry, and nonfiction. In any case, the pervasiveness of film study and concern about film among older adolescents can easily be capitalized on by teachers of senior high literature. What is *gained* and what is *lost* by perceiving reality through each medium can make for some most effective comparison-contrast classroom activities. You will find a wide range of possible uses of media in teaching English in Chapters Eleven and Twelve.

TACKLING LITERARY FORMS

A final matter of concern in teaching literature to older adolescents is the problem students may have in dealing with literary genres. When the form of the printed word gets in the way of readers' understanding, then the teacher had better be prepared to deal directly with the problem. Here are some suggestions for dealing with recurrent *formal* problems, and also for building a logical sequence in which the genres might be approached.

Novels

First of all, we think it wise to start with the novel or biography. By choosing the novel we pick the students up where they most probably *are*. First of all, longer prose fiction tells a story, and the overwhelming majority of young people enjoy stories. Whether or not they are superior readers, most younger students are accustomed to the narrative form, whether it appears printed or orally.

To implement the use of novels in early stages of literature instruction, the teacher should select ones that are conventionally written. As we define it, a conventionally written novel follows a clear chronological order in its development. The action involved is mostly of an *outer* nature; that is, physical activity predominates, and the reader is clearly aware of this. There are few flashbacks; those that are used are clearly identifiable, and the sequence of events is seldom interrupted for a long time. Characters are also developed without obscurity. Dialogue is regularly punctuated, and the thoughts of individuals are labeled as such.

We don't see the need to pursue the notion of conventionality in longer works of prose fiction. But the novel does offer one further advantage as an introductory form of literature. The development during the past forty-plus years of the well-written junior novel has provided us with a great *range* of materials for individualizing classroom instruction in the reading of literature. Hopefully, we all recognize the grim fact that not all readers at any grade level read with the same degree of proficiency. In the teaching of literature, the junior novel affords the teacher an additional and valuable instrument. Moreover, the junior novel most often portrays a protagonist in *adolescence,* moving through situations very close to the *literal* experience of young (or less mature) readers. This makes imaginative literature possible for a large number of students. It also allows the teacher to choose well-written but easy to read selections for students who have trouble in reading. She can also use them as the basis for exploration of more complex works on more mature topics.

Flexibility is something for which all teachers crave. With junior novels, plus longer but conventionally written novels on more adult topics (Kipling, London, Twain, and countless others) and finally the longer and more complex fictional works encountered at the college level, the teacher can work with students at several stages of development. By helping them find meaning and emotion (ranging from empathy and perception of meaning to assessment of artistic unity) in more or less conventionally written works, he can give them a sound basis for literary understanding.

Short Stories

The short story is an excellent transitional vehicle for moving students from "easier" to more difficult literary forms. (The term "easy" is a very slippery one when applied to the *reading* of literature—grade level assessments from readability formulae don't tell us enough about relative difficulty of most imaginative works.) While the short story is obviously *fiction*, exemplary works often contain special problems of which students will be largely unaware unless they are led to recognize and deal with them. Another problem is that there is considerably little adolescent fiction to be found in this abbreviated form. While there are undeniably some worthwhile collections of junior short stories available, the great majority of shorter fictional works studied at the secondary level are quite adult and sophisticated. Thus the teacher will frequently find himself faced with the inescapable responsibility of dealing with short fictional works that present one or more significant structural difficulties.

Opening paragraphs in most short stories are crucial to the understanding of the work. With *much* less room to maneuver than in a longer work, the writer of a short story must invest great significance in some relatively sparse and often trivial-seeming detail. The student who is not on the lookout for these opening clues will almost invariably develop a confused or distorted idea of the direction in which the work is moving.

Time sequences are juggled about with abandon in modern short stories. Since the writer is typically presenting only "a slice of life," he must often "play about with his clock," as E. M. Forster would say, in order to place in sharpest focus those details he wishes to emphasize. The result is often a series of abrupt transitions in scene, unexpected flashbacks, and puzzlingly underdeveloped situations. The student who is used to reading conventionally developed longer fictional works may be jarred by these sharp turns and bumps in the road.

Further complications exist in short stories, particularly in those written within the last fifty years. Freudian influences have led many writers to concern themselves increasingly with the exploitation of the inner nature of man and to devote a good deal of attention to the disturbed person's outlook on life. The result has been a great deal of experimentation with stream of consciousness, interior monologue, and other stylistic devices. Students who cannot follow such nuances will obviously have trouble grasping the contributions that certain characters make to the story as a whole. When writers add conscious ambiguity to the statements or reflections of their characters, the untrained reader becomes further confused.

Anticlimactic endings add to the difficulty in interpreting significance in short fiction. The student who has read longer, conventionally written prose works becomes accustomed to the piling up of a welter of evidence leading to a decisive climax. He learns to anticipate such inexorably moving plots and thus may be irritated and disconcerted by an ending that offers no resolution or triumphal confrontation. Hemingway's "The Killers" has often had this effect on high school students. They are vexed by the utter futility evinced by the two main characters in the closing lines of the story.

In the light of all these structural irregularities, the student who would become a careful and ultimately *satisfied* reader of well-written short fiction must come to two major realizations. First, he must perceive that most short stories feature *compression* of ideas. Much is said in a few words, but much is left for the reader to infer and relate to his own literal experience. A few lines in a short story can lead to a good deal of frequently wide-ranging reaction, and ambiguity of interpretation is always possible. It is in the student's impression of the significance of this compression of ideas and images that the reading of the short story can have its greatest value as a transitional activity. The reader finds himself going perceptively beyond the sparse details supplied him by the author.

Because of this compression, the great necessity for slow, careful reading must become gradually evident to the student. He must move away from the casual inspection and skimming that has probably characterized his reading of longer, conventionally structured novels. He must make meticulous note of *each* part, regardless how seemingly insignificant, as it relates to the whole.

Plays

Drama creates several problems in the teaching of literature, primarily because it is written not to be read silently, but to be *played*. Thus a reader must be able to *visualize* what is going on virtually from the first sentence in the text. Most often the playwright doesn't tell the reader what is happening; he lets the actor do it, and this makes for a tremendous amount of *omitted* detail that would generally be supplied by the writer of a novel, short story, or biography. In drama, especially modern drama, the writer doesn't tell the reader much of anything about the inner nature of the characters on stage (except, of course, in the soliloquy, a technique not used much these days). He really doesn't even *show* the reader too much; he relies on his actors to do this. If dramatic selections are to be read independently and silently, you need to be aware from the outset of this lack of significant fill-in information, and to do all in your power to compensate for it as the reading progresses.

Most plays begin with stage directions that describe the setting of the action to take place. When settings change, new stage directions are provided. Stage directions are not always easy to read. They are frequently spelled out in something less than complete sentences. They are usually set in italics, which can confuse people. They utilize abbreviations and technical stage terms for which some background must be provided. They use such symbols as U.L. (upper left) to denote where things are and/or where they will happen. These directions contain irregularities for a reader who is used to following a conventional prose-paragraph format. If a reader doesn't have a clear, graphic picture of the setting before the play begins, he may well become very confused by the subsequent *absence* of anything to remind him of what is there in the particular setting.

What you need to do, then, is pretty obvious: don't presume that your students have gained this graphic image from one, often hasty, reading. Do with settings what you should do with just about every component of a play: *use several reinforcement activities for the silent reading.* Discuss the setting with them. Draw it on the board. Have them sketch it on a piece of paper. Show them a photograph or model of one exactly similar if it is available (don't knock the old Globe Theater model!). If you have slides or filmstrips of the setting, parts of the play, or the entire play, use it as reinforcement. Remember, a play was written to be *seen*. Students who have trouble visualizing are really in a tough way when asked to read this genre.

The reinforcement approach, through oral and audiovisual activities, is needed throughout the study of dramatic selections. Much oral reading of parts can be helpful, and stop the reading occasionally to ask them and their classmates about various aspects of the lines. Don't forget that a character in a play is using facial expressions, gestures, and movement while he is speaking. Also, there may at times be simultaneous activity on stage during the lines; other characters may be moving about, coming and going, making side comments, and reacting kinetically to what is being said. Most of this action is never stated in print, so *somebody—you—*must indicate its occurrence and significance.

In many plays, there are ongoing stage directions that can present further comprehension problems. They are often very brief, even cryptic, and demand that a reader perceive much in few words. They also indicate a break in the speeches, calling for the reader to keep two things in mind—the speeches and the indicated action—at the same time. You must provide readiness for these devices and reinforce their impact through means similar to those suggested.

Like the short story writer, the playwright must be very careful about the *time* dimensions of his work. Sometimes a brief, concentrated time span is covered; at other times, gaps in time between the action are implied. The time durations and sequences are most important to the understanding of the total production, and you need to help students keep the time elements reconciled, especially in many of the well-known plays written in this century. Consider, for instance, the time problem in *Death of a Salesman*, in which Willie Loman exists in the real world of the present but continues to retreat into the remembered world of the past as the play progresses. Keeping "where" Willie is at a given point takes some careful reading, visualizing, discussing, and oral interpreting for a good many high school students. It is generally helpful to keep your students consistently abreast of the time component in a given selection.

One way of dealing with time problems, and at the same time helping the students in their need to *sustain* understanding of what is going on, might be to use the "progressive exercise" suggested earlier for use with novels. The three questions help with interpretation and keep readers on the track of what is going on. Since most plays break down into acts and scenes, the use of this approach is facilitated.

There is one further matter to be considered in the teaching of drama: that of *choice*. Much of the dramatic material assigned to teen-agers, especially for production in the schools, is archaic, sentimental, maudlin, and/or sterile. Hopefully the "Date with Judy," "Junior Miss" era is long gone in our secondary schools, and students are more free not only to read but to *perform* plays that are meaningful to them. The censorship issue doesn't seem to go away, however, and since much modern drama features tough, frank, searching treatments of the problems of our times, some taboos are almost inevitably present. We advocate neither a copout by the teacher nor a confrontation with the powers of the community. We would merely remind you that reality presented in dramatic form can be objectionable to some people and that your choices in this genre need to be considered carefully. Once they are made, however, don't forget the ongoing need for reinforcement activities of several kinds during and after the silent reading. For many of your students, dramatic selections will not be easy to read either silently or orally.

Poetry

For several reasons, poetry presents the greatest obstacle to the teacher who wants to lead his students to the effective reading of literature. One immediate reason is that poetry, unlike prose or drama, does not necessarily tell a story. Much of the poetry that young people usually must read, as early as junior high school, develops an abstract idea or establishes a proposition concerning human experience. Some poems are not even idea-centered; they merely create an aesthetic impression. Consider the impact of Ezra Pound's famous "In a Station of the Metro":

> *The apparition of these faces in the crowd;*
> *Petals on a wet, black bough.*[2]

The student who is looking for a story in this work is certainly doomed to disappointment. Because the *ways* of so many poems are simply not necessarily narrative ones, readers who are unprepared for this may well be troubled by a search that goes unrewarded. We should keep in mind that perception of aesthetic impact occurs in only a small minority of readers. In Pound's poem, there isn't really much else to be gained.

A further complication in the study of this form is that there is not much range in difficulty levels. There is little or no *transitional* poetry. While the junior novel has flourished during the past thirty years, the junior poem is still looking for a champion. Most poetry with which students contend is based on adult situations, represents abstract themes, and is complex in structure when compared to the conventionally written novel. Teachers trying to individualize instruction in poetry based on the reading abilities of their students have, in our opinion, a tough row to hoe. Since there is no appreciable fund of adolescent poetry to augment such instruction, the teacher must come to terms realistically with the reading problems the medium presents.

Probably the greatest difficulty to be found in the reading of poetry lies in the pronounced irregularity of its structure. By "irregularity" we mean

---

[2] *Personae* by Ezra Pound. Copyright 1926 by Ezra Pound. Reprinted by Permission of New Directions Publishing Corporation.

that the form of poetry is so vastly different from that which students are accustomed to reading that it continues to frustrate large numbers of them. We feel, incidentally, that teen-age boys do not really reject poetry because it is "fairy stuff" or "fruity"; this has simply become an institutionalized rationalization. The main reason boys retreat from poetry is that poetry is difficult to read and so many boys are inefficient readers. Another main reason why poetry has failed to interest and relate to young readers is that teachers have consistently emphasized the wrong elements in poetry; they have compulsively continued to putter about among the metrical ornaments of verse while neglecting to sense and deal with the real reading problems the form presents.

Of the numerous reading difficulties inherent in the poetic form, we will identify and illustrate only a few. Remember, though, that they are almost invariably occurring simultaneously in the work being studied. In other words, several aspects of reading a poem can be troubling a student *at the same time.*

One obvious structural irregularity is that, in order to create impressions through rhythmical patterns, the appearance of poetic lines differs sharply from that of prose fiction. In response to the charge that much of his poetry was difficult, the American poet E. A. Robinson was once quoted as saying, "If they would only read my sentences!" Of course, what Mr. Robinson failed to mention was that many of the conventional characteristics of prose sentence structure are missing in poetry. Each line is capitalized. Punctuation is irregular. Thoughts are often interrupted or ended *in medias res.* Lines are ended to accommodate rhyme rather than to facilitate syntactic flow. In fact, one of a young reader's major confusions in early bouts with poetry may stem from his wish to pursue the lilt of the poem rather than its *meaning.* When metrical analysis and identification of rhyme scheme become issues of paramount importance in the teaching of poetry, distorted reading can easily result.

Word order in sentence structure is a vital factor in the transmission of meaning in the English language. Linguists tell us that somewhere between seventy-five and eighty percent of the sentences produced in our language follow the subject-verb, subject-verb-object patterns. Therefore, the inversion of word order, the abrupt inclusion of single word and/or phrase modifiers, and other such machinations will create reading problems for the uninitiated. Notice in this poem by E. E. Cummings: first, the time it takes the poet to get to the subject of his sentence, and second, the ways in which he places his noun-modifier, subject-verb structures.

when serpents bargain for the right to squirm

e. e. cummings

when serpents bargain for the right to squirm
and the sun strikes to gain a living wage—
when thorns regard their roses with alarm
and rainbows are insured against old age

when every thrush may sing no new moon in
if all screech-owls have not okayed his voice
—and any wave signs on the dotted line
or else an ocean is compelled to close

when the oak begs permission of the birch
to make an acorn—valleys accuse their
mountains of having altitude—and march
denounces april as a saboteur

then we'll believe in that incredible
unanimal mankind(and not until)[3]

If we were to use a readability index that included a subordinate clause factor to judge the level of difficulty of this poem, that level would probably turn out to be quite high indeed.

In addition, poets often utilize *unusual words, dialects, and historical allusions* throughout their work. Ease of understanding is further reduced when such expressions appear in crucial places and are of central importance to the poet's purpose. In the third stanza of "Sailing to Byzantium," William Butler Yeats says:

"Oh sages standing in God's holy fire
As in the gold mosaic of a wall,
Come from the holy fire, perne in a gyre, (*emphasis mine*)
And be the singing-masters of my soul."[4]

If you don't know ancient Celtic you probably won't understand what the critics tell us is a most important phrase not only in this poem but in all of Yeats's work. Since this is not a book about literary scholarship, no explication of the phrase will appear. If you want to teach poems with such expressions, however, you ought to have reference materials available or be ready yourself to help students identify key meanings. Generally speaking, dialect can be consistently troublesome because it seldom occurs here and there, but usually permeates an entire work. It is important to remember in the study of English literature that strange dialects predominate in poetry written through the seventeenth century; that is, dialects strange for today's reader. *And this period of literature constitutes the first several months of study in chronologically oriented senior high school courses.*

Continual use of *historical and mythological allusions* is characteristic of most renowned poets from all eras and of all nationalities. When such allusions

---

[3] Copyright, 1948, by E. E. Cummings. Reprinted from his volume, *Complete Poems 1913–1962*, by permission of Harcourt Brace Jovanovich, Inc.

[4] Reprinted with permission of Macmillan Publishing Co., Inc. from *Collected Poems* by William Butler Yeats. Copyright 1928 by Macmillan Publishing Co., Inc., renewed 1956 by Georgie Yeats.

are unclear to the student, he often fails to perceive both the idea the poet is trying to communicate and the force with which he conveys it. Remember the quoted stanzas of Auden's "Musée des Beaux Arts" (p. 59). It happens that there's only one such allusion in the Auden poem. Where would we be in treating "The Waste Land" if we didn't know something about Eastern and Western culture through the ages?

Logically, we turn next to the whole matter of *figurative language* in poetry, which has always presented great obstacles to understanding for all but the most sophisticated of readers. One of the main problems in reading poetry is that poets juxtapose unusual objects and ideas with great frequency. T. S. Eliot's comparing of an evening sky with an etherized patient in "The Love Song of J. Alfred Prufrock" is probably one of the truly classic examples of this. Whenever meaning is to be conveyed by allusion a potential problem in communication exists. In setting up his association, the writer hopes that by comparing something less familiar, his main object or idea, with something *more* familiar to the reader, the reader will perceive the former idea more easily. The real problem is that in many instances the reader (and particularly the *young* reader) will not be as familiar with that part of the allusion as the writer had hoped. Thus, if the reader cannot conjure up a lucid and *complete* image of an etherized patient, then Eliot's comparison is really *defeated* in this instance, and the poet has confused where he hoped to clarify.

Much can be done with the analytical teaching of figurative language to help less mature readers with problems in understanding, as we can see. If we would teach *metaphor* for what it is, a basic widespread means of conveying information and ideas, then our students would probably have a better chance to deal with it successfully when they encounter it in poetry. S. I. Hayakawa has been claiming for a long time that metaphor is a fundamental component of our communication process. In everyday speech we juxtapose the unusual for clarification, for emphasis, for variety. We say, "I'm dying to meet him," "This box weighs a ton," "As dead as a doornail." Too much time, however, is spent by teachers in presenting simile, metaphor, conceit, and other devices purely as ornaments of poetry. Students memorize definitions for these terms, then sleuth about for their presence in works being read. If these same youngsters were first and forcefully shown the omnipresence of metaphor in *their own* language and the relationship of the figurative in everyday discourse to that in poetic works, they would probably understand better a greater number of the selections they read. This problem, already illustrated in "The Lottery" exercise, is also a recurrent one with older adolescents.

We would mention one final feature apparent in much verse which, if overlooked by the reader, will most certainly weaken its impact on him. Most writers of poetry quite often employ single words and patterns of words for the purpose of evoking emotional reaction, largely through their tonal patterns; that is, they depend heavily on *sounds* to produce ideas and emotions. Here is a short poem, "Dead Boy," by John Crowe Ransom, that employs such audio devices:

> The little cousin is dead, by foul subtraction,
> A green bough from Virginia's aged tree,
> And none of the county kin like the transaction
> Nor some of the world of outer dark, like me.
>
> A boy not beautiful, nor good, nor clever,
> A black cloud full of storms too hot for keeping,
> A sword beneath his mother's heart—yet never
> Woman bewept her babe as this is weeping.
>
> A pig with a pasty face, so I had said.
> Squealing for cookies, kinned by pure pretense
> With a noble house. But in a little man quite dead,
> I can see the forebears' antique lineaments.
>
> The elder men have strode by the box of death
> To the wide flag porch, and muttering low send round
> The fruit of the day. O friendly waste of breath!
> Their hearts are hurt with a deep dynastic wound.
>
> He was pale and little, the foolish neighbors say;
> The first-fruits, saith the Preacher, the Lord hath taken;
> But this was the old tree's late branch wrenched away,
> Grieving the sapless limbs, the shorn and shaken.[5]

If the reader does not respond to the grating, rasping sounds made by "the old tree's late branch wrenched away" in the next to last line of the final stanza, and to the quiet closing provided by the sibilants "S" and "SH" in the final line, then, in our opinion, he has missed something. But this kind of appreciative reaction may not come to large numbers of students. As teachers, we may help our students, through inductive approaches, to realize the significance of such juxtaposition, but we cannot and should not teach it by edict. It goes without saying, of course, that effective oral reading by the teacher can have a great influence in matters of poetic consideration such as this.

Nonfiction

Before leaving genres, let us consider nonfiction. This, we realize, many feel is not really literature, but we know older adolescents will have to cope with it frequently as they enter adulthood. Prose nonfiction has been quite generally

---

[5] Copyright 1927 by Alfred A. Knopf, Inc. and renewed 1955 by John Crowe Ransom. Reprinted from *Selected Poems*, Third Edition, Revised and Enlarged, by John Crowe Ransom, by permission of Alfred A. Knopf, Inc.

a bore to adolescents in the past, but so much of the recent Literature of Protest has come in nonfictional form that senior high school students probably read more of it now than ever before. The recent popularity of Eldridge Cleaver's *Soul on Ice* is an example of the new interest in this genre and illustrates a need for dealing with it in the classroom. It is highly relevant to older adolescents of today.

We have two brief suggestions to make about nonfiction. First, this is an excellent form for practice in a variety of reading skills. Consider some of them:

1. Dealing with word attack skills, especially with abstract and technical terminology;
2. Identifying sequences of details and ideas, especially cause-and-effect relationships;
3. Finding and identifying important facts in isolation;
4. Finding main ideas when expressed and implied;
5. Drawing inferences and making judgments, especially in the analyses of such persuasive pieces as propaganda tracts;
6. Relating rate to purpose, as in scanning and skimming activities;
7. Reading to find unifying ideas, as in the assessment of the total meaning of a long selection.

We contend that these skills *should* be dealt with, and this contention leads to our second suggestion: teach nonfiction for its *pragmatic* value. Most people read nonfiction not because it is beautiful or captivating or even because they want to. They read it because it contains information or ideas they *need to have*; i.e., it is of utilitarian value. With this in mind, reading assignments should be made with the clear understanding that they are a means to some necessary and practical end; that when completed by the reader, he will know something that he needs to know or can do something that he wants to do or do it better.

A related activity in using nonfiction is *debate over contemporary issues*. Experience convinces us that most older adolescents truly enjoy arguing. Capitalizing on this, we suggest selecting a debatable issue in class, stating the pro and con points of view, choosing up sides, and providing each group with nonfiction materials to help them support their arguments. The debate should be highly informal, and the class and teacher can interact during as well as after the presentation of the statements. The teacher should be ready to act as referee when the argument becomes heated. There are plenty of issues that can and are being debated by high school students today. The teacher should consider some likely ones and then search diligently for the nonfiction materials that will help student debaters in establishing their positions.

In such an activity as the informal debate, the reading of nonfiction clearly becomes a pragmatic tool: the students read the material *so they can do better in their arguments*. They can support their contentions with the printed statements of others and can qualify what might otherwise be empty, unsupported generalizations. Thus nonfiction becomes in the classroom what it will be in the overwhelming number of instances in adult life—a means to an end.

We firmly believe, then, that nonfiction should not be overlooked as a form of literature to be studied. Essays of various kinds can easily be related to several thematic units, in that they often provide *direct* statements on the themes in question. As a separate genre, nonfiction has both pragmatic and philosophical value.

While the pragmatic value of certain types of nonfiction is questionable, it should not be overlooked. By "pragmatic" we mean those materials with which the senior high school student will have to contend for the remainder of his adult life. They include such documents as insurance policies, income tax forms, real estate titles, bills of sale, and various legal documents. These materials feature unusual formats, abundant technical terms, and most of all, highly intricate syntactic structures (for instance, "The party of the first part ———"). Some highly worthwhile time can be spent introducing students to the various *styles* of these documents and providing them with opportunities to apply their comprehension skills to them. In terms of carry-over value into "real life," it is hard to do better.

While reading nonfictional works for their philosophical value does not offer the immediate practical awards described above, it can prove to be highly worthwhile and engrossing. Some of the great issues of our times, ones with which millions of young people are now intensely involved, are given broad and sometimes eloquent voice in nonfiction. Essays on war, pollution, military spending, and youth culture help to inform and persuade those who read them. And essays on more abstract themes such as racism, alienation, and credibility can do much to catalyze classroom interaction on matters that are being argued by youth in all corners of the United States—even as you read this book! We see, then, that nonfiction is not necessarily *dull*. When it treats matters of great immediate and sometimes emotional concern, it can be a highly exciting genre. *And there is plenty of it around today!* You don't need to purchase large, expensive textbooks if you want to teach pragmatic or philosophical nonfiction. There is an abundance of it in newspapers, magazines, political handouts, and advertising circulars. You can collect it, or you can have your students bring it in. With the amount of cheap printed material now available, a teacher who is able to evoke interest on a particular contemporary issue should have no trouble getting his students to gather relevant pieces of nonfiction. Some highly involving and informative student-initiated and -guided discussion can well develop from the reading and consideration of nonfiction in your classrooms. Don't be afraid to use it!

MULTIETHNIC LITERATURE

In the past few years the literature of various ethnic and racial minority groups has become increasingly interesting to both younger and older adolescents. Due in part to the increased consciousness of these groups themselves that their contributions to our literary heritage are important and essential, more multiethnic literature is being published than ever before. Increased awareness of the contributions of various groups to our developing society has been stressed by professional groups such as the Committee on Racism and Bias of the National Council of Teachers of English, as well as by the publishers themselves. Not only is more new literature being written and published, but literature that has been available for many years—some of it well-known to blacks, American Indians, Puerto Ricans, and Mexican Americans—is at last finding its way into literary anthologies. In some cases, librarians, teachers, and even minority communities have influenced both authors and publishers to make available more literature written by and about minority groups. Since much of this literature is coming into print so rapidly, we urge you to regard the books cited as examples of multiethnic literature you might wish to use either for individualized reading or for class study. We urge you to read as widely as you can, since more and more multiethnic literature is continually being made available and you will want to develop reading lists of your own.

A word of caution is in order, though. Some teachers working with Oriental, black, or Mexican-American children, once they discover multiethnic literature, try to force-feed a steady diet of it to minority group children. They mistakenly feel that black youngsters wish only to read biographies of black people, and Chinese-American youngsters, stories about Chinese-Americans. Until recently, the opportunity to do this type of reading was scarce. Little multiethnic literature was to be found in anthologies and paperbacks used in schools. In the early 1960s, Marjorie Smiley, a professor at Hunter College in New York City, began a major experiment using multiethnic literary anthologies she had developed for younger adolescents, in what she titled the Gateway English Program. Working with inner-city students and teachers in junior high schools in New York and Miami, Dr. Smiley constructed anthologies of poetry, short stories, essays, biographies, and autobiographies written by and about black, Puerto Rican, and other racial and ethnic minority groups. A basic rationale for the study was that minority group students would develop a stronger interest in reading if they could read and identify with protagonists who had overcome obstacles like the ones many of them were facing. In his book *We Have Tomorrow*, published in 1945, A. Bontemps collected a number of brief, inspiring biographies of young black people who had succeeded in breaking through the color barrier of the 1930s and had become army officers, lawyers, and engineers. Marjorie Smiley drew upon these, along with the biography of Jackie Robinson by Milton Shapiro as well as a variety of other sources, to build the *Gateway* anthologies. An evaluation, conducted after a tryout period of three years sponsored by the Research Foundation of the National Council of Teachers of English, showed conclusively that minority group students were stimulated by the type of literature used in the *Gateway* series and that they were more interested in reading, particularly reading more about members of minority groups. The *Gateway* series was followed rapidly by other literary anthologies based essentially on the same concept. The Holt *Impact* textbook series was developed by Charlotte K. Brooks, who later anthologized *The Outnumbered*, a collection of essays, stories, and poems about minority groups.

Multiethnic literature is fast becoming an integral part of the new elective programs in English described elsewhere in this book. Electives in Black Literature now exist in many senior high schools, and electives in Southwestern Literature, for example, now contain novels, stories, essays, and poetry of and about the American Indian and the Mexican-American.

Despite the recent recognition of the importance of multiethnic literature in school programs, you will need to be selective about the works you choose for your students. If you are working with younger adolescents or with older adolescents who are reading for unconscious enjoyment, you must use the same criteria in choosing multiethnic literature as you use in choosing good literature of any sort.

As Edgar Friedenberg wrote in *The Vanishing Adolescent*, one of the primary role tasks of adolescence is to define oneself as a person. Literature dealing with the search for identity provides the opportunity to participate in the solution of a personal problem by vicariously identifying with a character in a particular situation. This "situation" may have racial or ethnic dimensions, as in the junior novel *Lions in the Way*, by Bella Rodman, which describes the problems of a few black students who were the first to integrate a high school in a small southern town in 1959. Although there are a series of unpleasant incidents directed against the black students by a few hostile, white students and adults, the school is eventually integrated partly through the efforts of Robby Jones, the leader of the black students, and partly by means of a federal injunction.

As Barbara Dodds points out in *Negro Literature for High School Students*, concerning her collection of black literature chosen especially for English teachers:

> In their dealing with race, junior novels tend to be optimistic. They usually relate specific incidents that high school students are likely to meet, like discrimination in athletic or student activities. Since they describe specific instances of discrimination rather than the cumulative psychological effects of prejudice, junior novels frequently have a happy ending. Those included here can be effective in helping white and middle-class adolescents to understand Negro youths, for all show vividly the frustration and resentment of Negro youths when they are subjected to the common types of high school discrimination. Some of these novels may encourage white youths to stop discriminating; at least, these books can help make white youths to understand the feelings of their Negro classmates.
>
> Dealing as they do primarily with middle-class Negroes in integrated situations and often being written by white authors, junior novels do not reveal the explosive bitterness of the ghetto, the topic of many adult novels. Because junior novels

generally hold middle-class values and taboos—forbidding profane language, mention of sexual intercourse, or episodes of violence—they are unrealistic, or too "nice" at times.[6]

Multiethnic literature as it exists in junior novels and biographies especially written for younger adolescents is undoubtedly subject to some extent to the limitations of the junior novel. Changes are occurring, however, in a variety of ways. Junior novels for girls, for example, are becoming more realistic in their treatment of sex. Consider the variety of recent books dealing with unwed pregnancy, such as Felsen's *Two and the Town*, *Phoebe*, by Patricia Dizenzo, *Too Bad About the Haines Girl*, by Zoa Sherburne, *My Darling, My Hamburger*, by Paul Zindel, and *A Girl Like Me*, by Jeannette Eyerly. A few years ago, most of these books would have been unwelcome in any public or school library. There have been surprisingly few censorship incidents over these books.

Similarly, we are on the threshold of somewhat more realistic transition literature representing the "explosive bitterness" not only of the ghetto but of the barrios, the rural schools, and the Indian reservations as well. Even though we may be moving toward a new realism in transition literature, the new books for young people that are now being written will obviously need to be good *books* as well as good multiethnic books. There are several good multiethnic junior novels and biographies available now. A junior novel of considerable literary quality is *Julie's Heritage*, by Catherine Marshall. Julie, a black girl in a largely white high school, experiences racial prejudice when she and her boyfriend Dave are prevented from attending a school dance at a country club. A central conflict in the book involves Dave, who disagrees with Julie and who wishes to fight back after the country club incident, as well as the two other central black characters in the book, her friend Marilyn and her cousin George, who become embittered by their experiences. The book is valuable because of its sensitive treatment of Julie as she struggles to preserve her relationships with whites but to stay faithful to her black heritage.

And Now Miguel, a Newberry award-winning book of the 1950s, is valuable reading for younger students since it depicts with such sensitivity the life of a Spanish-American boy in New Mexico. Insights into culture pervade the book. The importance of the family and the relationships of the family to their Spanish origins and to sheepherding are key aspects in the development of Miguel, whose one great wish is to join his father under an older brother in the sheep camp in the Sangre de Cristo Mountains during the three-month grazing period. As the middle brother, Miguel must await the time when he is judged ready to enter a society in which roles are carefully defined and the places of children, men, and women are carefully prescribed. His older brother has already joined the men of the family. Krumgold carefully portrays the feelings of

---

[6] Barbara Dodds, *Negro Literature for High School Students*, National Council of Teachers of English (Urbana, Ill., 1968), p. 69.

Miguel as he participates in the "initiation rites" of the sheepshearing and his joy at being asked to join the men at the table at its conclusion. His movement from boyhood to manhood has begun.

In contrast to the variety of literature available about and by blacks in urban settings, it is more difficult to find good books available about Mexican-Americans in the city. In Frank Bonham's *Viva Chicano*, a Mexican-American boy, Kenny Duran, struggles to understand himself and those around him. He tries especially to understand his mother and stepfather, who offer him little hope or help and continue to threaten to return him to reform school. He continues to remember his own father, whom he lost at an early age, but who had stressed *la Raza* and his Spanish heritage. He searches to find this heritage as he also attempts to understand the prejudices displayed by some Anglos, who continue to refer to him as "greaser." Frank Bonham does an excellent job of sensitively portraying Kenny as he tries to stay in school despite fights with hostile Anglos, active gang warfare, and the drug scene. A short biography available for younger readers is *Caesar Chavez*, by Ruth Franchere, dealing with the well-known labor leader who has struggled to improve working conditions and pay for Chicano farm workers. Another biography for older readers is *Mighty Hard Road: The Story of Caesar Chavez*, by James J. Tarzian and Kathryn Crones.

Books for older adolescents include *Angel Loves Nobody*, by Richard Miles, a terrifying story about the excesses of racial hostilities and hatreds between Mexican-Americans and Anglos, in a mythical Los Angeles junior high school where Angel, a talented student, devises a deadly plan to assassinate all the teachers in the school. *Chicano*, a recent novel by Richard Vasquez, pictures Mexican-Americans in the barrios of Los Angeles attempting to hold on to the customs and beliefs of their heritage but uncomfortable and unhappy in attempts to adopt Anglo middle-class traditions and housing. Life in the barrios is depicted graphically, and prejudice again shows itself through the pursuits of Anglo sociology student David Stiver, who becomes ostracized after his forced marriage to Marianna, a young Chicano girl. Another adult novel with a somewhat similar theme is *Pocho*, by Jose Antonio Villarreal, which depicts the life of Richard Rubio, a pocho or child born of Mexican parents in the United States. The novel concerns Richard's attempts to adopt Anglo ways as he grows up in central California. In his search for identity, he fights to hold on to his own ways but at one point, when harassed by the police, even becomes a "tio Taco" or "Uncle Tom." Although this novel was written several years ago, it still seems to represent a vivid and accurate picture of many Mexican-American *pochos* in the Southwest today.

More junior novels concerning the Puerto Rican experience seem to have been written than adult novels. Many involve the problems of immigrating from Puerto Rico to a place on the mainland, more often than not, New York City. Such books for younger adolescents are *Tomas Takes Charge*, by Charlene Joy Talbot, and *That Bad Carlos* and *Candita's Choice*, by Mina Lewiton.

A somewhat more complex treatment of this theme is *The Girl from Puerto Rico*, by Hilda Colman.

Nonfiction, fiction, and poetry about and by American Indians is becoming more plentiful, some of it written especially for younger readers and some of it written for adults, but of special interest to adolescents and young adults.

Some junior novels involve the interaction of the American Indian with the white man, and some do not. In *Conquering Hero*, a young Sioux boy passes through the traditional "initiation rites" in attempting to win a wife and to gain the status of a man in his tribe. In *The Loon Feather*, by Lola Fuller, Oneta, daughter of Chief Tecumseh, returns to her tribe to help them in time of peril. In *Billy Lightfoot*, by Richard Erno, Billy runs away to school outside the reservation, to learn that he must first make a decision between basketball and painting and then a decision as to whether he can blend his choice to include his people and the Navaho way. In Conrad Richter's *A Light in the Forest*, a white boy who has grown up among Indians is taken by force back to the white settlement. The book is a sensitive treatment of his dilemma and ultimate rebellion. In Elliot Arnold's *Blood Brother*, Cochise, chief of the Chiricahua Apaches, leads his people relentlessly against the overpowering strength of the invading white man. A very well-written story, *Johnny Osage*, by Janice H. Giles, deals with the attempts to arrange a truce in a vicious war between the Osage and Cherokee in Oklahoma in the 1820s. *Laughing Boy*, by Oliver LaFarge, although written a number of years ago, remains a classic novel for many young people because of its sensitive portrayal of the development of love between Laughing Boy and Slim Girl as they grow up in the Navaho way.

Another novel that continues to be extremely popular with adolescents is Hal Borland's *When the Legends Die*. In a sensitively written novel, the growth of Tom Black Bull, a Ute Indian boy, is depicted as both a search for personal identity and an explanation of the Indian as an outsider. In *House Made of Dawn*, N. Scott Momaday paints a picture of Abel Francisco, a young Indian man trapped in the complexities of finding himself caught between Anglo, Spanish, and Indian cultural traditions in a small southern California town. It is a highly symbolic novel in which the influence of tribal oral tradition plays an important part. A suspenseful novel about a Kiowa Indian who becomes cynical enough to join a group of conniving whites in an attempt to buy up the mineral rights to Indian lands is Thomas Tall's *The Ordeal of Running Standing*.

Many have applauded the recent reissue of *Fig Tree John*, a classic novel about an Apache father and son in a temporary land of exile near California's Salton Sea. The novel is exceptionally well-researched and well-written and reveals much of the basic Apache character, especially as it deals in the adversities faced by Fig Tree John as he watches his son affected by the ways of other tribes, Mexicans, and the materialistic world of the whites. Oliver LaFarge, in reviewing *Fig Tree John* for the *Saturday Review* when it was first published, noted that Corle has taken "two of the great possible themes—

the functioning of the intellect in savagery and the adjustment of the Indian to the white world—salted them with action, spiced them into a sound love element, set them against a peculiar . . . background which throws them into sharp relief, and made the whole into a sensitive and delightful story." In the introduction to the new edition of *Fig Tree John*, Walter James Miller calls it one of our greatest novels about the predicament of the American Indian.

Nonfiction, especially biography and autobiography, is becoming especially important in multiethnic literature in that it is especially popular with adolescents and young adults. At the time of this writing, an historical volume concerning the mistreatment of American Indians by whites as told from the Indian point of view and based on contemporary reports, oral histories, and personal documents, is at the top of the best seller list. This book is *Bury My Heart at Wounded Knee*, by Dee Brown. Here is a book that can provide needed background for a variety of fiction and nonfiction about American Indians, as can the chapter "Go in Beauty" from the book *The New Indian*, by Stan Steiner. Vine De Loria, Jr., has written "an Indian manifesto" in *Custer Died for Your Sins*. His readable and bitter book is recommended nonfiction for a realistic view of Indian life—certainly one book that "tells it like it is" about American Indians.

Biography is a good way to achieve "imaginative entry" in helping your students to begin to read about other social or cultural groups. Biographies exist for all levels of reading and interest, and cover practically all groups. Such biographies and autobiographies as: *Born to Play Ball: Willie Mays's Own Story*, by Willie Mays as told to Charles Einstein; and *Ahdoolo! The Biography of Mathew A. Henson*, by Floyd Miller, tell the stories of a famous black baseball player and a famous black scientist, Mathew Henson, who was chief assistant to Perry in his struggle to reach the North Pole. *Thunder Rolling: The Story of Chief Joseph*, by Helen M. Miller, is a biography of suspense and excitement involving the chief of the Nez Perce Indians. Robert Silverberg has written a biography of an entire tribe in his *The Old Ones: Indians of the American Southwest*, a detailed history of the Pueblo Indians that includes maps, drawings, and a directory of historic sites. Perri Thomas's book *Down These Mean Streets*, the autobiography of a Puerto Rican boy growing up in Spanish Harlem, affords a good comparison with Claude Brown's *Manchild in the Promised Land,* the autobiography of a black boy growing up in Black Harlem. Two biographies concerned with Mexican-Americans in the Southwest (in addition to those of Caesar Chavez mentioned before) are *With a Pistol in His Hand*, by Americo Paredes, and *Among the Valiant*, by Raul Morin. Other nonfiction that illuminates the history and contemporary culture of the Mexican-American in the Southwest includes: *North from Mexico*, by Carey McWilliams; *Forgotten People*, by George Sanchez; *Mexican Americans: A Brief Look at Their History*, and *La Raza: The Mexican Americans,* by Stan Steiner; and *Mexican Americans in the Southwest*, by Ernesto Galarza *et al.*

In introducing your students to the literature of the many cultural groups who make up our society, you will need to range widely through such works as those described above and many others as well. Undoubtedly, one of your most difficult tasks will be judging which multiethnic literature will be appropriate for the students you teach. You should consider the following criteria—along with any other criteria you judge to be especially important:

1. Although our discussion has centered largely on black literature, Spanish-American literature, and literature of and about the American Indian because of their neglect in most of our school programs, multiethnic literature can be the literature of any minority ethnic group that differs from that of the dominant cultural group in the United States. In his book *Brothers under the Skin*, Carey McWilliams defines an ethnic group as "a people living competitively in relationship of superordination or subordination with respect to some other people or peoples within the same area or region."[7] Therefore, you might wish to develop multiethnic literature thematic units or reading ladders on Polish-American, Japanese-American, Chinese-American, or any other of the various ethnic groups that inhabit our land.

2. Since multiethnic literature has been neglected in literature programs, we propose that it be given a place and that the literature program be a balanced one including good writers from minority ethnic groups as well as those from the dominant culture. The goals of the literature program should be, as stated earlier, essentially to develop each child's capacity for engagement, interest, and enjoyment in reading.

3. Literature that casts minority group characters in negative stereotypes should be avoided. All blacks do not live in the inner city and eat soul food, nor do all Mexican-Americans speak with a Spanish accent and eat tacos and beans.

4. The books you select should be good books for adolescents and young adults to read, regardless of their multiethnic quality. Books like Kristin Hunter's *The Soul Brothers and Sister Lou*, *Fig Tree John*, by Edwin Corle, and *The Pearl*, by John Steinbeck, provide characters with whom all young people can identify, situations that are believable, and universality of experience that all can understand and share.

5. An essential issue in selecting multiethnic literature either for class study or for individualized reading concerns whether the literature is *by* or *about* ethnic minorities. Nancy L. Arnez recently showed the intensity of feeling on this issue:

> ... There is no possible way that whites can evaluate the black experience in or out of a literary context. They wear blinders because of their white perspective and the totally white quality of their lives. They can have but one approach to black literature. And that is to measure it in terms of the degree to which it reflects white life in American and white cultural values.

---

[7] Carey McWilliams, *Brothers under the Skin*, rev. ed. (Boston: Little, Brown and Company, 1964), p. 113.

No longer can black writers be concerned with such standards as universal appeal of themes, white-denoted excellence in technique, control, imagery, style and language. Black writing needs allusions to the black life style, experimentation with unique rhythms, different syntactical forms and new orthography in tune with speech patterns of black people. We need to look at the inventiveness of vocabulary and the real-life character of events, creativeness of expression and its focus on the humanness of man. What white man has the soul to tune in to the genius of black folk . . . ?[8]

Strong language? Perhaps, but certainly a view increasingly held by many ethnic minority writers, Indian, Puerto Rican, and Chicano as well as black. You should become familiar enough with the ethnic literature you are evaluating to know whether or not a particular book, poem, or short story has been written by a minority writer.

The case for including multiethnic literature in the literature program would seem obvious enough so that no case would need to be made for it. Only to the extent that our literature program reflects our true multiethnic heritage as a people, can we expect the unity that occurs through a balanced diversity. In addition, we can expect other assets from such a program. Black, Puerto Rican, Chicano, and American Indian children will be able to read about characters like themselves. Girls will be able to read about the careers and lives of women in literature. The cultural contributions of various ethnic groups to our society will become clear and, hopefully, the humanizing effect of literature will be of benefit to all.

LOOKING AT THE WHOLE THING

We propose the above strategies, styles, techniques, and patterns of organization as ways to help you develop your own literature program, e.g., the one that best fits the needs of your students and your community. Whatever the literature program has been in your school, it is probably changing and you are being called upon to be a part of that change. Although, as noted earlier, there is much we do not know about the ways young people grow in their interest in reading and in their appreciation of literature, certain principles have emerged from the empirical experience of teachers and literary scholars that we hope you will keep in mind as you develop your own techniques and build new programs.

---

[8] Nancy L. Arnez, "Enhancing the Black Self-Concept Through Literature," in *Black Self-Concept*, by James A. Banks and Jean D. Grambs, eds. (New York: McGraw-Hill Book Company, 1972), pp. 105–106.

Dwight Burton has noted an important principle for any act of literature teaching or for any proposal for a new literature program:

> Literature is liberating in the sense that it helps to free us from the inherent shackles fastened upon us by our society. Crucial in the quest for identity, as opposed to a deadening relating to the crowd, is the ability to shake off, when necessary, the emotional censors of society. One can accomplish this in the literary experience and therein lies the great enduring value of literature.[9]

In her Distinguished Lecture for the National Council of Teachers of English in 1970, Louise Rosenblatt discussed the reader's response as part of the interaction between reader and book on which she had first focused the attention of teachers in 1938, in *Literature as Exploration.* She recounted the story of the publisher who asked her to write a book on *How to Make Literature Relevant.* She pointed out, "My immediate response was, you can't *make* it relevant. Literature by its very nature is relevant."[10] Rosenblatt further noted the basic problem of literature "viewed as an object of study," obscuring the problem of most approaches to teaching literature wherein the "basic flaw" is that the reader, like Ralph Ellison's *Invisible Man,* is viewed as invisible by teachers.[11]

Many teachers have indeed treated their students as though they were "invisible men" by such practices as making them read and study in depth poems, essays, novels, and short stories for which they have had little interest or aptitude. In fact, studies of reading interest by George Norvell and others with a variety of student populations over the past quarter century have verified that many of the readings most frequently assigned in literature classes are not well liked by most students, and particularly by boys.[12]

Meanwhile, as a result of the "paperback revolution" occurring over the past three decades, a variety of books written especially for adolescents, as well as some adult books especially popular with adolescents, has become commonplace in many English programs, particularly in elective programs. The problem of differentiating between literature especially written for adolescents and that written especially for adults may not really be a problem at all. In the preface to a recent issue of the *Arizona English Bulletin* on the theme of "Adolescent Literature, Adolescent Reading and the English Class," editor Kenneth L. Donelson notes the difficulty he found in asking teachers working with adolescents to keep the distinction between literature written for teen-agers and that

---

[9] Dwight L. Burton, *Literature Study in the High Schools,* 3rd ed. (New York: Holt, Rinehart and Winston, Inc., 1970), pp. 5–6.

[10] Louise M. Rosenblatt, "Literature and the Invisible Reader," in *The Promise of English,* NCTE (Champaign, Ill., 1970), p. 5.

[11] *Ibid.,* p.6.

[12] George Norvell, *The Reading Interests of Young People* (Boston: D. C. Heath, 1947).

written for adults in mind when writing about the successes that they had had in bringing books and young people together:

> Originally, I intended to devote this issue to literature written specifically for young people, roughly grades five or six through ten or eleven, material fondly (or condescendingly) called "junior" or "adolescent" or "transitional" literature. But a fast reading of just the first two or three articles submitted revealed that restricting the issue to the original goal would hamper writers intersted in discussing *both* what students liked to read *and* what they might like to read. Since both adolescent and adult titles kept popping up, the issue was broadened to what now appears on the cover, doubtless a more clumsy but certainly a more accurate indication of the content therein. If comments on *Mr. and Mrs. Bo Jo Jones* and *The Pigman* and *The Outsiders* and *Durango Street* abound, so also do comments on *A Separate Peace* and *Siddhartha* and *Red Sky at Morning* and *Johnny Got His Gun* . . .
> . . . teachers who really want to help kids and who really believe that educational truism, start where a child is and then take him someplace, may discover that *Moby Dick* and *Pride and Prejudice* and *David Copperfield* are not the answers. Those teachers may discover, more surprisingly, that *A Separate Peace* and *To Kill a Mockingbird* and *Childhood's End* are not necessarily any more satisfactory answers. Just possibly, *The Outsiders* or *The Pigman* or *Durango Street* might help. That assumes, of course, that teachers really care. It also assumes that teachers are willing to read adolescent books to find answers. Is that too much to ask?[13]

That particular issue of the *Arizona English Bulletin* describes a variety of successful experiments and programs by teachers in several places in the country that attempt to bring children and books together, certainly for a variety of purposes, but essentially to bring the right book together with the right child at the right time. This particular philosophy of teaching literature is quite different from what most of you may have experienced either in your high school or in your university studies. Perhaps the reason why "individualized reading" courses are becoming more popular in junior and senior high schools has to do with the student's demand for meaning and relevance in his studies, as noted earlier. In any case, the bulletin mentioned represents a valuable compendium of both methods and materials for any teacher desiring to begin an individualized reading program or an elective course in which students are considered more than "invisible men" and are able to read a variety of materials representing their own interests and maturity levels, and still satisfy the requirements for English courses.[14]

---

[13] Kenneth L. Donelson, "Preface to the Issue," *Arizona English Bulletin* 14, No. 3 (April 1972): 1.

[14] *Ibid.*

Why have programs of "individualized reading" gained popularity with students in junior and senior high schools? In many cases, teachers have become aware of a vast network of underground books circulating throughout the schools, undoubtedly affecting students in a variety of significant ways and yet not discussed in any literature class or by the faculty members of the English departments. Teachers have become more conscious of the impact of certain books such as *Demian* and others mentioned earlier, which are obviously having considerable impact on many senior high school students. Many teachers have brought the "underground circuit" of books into their classrooms.

As today's secondary school students have come to examine and respect their own experience, they have sought meaning in their own world and their own lives. Walter Loban, in noting Socrates' comment that "the unexamined life is not worth living," proposes that literature has a special significance in helping young people in the search for order and meaning in their own lives:

> All life, as Socrates knew, is a search for meaning, a continuing struggle to find, among the fragmented moments of experience, some order and significance. Everyone questions life in various ways—through talk with friends, through contemplation silently and alone, through religion, philosophy, and the humanities. Among all the ways, literature is one of the most respected, and furthermore, is the only one with an established place in public education.
>
> Other arts make their appearance in the schools, but it is noteworthy that they are not required. There must be some reason that literature is assigned to reach all students, whereas music, art, the dance—all the other fine arts—are offered only as elective subjects. We agree that all the arts help to vivify and unify our experience. But we can also see that literature deals more directly, more comprehensively, with the human situation. Through literature we compare, contrast, and clarify our own experience of life with that of the author.... *However, because it can enlarge students' awareness of values and refine their discriminations among values, literature is a force of tremendous potential for education provided the responder is genuinely involved.*[15]

In this chapter, we have attempted to stimulate your thinking about one of the most complex learning processes in which your students will engage—the learning that will result from their involvement with imaginative literature. The philosophies, methods, techniques, and materials designed to help your students respond to literature represent our own particular biases and observations and what precious little research we have on this most complex of subjects. What we are urging you to do is to take a stand after you have examined the research and after you have watched your own students as they become involved with books. Also, carefully consider your own personal reading history. Hopefully all of this will prevent you from attempting to foist on your students literary works that you have read only with difficulty at age twenty-two. If we were

---

[15] Walter Loban, "Literature and the Examined Life," *English Journal* 59, No. 6 (Nov. 1970): 1086–1090.

to suggest a point of view toward the teaching of literature, it might be that proposed by Geoffrey Summerfield in *Creativity in English*. He quotes the poet May Swenson in her preface to *Poems to Solve:*

> Notice how a poet's *games* are called his "works"—and how the "work" you do to solve a poem is really *play*. The impulse and the motive for making a poem and for solving and enjoying a poem are quite alike: both include curiosity, alertness, joy and observation and invention.[16]

Summerfield proposes that the decision you make about what constitutes your "work" as a teacher and your students' "work" or "play" in the classroom is a very serious one. He challenges the assumption that "creative English" is *one* thing and serious work in English is *another*, that one "does the first on Thursday afternoon and the rest in every other English lesson."[17] In "creative English" you and your students will need to redefine what all of you have usually conceived of as work. Together, in the planning of individualized reading programs, you may well find that the *playful* aspects of creativity will contribute most to their learning and to their involvement both with literature and with life itself. The literature program in your classroom will then serve to release and engage their energies in creative response in understanding that "work" is, in May Swenson's sense, not "work" as they had thought of it at all, but the engagement of the imagination in "curiosity, alertness, joy, observation," and perhaps most important of all, "invention."

If you have been reading biographies or stories with particularly good character development, get the students involved in what it's like being a biographer. Have each student go to a cemetery, or better yet, plan a trip so that the whole class goes to the same cemetery. Then have each student select a tombstone and write down the name and dates shown on it. For a writing assignment, have the student find out all he can about this person and write a biography in the form of a short essay, or else an epitaph in the form of a poem in the style of *Spoon River Anthology*. This kind of assignment can involve students in a variety of kinds of research—courthouse records, interviews with family and friends, old newspaper clippings, and so forth. If all of the students went to the same cemetery, they might find people who had been friends or enemies in life; rich people buried beside poor; people who had been murdered, which could be stories in themselves; people who had lived rich, fulfilled lives; people who had lived desperately. They could imagine (if they could not actually find out) what they looked like, how they idled away their time, how they came to be what they were. This could lead to discussions of what people live for and what they die for—something with which our literary heritage is filled. This could lead into and out of various forms of literature;

---

[16] May Swenson, *Poems to Solve* (New York: Charles Scribner & Sons, 1966), pp. 17–18.

[17] Geoffrey Summerfield, *Creativity in English*, National Council of Teachers of English (Champaign, Ill., 1968), p. 67.

it could lead to values clarification; it could lead to added awareness of what it is like to be human, and of how we relate to the scheme of things.

If James McCrimmon's statement that "the prerequisite to writing is thinking and the prerequisite to thinking is observation" is true, then the study of literature and writing must get back to a great deal of observation. One of the marks of a good writer is that he pays close attention to significant detail— how a character talks, dresses, acts, how he furrows his brows, drums his fingers, or shows what he is thinking or feeling through what he does. A good writer can describe a room so well that you can actually see it, or a meal with such finesse that you actually seem to smell and taste the food. Students see things every day that can be the basis for detailed observation, which can lead to thinking and writing and to paying closer attention to detail in their reading. After reading a particularly descriptive passage in a novel or poem, have the students take a walk around their neighborhood, city, church, park, or anywhere. Ask each one to pick out one thing that catches his attention—a particular tree or interesting building, an unusual stained glass window, or a person. Then have him try to find out all he can about this particular person, place, or thing. This, again, will involve research. (If he has picked out something that has caught his attention and is particularly interesting to him, he will want to find out more about it.) With this raw material, he can create a scene or a character that might fit into a short story or poem of his own or that might relate to a scene or person in something he is reading. This is the way such projects as the *The Foxfire Book* got their start.

In other words, be constantly cognizant of activities that make the "act of writing and experiencing literature" a concrete experience for the student. Keep in mind that you must try to extend awareness and provide opportunities for students to become actively engaged not only in reading but in creating literary experiences.

ADOLESCENT WORKS GUARANTEED TO "HOOK" SOME OF YOUR STUDENTS

Author	Title
Annixter, Paul and Jane	*Swiftwater, Windigo*
Armstrong, William H.	*Sounder*
Ball, Zachary	*Bristle Face*
Benary, Isbert Margot	*The Ark*
Bennett, Jack	*Jamie*
Birmingham, John (ed.)	*Our Time Is Now*
Bonham, Frank	*Durango Street, The Nitty Gritty, Viva Chicano*
Bordeus, Dennis	*Mysterious Worlds*
Brink, Carol	*Caddie Woodlawn, Snow in the River*
Bro, Marguerite Harmon	*Sarah*
Burch, Robert	*Queenie Peavie*
Catton, Bruce	*Banners at Shenandoah*

Caudill, Rebecca	*The Far-Off Land*
Cavanna, Betty	*Almost Like Sisters, The Boy Next Door*
Chute, Marchette	*Innocent Wayfaring*
Clapp, Patricia	*Jane-Emily*
Clark, Anne Nolan	*Santiago*
Cohen, Joel H.	*Hammerin' Hank of the Braves*
Cole, Stephen	*Pitcher and I*
Colman, Hila	*Car-Crazy Girl, Classmates by Request*
Craig, Margaret	*It Could Happen to Anyone*
Cunningham, Julia	*Drop Dead*
Daly, Maureen	*Seventeenth Summer*
Dizenzo, Patricia	*Phoebe*
Donovan, John	*I'll Get There, It Better Be Worth the Trip*
DuJardin, Rosamond	*Practically Seventeen*
Emery, Ann	*The Losing Game*
Eyerly, Jeannette	*Drop-Out, Escape from Nowhere, A Girl Like Me*
Fast, Howard	*April Morning*
Felson, Henry	*Boy Gets Car, Hot Rod, Street Rod, Two and the Town*
Forbes, Esther	*Johnny Tremaine*
Freedman, Nancy and Benedict	*Mrs. Mike*
Fuller, Lola	*Leon Feather*
Gault, William C.	*Dirt Tract Summer*
Gipson, Fred	*Old Yeller, Savage Sam*
Graham, Lorenz	*South Town*
Gray, Elizabeth J.	*Adam of the Road*
Green, Hannah	*I Never Promised You a Rose Garden*
Haggard, Elizabeth	*Nobody Waved Goodbye*
Hall, Lynn	*Sticks and Stones*
Hamilton, Virginia	*The House of Dies Drear*
Head, Ann	*Mr. and Mrs. Bo Jo Jones*
Hentoff, Nat	*I'm Really Dragged But Nothing Gets Me Down, Jazz Country*
Hinton, S. E.	*The Outsiders; That Was Then, This Is Now*
Hintze, Naomia	*You'll Like My Mother*
Hoffman, Peggy	*Shift to High*
Hunter, Kristin	*The Soul Brothers and Sister Lou*
James, Will	*Smoky the Cowhorse*
Johnson, Anabel and Edgar	*Count Me Gone*
Kelly, Eric	*Trumpeter of Krakow*
Keyes, David	*Flowers for Algernon*
Kingman, Lee	*The Peter Pan Bag*
Knight, Eric	*Lassie Come Home*
Krumgold, Joseph	*And Now Miguel, Henry 3*
Laing, Frederick	*Ask Me If I Love You Now*

Lambert, Jane	*The Odd Ones*
L'Angle, Madeleine	*The Arm of the Starfish, A Wrinkle in Time*
Lipsyte, Robert	*The Contender*
MacLeod, Ruth	*Buenos Dias, Teacher*
Maxwell, Edith	*Just Dial a Number*
Mays, Willie	*Born to Play Ball*
McKay, Robert	*Canary Red, David's Song*
Merrill, Jean	*The Pushcart War*
Miller, Helen	*Thunder Rolling: The Story of Chief Joseph*
Morris, Jeannie	*Brian Piccolo: A Short Season*
Murphy, Robert	*The Pond*
Neufeld, John	*Lisa Bright and Dark*
Neville, Emily	*It's Like This, Cat*
North, Sterling	*Wolflings*
Norton, Andre	*Catseye, Lord of Thunder*
O'Dell, Scott	*The King's Fifth*
Olson, Gene	*Bailey and the Bearcat*
Perry, Dick	*Raymond and Me That Summer*
Potok, Chaim	*The Chosen, The Promise*
Rawlings, Marjorie	*The Yearling*
Richter, Conrad	*Light in the Forest*
Rodman, Bella	*Lion in the Way*
Russell, Bill	*Go Up for Glory*
Sandoz, Marie	*The Storycatcher*
Sayers, Gale	*I Am Third*
Schapiro, Milton	*Jackie Robinson of the Brooklyn Dodgers*
Schollander, D., and Savage, D.	*Deep Water*
Scholtz, Jackson	*Dugout Tycoon*
Sherburne, Zoa	*River and Her Feet, Too Bad About the Haines Girl*
Shotwell, Louisa R.	*Roosevelt Grady*
Speare, Elizabeth George	*The Witch of Blackbird Pond*
Sterling, Dorothy	*Mary Jane*
Stirling, Nora	*You Would If You Loved Me*
Stoltz, Mary	*A Love for a Season, Ready or Not, Who Wants Music on Monday?*
Street, James	*Goodbye, My Lady*
Sture, Vasa Mary	*My Friend Flicka*
Summers, James L.	*The Shelter Trap*
Swarthout, Glendon	*Bless the Beasts and Children*
Thompson, Jean	*House of Tomorrow*
Trevino, Elizabeth	*I, Juan De Pareja*
Tunis, John	*His Enemy, His Friend, Silence Over Dunkerque*
Ullman, James Ramsey	*Banner in the Sky*
Walden, Elizabeth Amelia	*Race the Wild Wind*

Walker, Mildred	*Winter Wheat*
Witton, Dorothy	*Crossroads for Chela*
Wojciechowska, Maia	*Don't Play Dead Before You Have to, Shadow of the Bull, Tuned Out*
Yates, Elizabeth	*Patterns on the Wall*
Young, Bob and Jon	*Across the Tracks*
Zindel, Paul	*I Never Loved Your Mind, My Darling, My Hamburger, The Pigman*

ADULT NOVELS, BIOGRAPHIES, AND OTHER NONFICTION GUARANTEED TO "HOOK" SOME OF YOUR STUDENTS

Author	**Title**
Adamson, Joy	*Born Free*
Agee, James	*A Death in the Family, Let Us Now Praise Famous Men*
Angelou, Maya	*I Know Why the Caged Bird Sings*
Baldwin, James	*The Fire Next Time, Nobody Knows My Name, Go Tell it on the Mountain*
Borland, Hal	*When the Legends Die*
Bradbury, Ray	*Fahrenheit 451*
Bradford, Richard	*Red Sky at Morning*
Braithwaite, E. R.	*To Sir with Love*
Bronte, Charlotte	*Jane Eyre*
Brown, Claude	*Manchild in the Promised Land*
Brown, Dee	*Bury My Heart at Wounded Knee*
Burgess, Anthony	*A Clockwork Orange*
Clark, Walter von Tilburg	*The Ox-Bow Incident*
Corle, Edwin	*Fig Tree John*
Crichton, Michael	*The Andromeda Strain*
Denby, William	*Battlecreek*
Dickens, Charles	*David Copperfield, A Tale of Two Cities*
Ellison, Ralph	*Invisible Man*
Flaubert, Gustav	*Madame Bovary*
Golding, William	*Lord of the Flies*
Gregory, Dick	*Nigger*
Griffin, John	*Black Like Me*
Heinlein, Robert	*Stranger in a Strange Land*
Heller, Joseph	*Catch 22*
Hemingway, Ernest	*A Farewell to Arms, For Whom the Bell Tolls, A Moveable Feast, The Old Man and the Sea, The Sun Also Rises*
Hersey, John	*The Algiers Motel, Hiroshima, A Single Pebble, Incident*
Hesse, Herman	*Siddhartha, Demian*
Hughes, Langston	*Not without Laughter*
Katz, Elizabeth	*A Patch of Blue*

Kellogg, Marjorie	*Tell Me that You Love Me, Junie Moon*
Kesey, Ken	*One Flew Over the Cuckoo's Nest*
Keyes, Daniel	*Flowers for Algernon*
Knowles, John	*A Separate Peace*
LaFarge, Oliver	*Laughing Boy*
Lee, Harper	*To Kill a Mockingbird*
McCullers, Carson	*The Heart Is a Lonely Hunter*
Malamud, Bernard	*The Assistant, The Fixer*
Miles, Richard	*Angel Loves Nobody*
Momaday, N. Scott	*House Made of Dawn*
Morin, Raul	*Among the Valiant*
Orwell, George	*1984, Animal Farm*
Parades, Americo	*With a Pistol in His Hand*
Paton, Alan	*Cry the Beloved Country*
Plath, Sylvia	*The Bell Jar*
Potak, Chaim	*The Promise, The Chosen*
Salinger, J. D.	*Catcher in the Rye*
Solzhenitsyn, Alexander	*One Day in the Life of Ivan Denisovich*
Steinbeck, John	*The Grapes of Wrath, Travels with Charley, The Pearl*
Tarizan, James J., and Cramer, Kathryn	*Caesar Chavez*
Thomas, Perri	*Down These Mean Streets*
Toomer, Jean	*Cane*
Trumbo, Dalton	*Johnny Got His Gun*
Vasquez, Richard	*Chicano*
Villaneal, Jose Antonio	*Pocho*
Vonnegut, Kurt	*Cat's Cradle*
Weston, John	*Hail Hero!*
Wiesel, Elie	*Night*
Wright, Richard	*Black Boy*

Part III

What Do We See in the Language We Use?

Chapter 6

A First Look at Elements of Our Language

WHAT ABOUT LANGUAGE?

In the beginning was the Word, and the Word was:

(a) a noun; (b) an adjective; (c) God; (d) that depends
(Select the right answer)

If the foregoing exercise excites your "teacher-test-taking-tendencies," then you have no need to read this section. All you need is a "hot" grammar book with a teacher's manual that gives the correct answers to all of the exercises. If the exercise makes you mildly curious or stimulates your thinking about the implications of the "answers" as well as of the question, then you have no need to read this section either. All you need is some kids and some "cool" symbols—written, spoken, drawn, or otherwise. Who, then, *should* read this section? That depends. Perhaps you should read it to find out. Maybe a few more clues will help you to decide.

Our aim is to pose some more questions about language—why "teach" it, to whom, for what purpose? How you answer the questions will determine what you do about "it" with "them" in the classroom. The purpose then, is to help you consider why, how, when, where, and what aspects of language(s) can be introduced as topics of exploration. Various approaches and situations are presented here for your consideration. The decision as to which ones are appropriate for *you* depends, of course, on you, your audience, your purpose, and your school—your "educational context."

IS LANGUAGE "HOT" OR "COOL"?

"A hot medium," according to Marshall McLuhan, "is one that extends one single sense in 'high definition.' High definition is a state of being well-filled with data." Most high school language books are hot. Since most English teachers use these books, most language instruction is hot. It heats up to a mere listing of rules and regulations about structure and usage, with little variety in approach or technique. "Hot linguistics," then, is well-filled with data concerning structure and systems of language and technical "input" regarding morphology, phonology, and syntax. Some like it hot because it is easier to grade papers if you use a "hot" theory; it is mechanical; it is therefore easily translated into behavioral objectives. "Hot linguistics" is school language. It provides for what Charlton Laird has termed "intellectual and social toilet training" in language. This is not to say that toilet training is unnecessary, but it isn't the ONLY intellectual and social training we should engage in.

By contrast, "a cool medium" has "low definition," McLuhan says, because "so little information is given and so much has to be filled in or completed by the audience." "Cool linguistics," then, is the study of language as human behavior. It is the study of the communication of thoughts, feelings, ideas, and desires by any means—grunts, groans, gestures, scribbles, or other symbols. It is the study of what Charles Weingartner has termed "human meaning-making processes" and the effects of those processes. This is the language study of the real world—advertising, politics, the psychoanalyst's couch, and the mass media. It requires a great deal of student involvement. It is more difficult to plan and even more difficult, if not impossible, to write in behavioral terms. It has humanistic objectives.

Both "hot" and "cool" linguistics are being taught in the schools today. The development of each type parallels the curious transitions that have occurred in the English curriculum as a whole. Most of its history is a dreary account of emotional reactions to misinformation and misguided purposes and projects that seldom reached their goals. Therefore, we should not look at the history of language study in our schools in hopes of repeating ourselves, nor should we look at it for inspiration. At most, it should give us a perspective. As Michael Katz, in *School Reform: Past and Present*, remarks about education in general, history gives us

> ... a liberating perspective in a manner similar to psychoanalysis. Both bring us back to the origins of our problems, and, by some strange chemistry of our nature, it would seem that only by understanding their origins can we begin to overcome them.[1]

This is not the place to go into a lengthy discussion of the history of language study, for that has been done well and thoroughly elsewhere. However, a

---

[1] Michael Katz, *School Reform: Past and Present* (Boston: Little, Brown & Co., Inc., 1971), p. 2.

brief analysis of some of the origins of our problems might help us to overcome them.

English teachers who have pushed pronouns, diagrammed sentences, unsplit split infinitives, and dabbled with dangling modifiers have consistently failed to convince students that these mind-boggling activities make sense. As any psychoanalyst knows, consistent failure develops unhealthy self-concepts and often leads to neurotic behavior. Many English teachers, whether they admit it or not, have unhealthy self-concepts in view of their consistent failures, and they neurotically keep pursuing these same failures. Or, they blame the students, rationalizing that *they* are the ones who "really" failed—not the teacher.

Parents have also added to the teachers' frustration by encouraging them to continue this mindlessness. It's part of the "I-had-to-walk-a-mile-in-the-snow-so-why-can't-you-kid" syndrome. Many parents feel that grammar study is the only practical part of English instruction. Few see much use in their child studying Shakespeare or Hawthorne or the mysteries of poetry. After all, how will this help the kid make a living in this world of technology and skill? They want their child to get the basics—the really "useful" stuff—that is, the skill to write and speak "correct" English.

If parents don't exert this pressure on the English teacher, the other faculty members do. A common complaint heard daily in teachers' lounges is, "My students can't even write a complete sentence, for pity's sake! When are you English teachers going to quit fooling around with film-making and those other frills, and teach them something useful!" To them, the subject of language is considered easy. It's fixed like geometry. After all, there are definite rules (which most parents and many teachers have forgotten). So teach them! Rarely do you hear parents expounding such directives to chemistry or history teachers. Those areas are not in the public domain, but language is.

English teachers are rightfully frustrated. They are in the middle—the students and perhaps their own convictions screaming on one side, with parents and other teachers shrieking on the other. Not only is this the origin of our problem, it *is* the problem.

WHAT DOES LANGUAGE MEAN TO OTHERS?

Since language is in the public domain, many people other than English teachers have been involved in its study. Writers, psychologists, and anthropologists have formulated a constellation of definitions, each adding facets to its meaning. These definitions and extensions of language study have enriched the possibilities of language pursuits in the classroom. Here are a few definitions of language:

> *Language is a purely human and noninstinctive method of communicating ideas, emotions, and desires by means of a system of voluntarily-produced symbols.*
>
> EDWIN SAPIR
> *Language*

Language—the system of various noises humans produce with their lungs, throats, tongues, teeth, and lips systematically standing for specified happenings in their nervous system.

S. I. HAYAKAWA
Language in Thought and Action

Language is a bridge between man and his environment, between man and his fellow man. It most clearly distinguishes men from all other animals. It is what makes men truly human. It conveys thoughts, feelings, desires, attitudes, sharing in traditions, conventions, knowledge and superstitions of man's culture. It is arbitrary sounds and marks which convey accurate or misleading information, arouses fear, gratitude, passion, sets machines in motion, topples governments, starts wars and revolutions. It covers not only writing and speech, but certain "paralinguistic" phenomena which accompany or replace speech: gestures, facial expressions, significant feature of context. (condensed)

MAX BLACK
The Labyrinth of Language

Language—the study of our ways of perceiving reality.

POSTMAN and WEINGARTNER
Teaching as a Subversive Activity

Language is but the instrument conveying to us things useful to know.

JOHN MILTON (1614)
Education Words (1847)

After studying these various definitions of language, what are some of the common elements in the definitions? What do these common elements stress about language? Each definition emphasizes a different aspect of language. What are some of the differences? Which definition seems nearest to what language means to you?

WHAT DOES LANGUAGE MEAN TO YOU?

Think about that question. Attempt to answer it. The question was not put there simply to make a nice subtitle, but to elicit some response from you.

What *does* "language" mean to you?

Does it mean the same thing as "linguistics"?

Do both of these terms mean the same thing as "communication"?

If you feel that there is a shade of difference in meaning of these terms, how are they different? How are they similar?

What do you think students should know about language? About linguistics? About communication?

Why?

Should all students of various abilities and backgrounds know the same things about language?

What should all students know? Why?

Who should know different things?

What are these "different" things?

What do students already know about language/linguistics/communication?

How do you know? How can you find out?

Does this make a difference in what you should "teach" them about language/linguistics/communication?

Should language/linguistics/communication be taught in isolation; that is, as a separate course?

Why, or why not?

Check some of your local schools and list the language courses and course descriptions that are offered.

What aspects of language seem to be "taught"?

What aspects seem to be ignored in the classroom?

Is this significant? Why, or why not?

Talk to some English teachers and find out what they think should be taught about language/linguistics/communication.

What do *they* think kids need to know?

Ask them if the students seem to make the same mistakes repeatedly in usage, grammar, and other matters.

Ask the teachers what they try to do about this problem.

Interview some students in junior and senior high schools.

Ask them what they've "learned" about language.

Ask them what they think about the study of language in their courses.

Ask them to tell you the most significant thing they've learned about languages.

Do these answers from teachers or students confirm any of your thoughts about the teaching of language? What?

Do they confirm any of your notions? Which ones?

So what?

You will not find the answers to these questions in the back of this book. You will find them by talking to teachers, kids, and yourself. Consider these answers and their implications before reading on.

WHAT DO YOU KNOW ABOUT STUDENTS?

If you accept Postman and Weingartner's definition that the study of language is the study of our ways of perceiving reality, then you should know something about perception and reality. In other words, if you are going to work with kids, then you should realize that each of them will perceive differently than you do, depending upon their backgrounds and exp rience—their realities.

Much research has been conducted in perception. Victor Lowenfeld, in *Creative and Mental Growth*, offers some interesting concepts for the art teacher that could be applied just as well to the English teacher. He suggests that there are two distinct creative types, based upon two different reactions toward the world of experiences, which he calls the *visual type* and the *haptic type*.

The *visual type* is the observer. He has the ability to see things first as a whole, then analyzes this total awareness into an awareness of details or partial impressions, and finally synthesizes these parts into a new whole. Further, the visual type has a tendency to transform physical experiences into visual experiences. If he were put into a dark room and given an object, he would touch, smell, perhaps taste it, and would translate this sensual experience into a visual one—sketching in his mind what the object looks like to determine what it is. Lowenfeld compares him to a spectator who observes and analyzes the outside world.

The *haptic*-minded person is not satisfied being a spectator. He must participate in the game. He is a subjective type; thus, all experiences have no meaning to him unless he can place himself in a value relationship to the outside world. If a haptic-minded person were placed in a dark room with an object, he would not transform the tactile or kinesthetic experiences into visual ones. He would be satisfied just with the physical experience. Further, Lowenfeld points out, he would arrive at a synthesis of these partial impressions "only when he becomes emotionally interested in the object itself." He is not analytical, not interested in the abstract, but only interested in the concrete experience insofar as that experience relates directly to him.

Another area of research that has direct bearing on the teaching of language has been concerned with the sociological determinants of perception and their relationships with language, social class, and language development of children. Basil Bernstein, in his article "Social Structure, Language and Learning," presents an interesting account of how the special type of social relationships of lower working-class children is the cause for the lack of verbal versatility, and that this lack is not a consequence of a deficiency of intelligence. The social relationships mark out a pattern of stimuli that forms the child's learning pattern, his perception, and his language. All three work back and forth to reinforce the others. The child is not forced to talk about abstractions. Most of what he hears are concrete commands or concrete accounts of what is happening in his immediate environment. Bernstein has labeled the linguistic habits of lower working-class children as "restricted codes." If a speaker is using a *restricted code*, the range of alternatives will be small and the pattern of organizing elements considerably reduced. He will use "ritualistic modes of communication . . . the sequences will tend to be dislocated, disjunctive . . . point to the concrete, the descriptive, the narrative . . . and nonverbal signals will be an important source of significant changes in meanings such that the verbal sequences are relatively impersonal; i.e., not individuated."

Bernstein calls the linguistic codes of other social classes "elaborated codes." Speakers or writers who use these codes are versatile, are able to use a wide range of alternatives in expressing themselves, and know a variety of patterns of organizing elements. They write and talk about abstract ideas and do not have to depend on nonverbal signals to modify what they have to say because they can individuate their verbal sequences.

No school, so far as we know, designates student groups by the way in which they perceive—at least, not by the way in which Lowenfeld distinguished perception types. However, if you consider the usual manner in which classes are designated, i.e., by "academic performance (ability)," and if you think of the language abilities of these groups, then we might very well be grouping them in a "Lowenfeldian/Bernsteinean" manner.

If you spend any time observing "basic English classes," you come to realize that most of the students do not write "grammatically correct" English consistently. Many do not speak the "standard dialect." The students are limited, it seems, in their ability to express what they think about concepts, literature, or personal experiences. Yet, the "advanced" or "academically talented" students usually do write and speak "good English." Their language is different in that they are able to understand complex ideas and experiences and translate them into verbal expressions. Further, if you observe the general classroom atmosphere of these different ability groups, the basic (low ability) students tend to be more physically active. Their attention span is relatively brief, which makes it difficult for the teacher to hold and sustain their concentration. They are not interested in the detailed analysis of a problem, a poem, or a language concept. As more emphasis is placed on what Piaget calls "formal operations" in the senior high school, these students become more frustrated and less interested because they are restricted to "concrete operations." They often become disciplinary and academic "problems" to teachers. They are *haptic*-minded, dependent upon *restricted codes* to cope with situations demanding elaborated codes.

On the other hand, "advanced" students can become engaged for longer periods of time in "minding," in "noodling" with ideas, concepts, and abstractions without having to be as physically involved. They are *visually*-minded and do quite well in dealing with and producing the elaborated codes of the classroom.

As Bernstein noted:

> ... attempts to change the system of spoken language of children from certain environments will meet with great resistance, passive and active. It is an attempt to change a pattern of learning, a system of orientation, which language originally elicited and progressively reinforced. To ask the pupil to use language differently, to qualify verbally his individual experience, to expand his vocabulary,

to increase the length of his verbal planning function, to generalize, to be sensitive to the implications of number, or order a verbally presented arithmetic problem, these requests when made to a public (restricted) language user are very different from when they are made to a formal (elaborate) language user. For the latter, it is a situation of *linguistic development* whilst for the former it is one of linguistic change. Two different psychological states underlie these situations. The public (restricted) language speaker is called upon to make responses to which he is neither oriented nor sensitized. His natural responses are unacceptable. It is a bewildering, perplexing, isolated, and utterly defenseless position which ensures almost certain failure unless the teacher is very sensitive to the child's fundamental predicament.[2]

It is not enough for you to be aware of these language problems of your students. You must decide what you plan to do about it. Are you going to attempt to teach these particular students a "second language," using as your rationale that they need a second language to function and to be accepted in other social dialect groups? Do you think this rationale will provide sufficient motivation for your students? Because these students have different language problems, should they be taught differently? Do they need to know the same kinds of things about language that advanced students do? How can you find out their way of perceiving reality? What do you know about their social background and all of the ramifications involved in that background?

If you believe that it is necessary to teach such students a "second language," you will find yourself in the company of some notable linguists, many of whom have expressed their ideas in a number of sources.[3] However, if you question the notion of attempting to make a student bidialectal, you will find evidence that delineates the failures of such programs. James Sledd, in his rollicking but scathing review of the work of dialecticians, notes:

> It is sad to report that the results of such vast activity have been disproportionately small. The biloquialists themselves do not claim to have produced substantial numbers of psychologically undamaged doublespeakers, whose mastery of whitey's talk has won them jobs which otherwise would have been denied them. In fact, the complete bidialectal, with undiminished control of his vernacular and a good mastery of the standard language, is apparently as mythical as the unicorn; no authenticated specimens have been reported. Even the means to approximate the ideal of doublespeaking are admittedly lacking, for "the need for teaching materials preceded any strongly felt need for theoretical bases or

---

[2] Basil Bernstein, "Social Structure, Language, and Learning," in *The Psychology of Language, Thought and Instruction*, ed. John P. DeCecco (New York: Holt, Rinehart and Winston, 1967), p. 99.

[3] See especially *Teaching Standard English in the Inner City*, ed. Roger Shuy and Ralph W. Fasold; *The Florida Reporter* 1969 special issue on "Linguistic-Cultural Differences and American Education"; the Report of the Twentieth Annual Round Table Meeting at Georgetown, "Linguistics and the Teaching of Standard English to Speakers of Other Languages Or Dialects"; and Frederick Williams's anthology *Language and Poverty: Perspectives on a Theme*.

empirical research upon which such materials could be based" (Fasold and Shuy). Consequently there are relatively few teaching materials available and those that do exist differ in theory, method, content, and arrangement.[4]

Sledd comments, however, that the dialecticians' favorite rebuttal is the question, "If not biloquialism, what?" He suggests that English teachers must impress upon their students some higher ambition than to "get ahead," which seems to be one of the main reasons for teaching a student a "second language." He believes that teachers, as politically active citizens, should do whatever possible to end the social isolation of "substandard speakers, so the differences in speech, if they don't disappear themselves, will lose their stigmatizing quality." He stresses that English teachers should point out to students how society uses language "as its most insidious means of control, how we are led to judge others—and ourselves—by criteria which have no real bearing on actual worth." Sledd emphatically states that "no harsh, head-on attempt to *change* their language, to make them speak and write like us [should be made]. If they value our world and what it offers, then they will take the initiative in change, and we can cautiously help them. But we must stop acting as the watch-dogs of middle-class correctness. . . ."

Sledd's suggestions parallel the philosophy of the authors of this book and include the types of language study we feel are necessary. Prescriptive teaching of language is not meaningful, nor has it proven successful with most students— especially with the "disadvantaged" student.

From all of this, we can make some generalizations about student groups and approaches to teaching them language:

1. If your school groups students according to academic performance (ability grouping), you will usually have three groups: basic, average, and advanced (or other similar labels). If your school groups the students heterogeneously, then you will likely have all three types within each class.
2. Basic students will more than likely display the characteristics of haptic-minded, restricted language-users.
3. Average students will be a mixture of haptic/visually-minded students who are both restricted and elaborated speakers of language.
4. Advanced students will be much like your average students, but they will be able to sustain attention for longer periods of time, and they will display the characteristics of the visually-minded person. They will be willing to work and will want to achieve.
5. Your work with basic students will have to be literally engaging. You must get them involved physically to keep their attention for even a short span of time. The work must be concrete, not abstract. There must be a variety of activities, which must be related to them directly—constantly! Though these students are the ones who need the most help in the development of

---

[4] James Sledd, "Doublespeak: Dialectology in the Service of Big Brother," *College English* 33, No. 4 (Jan. 1972): 440–441.

communication skills, they will be the most resistant. They will take your greatest patience and demand your most creativity.

6. Your approach with so-called "average" students should be much like that used with the basic students. Your illustrations, materials, and production requirements can be on a higher level, but the content must remain engaging while practical.

7. You can be more abstract with your advanced students and more demanding by placing more of the responsibility for production on them. Their intellectual needs are different, but their interests cross over ability levels. Advanced kids often react *adversely* to overly haptic approaches. They consider games "kid stuff." Little time, if any, should be expended on grammar and usage, and much more on the dynamics of human meaning-making processes with their psychological and social implications.

WHY SHOULD YOU TEACH LANGUAGE?

The reason usually given for teaching language—which, in schools, most often means grammar and usage—is to improve writing. "Correct English," or the ability to write grammatically correct sentences with no solecisms, we are told, is the mark of a literate man.

One of the most thoroughly investigated problems in the teaching of written composition, then, concerns the merits of formal grammar instruction as an aid in composition. Almost no researcher has found any correlation between knowledge of traditional grammar and quality of composition. After reviewing study after study, the Braddock Committee (The National Council of Teachers of English Committee on the State of the Knowledge about Composition) reported: ". . . the conclusion can be stated in strong and unqualified terms: the teaching of formal grammar has a negligible or, because it usually displaces some instruction and practice in actual composition, even harmful effect on the improvement of writing." (pp. 37–38)[5]

With the advent of structural and generative-transformational grammar in our schools, further research was conducted to see if these new approaches had an effect on writing performance. In 1969, Pooley and Golub reported: "There is no guarantee that students who are taught these concepts will write better compositions. However, there is some indication that students who learn the generative-transformational grammatical process will tend to produce the kinds of varied and dense structures characteristic of professional discourse."

But the Educational Testing Service Writing Panel, when formulating the *Writing Objectives* for the National Assessment Program in 1969, rejected both

---

[5] R. Braddock, R. Lloyd-Jones, and L. Schoer, *Research in Written Composition* (Champaign, Ill.: National Council of Teachers of English, 1963), pp. 37–38.

grammar and vocabulary as criteria, recognizing "the existence of conflicting approaches to grammar and sentence structure . . . and that the teaching of grammar had little or no effect on a student's written expression." (p. 5)[6]

Usage has also been related to composition in an attempt to show that the study of "correctness" will eliminate "incorrectness" in students' writing performance. Deighton observed that "after four years of high school study, twelfth grade students still make the same mistakes [in usage] they made in the ninth grade."[7]

The National Council of Teachers of English advised in 1964 that "instead of teaching rules for the avoidance of errors, pupils must be taught to observe and understand the way in which their language operates today for all the various needs of communication." The NCTE has been advising this ever since it was organized in 1912. James Hosic, one of the cofounders of the National Council, reported the activities of the newly joined committees, now known as the National Joint Committee of Thirty, in *Reorganization of English in Secondary Schools*. The Committee stated that the first aim of English instruction should be "to give the pupils command of the art of communication in speech and writing."[8] It is apparent that for students to command the art of communication, some study beyond grammar is necessary. As Walter Loban observed:

> From my own research I know that the difference between effective and noneffective users of language does not appear in their control of grammatical sentence patterns, for all pupils know these before they enter school. Not grammatical sentence patterns but what is done to achieve greater flexibility and modification of ideas within these patterns proves to be the real measure of proficiency with language. . . . We can see that much more needs to be done to link language with thinking.[9]

What kind of language study will link with thinking? *The Encyclopedia of Educational Research* (1960) makes some suggestions:

> To emphasize and clarify the relationship of words to human behavior. The psychological and social aspects of language; observation of language usages to achieve social standing, express private experiences, and control the behavior of others; the social implications of such phenomena as slang, shoptalk, localism, and euphemism; multiple-meanings as related to particular

---

[6] Committee on Assessing the Progress of Education, *National Assessment of Education Progress: Writing Objectives* (Ann Arbor, Mich.: National Assessment Office, 1969), p. 5.

[7] Lee Deighton, "The Survival of the English Teacher," *ETC.* 10, No. 2 (Winter 1953): 99.

[8] J. F. Hosic, *Reorganization of English in Secondary Schools*, U.S.O.E. Bulletin No. 2 (Washington, D.C.: U.S. Government Printing Office, 1917), p. 30.

[9] W. Loban, "What Language Reveals," in *Language and Meaning*, ed. J. B. MacDonald (Washington, D.C.: N.E.A. Association for Supervision and Curriculum Development, 1966), pp. 71–72.

contexts in which language is used—these are among the relationships between language and behavior which need to be established. The objective further requires the development of insights into the symbolic nature of language, the relationship between words and things, the uses and dangers of the process of abstraction, the literal and metaphorical uses of words, and distinctions between language which reports verifiable fact and that which conveys inferences and judgments.[10]

This type of language study emphasizes the world in which students will have to survive. If students never read another poem or write another theme, they will continue to be language users, senders and receivers of communication, for the rest of their lives. The emphasis is on critical thinking and the process of meaning-making. This is the link that Loban called for. "Correctness" can no longer be the major criterion, nor the only content of language courses. Teachers should waste no time on usage unless students ask particular questions about specific matters, and grammar should be offered only as an elective to the student who is particularly interested in it (a few are). If you find that your students make errors in difficult verb agreement situations or mood situations, that is the time to discuss usage with them. If you find they need work on sentence construction and variety *in their compositions,* that is the time to give them that work. Procedures and techniques to develop these abilities are discussed in Section IV, for this should be employed as part of style development in the rhetorical process, not as rule learning or workbook skill-kill. This work should not be done in isolation just to cover the "next" lesson in a textbook.

Usage matters should stem from a communication context in which students must consider what their purpose is, who they are, and who their audience is. As Robert Pooley wrote forty years ago: "Good English is that form of speech which is appropriate to the purpose of the speaker, true to the language as it is, and comfortable to the speaker and listener. It is the product of custom, neither cramped by rule nor freed from all restraint; it is never fixed, but changes with the organic life of the language." Most traditional textbooks approach usage with a list of rules of "don'ts," not as a function of purposes and strategies required by a particular communication situation. Dialect problems get mixed in with both syntax and usage. The point seems to be that when speakers or writers make usage and syntactic errors and they don't "know" it—then, that's a social dialect, or more precisely, an "ideolect" problem. But if they make the mistake *on purpose*, they are assuming a *persona* to communicate with a certain audience. Politicians and advertisers, perhaps the best language manipulators, do this. Do they have a "usage" problem? Or, are they using "usage problems" to their advantage? Sometimes it is more polite, more political, and more profitable to be grammatically *incorrect*. At other times, it can be disastrous. It all depends. If we want our students to be versatile language manipulators

[10] *Encyclopedia of Educational Research*, 3rd ed., ed. Chester W. Harris (New York: Macmillan, 1960), p. 458.

PART III   **What do we see in the language we use?**

and translators, then they must know "correct" *and* "incorrect" usage so that they can use either type, depending upon their needs at different times. Thus, the following basic concepts about language should determine what we do in the classroom:

1. *Language is behavior.* Its effectiveness is measured in terms of purpose, the situation, the user, the audience, and the subject matter. Therefore, language cannot be taught prescriptively since the prescription will fail to keep up with the actual practice of the culture and may not be appropriate for situations within that culture.
2. *Language is shaped by its culture.* It varies from culture to culture. Further, language shapes reality for its culture, acting as a set of "goggles" through which reality is perceived. Therefore, language study should include the analysis of the culture and subculture groups, and how these groups are used by and create their languages.
3. *Language is total perception.* Its parts—the word, the sentence, or the paragraph—have no meaning apart from the total context of a situation.
4. *Language is a symbol system.* Language can mean different things to different people. It is arbitrary and constantly changing. Therefore, language textbooks are of very little help since they become frozen in terms of time and space, while the realities of a constantly changing language environment continue. Language teaching, therefore, requires the teacher to constantly change by creating materials and developing approaches that keep abreast of the current language scene.

HOW DO YOU TEACH LANGUAGE?

Before discussing and demonstrating some specific ideas for the teaching of language, some general principles should be related.

First, *proceed from the known to the unknown.* In order to do this, the teacher must find out what the students already know—in this case, what they already know about language. What has their past instruction included and excluded? What kind of sociological factors have influenced their experience and the varieties of language experience? What kind(s) of grammar have they been taught? What textbooks have they used in the past? What do they know about the history of their language? Can they describe and relate to you how their slang words and expressions were derived? Who influences their language —how much do they feel their parents have influenced them? What about their peers, the cult groups, the advertising media? What do they know about the sounds of their language? How much do they know about other languages? One way to find out, of course, is to ask. An initial oral discussion with the class might reveal not only to you but to them how little they do in fact know about their language. Or, you might prepare a language awareness inventory.

This kind of initial exploration will help you plan your instruction and also involve the students in the exploration of some of the unknown regions of language to be studied.

Second, *proceed from analysis to synthesis.* As the result of your discussions or inventory, it will be evident to you and the students that there are gaps in their knowledge about language. Language as a whole has many aspects. It can be as simple (?) as word analysis (prefix, suffix, and root—analysis of sounds in the words—analysis of symbolic manifestations of the word), or as complex as the analysis of language as a symbol system—historically, semantically. There is an exception in syntax. In working with sentence building, begin with synthesis and work back to analysis. Analysis then helps us view the complex whole, noticing similarities and differences in the process of synthesizing. Teaching and learning should be a mixture of both analysis and synthesis.

Third, *proceed from the simple to the complex.* This should be determined from the *students'* point of view. It is not easy for teachers to put themselves in a student's position of learning something for the first time, especially in an area in which the teacher has spent many years of specialized study. What might seem basic to the teacher is, in fact, a complex notion to the student. Teachers often act as if *they* are cumulative. This can happen even in a single day's lesson. By the time a teacher has taught the same lesson four times, he feels that the fifth period class already knows much of what he has said in the first four periods, so he begins to shorten, modify, and leave out fundamental ideas. After he has taught it twenty years . . .

Fourth, *proceed from the whole to the part.* Even deciding the whole can be difficult if you do not keep the student in mind. The "whole" for basic students should be smaller than the "whole" for advanced students. If you give the basic student too much material all at once, he can't relate to it and it makes no sense to him. Further, the teacher must relate the whole, however large or small, to the student and his experience. He needs to begin with language as human behavior, as a symbol system, and show the student how it uses him and he uses it.

Fifth, *proceed from the concrete to the abstract.* As was stated earlier, most of us are haptic-minded. If someone expounds about a theory, we usually ask him to give an example. It is easier to learn a new dance step if someone shows you how to do it rather than describes it. In order to relate abstract ideas, use concrete examples, demonstrations, or objects. If you are discussing propaganda techniques in language, show examples of advertising, or play tapes of political candidates' speeches. Use concrete objects, activities, and examples as much as possible to lead to the generalizations or abstractions.

Sixth, *proceed from the particular to the general.* If you want students to derive a general principle about some aspect of language, analyze particular examples from which the principle can be derived inductively. It's easier.

Then move back deductively, in order for the students to demonstrate their knowledge of the principle by their own production of examples.

Seventh, *proceed from the empirical to the rational.* Empirical knowledge is based on observation and experience. This is getting back to what we know from what we have seen, noticed, or felt in our lives. Most people don't think much about language. Very few think enough about it to rationalize, theorize, and write books about it. However, all of us use language daily in a variety of situations that profoundly affect our lives. You should focus on these situations in order to stimulate thinking.

Chapter 7

Pointing Out How Meaning Evolves

Since we have been stressing the necessity of concrete examples and demonstrations throughout this book, we offer the following dialogues and lessons to demonstrate some ways to teach a variety of language concepts. First, here is a shortened transcript of some tapes made in an actual classroom:

Making a "peace" sign with her hand, the teacher asks:
John, what does this mean to you?

John: "Peace."

Teacher: How do you know?

John: Its use.

Teacher: How did you figure out how it was used?

John: Well, I just noticed that when people do that, other people know that it means "peace."

Teacher: What's another word for "noticed?" Did you do more than just "notice?"

John: I guess another word is looked or observed.

Teacher: So through observation you figured out what was meant by this symbol. Suppose I said that it means "war," and I just did it one time and said it one time, while everyone else is saying that it means "peace." Have I changed the symbol? The gesture?

John: No.

Teacher: Have I changed the "meaning?"

John: No, you might have changed the meaning for you but not for most people because most people know that it really means "peace."

Teacher: What if I convince enough people that it stands for "war." Then would it *really* mean "war?"

John: I'm not sure. Maybe.

Teacher: Has this symbol always meant "peace?" Has it stood for anything else?

Bill: Yeah, Churchill used to do that all the time and I think it meant "victory."

Teacher: Then is meaning sort of arbitrary? Does meaning depend upon *who* is giving the meaning to it? Things do not have meaning in themselves. People *give* meaning to things. And if we get enough people to agree that it means something, we have established a pattern that becomes predictable.

For example, here's another gesture. (*Puts arm out with hand at right angle.*) Suppose I am standing in the middle of the street. I do not have a uniform on or any other thing that would be symbolic, and you are driving down the street toward me and I use this signal. What would this mean to you?

Nancy: "Stop."

Teacher: How do you know?

Nancy: Well, like John, I've observed that when it's done, something happens. People stop.

Teacher: Right. And if I am in the middle of the street, I am assuming that you will understand what I mean. If you don't, then I've had it. Okay, Nancy, you have also observed a pattern. What is another gesture or nonverbal act which you can do that symbolizes something?

A girl, Joyce, demonstrates someone with head bowed.

Teacher: Don, what does that mean to you?

Don: She's praying.

Teacher: Are there other ways to demonstrate that?

Don: Yeah. You can kneel, or fold your hands.

Teacher: What position do the Moslems get into when they pray?

Don: Well, they sort of lie down while they are kneeling.

Teacher: What if someone did that in a restaurant? What would the other people's reaction be, do you think?

Don: They'd probably think that he was some kind of nut.

Teacher: Do symbols take on different meanings in different places, then?

The discussion then moved on to concrete objects that are used as symbols—wedding rings, flags, signs, signals. The point made here was that people become very emotionally involved with symbols. Further, you cannot always rely on symbols. If the wedding ring is removed, does that "mean" that you are no longer married? Or, if you wear one, does it mean that you are? Why do some people get upset when they see a flag hung upside down or backward? What kind of symbols do men live and die for? Then, the discussion moved on to written symbols—some of which are "universal" and some of which are "culture" bound. Music is an example of the former type. It can be read or understood by many culture groups. Another example, but with a shade of difference, is the symbol △. When asked what this "meant," most of the students said, "triangle." It was brought out that it also means "evergreen tree" in botany, and "heat" in chemistry. The meanings you assign to symbols are related to your background, knowledge, experience, and the context in which they are used. After talking about a variety of written symbols, the teacher asked:

Angela, how would you symbolize yourself?

Angela: My name.

Teacher: Okay. You are Angela. (*Writes her name on the board and, pointing to the board*) Is this Angela Turner? No. That (*pointing to the student*) is Angela Turner. This is merely a symbol of her name. What if Angela doesn't know how to make that symbol, but uses an "X" in place of it, does the "X" mean the same thing as "Angela Turner"?

Betty: Yes. Some people use that for their legal signature.

Teacher: What if all of you couldn't write your name and you were going to turn in papers to me, and everyone used an "X"? How would I know whose paper I had? Does that symbol have any meaning for me if thirty of you use it to stand for John Cox or Shannon Gridley? What is another system we could use?

Pat: You could use numbers. Most companies identify you by your credit card number or your social security number.

Teacher: Do you think you could remember all of those numbers as easily as you seem to remember names?

Pat: No.

Teacher: Why not?

Pat: Because you associate names with people. I mean some people just look like a Carol or a Mary. I don't think people would look like a 3 or a 4.

Angela: But if we were used to that system, then it wouldn't seem hard or unusual. I know a lot of my friends' telephone numbers, and that sort of stands for the person I want to call.

Teacher: And have you noticed that telephone numbers, and social security numbers, and so forth have certain patterns. And do these patterns help you remember them?

Angela: Social security numbers always have three digits, then two, then four more. The first three numbers of a telephone number usually indicate an area of town.

The next lessons reinforced this idea of patterns. In fact, these two concepts—that language is symbolic and is patterned, and that man is a pattern-planner and symbol-maker—might be the unifying element in the humanistic study of "new English," for it applies not only to language, but also to literature, composition, and nonprinted media. Meaning is what holds the whole English language together, and discovering and making patterns of meaning (symbolizing) is what the kids should be doing.

In the previous dialogue, the concept of man as symbol-maker was stressed and the concept of pattern-maker was introduced. In the following dialogue, patterns will be stressed and symbol manipulation will be introduced.

Using an overhead projector, the teacher puts an assortment of buttons of different sizes on the lighted area of the projector, and the buttons are silhouetted on the screen.

Teacher: Randy, will you come up here and arrange these buttons in some kind of pattern?

(*Randy manipulates the buttons and forms a design.*)

Teacher: What kind of pattern do you see in this arrangement, Joan?

Joan: There is a pattern, like there is a triangle with a tail on one end.

Teacher: Okay. Carl, do you see any pattern?

Carl: I see an arrow.

Teacher: All right, Carl, you come up and put them in another pattern.

(*Carl arranges the buttons of like size in rows, with the largest buttons in the bottom row, the next largest ones in a second row, and so forth, in pyramid style.*)

Teacher: Fine. How has Carl arranged the buttons?

Jan: He's done it according to size.

Teacher: Could you think of another way, Jan?

Jan: Well, you could arrange it like little, little, big—little, little, big. That would be a pattern.

Teacher: Very good. Let's go back to what we were talking about the other day. It seems that man is not only a symbol-using and symbol-making animal, but he also figures out ways to help him remember things. How do you remember things? How do you remember your symbols? How is knowledge or information organized? Ralph, can you give me an example of how man has organized some part of his knowledge in science?

Ralph: Chemical elements are organized on a chart.

Teacher: And how is that chart organized? Is it according to the alphabet, or is it according to when the elements were discovered?

Ralph: No. It's according to atomic weight.

Teacher: Why is it organized in that way? Would it be better to do it alphabetically?

Ralph: It just makes more sense, or it's more useful to do it by atomic weight.

Teacher: Let's analyze something else that you use every day and figure out how it's organized or patterned. Can you think of anything?

Tara: A newspaper.

Teacher: How is it organized?

Tara: Well, the TV programs and movies and stuff are in one section, and the comics are in a section, and the sports pages are together.

Teacher: Okay. Let's talk about the TV programs. How are they organized?

Pat: By time.

Teacher: Within the time organization, how is it further organized?

Pat: By channel.

Teacher: Does that make sense? Why don't they do it just by channel? For example, have Channel 2 and all of the programs listed according to the alphabet. Like: Channel 2, "All in the Family," 8:30 p.m. Saturday?

CeCe: It would be harder to find what you want. I mean you usually look at the clock and say, "What's on the TV now?"

Teacher: The people who make up the TV program listing want it to be useful, so they've figured out the purpose of this listing and organized it according to the easiest way it could be used by most people. All right, the way we organize something, then, depends upon our purpose. Let's relate this to symbols.

(The teacher has a flannel board with three felt symbols on it: the numbers 1, 2, and 3. If possible [with basic kids], each student should also have a small flannel board with the same felt symbols.)

Teacher: How could we arrange these three symbols?

Ellen: Just the way they are. That is, 1, 2, 3.

Teacher: If you leave them the way they are, how are they arranged? Do you have a sequence or a pattern?

Ellen: From smallest to largest number.

Teacher: Good. Cathy, is there another way we could arrange these three numbers?

Cathy: Just the opposite. 3, 2, 1.

Teacher: And what kind of pattern is that?

Cathy: From largest to smallest.

Teacher: Right. Now you notice that the numbers 1 and 3 are blue and the number 2 is yellow. If I put the blue numbers together like $\frac{1}{3}$, and put the yellow number in another column, could you predict what the next yellow number will be?

Don: 4.

Teacher: How do you know?

Don: Because the blue numbers are odd numbers and the yellow number is an even number, so the next even number is 4.

Teacher: We have been looking at these symbols as individual or separate numbers. Suppose we put the three of them together to form one number. How many ways can you rearrange them?

Various members of the class: 123, 213, 312, 132, 231, 321, . . . , etc.

Teacher: Wow, you can get quite a variety of combinations, using the same three symbols. Are all of the combinations different?

Joe: Yes.

Teacher: How do you know they are all different? You are using the same three numbers!

Joe: Well, the form of the number remains the same, but it means something different when it's in a different place.

Teacher: So position of the numbers changes the "meaning" of the symbols. What does "3" mean when it's in this right position? (123)

Joe: "3." Like three ones or units.

Teacher: And when it is in this position? (132)

Joe: It means "30," or three tens.

Teacher: And here? (321)

Joe: "300."

Teacher: You know this because you know our number system, which is based on patterns and positions of symbols. Is our language something like this? Here I have the words "one," "two," "three." Is this another way to represent these symbols (the numbers)?

Angela: Yes.

Teacher: And do these combinations stand for anything? That is, what are letters and words?

Angela: I don't know what you mean, but is it something like when you wrote my name on the board and that name should stand for me?

Teacher: That's right. Words are symbols. They represent objects. Like you can't sit on the word "chair" or eat the word "apple." And the letters stand for the sounds we make when we use them in our talking. So, written words are symbols for our spoken words, which in turn are symbols for the objects and actions in the "real world." And just like the numbers symbols, the pattern or sequence in which you put the letters or the words changes their "meaning." The form of that letter or word may not change, but its function changes. For example, these three letters—S, A, W—can be put into two patterns: saw, and was. They mean different things—we know that because they are arranged in a different pattern. Now—the word "saw" can mean different things according to where it is placed in a sentence. For example, "I saw you yesterday," and "I bought a new saw." How is it used in the first sentence, John?

John: It tells me what you did. It's a verb. And in the second, it tells me what you bought—an object—something you cut wood with.

Teacher: Right. You can see that man is not only a symbol-maker, but he is also a pattern-maker. He puts his symbols into patterns to fit his purpose. He also uses symbols and patterns in a conventional way, or a way that other people use them, so he can be understood or so he can communicate.

From these initial lessons, the teacher and the students can continue in a number of directions. One way might lead to the study of basic sentence patterns, which would necessitate a discussion and analysis of the four form classes of words in order to make the patterns. Another avenue might be historical: to see how man had developed these patterns of language, how he has changed them, and why. Still another avenue might be how our culture shapes patterns and how different cultures have different patterns. Why and how are foreign languages different (words, vocabulary, sentence structure, sounds, symbols)? Within a single country, how have different culture groups and different social groups created their own distinct patterns? Yet another way might be how you construct your patterns (strategies) to fit your purpose of communication with someone in another culture group (age, race, social, alien). This leads naturally to the emotional and psychological uses of language (semantics and the function of syntax).

To illustrate some of the directions just mentioned, the following detailed units were written. They incorporate the principles of teaching listed in the previous chapter, and also develop the concepts of language presented earlier. They involve the students in oral language, media projects, and activities that go beyond pencil-and-paper work in exploring language as they use it in their world.

Before students become involved with the study of special topics of language, they should first understand the nature of language and some principles of general semantics. The following lessons, based on materials developed by the Florida State University Curriculum Study Center, demonstrate how this topic can be approached.

THE NATURE OF LANGUAGE

Objective

To demonstrate the two functions of language—the referential function and the expressive function.

To the Teacher

1. Distribute the selection in the student materials, "Is She Skinny, Thin or Svelte?" Explain to the students that they are to follow along as you read it aloud. Before beginning the selection, write on the board (if possible, do this before the class enters the room) the following phrases: lawyer or attorney, policeman or pig, adolescent or juvenile, skinny or slender, firm or pigheaded. Ask students to look at these phrases. [Even a cursory glance tells us that, even though they seem to mean the same thing, they are quite different. A man would rather be called a policeman than a pig; a teen-ager would rather be called an adolescent than a juvenile; a person would rather be slender than skinny, firm rather than pigheaded. In the selection to be studied today, Professor Hayakawa talks about this double function of language.]

2. Read the first part of the selection orally as the students follow along with you. Explain any terms or words that seem to be too difficult for the class.
   a) What incident or happening caused the remarks in the examples at the beginning of the essay?
   (1: Someone refuses to change his mind; he is firm, obstinate, or pigheaded. 2: Someone is angry about something; he is either

indignant, annoyed, or making a fuss about something. 3: Someone thinks highly of herself; she is beautiful, has quite good features, or isn't bad looking if you like that type. 4: Someone likes to talk; he is sparkling, usually talkative, or drunk. 5: Someone thinks he is a writer; he is a creative writer, has a journalistic flair, or is a prosperous hack. 6: Someone is extremely careful about something; he is fastidious, fussy, or "an old woman.")

b) What is the referential function of language? (The use of language to point to facts observable in the external world, that is, the use of language to make factual statements about things in the world around us.)

c) What determines the way we express these facts? (The way we feel about what we are speaking of. For example, if we admire a person's resistance to change, he is "firm"; if we are critical of him, he is "obstinate"; and if we become angry at his resistance, he is "a pig-headed fool.")

d) What is the *expressive function* of language? (To reveal our own feelings toward the facts we state.)

3. Complete the reading of the essay to the students, following it with a discussion centering around the following questions:

a) Give an example of a purely referential statement. (Water freezes at 32°F. I am 5 ft. 10 in. tall. She weighs 120 pounds.)

b) Give an example of purely expressive language. (I'm sitting on top of the world! Oh boy, I am happy as a lark!)

c) What is the expressive language in the statement about the Jones–Smith–Harrison Act? (· · · in reckless disregard of the public welfare, invited national chaos · · · the vicious · · · Act.)

d) What is the referential language in this statement? (The President signed the Jones–Smith–Harrison Act.)

e) What is the expressive language in the advertisement concerning the Fleetwind? (Every single phrase except the one that says the car has eight cylinders. *Note:* Have the students mention each phrase separately.)

f) Can the student think of other examples of expressive language used in advertising by citing specific ads?

g) What important concept can we state concerning the double function of language? (The double function of language is important because expressive language tells us how a person feels toward his subject, which in turn, allows us to discover if he is "coloring" his facts and speaking from emotion rather than reason. It allows us to see if his "map" represents the territory he is describing or if he is creating a map of a "made-up" territory. We must watch for this in our own speaking and writing because we often talk as if we are stating facts, when, in truth, we are stating opinions. What is dangerous is that we operate or act on opinions rather than on facts. This can have dangerous consequences. It can cause wars, for example.)

Assignment

1. Write the following sentences on the board. Have the students copy them in their notebooks, and ask them to compare the different meanings of the word *dog* in each of the sentences:

   a) A dog is man's best friend.
   b) He leads a dog's life.
   c) You are a dirty dog!
   d) He is always putting on the dog.
   e) Let sleeping dogs lie.

2. Have the students construct five sentences in which they use the same word in five different contexts, with five different meanings.

3. Have the student "conjugate" some words in the same way as Hayakawa did in his essay. Have them write at least ten words and give variations of their "meanings." (*Examples:* horse-nag; stingy-thrifty; etc.)

4. Assign for reading the selection in the student materials, "Theories of Language Origin." Explain to the students that since we have been discussing language, they may be interested in some of the theories of how language began. Allow the rest of the period for the students to work on this assignment.

Objective

To look at language as a system of symbols through which we can achieve a certain amount of communication.

To the Teacher

1. Explain to the students that their reading assignment, "The Origin of Language," offered several theories of how man created his language. Ask the question, "Have any of the theories been proven?" (The answer is no.) Question the seriousness of this essay. What is it about the writing that makes us think the author was really ridiculing the many theories of language development? (Such names for the theories as the "Ding-Dong" theory, the "Bow-Wow" theory, the "Pooh-Pooh" theory, and the "Yum-Yum" theory, suggest a kind of comic treatment.) Have the students note the first paragraph. Select the principal statements in this paragraph. (Language is man's finest invention. All races of man, even the most primitive, have a fully developed language system. Each system is sufficient for that society. Some societies have no written language, but all have a spoken one. No one really knows how language came about.)

2. Discuss the ideas behind each of the theories and the reason each theory was discarded. (The "Ding-Dong" theory: based on the notion that every object has a sound and man identifies the object by its sound. Its drawback is that all objects do not have sounds. A rock, for example,

does not have sound, nor does a mountain, nor a flower. The "Bow-Wow" theory: based on the view that man copied the sounds of the animals around him for the sounds in his language. Its drawback is that it accounts for only a very few words. What animal makes a sound for the word *poetry*, or *language*, or *water*? The "Pooh-Pooh" theory: based on the notion that man makes certain sounds by instinct, and because everybody makes these sounds, they have meaning. Modern science denies this theory. If our language were wholly instinctive, then a baby born of American parents would speak English even if he had never heard English being spoken. This, of course, is not true. An American child will speak French if he is raised in a French-speaking home. The "Yum-Yum" theory: holds that man's words come from the positioning of his tongue, which imitates the gestures man makes with his hands and legs. This theory, like the others, cannot be proven scientifically.)

3. Ask the students which theory they think is nearest the truth of how language developed. (Answers will vary, but some good discussion may come of this question. Allow the students to state their reasons for thinking a theory is possibly true.) Conclude the discussion by suggesting or leading a student to suggest that parts of all the theories are true, but none of them adequately explains the origin of language.

4. Explain that for the present the class will concentrate on written communication. A possible transition between the study of theories of the origin of language into a study of the ways we communicate may be as follows:

"Man, we have learned, does have a language, wherever he lives. People in every society are able to speak among themselves, and most societies have some form of written language. Of course, there are other ways we can communicate besides using written language. We will now consider some of those ways before going further into our study of language."

5. Get out your copy of the *Kaiser Aluminum News Bulletin*, "Communications," by Don Fabun. Turn to page 5.

6. Explain that on this page, the question being asked is one we all must ask ourselves each time we try to communicate with someone. As an example: I (or mention some student's name) have had an experience. This experience happened "outside the skin," but by having the experience, we get it "inside the skin." Now, the question is, how do we get it back outside the skin and possibly inside somebody else's skin? Suppose someone (a student) on his way home saw two dogs fighting over a bone. The experience happened outside his skin. By seeing it, the experience becomes a part of him or gets "inside his skin." Today, he (this student) wants to tell someone about the experience he has had. He wants to tell it in such a way that the experience gets back outside *his* skin and inside someone else's skin. How can he recreate this experience so that his listener has the same experience?

7. Have one of your students read the page (5) to the class. This will reinforce the teacher's explanation. Have the students notice that the

author of this bulletin uses heavy black, boldface type for important concepts. Reread the important statement on this page to the class. At this point, the teacher should explain very carefully this concept: *When we tell someone about an experience we have had, we create a new experience entirely. We cannot possibly, by telling someone of an experience, speak so that what we say becomes a carbon copy of our original experience. The more we learn about language and how it is used, the closer we can come to recreating this experience, but we can never achieve it entirely. This is why the words we choose create a new event entirely.*

8. Read pages 6 through 12. These pages explain some of the reasons why words create a new experience entirely. Discuss these pages with the students, having them copy in their notebooks the boldface portions.

To the Teacher

1. Read page 15 of the *Kaiser Bulletin*. Explain, when the reading is completed, that the author says there are two ways in which individuals can communicate. They are mentioned on this page. What are they? (Actual physical touch and by visible movements of some part of the body.) What are some examples of these two ways? (Examples are listed in columns.)

2. Read page 16. Two more ways are given. Explain that spoken symbols are what Professor Thorndyke calls "puffs of air." The description of how we visualize symbols is simply the description of *what takes place when we see something*. The teacher should not spend time trying to give a physiological explanation of this phenomenon.

3. From the pictures on pages 16 and 17, how many visual symbols can the student recognize?

4. Explain that the most common visual symbols are *words*. Words seem to give us more trouble than any other symbol we use for communication. Since language is made up of words, words become part of the nature of language. Read page 18 of the *Kaiser Bulletin*. This is a short essay on words. Read through this with the students. This is an important introduction to the next phase of the unit: *The Problem of Meaning*. Read to them page 19, which is a summary statement, but this statement may prove difficult for them to understand. Point out the last two sentences (in boldface type) on page 19. Have the students copy these statements in their notebooks. Tell them that these statements are extremely important.

5. After reading through pages 18 and 19 with the students, discuss the essay in the following manner:
   a) How many possible left-to-right combinations can the letters S-T-A-R have? (The answer is 24.) How many of these combinations create the word *star*? (The answer is one). How does the

author describe the process of writing or typing such a word? (The patterns we create in our nervous systems and transmit to our muscles instruct them to arrange the letters into the word *star*.) Does it matter if this word is small or large? Written or printed? (No—it is still the word *star*.) Is learning that S-T-A-R is the word *star* instinctive with us, or do we have to learn it? (We must learn it, just as we have to be taught to recognize a cup and saucer.)

b) In the use of words for communications, which is more important: spelling or meaning? (The spelling.) Why is the meaning not as important? (Because the meaning is *not the word*, but depends on how the person is using it.) Which changes most often: the spelling or the meaning? (The meaning changes with speakers, regions, contexts, and time. Spellings change but slowly over a period of time, and when they do, the pattern remains much the same.)

c) From what has been studied so far, how would the statement on page 19 be explained: "Common words cannot have meanings in themselves—only people can have meanings"? (People have the power to give any meaning to any word.) Is there any relation between this idea and the concept of idea-bound words? (Yes, words that are idea-bound have been given particular meanings by those people for whom the words have become idea-bound. This is why the word *foreigner*, to some people, really *means* a dangerous or evil person. To these people, a foreigner is not just someone to be watched closely; he cannot be trusted; he is dangerous.)

d) From this short essay on words (page 18), what major concept on the nature of language can we develop? (The words of a language have no meaning in themselves; only the people who speak that language give the words meaning.)

6. Write the word *elephant* on the chalkboard, and opposite it write the word *language*. Ask several students each to give you one characteristic of an *elephant*. Ask other students each to give you one characteristic of a *language*. Write these in columns underneath each word. About five characteristics will be enough. (Possible characteristics of an elephant are huge, four legs, a trunk, usually gray, big ears, tusks, etc. Characteristics of a language are: words, sounds, sentences, letters of an alphabet, punctuation marks, etc.) When five characteristics have been mentioned, ask the students if they have named all the characteristics of either an elephant or a language? (Naturally not.) Is it possible to name all the characteristics? (Probably not.)

7. Keeping this in mind, the students will now read "The Parable of the Blind Men and the Elephant," in the *Kaiser Bulletin* (page 13).

8. When they have finished reading it, ask the students to relate "man and his language" to the "blind men and the elephant." (If this question seems to give the class too much difficulty, have them read the paragraph on the next page on the "composite elephant." This should give them an idea out of which to develop the relationship we are searching for.

Man and his language is much like the blind men and the elephant in that: 1) our language is an outgrowth of our experiences; 2) our understanding of the way language operates is usually piecemeal, much like the blind men's conception of the elephant; 3) through the use of language we explain strange things by referring to something familiar; 4) like the blind men, we sometimes do not care to consider the reasons why we disagree with somebody, and 5) like the blind men, we sometimes look at only a small portion of the total act of communication.)

9. Have the students rename all the synonyms the blind men gave to the elephant. Were these synonyms familiar objects to the blind men? (They must have been; otherwise, the blind men would not have related the elephant to these things.)

10. Did each of the blind men think he was speaking the truth about the elephant? (Yes.) Was he willing to change his mind? (No.) How is this like people today?

11. At this point, the teacher should deliver a short lecture, incorporating the following information into it in any way she desires:

[Each of the blind men thought he was speaking the truth, that his conception of the elephant was real. In other words, we sometimes use language as though we were blind. What we say or write may not be true at all, may be only partly true, or, if we are lucky and careful, may approach closely to the truth.]

Ask the students if they can, from their study of poetry, explain the type of language each blind man used to describe the elephant. They used comparisons, and in the study of poetry, two ways of comparing things were mentioned. What were they? (Metaphors and similes.) Which of these comparisons did the blind men use? (Similes.) What is the language called that includes all types of figures of speech and what Hayakawa called "expressive language"? (Metaphorical language.)

The teacher continues her lecture:

[Metaphorical language is not used just in poetry. It is used in almost every situation where communication is attempted. We call this type of language *imaginative* language, which not only includes metaphorical language, but the style and structure of what we say or write. Whenever we open our mouths to speak, we are being imaginative. Every sentence is a new sentence; we have created it; it may never be spoken again. Especially when we are trying to communicate, we are forced to be imaginative. We try to find comparisons so that we can explain things better. We try to relate our experiences with experiences familiar to others, so they will understand us. Our talking and writing would be really drab if we did not use our imagination to dress up our language. But . . . (*Ask the students if they remember what Hayakawa said about expressive language.*) (Expressive language is the words we choose to show our feelings toward our subject. We must be able to understand when language is *expressive* and when it is *referential*.)]

12. Explain that as an overnight assignment, you will give the students a statement that is not imaginative at all. It has not had any imagination applied to it. The students are to add to this statement, ending with not more than *three* sentences.

Write the following statement on the board: *The boy bought a loaf of bread.* Explain the assignment further: The students are to take this one simple statement—call it a *kernel sentence*—and expand it by using imaginative, but not expressive, language (metaphors, similes, descriptions, etc.) Have the students look at the statement. Explain again that this is just the factual outline. Ask the students: what questions are left unanswered by just this simple statement?

Examples:

Why did the boy buy the bread?
Who is the boy?
What does he look like?
What kind of personality does he have?
Where did he come from?
Was it a big or a little loaf of bread?
What circumstances make this an important statement?

Explain again that only three sentences are to be written, but that the students may broaden the first sentence if they like. In fact, the bare statement should be stretched out. Ask for a phrase from the students or supply one, such as the following, to help the students start on the assignment:

Lost and lonely, the boy bought a loaf of bread.

If time remains, allow the students to begin work on the assignment.

Objective

To show that statements are embellished by the speaker's or writer's ability to use his imagination to create clearer images in the minds of his audience.

To the Teacher

1. The first step in today's lesson is a review of the homework assignment. We are not concerned here with the literary quality of the work, but only with the imaginative use of language, or, to put it another way, with the student's attempts at embellishing a brief statement to create a more complete image in the minds of his audience. It is not expected that any student will carry the statement as far as the example given below, but he should see how much more communication is apt to take place when an imaginative use of language is involved. One important aspect of this type of creativity is the effect of praise on the student. The teacher should refrain as much as possible from direct criticism of the student's work. *No criticism of his use of trite or hackneyed phrases should take place at this time.* This does not mean that the student should not be made aware of the triteness, but the teacher must be very careful not to stifle his imagination by condemning him for a phrase that is, in truth, original with him.

2. Write the original statement on the board:

The boy bought a loaf of bread.

3. Ask a student to add a phrase to this:

Lost and lonely, the boy bought a loaf of bread.

4. Ask several students to add phrases. As an example of what could occur, the following will suffice:

Lost and lonely, his face showing signs of fright, the five-year-old boy, red-faced and drippy-nosed, hobbled into the store, stopped, and with eyes popping like a fish's, looked at the tobacco-stained floor. Finally, hunching his shoulders, he started to speak, but no words came.

He wiped his nose on the sleeve of his shirt, black with an accumulation of days of dirt, the cuffs spotted and shiny-slick, the front hanging open, forming an upside-down V from the one button at his neck. He walked to the bread rack, pulling one leg behind the other as though one of them was useless, selected the smallest loaf, and placed twenty-one cents (two dimes and a penny) on the chipped and rutted counter.

5. When the students' embellishments have been added to the statement, ask the students what the difference is between the embellished statement and the original fact. (It is hoped the students will grasp the concept that the more details we give, the clearer the images we create in the minds of our readers and listeners.)

6. Would two people see the boy in the same way? That is, would the language of two people describing the boy be the same? (No.) Why? (We describe things in terms of our own experiences and our ability to use the language. Choice of words depends on knowledge and on the imagination.)

7. Refer to Hayakawa's paragraph on the *expressive function* of language. In the embellished statement on the chalkboard, is there an expressive function in the language the students used? (There should not be, if the students have not allowed themselves to state their feelings about the boy. In the example given above, the embellishment adds to the picture we are trying to create; it rounds out the idea for the audience. There is nothing in the embellishment that tells how the author feels toward the boy or the episode, if we accept his description as true. Naturally, our choice of words sets the tone of our writing, and if the author is being critical of a disregard for the poor by painting a *true* picture of *real life*, he is achieving the same result as that achieved through language such as Hayakawa called *expressive*. But imaginative language does not necessarily have to have an expressive function.)

8. To reinforce this concept of language as imaginative, distribute *America A* from the student materials. The students should not see *America B* at this time. (*America A* is the barest outline, the straight report, so to speak. *America B* is the same statement but expanded into an imaginative picture by one of America's most imaginative authors, Thomas Wolfe.)

9. Have the students read *America A*. With no discussion, distribute *America B*. Explain to them that *America B* is an embellished version of *America A*. Ask the students which version tells them more about America; that is, which version creates the clearer image in their minds? Did Wolfe's imagination distort the picture of America? Have them take one sentence from Wolfe's writing and rewrite it as a man who disliked America might do. Wolfe, it can be seen from this passage, saw only beauty. He did not want, at this point of his narrative, to show us the dirt and filth that are also a part of any country. But suppose he had wanted to do this; what are some of the phrases he might use as replacements for the ones he did write?

    Example:

    Behold those creeping monsters of the jungle East,
    strewn like skeletons through the field of night.

10. Explain that on the following day, a complete recapitulation of what has been studied thus far will take place. At this point, the class will move into the second phase of their study of language: *The Problem of Meaning*. How do we make certain our words mean what we think they do? Explain that this question is not so easily answered as people might think, and that for the next two weeks, the class will try to answer it as fully as possible.

11. As a beginning point in the study of *The Problem of Meaning*, distribute *Main Street A* to one half of the class, and *Main Street B* to the other half. No mention is to be made that these are two different readings, or that one is the correct excerpt and the other is not. Students are to underline phrases or words that describe Main Street. These are the words the author has chosen to create images in our minds—the kind of images he wishes his readers to have. At first glance, it may appear that this assignment is only a repeat of the previous exercise involving *America A* and *America B*. The *Main Street* assignment, however, is a bridge between the previous study of the *Nature of Language* and a study of *Abstractions*, the first problem in meaning that will be taken up in this unit.

12. If time remains, the students should be allowed to work on the assignment until class ends.

THE PROBLEM OF MEANING

Objective

To review and supplement the student's knowledge of abstraction, especially the *ladder of abstraction*.

To the Teacher

1. Immediately after the class is assembled, the teacher asks a student to read the first sentence of his *Main Street B* excerpt.

2. She then asks a student to read the first sentence from his *Main Street A* excerpt.
   a) What was the difference? (One word: "despaired" in the *A* excerpt; "happy" in the *B* excerpt.)
   [Notice that this first sentence sets the tone for the remainder of the excerpt. The word "despaired" tells us that what is going to follow is to be a very unendearing picture of Main Street. The word "happy" tells us that the description in excerpt *B* will be in terms of beauty and contentment.]

3. The teacher selects certain passages and repeats the process—first, *Main Street B*; then, *Main Street A*. The idea is to show the students how our choice of words creates an effect upon our reader. Here is the same street seen from two different points of view. As the two points of view are read, the discussion should center around their differences. How did the authors express themselves? (In many cases, an adjective denoting beauty was used in place of the disparaging modifier. In some cases (as in paragraph 8), the whole idea has been changed. Mention should be made of the sameness of the description of the Bon Ton Store (paragraph 19). In *Main Street B*, this store does not stand out from the others; in *Main Street A*, it almost appears that it does not belong in the same story.

4. Ask the students which excerpt they enjoyed reading more. The majority will probably say *Main Street A*, and the teacher should tell them that is the correct excerpt from the novel *Main Street*, by Sinclair Lewis.

5. Emphasize "point of view" as important in choosing our language. It is how we think about something that leads us to choose certain words and phrases. Remember, we are always trying to communicate with others, and in many cases we want them to "feel" the same as we do about something.

6. Explain to the students that Carol has come from a big city in the East. We are seeing Main Street from her viewpoint. From Carol's viewpoint, what kind of Main Street does she think a town should have? Looking at *Main Street B*, can we suggest anything about the Carol of this excerpt? Where do you suppose she came from?

7. Now, explain to the students that they are going to have to allow their imaginations to work overtime for the next moment or two. Suppose Carol-A is looking at Main Street in 1930, immediately upon her arrival in town. In 1950, Carol-A looks at Main Street and sees it as it is described in *Main Street B*. Is the town the same in 1950 as it was in 1930? (No.) Is Carol-1950 the same as Carol-1930? (No.) We have concluded that Carol in *Main Street A* is not the same as Carol in *Main Street B*, if both are looking at the street on the same day. When we say that Carol-1930 is not the same as Carol-1950, we are not saying that there are two Carols, but rather that the first Carol has changed and is not the same as she was in 1930.

8. Ask a student what his favorite book is at the present time. Then ask him what his favorite book was when he was eight or ten years old. Is he the same person now as he was then? If he were the same, his favorite book would be the same. Ask the same or similar questions to two or three other students. From this discussion, bring forth the formula: X_1 is not X_2.

    [At this point we are leading into the study of *Abstraction*. This is a fairly difficult concept to get across to students. In the amount of time we have here, we do not have time even to hope to cover completely the principles and practices of abstraction. What we will try to do is develop the concept in this unit. The work will be kept as simple as possible. The teacher will note that so far in this unit, we have hardly mentioned terms but have looked on language as something we use every day, not as an involved theory of communication. This is as it should be.]

9. Put the name of a student on the chalkboard. Ask that student the following questions and then place answers beneath his name:

    John Brown

    1. How old are you?   Age 14
    2. What grade are you in?   Grade 10
    3. What kind of movies do you like?   Monster movies
    4. What is your hobby?   Building model cars
    5. What is your favorite book?   *Red Badge of Courage*
    6. What is your favorite food?   Roast beef

10. Now stand in front of the chalkboard and ask another student to tell you all that the name John Brown means to him. Mention that the words "John Brown" stand for all these things. It also stands for many others: the atoms and neutrons that he is made up of, the headache he may have, everything he is thinking about, the people around him, and so on.

    John Brown is also a "student," a "son," perhaps a "football player," someone's "boyfriend." "John Brown" means something different to all of these people who have different relationships with him. Explain that it is impossible to know the title "John Brown." Suppose that John Brown is, at this moment, thinking about football practice, or baseball, or the movie he will see tonight. Five minutes ago he was thinking about the English lesson, or borrowing his father's car, or some other thing. Point out that the John Brown of NOW is not the same John Brown of five minutes ago. One slight change makes the two John Browns different: John Brown$_1$ is not John Brown$_2$. At every moment, John Brown is unique. There is nothing else like him in the universe. He is never the same John Brown; we continually call him John Brown, but we forget, in doing so, about the changes that take place around and in him all during his life.

11. Now write the word *boy* on the board. Explain the following:

Now look at the word *boy*. (*Put the word on the board.*) John Brown is a boy. He is similar to other boys. But notice that all boys are not fourteen years old; all boys are not in the tenth grade; all boys do not like monster movies, and so on. Thus, we can say more specific things about John Brown than we can say about boy. When we say *boy*, what are the characteristics we see in this idea? We classify John Brown as a boy because he has all these characteristics of *boy*, but *boy* does not have all of John Brown's characteristics. *John Brown* and *boy* are, thus, ideas. (Do not confuse this with our concept of idea-bound words.) Now, we are talking about facts, rather than idea-bound words.

Now, on a higher level we have the idea *human*. At this level, the characteristics become even more generalized than at the level of *boy*. Up the ladder one more step, we come to the idea of *mammal*. Notice that here the idea is a group of creatures who suckle their young who are born rather than hatched. Another step up the ladder, and we have *biped*—two-legged creatures. Notice that everything we can say about bipeds can apply to all mammals, all humans, all boys, and one John Brown. Notice, too, that we cannot say as much about bipeds as we do about mammals or about humans, or about boys, or about one John Brown. Taking another step up the ladder, the idea is *animal*—a thing with some form of nervous system. Above this comes *organism*, which includes all living things.

Depending on what we wish to say, we make selections from the ladder. The teacher should write the ladder items on the board:

Organism
Animal
Mammal
Biped
Human
Boy
John Brown

The farther down the ladder we go, the more specific we become. So when we select John Brown from all these ideas, we have taken the most specific level and we can say more things about John Brown than we can about any of the classifications above him on the ladder. (Write beside the classifications: *Levels of Abstraction*.)

Each of the classifications is a level on which we classify the ideas we have. Our experience gives us these ideas. Relate to the students that too often we attempt to communicate by talking or writing on the highest level of abstraction—like talking about "my pet"—and that in doing so, we do not communicate very well. In talking or writing about pets, we may not get into too much trouble, but when we talk or write about people or events on this high level of abstraction, misunderstandings and prejudices sometimes develop and take control. Many people talk in terms of *classes*, which is a high level of abstraction. How many times have the students heard such statements as, "Jews are stingy," or "Teen-agers are reckless"? Can the students think of any examples? The problem with this type of thinking is that a person making such a statement tends to notice *only* the *similarities* of a *few* people in those classes, and he neglects the *differences*; he does not go down the ladder of abstraction. This is the type of person who, if he met John Brown, would neglect all of the characteristics that make John Brown unique; he would equate one characteristic of John Brown with a class—like teen-ager—and would then react to one of John Brown's labels rather than to John Brown as a unique person.

Assignment

Hand out the exercise on Abstraction in the student materials for them to work on as an overnight assignment.

Objective

To understand how the misuse of an abstraction ladder affects us in our process of living and communicating with other people.

To the Teacher

1. First, go over the homework and answer any questions the students may have about the ladder of abstraction.
   The key to the exercise is as follows:

I. Organism	II. Organism
Animal	Animal
Biped	Mammal
Fowl	Quadruped
Chicken	Horse
Hen	Mare
Myrtle	Clarabelle

2. Write on the board:
   John Doe was just released from the penitentiary.

3. Ask the students what some people would immediately conclude about John Doe; that is, what *inferences* would they draw from the fact that he

has been in the penitentiary? (John Doe is an ex-convict. John Doe is a criminal, and therefore, he is dangerous. He will probably commit other crimes.)

4. If John Doe applies for a job, what kind of inferences might his prospective employer draw? (Because he committed one crime, he is probably not trustworthy; therefore, he would not be employed.)

5. Do you think John Doe would get a job from this employer? (No.)

6. Ask students what rule they learned yesterday that should stop the employer from climbing the ladder of abstraction too fast; that is, stop him from drawing the wrong inferences. (Actually, there are two rules. The one that is related to the abstraction ladder is *John Doe$_1$ is not John Doe$_2$*. The other relates to the "when index": *John Doe$_{19\_\_}$ is not John Doe$_{today}$*.

7. Ask a student to explain these rules again. (The John Doe who went to prison is classified as an "ex-convict." But John Doe is a unique individual; he should not be classified or lumped together. Further, the John Doe who entered prison is not the same John Doe who has just been released from prison after serving his term.)

   [John Doe may have completely changed, and may even have been unjustly convicted in the first place. Nevertheless, he may never get a job because people have a tendency to misuse the ladder of abstraction. In fact, by misusing the ladder of abstraction in terms of John Doe, we may force him to commit another crime. He may come to the conclusion that since everyone thinks he's a criminal, he might just as well be one.]

8. What kind of ladder would some people build in terms of this John Doe? (They would see a *convict*, instead of a *man*, on their ladder. *Convict* would mean *criminal* to them. Therefore, John Doe is still a criminal; therefore, he is not to be trusted, not to be employed, always to be shunned as someone dangerous.) Is the person who builds this type of ladder making an accurate "map" of the "territory?" (No.)

9. Read page 46 in the *Kaiser Bulletin*. Let the students read the last part of the employment application printed on that page. (Here is an example of an employer making errors in abstraction. The employer should have learned more about the man. Look at his good points. *Should a man be condemned for life because he makes two or three mistakes?*

10. Ask students how the misuse of abstractions may apply in the following situations:
    a) When he answered the door, Mr. Brown had a cocktail glass in his hand.
    b) Johnny Jones carries a cigarette lighter in his pocket.
    c) I saw the police talking to Frank Allen last night.
    d) On Sunday, Mr. So-and-So was still in bed at noon.
    e) Biff Doe was carrying a box for his teacher yesterday, and today he got an A on his paper.

11. Ask students what could be the truth in each of these situations.

12. Ask for other examples of ladder-climbing by people. In what ways are parents guilty of errors in abstraction, especially pertaining to their children?

13. Tie in the discussion with what was termed "idea-bound words." Notice that in every case, an idea-bound word is an error in abstraction. Previously, in the exercise on idea-bound words, we mentioned such situations as:

He lives on Fourth Street; therefore, he must be evil.

It is the foreigners who have ruined the country.

(Fourth Street in the first sentence is abstracted to mean "a place of evil." Further up the ladder, the abstraction becomes "people who live on Fourth Street." From this, we climb to Fourth Street–evil place; evil place–evil people; people on Fourth Street–evil people.)

[At this point, the discussion will move to the differences between *facts* and *inferences*. In the cases cited and in those brought up by the students, inferences were involved in our ladder-climbing. Facts were not considered. We only inferred from what we had heard or seen that such-and-such was true. Mr. Brown had a cocktail glass in his hand, so we might have inferred that he was an alcoholic, or at least that he was drinking alcoholic beverages. Johnny Jones carries a cigarette lighter in his pocket, so he must smoke. (Or, is he an arsonist? Did any student's imagination take him to this conclusion?) The police talked to Frank Allen, so he must have committed a crime. (Or, was it a member of his family who was in trouble?) Mr. So-and-So sleeps late on Sunday, so he must not be a Christian or a churchgoer. Biff Doe carried a box for his teacher, and only because of his "apple-polishing" was he given an A.]

14. On page 36 of the *Kaiser Bulletin* is an exercise in the drawing of inferences without consideration of the facts. Have the students look at the picture for two or three minutes. Then orally ask the students the eleven questions listed below the picture. Have them write the answers they think appropriate. Then turn to page 38 and discuss the answers. (Notice that every statement in the exercise is false. The family may own the television set, but we cannot know this from the picture. It may be a borrowed or rented one.)

15. Notice the *Peanuts* cartoon on page 37. Notice that Linus has seen something that looks like a porcupine. He infers that it is a porcupine. Lucy explains that it is only a bush. Linus, in this cartoon, represents something typical about people. Ask the students if they can guess the meaning of Linus's remark, "Stop looking at me!", in the last panel. (People, even when shown that their inferences are wrong, sometimes continue with their same erroneous beliefs and suppositions. Linus has been told his "porcupine" is a bush, but he prefers to continue his belief that it is a real porcupine.)

16. Turn to page 37 and read orally to the students the essay "As a Matter of Fact." Go through the exercise with them at the end of the article on page 38.

Assignment

Have the students write a theme, giving them the following directions: "Write a theme based on this event—'A man is lying down on a park bench.' Describe how three passersby react to this event; that is, describe what inferences they make about this man and his situation. Then have the man relate to someone the reason why he was lying on a bench in the park. Set up a framework for your theme so that these three people know this man in some way—maybe someone who works with him, a relative, and a friend. Have them all come together in some way, after they have related their 'stories,' to hear what the man has to say about what 'really happened.'" Give the students a couple of days to work on this.

Objective

To distinguish between fact and inference, and to consider the misuse of the "absolute *is*."

1. Discuss the article "As a Matter of Fact," using the following questions as guides:
  a) Distinguish between *fact* and *inference*.
  b) What is meant by a fact being something that is socially agreed upon?
  c) Give some examples of this type of fact.
  d) How are facts related to time? Give some examples.
  e) Discuss inferences in terms of "higher or lower possibilities."

2. Project the essay "The Trouble with Is, Is Is," pages 39–41, and read it with the students.

This initial study of the nature of language and general semantics lays the foundation for students to "sleuth around" in a variety of language situations and to apply their knowledge of general language problems to specific areas. A unit that would follow naturally from the one just described would be "The Language of Advertising."

LANGUAGE IN ADVERTISING, OR
"BUY IT, YOU'LL LIKE IT"[1]

Statement of the Problem

Every day television, radio, newspapers, and billboards constantly bombard students with advertising propaganda. "It's the sex-appeal toothpaste,"

---

[1] Reproduced by permission of John Cullum, Jr., of Sanford, Fla. Unpublished manuscript.

"the kissing gum," "walk a mile for it," "try it, you'll like it," and, the Madison Avenue ad-men hope, buy it.

The language used in advertising is of a very special nature. It must be powerful, persuasive, and interesting. It must appeal most to the group by which its product will be bought, and it must provide a reason for purchasing its product instead of a competitor's product.

This unit will show students the devices used by advertisers, the very special nature of the language they use, and the manner in which they turn the credulity of their audience into profit dollars. The unit will focus primarily on the way language is used (and in some cases abused) and will alert students to the special nature of this language (what is AT-7, anyway?). The unit will include the use of the media, the VTR, the opaque projector, class discussion, and student demonstration.

General Objectives of the Unit
After the completion of this unit, the student:

1. Will use critical thinking skills in reading advertising:
   a) Distinguishes between fact and opinion in advertisements.
   b) Distinguishes between valid and invalid advertisements.
   c) Identifies errors in the logic of advertisements.

2. Comprehends the descriptive vocabulary of advertising:
   a) Saturation
   b) Animation
   c) Copy platform
   d) Corporate campaign
   e) Puffed-up ads
   f) Logo
   g) Vague references
   h) Testimonial
   i) False claims
   j) Unique selling proposition

3. Evaluates two commercially generated advertisements.
   a) Audiovisual advertisements
   b) Aural advertisements
   c) Visual advertisements

4. Discriminates between the types of language used in advertisements.
   a) Audiovisual advertisements
   b) Aural advertisements
   c) Visual advertisements

5. Writes an advertisement designed to sell a real or imaginary product.

6. Demonstrates the advertisement he has written.
   a) Videotape recorder
   b) Soundtape recorder
   c) Graphic arts

7. Evaluates student-generated advertisements in terms of language use.

Statement of Special Concentration

This unit will focus on the ways advertisers use language, whether on television, radio, magazines, or billboards. Special attention will be given to the manner some advertisers twist language, using false claims, "puffed-up" claims, or suggestions ("Sure, buddy, even fat, bald, and ugly *you* can get the chick—just rub some of this stuff with ZN-8 in it on your hair.")

Critical thinking skills will be developed, in the area of advertisements, so students can sift through the maze of insincerities and decide upon a product for its own merits and not those extolled by an ad-man, whose purpose may be only to expand the profit margin of his client (and bulge his own pockets a bit in the process!).

Initiating Activities

The initial introduction of this unit is designed to follow any previous unit and will take as much time as the individual teacher wishes to spend on it. The period "in limbo" between two units may be as much as one full period, or as little as fifteen or twenty minutes. The flexibility, therefore, will permit the teacher to conduct the following discussion as time allows.

The teacher should give a brief explanation of the unit, touching briefly on the general objectives outlined above, and explain the following premises:

1. Advertisements use language to "lure" customers.

2. Ads sometimes use language that is vague and misleading. For example, one soap manufacturer claims an ingredient given a code name that, for all the consumer knows, could very easily be animal fat or reclaimed crankcase oil.

3. Not *all* advertisements use language in this manner. Some rely on the use of humor, some establish a slogan, and some a price enticement.

4. Advertisements must appeal to the group for which their product is manufactured.

Ask the following, or similar, "kick-off" questions. These may be discussed with the class as a whole, or the teacher may wish to break the class into small discussion groups and compare answers (and arguments) later.

1. Who makes the best mouthwash, and why?
   Sample answers:
   a) "Listerine, because it kills germs."
   b) "Lavoris, because nine out of ten dentists use it."
   c) "Hell, teach, we can't even afford toothpaste!"

2. What is the best bath soap, and why?
   Sample answers:
   a) "Dial . . . 'cause it keeps you fresh 'round the clock."
   b) "Zest . . . it's got that AT-7 stuff in it, so it must be good."

c) "Irish Spring . . . it's for real he-men."
d) "Soap?"

3. Who makes the most popular soft drink, and why is it the most popular?
Sample answers:
a) "Coke, 'cause everybody knows it's the real thing."
b) "Pepsi . . . you've got a lot to live when you drink Pepsi."
c) "7-up . . . 'cause it's the uncola."

4. What is the best headache pain reliever, and why is it the best?
Sample answers:
a) "Excedrin . . . it's stronger."
b) "Bayer Aspirin . . . it's pure aspirin, and everybody knows aspirin is the best pain reliever!"
c) "Bufferin . . . it gets to your headache faster."
d) "180-proof grain alcohol . . . two drinks and you don't feel a thing."

5. What is the most popular cigarette, and why?
Sample answers:
a) "Winston . . . 'cause it tastes good, like a cigarette should."
b) "Salem . . . 'cause it's fresh as springtime."
c) "Marlboro . . . 'cause they're for real men."
d) "Picayunes . . . 'cause they're only a quarter a pack."

If you're lucky enough to get answers similar to these, you can easily draw a relation to how ads influence opinions and how language influences advertising. It should be easy to start a discussion on why students answered as they did. The most popular product, you may wish to point out, is the product whose advertising best fits the premises on page __.

DEVELOPMENTAL ACTIVITIES

First Day

Begin with the initiating activities outlined above.

Specific Objectives

(all specific objectives are keyed to the general objectives)
The student:

1.1 Evaluates advertised products
1.2 Discusses fact and opinion contained in product advertisements
1.3 Evaluates the effectiveness of product ads
1.4 Identifies errors in the logic of some advertisements
1.5 Begins to evaluate advertisements critically

Second Day

The Vocabulary of Advertising

The teacher should evaluate each of the following terms while discussing them with the students. Ask the students for examples they have heard, seen, or read in the media. Tape recordings or videotape recordings may be used in conjunction with the discussion, and samples of representative ads are mentioned in most definitions. If a VTR or tape recorder is not available, a portable television set may be used after the discussion to place emphasis on several forms, and to provide motivation and reinforcement.

a) **Saturation:** Heavy bombardment of broadcast audiences with an advertising message. Explain that saturation is one technique copywriters use to familiarize their audiences with the product. Glim (see bibliography) says that the substitute for inspiration is saturation, and that the first principle of saturation is to mate what the product offers with what the public wants. This means that the copywriter needs facts about the product—and facts about those who are prospective purchasers of the product.

Ask students to give examples of saturation advertising. These include all those ads that most readily come to mind whose messages are constantly repeated, perhaps a dozen times an evening.

b) **Animation:** Communication of the advertising message by the use of frame-at-a-time photography, which gives the illusion of movement when viewed at projection speed (24 fps). Copywriters can focus attention on a word or a slogan when it appears in animation, and the field is only limited by the animator's imagination. The Jolly Green Giant has "ho-hoed" that company's products into the land of the jolly long green, and countless animated heroes and heroines have transformed the breakfast food companies into industrial giants.

c) **Copy Platform:** The basic creative plan of an advertising firm to exploit particular reputed values of a product. Most copy platforms are based on the idea that "ours has something that theirs doesn't" or "this quality of ours is better than that of theirs."

For example, Crisco's copy platform is "It's not greasy," American Motors' is "buyer protection," and Palmolive dishwashing liquid's is "It softens your hands while you do the dishes." All advertising for the product during a platform period conforms to the platform. Point out that the platform uses language powerfully—it presents, simply, a feature that everyone would consider important for the product to have. Crisco's "not greasy" is an example; nobody would buy a cooking compound whose copy platform was "it's the greasiest," because this is a quality that most people consider to be undesirable in cooking oils. Stress that language is used in the copy platform, in order to bring a relation of the product to people. The copywriter selects a position or a positive quality and connects that quality, through his ads, to the product.

d) Corporate Campaign: This advertising campaign is charged with developing a complete corporate image, as apart from selling a particular product. Some large corporations use this technique to "sell the company" rather than its product. Language usage in this form of advertising relies heavily on instilling trust and loyalty in its audience. For example, monopolistic companies such as utility companies often advertise in this manner. Their purpose is to portray their understanding of humanistic problems, i.e., pollution, crime. One company states, "We're planning for tomorrow"; another, "We can do more for you," and, the old standby, "Progress is our most important product." Examples are: Dodge ("Depend on it"), Zenith ("The quality goes in before the name goes on"), Standard Oil ("We're doing something about pollution"), and Mercedes-Benz ("Eight decades of engineering excellence"). Ask students to name others and discuss the values the advertiser is trying to communicate.

e) Puffed-up Advertisements: These ads use language to tell the benefits of their products in a vague manner. The ads include the use of a miracle ingredient or property so special that no other companies can use them. For example, one product claims the use of an additive such as B-1; another, one such as B-2; and still another, one such as X-5; one detergent is said to contain "all-fabric brighteners and lemon-freshened borax."

Ask students to give examples of some puffed-up ads and try to guess what the miracle ingredient is. Ask students why advertisers use language in this tricky way.

f) Logo (Logotype): A form of saturation and corporate image campaign. The logo is a graphic design, usually incorporating the manufacturer's name. When a viewer sees the logo, he thinks of the company and its product.

This may well be the simplest, but most powerful use of language by the advertiser. By incorporating an indistinguishable design and the name of the company, the audience immediately associates the logo with the company, and the company's product. Many ads on television devote the last second or two to the screening of their logo, presumably reinforcing the product-producer relation to the viewer. Examples of familiar logos include Bud, Coca-Cola, DuPont, RCA, etc. Ask students to give examples of other logos and tell why they feel that companies devote time on the screen (at nearly $1,000 a second) to the logo.

g) Vague Reference: This type of advertisement skillfully uses language to make an indirect inference—an inference that the ad does not openly state, but subtly suggests. Examples of vague reference include shaving lotion commercials (they always get the girl—*if* they have splashed on the right scent), beer commercials (relaxation), and cigarette ads (he-man image).

h) Testimonial: A statement given by a supposedly nonbiased individual supporting claims made by a manufacturer. The early trend was to use well-known personalities (radio, TV, movies, sports) but the trend is enlarging now to include the ordinary "man on the street." Examples include Lifesaver gum ("Pretty good idea, mister, but you left out the hole"), Crisco oil ("Honey, what kind of oil do you use to fry your fried chicken?"), and Ban deodorant ("Does your antiperspirant keep you dry?"). Ask students to evaluate these testimonials—why do they show only the positive? Ask them if they think they are real on-the-street interviews, or rigged fakes. Have a couple of students reenact an interview.

    i) False Claims: These are claims made by an advertiser that generally offer something very exciting and very difficult to the consumer, usually focusing on skills or self-improvement.

    Bring in some pulp magazines such as *True Story, True Romances,* or *Detective Stories.* Usually representative ads will be easy to find. These ads usually present, in bold or striking type, or attractive language, something for (virtually) nothing. The price at first appears to be very small or the skill or attribute very easy to obtain. For example, in one issue of *True Story* I found the following claims:

    $350.00 for your child's photo"
    "Lose 5 pounds overnight—only $1.00"
    "Play Guitar in 7 Days"
    "50 Towels—$1.00"
    "Add 3 inches to your bust in 8 days"
    "We guarantee publishing contract"
    "Free blitz diet" . . . read on, it's only $1.00
    "8 stereo tapes—only $1" . . . just agree to buy "only" 24 in 2 years
        at list price.

By showing students these ads, you can focus on the use of language as a "lure." Each ad begins with an amazing claim or offer, usually in type much larger than the body of the ad, and written in strong, persuasive words—offering you a deal you just can't turn down. J. N. Hook (see bibliography) states that nothing more clearly demonstrates the low caliber of the pulps than their advertisements; just as a man is known by the company he keeps, so a magazine is known by the advertisements it runs. Citing a unit on magazines, he concludes that "sophomores quickly saw how gullible people would be who would believe these claims; since the sophomores did not want to be classified on such a low mental level, they agreed that these magazines were not for them." Ask students to evaluate some of these ads. Ask them how language is used in these ads, and to contrast the language used in other, higher-grade magazines.

    j) Unique Selling Proposition: The claimed superiority of an advertised product. This is similar to copy platform (see page 150). The advertiser extols the virtues of his product in terms of the inferiority of a competitor's product. Examples include Excedrin ("Better than aspirin"), Contac ("Better than other so-called cold remedies"), Maxwell Instant ("We tested against fresh-perked, and we won"). Ask students to evaluate the products that claim superiority. Are they really better? How do they use language to influence your opinion?

Specific Objectives

Students will:

2.1 Discuss each ad-type in terms of commercials or advertisements they have seen recently.

2.2 Demonstrate their understanding of the different types of advertisements, and the techniques used in them, by identifying the types and defining the techniques.

2.3 Give an example of each type of ad.

2.4 Differentiate between language levels in different types of ads.

Student Assignment

Ask students to bring in one ad from a magazine showing one or more of the above characteristics. Tell them to be able to explain to the class which characteristic it uses, and why they feel it uses language in this manner.

Third Day

Materials needed:
Handout number 1 (see appendix)
Equipment needed:
Opaque projector

Briefly review the types of advertisements and pass out handout number 1. With an opaque projector, show the ads the students have brought in. Have each student explain his ad—how it uses language and why he feels it does so. Each ad should spark a discussion from the class— if it doesn't, start it yourself by asking the following questions:

a) Does this ad use language in a special way?

b) What is it?

c) Why do you think it uses language in this manner?

d) To whom do you think this ad is supposed to appeal?

e) Does the language suggest a particular audience?

f) How? Why?

g) Would you buy the product for yourself over a competitor's product? Why? Why not?

Assignment

Have the students watch TV (that should be an easy assignment!). Tell them to pay close attention to the commercials, and to the way advertisers use language—ask them to write down a few notes or ideas concerning commercials.

Specific Objectives

3.1 Students will discuss the use of language in advertisements.

3.2 Students will evaluate commercially generated advertisements in terms of language use.

3.3 Students will evaluate commercially generated advertisements in terms of language effectiveness.

3.4 Students will evaluate commercially generated advertisements in terms of audience appeal.

Fourth Day

Television Advertisements

Opening Discussion Questions:

a) How is television a different medium for advertisers than magazines? (It is possible, through television, to actually show a product and demonstrate its effectiveness. It makes use of an additional sense, sight. With the recent popularity of color receivers, it can show colors as vividly as life. Action can be seen, as well as heard.)

b) Is television more effective than magazines? How? (Television is generally regarded as the most effective medium for advertisers. Because it requires total submission, the audience must be involved.)

c) What advantages does television have over magazines or other forms of advertisement communication?

d) Are there any disadvantages to TV ads? (Advertising is limited to large businesses, and there is a lack of permanence (saturation, however, attempts this).)

Materials:

Handout, "Look, Ma"

Lecture/Discussion Notes:

"Look, Ma" is a television ad first screened in 1958, which has continued, with slight variation, until the present. I include this ad for use with students because of its longevity and its use of several techniques used in many ads, as outlined on pages 150 through 152. For example: "Fluoristan—a special fluoride formula," "the decay fighter," "that dentists put right on your teeth," "switch from ordinary toothpaste," "cut your family's cavities in half." The ad is loaded with advertising devices, and by the use of these language forms has made Crest the number-one-selling toothpaste in America. (An interesting note: Procter and Gamble, Crest's parent company, spends over $100 million per year on TV advertisements—only *two* other corporations in America spend that much.)

Discussion Questions on "Look, Ma":

a) How does this advertisement use language to make the viewer want to go right out and buy Crest?

b) Is this advertisement effective?

c) If the same advertisement were to be on radio could it be as effective? Why? Why not?

d) What would have to be changed if this were a radio advertisement?

e) What are the facts and opinions in this advertisement?

Ask students to contribute to a discussion about current television ads. Since this was their homework assignment, most should be able to remember at least one ad, but many will probably have the same ads. Discuss how language was used in these ads.

Specific Objectives

Students will:

2.5 Use the descriptive vocabulary of advertising in class discussions.
3.5 Identify specific language uses in a commercially generated advertisement.
3.6 Discuss language effectiveness in a commercially generated advertisement.
4.1 Discuss differences between the promotion of the same advertisement by different media.
1.2 Discuss fact and opinion contained in product advertisements.

Fifth Day

Students are probably ready for a change of pace. I have included, in the appendices, the script for a slide/tape presentation on advertising. If you have the time to make a slide/tape, do it. It can be used by others in your school and may be kept for years. If you do not wish to use an S/T, bring in a portable TV set and watch some advertisements with your students. You'll probably hit a few game shows, which are almost 100% advertising, as the offstage announcer tells the contestants what they have (or could have) won. If your classes are later on in the afternoon, the soap operas have some dandy commercials for language use study. Turn the sound down and discuss the ad while the program is going on; when it comes time for a "station break," turn the volume up and catch the barrage of ads.

Specific Objectives

The student will:

2.5 Use the descriptive vocabulary of advertising in class discussions.
3.5 Identify specific language uses in a commercially generated advertisement.

3.6 Discuss language effectiveness in a commercially generated advertisement.

1.2 Discuss fact and opinion contained in product advertisements.

Sixth Day

A Copywriter Is Born!

As an action project, use "Look, Ma" as an example of television script writing and have students break up into small groups (no more than four, if possible) and write an original script of their own. Explain that their commercial, complete with props and all, will be filmed by a videotape recorder and they will actually be able to see themselves on television. Tell them to pick a real or imagined product and make a one-minute script, similar in mechanics to "Look, Ma," carefully using language to sell their product.

Emphasize that it is very important to have a carefully planned script. Circulate around to each group and help them get started—if they have an idea, they will probably want your opinion; give it honestly. Show them how to make props, but keep them simple. A few felt markers and scraps of poster board should be all that you need to provide. Tell each group to bring specific props (i.e., a can of Crisco, a roll of tissue, etc.) to class tomorrow, and assign at least two members of each group to be responsible for bringing them (you know at least one of them will forget!). Go to bed early tonight!

Specific Objectives

The students will:

5.1 Write an advertisement designed to sell a real or imagined product.

Seventh Day

VTR Day!

Today is the day you decide to resign and become a plumber.

Give each group about fifteen minutes to refine anything they wish to refine on their advertisements, and let them practice a couple of times before filming them. Have them make two copies of their script; one for them, and the other for you; read over each script carefully before filming it. They may want a close-up of something, then a quick shot of something else. Since you are the cameraman, you must be aware of their wishes.

It may be a good idea to take each group twice—once to get over the camera-giggles, and once for real.

Equipment: Videotape recorder. If your school does not have access to a VTR, tape the commercials on a tape recorder, and alter the assignment slightly. Have them write a radio ad instead of a television ad. Since you are going to be filming about forty groups today, bring along some of your favorite pain reliever. (Aspirin?)

Specific Objectives

The students will:

6.1 Demonstrate the advertisements they have written.

Eighth Day

"Let's look at what we've done, teach."
      Play the videotapes for the class.   Evaluate each ad after it has been shown.   Ask students the following questions:

a) Is language used effectively?

b) What type of advertisement is this?

c) Does it influence your opinion in any way?

d) Why?   Why not?

Keep the discussions brief, because you have about ten of these ads to show and discuss, giving you about five minutes per ad.   Let the students do most of the talking; if you've done a good job over the last seven days, they'll know what they're talking about (besides, you need the rest!).

Specific Objectives

The students will:

7.1 Evaluate student-generated advertisements in terms of language use.
2.5 Use the descriptive vocabulary of advertising in class discussions.
3.7 Identify specific language uses in student-generated advertisements.
3.8 Discuss language effectiveness in student-generated advertisements.
1.2 Discuss fact and opinion contained in student-generated advertisements.

Ninth Day

Call a local radio station or newspaper office.   Ask someone from the advertising department to come out and talk to your class about language in advertising.   Generally someone will be happy to come, as this is good public relations, provided you give him adequate notice.   Let him discuss with the students the ways language is used by advertisers.   If he is from a TV station, tell him you can obtain a videotape recorder or 16mm projector, since he may wish to bring some samples.   If he is from a radio station, tell him you have a tape recorder; radio stations use hundreds of ads every day, and he will probably want to bring a few samples.

      Encourage the students to ask questions; they may want to show him their ads.   It would also be a good idea to record this man's talk on videotape, for use later.

Specific Objectives

The student:

8.1 Listens to a presentation by a professional ad-man.
8.2 Asks questions about the manner in which language is used in advertising.

Tenth Day

Culminating Activities

Start with a short discussion about your guest speaker. Touch on the way language is used in advertising and ask students to review quickly the types of ads and language used.

Test: Give them an essay test, requiring students to evaluate a written advertisement in terms of what they have learned over the past two weeks.

APPENDIX

Slide/Tape Presentation

Slide No.	Text	Slide description	Music
1	Every day you are bombarded with hundreds of advertisements, enticing you to buy one product or the other. ●	collage of ads	Bring up "American in Paris" then fade to background level.
2	It's the sex appeal ● toothpaste! //	Ultra-brite ad	
3	the ● kissing gum! //	Certs ad	
4	●walk a mile for it! //	Camel ad	
5	●try it you'll like it! //	Alka Seltzer ad	
6	and, // the Madison Ave. ad men ● hope, // buy it.	person at counter of store	sound of cash register, superimposed.
7	●The language used in advertising	"Language Use" on card	
8	is of a very special nature, // for example //●	Cigarette ad with tar and nicotine figures	Superimpose ambulance siren. Fade.

Slide No.	Text	Slide description	Music
9	this ad cashes in on the recent findings of the surgeon general. // ● Note the key words //	Same ad with arrows on *Low Tar*	
10	This ad promises low tar // ● but full flavor	switch arrow to "full flavor"	
11	This ad uses language ● "scare tactics,"	"Scare tactics" on card	
12	to try to sell their product.	slide 8	
13	Another cigarette company ● uses a different approach. //	KOOL ad	
14	This ad says // ● come all the way up to kool-extra coolness	KOOL ad with arrow on extra coolness	
15	This use of language is called // ● the prestige approach	Title card: "Prestige Approach"	
16	This approach sells ● shirts //	Shirt ad	
17	●Perfume //	Perfume ad	
18	●Liquor //	Liquor ad	
19	●Cars	Car ad	
20	and countless ● other articles. // Another approach becoming more popular within the last few years is ●	Collage of above ads	
21	The sex-appeal ad //	Title card: "Sex Appeal"	Fade-in music "The Stripper" Quick fade-out

Slide No.	Text	Slide description	Music
22	These ads are becoming more popular in their merchandising. They sell toothpaste ●	Slide No.	
23	●Clothes //	Clothing ad	
24	●Shaving cream //	Noxzema ad	
25	●Chewing gum //	Certs gum ad	
26	●and suntan lotion. // These are only a few ways that advertisers use language. // Can you think of ●	Suntan lotion ad	
27	Other ways ads use language?	Title card: "Other ways ads use language"	Bring up volume, ten seconds, then fade all.

// = pause
● = slide change

Handout number 1

The Vocabulary of Advertising

Saturation: Heavy bombardment of broadcast audiences with an advertising message. Examples: _____

_____ .

Animation: Communication of the advertising message by the use of frame-at-a-time photography, which gives the illusion of movement when viewed at projection speed.   Examples:

_____ .

Copy Platform: The basic creative plan of an advertising firm to exploit particular reputed values of a product.   Examples: _____

_____ .

Corporate *Campaign:*	An advertising campaign charged with developing a complete corporate image, as apart from selling a particular product. Examples: ——————————————————————.
Puffed-Up *Ads:*	Ads that use language to tell the benefits of their products in a vague manner. Examples: ——————————————————— ——————————————————————.
Logo *(Logotype):*	A form of saturation and corporate image campaign. The logo is a graphic design, usually incorporating the manufacturer's name. Examples: ——————————————————— ——————————————————————.
Vague *Reference:*	A type of advertisement that skillfully uses language to make an indirect inference—an inference that the ad does not openly state, but subtly suggests. Examples: ————————— ——————————————————————.
Testimonial:	A statement given by a supposedly nonbiased individual supporting claims made by the manufacturer. Examples: ——————————————————————.
False Claims:	Claims made by an advertiser that generally offer something very exciting and very difficult to the consumer, usually focusing on skills or self-improvement. Examples: —————— ——————————————————————.
Unique Selling *Proposition:*	The claimed superiority of an advertised product. Examples: ——————————————————————.

TEACHER'S BIBLIOGRAPHY

Diamant, Lincoln. *Television's Classic Commercials.* New York: Hastings House, 1971.

Durkee, Burton R. *How to Make Advertising Work.* New York: McGraw-Hill, Inc., 1967.

Glim, Aesop. *How Advertising Is Written—And Why.* New York: Dover Publications, Inc., 1961.

Hook, J. N. *The Teaching of High School English.* New York: Ronald Press Co., 1965.

Houck, John W. *Outdoor Advertising.* Notre Dame, Ind.: University of Notre Dame Press, 1969.

MATERIALS

1. Magazines, or advertisements from magazines. Include many different titles, as some advertisers and some types of advertisements occur only in "pulp" magazines. Suggested magazines: *True, Reader's Digest, Time, True Story, Newsweek,* among others.

2. Handout, "The Vocabulary of Advertising" (see pages 150–152). This handout lists ad forms and provides a space for examples.

3. Handout, "Look, Ma!" This is a television ad script first screened in 1958. The material can be obtained from a local television station, and copies duplicated; this is used during the fourth day (pages 154–155).

4. Slide/tape presentation. The script is shown on pages 158–161. You will need the following materials to make this presentation:
   a) Tape recorder (preferably stereo).
   b) Kodak Visual-Maker (available through your media center, or the county media center).
   c) Two rolls of Kodachrome-X film for slides.
   d) Seven flashcubes.
   e) Appropriate magazine pictures. These may be found in *Reader's Digest, Ladies' Home Journal, Redbook,* and *Newsweek,* among others.

5. Felt markers and poster board. These will be used on the sixth day of instruction (see page 156).

6. A Videotape Recorder (VTR). This will be used on the seventh day. This is available through your school's media center or the county media center.

7. A slide projector.

8. Printed test. This is an essay test and it can be made up for use with any radio, television, or magazine ad.

"The Language of Advertising" could be followed by a cluster of units designed around similar concepts; for example, "The Language of the Locker Room," "The Language of the Street," "The Language of Sports," "The Language of Games," "The Language of Politics," or "The Language of the Military." Here is a sample unit based on the latter:

THE LANGUAGE OF THE MILITARY[2]

Statement of the Problem

The military, like most subgroups in our culture, has its own language. Each branch of the armed forces has also developed its own system (dialect)

---

[2] Reproduced by permission of Leslie Topper, of Rockledge, Fla. Unpublished manuscript.

within the larger military framework. The special terms and abbreviations have been devised to save time and to avoid confusion, though to non-military persons these expressions and codes seem to confuse more than they clarify. Many students, especially boys, will probably have their chance to learn the language of the military. The purpose of the unit is not to indoctrinate students for military service, but to engage them in the study of a specialized kind of language in order for them to explore yet another realm of language that has been formed by special groups for specific purposes.

General Objectives of the Unit

1. To develop the student's understanding of language forms.
2. To develop the student's understanding of usage in language.
3. To develop the student's ability to write on different levels according to his audience.
4. To develop the student's understanding of the purpose/purposes of language.
5. To develop the student's understanding of language and communication.
6. To develop the student's understanding of the importance of language study.

Level: Secondary

First Day

Objectives

1. To develop the student's understanding of the forms of language and how forms vary according to purpose.
2. To develop the student's awareness of the usage of language.
3. To give the student the experience of developing his own forms of language to meet a specified purpose.

Lesson Plan

Write the terms "ID Card" and "Identification Card" on the board. Question the students:

What advantages does the first term have over the second term?
Why do people use abbreviations?
What are some common abbreviations? (states, organizations, titles, directions, etc.)
Why is it sometimes necessary to be brief and quick in communicating?
Why might the military find it necessary to save time and also be efficient?

Give the students some military abbreviations (point out that the military pronounces these abbreviations (acronyms) and uses them just like words):

OPNAV—Naval Operations
JAG—Judge Advocate General
ACDUTRA—Active Duty Training

The following abbreviations are used in addresses as well as for titles:

COMCARIBSEAFRON—Commander of the Caribbean Sea Frontier
COMCRUDESLANT—Commander of the Cruiser Destroyer Forces in the Atlantic
CINCNAVOPSPAC—Commander-in-chief of Naval Operations in the Pacific

The Navy uses these terms for several reasons:

1. To save time.

2. To avoid confusion. The person who is CNO (Chief of Naval Operations) might be Admiral Jones this week and Admiral Edwards next week, since people are moved from duty to duty. If you wanted to get something to the CNO for action and you sent it to Admiral Jones—he might be COMCARIBSEAFRON by this time and can't take the action required, since it is the CNO's responsibility. You use the title to indicate *the* person who has the responsibilities of that title or position, whatever his name might be.

If CNO is Chief of Naval Operations, what is VCNO? ACNO?
If BUPERS is Bureau of Personnel, what is BUMED? BUSHIPS? BUWEPS?
At all naval bases and on all ships, people have titles that indicate their duties and responsibilities:

Commanding Officer—CO
Executive Officer—XO
Command Duty Officer—CDO
Master at Arms—MAA
Shore Patrol—SP
Military Police—MP
Communications Watch Officer—CWO

How could you abbreviate the positions here at school so that, if the principal were replaced, you would still be referring to the principal or the person with those responsibilities?

Have the students come up with abbreviations for the positions at their school:

Principal
Assistant Principal
Vice Principal

Dean of Men
Dean of Women
Counselors
Department heads
Teachers of specific subjects

The military also uses abbreviations to indicate grade or level, from bottom to top or vice versa.

Navy Officers:

Ensign—ENS
Lieutenant Junior Grade—LTJG
Lieutenant—LT
Lieutenant Commander—LCDR
Commander—CDR
Captain—CAPT
Rear Admiral—RADM
Vice Admiral—VADM
Admiral—ADM

Navy Enlisted:

Seaman Recruit—SR
Seaman Apprentice—SA
Seaman—SN
Petty Officer, Third Class—PO3
Petty Officer, Second Class—PO2
Petty Officer, First Class—PO1
Chief Petty Officer—CPO

What abbreviations could you use to indicate whether a student was a freshman, a sophomore, a junior, or a senior?

Second Day

Objectives

1. To develop the student's understanding of language forms and usage.

2. To give the student experience in using a form of language he has developed for a specific purpose.

Materials:

Handout

Lesson Plan

Review the system of abbreviations the students developed yesterday—finish it up if necessary. Give them a handout containing sentences to be rewritten according to the system they have developed. When they have finished, go over the papers and discuss any problems or questions.

Handout

Rewrite the following sentences, using the system of abbreviations you have developed:

1. If you want information on summer school, see any counselor.

2. The discipline problems of the school are handled by the Dean of Men and the Dean of Women.

3. Sally King, who is a freshman, and Jack Brent, who is a senior, went to a meeting of the Journalism Club, which is sponsored by Mrs. Cortney, the English Department head.

4. Mr. Sizemore, who is a mathematics teacher, Miss Reginald, who is a biology teacher, Mrs. Hendrix, who is an art teacher, and Mr. Night, who is a Spanish teacher, attended a meeting in Miami.

5. Three freshman students, Jane Coniff, Rex Young, and Carole Simon, and two sophomore students, Paul Stevens and Bob Franklin, and one junior student, Max Dayton, represented the Drama Club at the convention in Jacksonville.

6. Mr. Baxter, principal of Rockledge High School, and Mr. Barton, principal of Cocoa High School, met today to discuss the possibility of exchange panels of students for the student government activities week.

7. Jack Manin, a senior class member, spoke to the members of the junior class today.

8. He transferred from King High School in New York City to Cocoa High School in Florida.

Sample Key

(Depends on the system the students have set up)

1. If you want info on summer school, see any CON.

2. The discipline problems of the school are handled by the DM and the DW.

3. FR Sally King and SR Jack Brent went to a meeting of the JOURNCB, which is sponsored by Mrs. Cortney, DHENGDEPT.

4. MATT Sizemore, BIOT Reginald, ARTT Hendrix, and SPAT Night attended the meeting in MA.

5. FR Jane Coniff, FR Rex Young, FR Carole Simon, SO Paul Stevens, SO Bob Franklin, and JR Max Dayton represented the DRACB at the convention in JAX.

6. RHS PN Baxter and CHS PN Barton met today to discuss the possibility of exchange panels of students for the STUGOVACTWK.

7. SR Jack Manin spoke to the JR Class today.

8. He transferred from KHS in NYC to CHS in FLA.

Third Day

Objectives

1. To develop the student's understanding of language forms and usage.

2. To develop the student's awareness of problems of form and usage in language.

3. To give the student practice in using a specific form of language.

Materials:

Handout

Lesson Plan

Can brevity and efficiency—the concept of saving time and confusion—be carried over into telling time and dates? If I tell you to meet me at six tomorrow at the pier to go fishing—what is wrong with that? (How do you know if I meant six in the morning or six at night, unless I say A.M. or P.M., or morning or evening?) How has the military solved that problem? What system of time do some universities and companies use? (The twenty-four-hour clock.)

Explain the twenty-four-hour clock.

Tell them that in the service, enlisted radio announcers often announce the time as 1600 (pronounced "sixteen hundred," not "one thousand six hundred") and then add, "Now for all you officers out there, that's when the big hand is on the twelve and the little hand is on the four." What time is 1800? 0600? 2400?

Explain how the military handles dates:

January 21, 1972	21JAN72
August 16, 1967	16AUG67
July 4, 1976	04JUL76

Handout

Rewrite the following sentences using the military system for time and dates:

1. Today's date is September 17, 1974.

2. We signed the agreement at two o'clock in the afternoon on February 24, 1973.

3. The convention will run from eight o'clock in the evening on November 25, 1974, until ten o'clock in the morning on November 30, 1974.

4. You are to report in at 9 P.M. on the thirteenth of April, 1975.

5. Janis and Tim will be married at nine in the morning on Valentine's day.

6. On Halloween, I will go to two parties—one at 12 noon and one at 8 P.M.

7. His class ran from 1:50 until 4:45.

8. He failed to report in for duty before eleven o'clock in the evening on the eighth of July last year.

9. Cinderella was cautioned by her fairy godmother to return before midnight, or her carriage would turn into a pumpkin.

10. Many parents set a 10:30 curfew for their children.

Key

1. Today's date is 17SEP72.

2. We signed the agreement at 1400 24FEB71.

3. The convention will run from 2000 25NOV72 until 1000 30NOV72.

4. You are to report in at 2100 13APR73.

5. Janis and Tim will be married at 0900 14FEB73.

6. On 31OCT72, I will go to two parties—one at 1200 and one at 2000.

7. His class ran from 1350 until 1645.

8. He failed to report in for duty before 2300 08JUL71.

9. Cinderella was cautioned by her fairy godmother to return before 2400, or her carriage would turn into a pumpkin.

10. Many parents set a 2230 curfew for their children.

When the students have finished the sentences, go over them and discuss any problems or questions.

Fourth Day

Objectives

1. To develop the student's understanding of how different meanings are intended by words according to the purpose or the situation involved.

2. To enable the student to understand the problems intended in differences in vocabulary or vocabulary meanings in dialects, organizations, or other languages.

3. To develop the student's understanding of word usage.

4. To develop the student's understanding of the varied purposes of a language.

Materials:

Two handouts

Lesson Plan

Give the students a handout with military terms on it.   Go over the meanings of the terms while the students fill in these meanings on their sheets.

Terms

Goes aboard—gets on ship or goes in building
Goes ashore—leaves ship or building
Bow—front
Stern—rear
Forward—to the front
Aft—to the rear
Decks—floors
Bulkheads—walls
Overhead—ceiling
Ladder—stairway, stairs
Door—door
Hatch—opening from one level to the next
Passageway—hallway
Smoking lamp is lit—you have permission to smoke
Smoking lamp is out—you cannot smoke now
Compartment—room
Secure—fasten down, take care of, nail down, put away, put in place
Swab the deck—scrub the floor
Hit the deck—get out of bed
Rack or bunk—bed
Turn to—go to bed; look sharp or alert
Afloat—moving on the water
Below—downstairs
Light the galley range—turn on the stove
Head—bathroom
UA—unauthorized absence
AWOL—absent without leave
SP—shore patrol
Liberty—free time (short)
Leave—free time (long, such as several days or more)
Kitchen—galley

Handout No. 2—Give the students the following handout:
Rewrite this paragraph, using military terms.

The first thing every morning at five o'clock, seaman recruit Gopher gets out of his bed and goes downstairs to the kitchen. The stairs are located right outside of his room, so he usually manages to do this without too much trouble. If the ship is moving on the water, he sometimes falls down three or four times in the hall, but he is getting a little better at this now. When he gets to the kitchen, he lights the stove and immediately begins scrubbing the floor. When he is finished, he puts away the bucket and mop and takes a look at the Plan of the Day nailed to the wall. If he has a busy schedule that day he generally swears at the ceiling for ten minutes, but if he has some free time scheduled, he does a few hops and skips across the floor singing "Popeye the Sailor Man." Then he searches the front end and the back end of the ship for his friend seaman apprentice Newman. They stand and discuss all the things they will do when they walk off the ship in the afternoon for their free time. As always, the commanding officer or the executive officer comes along and catches them loafing. He tells them to shape up or ship out, or the only way they will get off the ship is if they go without permission and with the shore patrol running after them. He then orders them to perform some easy task—like painting all of the walls on the ship or waxing all of the floors. Life in the Navy isn't always a bed of roses for seaman recruit Gopher and seaman apprentice Newman.

Key

The first thing every day at 0500, SR Gopher hits the deck and goes below to the galley. The ladder is located right outside his compartment, so he usually manages to do this without too much trouble. If the ship is afloat, he sometimes falls down three or four times in the passageway, but he is getting a little better at this now. When he gets to the galley, he lights the galley range and immediately begins swabbing the deck. When he is finished, he secures the bucket and swab and takes a look at the POD secured to the bulkhead. If he has a busy schedule that day he generally swears at the overhead for ten minutes, but if he has some liberty scheduled, he does a few hops and skips across the deck singing "Popeye the Sailor Man." Then he searches fore and aft/the bow and the stern for his friend, SA Newman. They stand and discuss all the things they will do when they go ashore in the afternoon for their liberty. As always, the CO or the XO comes along and catches them loafing. He tells them to shape up or ship out, or the only way they will go ashore is if they go AWOL/UA with the SP running after them. He then orders them to perform some easy task—like painting all of the bulkheads on the ship or waxing all of the decks. Life in the Navy isn't always a bed of roses for SR Gopher and SA Newman.

When the students finish their paragraphs, have them read a few to the class. Discuss some of the problems involved in trying to replace ordinary words and phrases with military words and phrases. Question them.

Why do you think the military has developed its own language?

Do you know groups of people who have their own vocabularies or languages? (Jewish, mountain people, Gullah in Charleston, blacks, any dialects.)

Why do you think these people have different vocabularies?

Homework Assignment

Have the students write a brief description of their rooms at home, or any rooms at home, using the military vocabulary given in their handouts.

Fifth Day

Objectives

1. To develop the student's ability to rephrase ideas.

2. To develop the student's ability to understand how words can be used to convey different meanings in different situations.

3. To develop the student's understanding of why it is often necessary to be precise with his language in order to bring about a desired response.

4. To develop a student's understanding of why it is essential for both parties to understand a language before they can communicate effectively.

5. To develop the student's understanding of the various purposes of language.

6. To develop the student's understanding of the importance of language study.

Materials:

Handout

Lesson Plan

Have the students attempt to give military commands for the following phrases—maybe there are war movie buffs or ROTC members in your class. If you wanted a group of people to do the following things, how would you rephrase the directions to make them military commands?

Try to get lined up in a straight line now	Fall in
You all can relax and enjoy yourselves now	At ease
You all try to stand up straight and look intelligent and alert	Attention
You all can get out of line now and go home	Fall out
Turn your eyes to the right (or left) to look at the general	Eyes right/eyes left

Everybody raise their hands and salute the general	Hand salute
Turn to the left (or right)	Left face/right face
Turn to face the rear	About face
While you are marching, march to the right (or left)	By the right/left flank march
Begin marching forward now	Forward march
Stop where you are	Halt
March but don't go anywhere	Mark time
Turn around and march in the opposite direction	To the rear march

Explain to the students—or have a member of ROTC explain to them—a little bit about marching: always start out on your left foot, and call "left"; most commands are given so that the last word of the command falls on a right foot step. Question them.

Do you think anyone enjoys marching or drilling? Why, or why not?

How can you prove that people like to drill or march or like to watch others drill or march? (Drill teams, parades, etc.)

Why is it necessary to be precise in giving commands for drilling?

Homework Assignment

Give the students a handout containing the military commands. Have them try to write out one-minute drill patterns. Instruct them to try out their drill patterns at home to see if they work.

Sixth Day

Objectives

1. To develop the student's ability to rephrase ideas.

2. To develop the student's ability to understand how words can convey different meanings, depending on the situation.

3. To develop the student's understanding of why it is essential for both parties to understand a language before they can communicate effectively.

4. To develop the student's understanding of the various purposes of language.

5. To develop the student's understanding of the importance of language study.

Lesson Plan

Have a few students form groups and try out their drill patterns. Discuss the need for preciseness, clarity, and timing. Discuss the problems that occur when these things aren't considered.

What is the specific purpose of any command? (It is to get a specific thing accomplished in a specific manner at a specific time. All commands have a specific purpose in mind.)

Seventh Day

Objectives

1. To develop the student's understanding of language usage.

2. To develop the student's understanding of the purpose of language.

3. To develop the student's understanding of effective communication.

4. To develop the student's understanding of the importance of language study.

5. To develop the student's understanding of language and communication.

Materials:

Handout (TEST)

Lesson Plan

Give the students the following test, then collect the papers and grade them with a letter grade:

1. Does all language have a purpose?

2. What is language?

3. What is communication?

4. What are some of the purposes of language? (To inform, to entertain, to gain information, to get something done, to reward, to punish, to explain, etc.)

5. Is language necessary? Why, or why not?

6. If you made up your own language, didn't tell anyone about it, and tried to use it to communicate with people, what are some of the problems you would have?

7. Why is the study of language important?

Eighth Day

Objectives

1. To develop the student's understanding of usage.

2. To develop the student's understanding of the purpose of language.

3. To develop the student's understanding of effective communication.

4. To develop the student's understanding of the importance of language study.

5. To develop the student's understanding of language and communication.

Lesson Plan

Discuss the test given the day before—discuss aspects of language and communication, their purposes, their importance, the problems involved, the importance of language study, and any questions the students have.

Ninth Day

Objectives

1. To develop the student's ability to use different language forms.

2. To develop the student's ability to use words to convey different meanings, according to the situation or the audience.

3. To develop the student's understanding of usage.

Lesson Plan

Have the students write a short poem, a brief description of something they have done (a shopping trip, a tour of Disney World, a party or movie), or something else they want to write about, using some of the abbreviations and terms they have learned in this unit.

Tenth Day

Objectives

1. To develop the student's ability to use different language forms.

2. To develop the student's understanding of usage.

Lesson Plan

Discuss the assignments from the day before with the class. Deal with any problems or questions the students have.

Eleventh Day

Objectives

1. To develop the student's understanding of the problems involved in language forms.

2. To develop the student's awareness of advantages and disadvantages of certain language forms or styles.

3. To develop the student's understanding of the different levels of language (differences in form and usage depending on the audience or situation).

4. To develop the student's awareness of the purpose of language.

5. To develop the student's ability to write on a level appropriate to his audience.

Lesson Plan

Discuss the advantages and disadvantages of military language.

1. Practical point of view—military viewpoint.

2. Brevity, lack of inspiration or beauty—poet's or writer's point of view.

Discuss how language changes forms and purposes according to the audience. Point out (or have the students point out) differences in usage, form, style, and purpose in talking with friends, the principal, teachers, parents, a minister, or a policeman. Discuss the differences in written or oral communication employed with each of these audiences.

Homework Assignment

Select two audiences from the following: parents, friends, minister, principal, teacher, policeman. Write two paragraphs—one to each audience—telling them about a particularly wild party you attended last week. Assume that they have asked you about the party.

Twelfth Day

Objectives

1. To develop the student's understanding of the problems involved in language forms.

2. To develop the student's awareness of the advantages and disadvantages of certain language forms or styles.

3. To develop the student's understanding of the different levels of language.

4. To develop the student's awareness of the purpose of language.

5. To develop the student's ability to write on a level appropriate to his audience.

Lesson Plan

Have the students share their paragraphs with the rest of the class, or collect them and read a few to the class. Discuss the differences in usage and form.
Why do these differences exist?

Can we say that knowing your audience and your purpose is important before you begin to communicate to others?

What was the purpose or purposes of your paragraph? To inform, to entertain, to explain, to punish?

What does the level on which you write or speak depend on?

The previous two units are prototypes of a series of units based around similar concepts that could comprise a full year's study. Another cluster of units could be developed around "foreign" languages or dialects, which could reveal other aspects of language. "The Language of the Tepee," for example, could consider totem poles, dances, and sign languages, as well as the variety of dialects represented by the various Indian tribes. "The Language of the Pagoda: Canton Jargon" could focus on pictographic writing and the importance of sounds in that particular culture group. This could lead naturally to the study of sounds in our own language.

BIBLIOGRAPHY

Francis, W. Nelson. *The Structure of American English.* New York: Ronald Press Co., 1958.

Gunn, George H. *The Perception of American Speech.* Baton Rouge: Louisiana State University, 1969.

Haas, W., ed. *Alphabets for English.* Manchester, England: Manchester University Press, 1969.

Herdon, Jeanne H. *A Survey of Modern Grammars.* New York: Holt, Rinehart & Winston, Inc., 1970.

Kaiser, Rolf. *Medieval English.* Berlin: 1958.

Wise, Claude Merton. *Applied Phonetics.* Englewood Cliffs, N.J.: Prentice-Hall, Inc., 1965.

Materials

To supplement these suggestions, the following materials represent some of the best language books on the market. They view language as human behavior; they are communication-centered; they incorporate a wide range of activities to help students explore "cool" language:

Anderson, Freeman *et al. New Directions in English.* New York: Harper & Row. Language and composition series that uses interesting readings to develop concepts of semantics, dialects, media, and metaphor; excellent teacher's manuals.

Born, Thomas. *Understanding Language Series.* Middletown, Conn.: American Education Publications. Designed for grades 7–9, an inexpensive four-book series on semantics that uses cartoon characters, puzzles, and many motivational devices.

English Unit Books. Middletown, Conn.: American Education Publications. Several little booklets printed on comic book paper, full of ideas and activities for the junior high teacher. Titles include: "Imagination," "Perception in Thinking and Writing," and "The English Language."

Glatthorn, Alan *et al. The Dynamics of Language.* Boston: D.C. Heath & Company. Six books for grades 7–12 that explore such topics as varieties of communication—machine, animal, human, nonverbal, verbal, visual modes, dialects, lexicography, and composition.

Language of Man Series. Evanston, Ill.: McDougal, Littell & Co. Six books for junior and senior high school that cover Semantics, Mass Media, Perception, Language and Politics, Advertising, Dialects, Role-playing, Origins and Development of Language; paperback.

Postman, Neil. *The New English Series.* New York: Holt, Rinehart & Winston, Inc. Six books for grades 7–12 that can be used with students of any ability level; problem-solving oriented.

In addition to these commercial publications, many of the curriculum centers (e.g., Nebraska, Oregon, Florida State) have developed units in all areas of language from a variety of approaches and with a variety of students in mind. See the ERIC catalogues for a list of available materials.

So What?

We have presented these sample units and lessons to demonstrate to you that language study can be exciting as well as meaningful. Hopefully, you can see that there is much more to language study than grammar and usage drills. Our purpose, as we stated earlier, was to pose some questions about language and to suggest rationales and strategies to help you determine your own answers. We promised no answers because answers are not in a book; they are in *you.*

Part IV

When and How Do We Compose in Communication?

Chapter 8

Establishing Purposes for Communicating

Like so many key words in the teaching of English, "composition" can have a variety of meanings. One of these has been for many years anathema to adolescents in school settings. Instead of proffering this unpleasant definition, the following is a description of a setting in which *this* meaning for the term is operational. The situation is this:

It is toward the end of the first week of school. The books have been passed out, the seats have been chosen, and a selection of literature has been assigned, to be read mostly in class. Now the English teacher, who sincerely wishes to develop improved writing among her students, intones: "For next Friday, I want you to pass in a 500-word theme on 'The Advantages of Living in This Community.' Please make it neat. Late papers will lose credit." After making the assignment, the teacher may set out some guidelines for successful papers, along with the penalties for such things as misspelling, comma splices, and sentence fragments. Discussion of the assignment is then laid to rest, and attention is restored to the task at hand—reading and explicating the current literary selection.

A critical assessment of certain characteristics of the assignment will, hopefully, both identify some problems in much of what has passed for composition instruction and also lead to a more meaningful definition of the term for today's students. First of all, the assignment is *isolated*. It has no context in the personal or curricular world of the student. While other work in English goes on, it has the appearance of being "tacked on." Little or no interactive classroom experience has preceded it; chances are that little will be done with it afterward save some red-penciling by the teacher.

The topic, as presented, is rather *sterile*. How many students have thought much about the major advantages of composition? Since they are probably not involved in serious civic endeavors or directly affected by the decisions of community leaders, it is usually difficult for them to relate to a topic such as this. Where do they find information for the development of the topic? Whom do they talk to? Where is the data? Almost assuredly they will wind up looking through some secondary source such as an encyclopedia. What they "learn" from it will do little to increase their understanding of various community matters.

The assignment may also present a political problem. What if, at his stage of maturity, the student sees more disadvantages than advantages of living in this community? Will he be allowed to say so, especially in the light of the assigned topic (note that the word "advantages" was used in the title of the assignment)? What if one of the reasons for his dislike of the community is his lack of interest in his *school*—surely one of the community's most important institutions, at least in his eyes? Can he say so without causing some negative reaction from his teacher, or must he (like *all* students) "play the game"?

As the parameters for success in the assignment are revealed, the students may well be led to a logical conclusion: their vital responsibility is to state something in writing that is free of errors. A desire for purity in *form* becomes the most important goal; *what* is said is necessarily a lesser goal.

If the recognized goal is *form*, with no "instructional framework" for this particular assignment, the student is probably correct in assuming that the paper is one more obstacle in his path to a diploma. It is a piece of "busy work" that he will probably complete with little interest or *enthusiasm*. It will be treated perfunctorily, returned by the teacher with some sort of a grade, and then probably filed in the trash can. When he has completed several similar writing tasks, he will have met his class requirements and can go on to more of them at the next grade level. What he (and possibly his teacher) may not have considered during this experience is that he is being *tested* on something he has not been taught, at least not in the context described here. Other, better assignments are needed.

THE COMPOSITION PROCESS: INVOLVING THE STUDENT

We can look at the term "composition" from a different perspective, one that can be more easily related to means of *involving* the student in his task. It is our firm belief that there is a vitally significant difference between the terms "writing" and "composition" in the secondary English curriculum. To write is to produce characters on a blank page with a pencil or pen. To compose is to involve oneself in a vastly more complex process.

There is a large measure of skill involved in writing. The creation of curlicues and flourishes on a page can be perfected with practice. Developing ability in composition, however, demands understanding as well as a willingness to develop an idea. A time-honored claim bears repeating at this point: "You can't write writing." If composition must be *about* something, then there obviously must be some prior awareness on the part of the composer of that which he will compose. Furthermore, the writer must have some meaningful commitment to his composition; that is, he must sincerely want to compose something. Without adequate background information and desire, significant composition cannot take place.

Another proposition needs to be stated at this point: writing is only one way of composing. If composition is the act of putting things together to develop a basic concept or placing order on a variety of elements such as content, stance, or conclusion, then we must consider other "ordering" activities as composition. The development in or out of class of such productions as the montage, the collage, the slide-tape presentation, the speech essay, the ballad, the improvised dramatic activity, and the film are all representative forms of composition, and the process through which they are developed needs to be considered as one of composition. It is a highly artistic and highly individualistic process. We need to move away from rigid definitions of composition in order to assist the student in getting involved in a variety of media, so that he can better learn the composition process. This means a development and an acceptance of more than the assembling of student-written words as legitimate composition processes. Such development and acceptance will also help him to perceive the putting together of words with other media with which he is probably more familiar (still pictures, motion pictures, music) as he builds his statement about a given topic.

In a later section of this book, the means of putting together nonprinted kinds of compositions are described in detail. In this discussion they illustrate a broader concept of composition that we wish to propose before describing a variety of composition techniques. The presentation of several classroom experiences *before* actual completion of a written (or other) product is the most vital component of this concept. In describing this kind of instruction, let us reverse the order of activities stipulated in the assignment described earlier. In that instance, the writing took place first. A composition assignment was given to the student, and any activities related to it would necessarily take place only after the actual writing had been done. In the scheme *we* would propose, composition, written or otherwise, would come subsequently. Discussing, reading, viewing, listening, information gathering, and other activities that can enrich the writer's experience would take place previously, all designed to direct the student in his task of arranging things so as to achieve the conclusions and the effects he wishes. The act of producing the composition would flow naturally from previous activity, and would be both a learning experience and an art.

Another preliminary thought: the teacher needs to consider his (her) role as *leader* in composition activity. All too often, topics for writing arise solely from the teacher's own interests, background, current crusades, and what have you. The teaching of composition offers an excellent opportunity for the building of student-centered approaches. In Part V of this book, we offer several suggestions for student-initiated activities. Beyond this, however, lies the basic notion that if students are ever to write meaningful statements, then they must become actively involved in the choice of topics. Thus the teacher needs to be alert to *any* reasonable possibility for student choice, rather than prescribe a a topic or series of topics on which all students must write.

It may seem, from these comments, that the authors are somehow against writing. Such is not the case! The techniques for inspiring, organizing, and completing composition should *all* be made relevant to the written form. It is the overemphasis on demand for production without either incentive or preparation to which we object. In the real world, the great majority of students will do considerably less writing than they will reading, speaking, listening, or viewing. Those who do want more advanced work in precise forms of composition will almost assuredly have ample opportunity for it after their secondary school years. What we really wish to do is put *formal* written composition (a term that will be discussed more fully later in this section) into proper perspective. We prefer to create situations and opportunities in which the act of composition, especially in writing, will be most profitable and enjoyable for secondary school students.

Before meaningful composition work can be initiated, the teacher, with the students, should pursue an honest answer to the question "why?" Why should people learn to compose? What good will it do? Why compose on this particular occasion? These are all legitimate questions, and they need to be answered openly and searchingly in class. Indeed, the introductory class sessions in composition may well be structured around these questions. This can be done in the middle and junior high grades, and students should be reminded, as dramatically as possible, of the reasons for composition during subsequent school years. Without answering the "why" question, it is probable that composition will devolve into a mere finger exercise and a meaningless pretense at self-expression.

One possibly effective means of moving toward such an answer could be through class discussions and role playing activities that both identify the necessity for communication among humans and place composition in proper perspective. The "why do we communicate?" question can be vividly considered through dramatic activities of various kinds. Awareness of the relationship between nonverbal and verbal symbols can help students understand just where man would be without the ability to *use* his language. As we move our students toward rationales for *composition*, we must be able to illustrate clearly some specific reasons for communicating. A set of dramatic experiences for use in class can be one effective way of doing this.

For example, as the teacher is introducing a particular subject, an interrupter (either a student or another "plant") can ask to be heard and then tell a joke. After restoring order, the teacher proceeds with what she is doing only to be interrupted again, this time by a school official who gives clear, precise details on the students' responsibilities in an upcoming activity. When this person has completed his statement, he leaves, and the teacher continues with her original presentation only to be interrupted one final time. This time, the interrupter is a high ranking school official, entering to levy a penalty on the class and then to defend his reasons for the decision to punish. The penalty is totally unexpected and ostensibly unfair. Without allowing a chance for rejoinder, the official leaves, and for a short while the teacher allows pandemonium to reign. Then, when order has been restored, she asks the class what was the nature of the three kinds of communication they have just heard. A tape recording, made during the performances, can be a most helpful adjunct to the ensuing discussion.

After assuring the students that they were not *really* being penalized by the school official, the teacher should help them delineate the three kinds of communication in which they have just been involved—to give and receive pleasure, to explain, and to punish. A playback of the individual presentations on tape can assist the students in their analyzing. The teacher might reinforce the conclusions reached by asking several students to prepare an example of one of these three forms of communication, present it to the class, and ask the class to identify the kind of communication presented, noting especially the *particulars* of the presentation. Once again, video or audio taping of the presentation can be valuable for needed playback.

This total class experience can lead to the formulation of certain generalizations with the students. First, the concepts were arrived at *inductively*. No generalizations were foisted off on them. In their analysis they moved from the example, to its meaning to them, and ultimately to its generalized nature: pleasure, explanation, or persuasion.

To make such an experience even *more* affective, the teacher can allow the students to choose their own topic for role playing. A kind of "what's happening around here?" inventory can frequently reveal what's on the students' minds. Careful listening by the teacher to between-classes hallway conversations can also be revealing. Once the teacher has allowed, indeed encouraged, the members of her class to reveal their present, immediate concerns, *development* of these concerns into a topic for further exploration (i.e., composition) can take place, often in a most enthusiastic manner.

A second principle of communication relates to the *dramatic* dimension. Communication demands people and a situation that is meaningful to them. (This concept will be expanded shortly in the discussion of the speaking voice.) Communication to an audience must be *relevant*. It must affect the audience in a way that is significant to them. And of course, communication must be, to some degree, *composed;* it must be put together in some systematic way in order to make a statement both intelligible and, when needed, affectionate. We see, then, that composition means thinking about the nature and arrangement of the communicative act. In a joke, for instance, the punch line has to occur at just the right spot to make people laugh and to make the joke successful. In giving a set of directions, certain steps must come before others in order to ensure that the procedure is perceived and executed properly.

In the class activity described here, one other point can appropriately be made about the total experience in which the students were involved. Communication through words is largely a pragmatic undertaking. It is not an end in itself, but a means to an end, and three major means are those already indicated. Thus the relative beauty, or *form*, of the groups of words is typically of secondary importance. The main purpose of communication is to reach others. In their analysis of the three different interrupters, the students will need to evaluate the efficacy of their communication.

You can take the "why" question a step further, by demonstrating for the students the differences between private and public utterances. It should be easy for everyone to agree that we all maintain a good deal of communication within ourselves. We continue these "internal dialogues" while we are perceiving the world around us. We internally evaluate them by drawing inferences and making judgments as we go through the day. Much of this private communication we keep to ourselves. It isn't necessary or even desirable to share it with others. There do occur situations, however, in which our privately held ideas or impressions need to be made public; that is, we sometimes feel the need to share them. At these points we need to impose some kind of order on the thoughts that have been racing helter-skelter through our heads, and when we express them in particular words, phrases, or sentences, we are making an educated guess that our thoughts are communicable and that we know the specific nature of the audience with whom we are attempting to communicate.

To demonstrate this to an English class, the teacher can show the students an enlarged picture of an action situation. Some of the pictures in the Leavitt and Sohn *Stop, Look, and Write* series are excellent for this purpose,[1] as are several in Dunning, Lueders, and Smith's poetry anthology *Reflections on a Gift of Watermelon Pickle*.[2] Perhaps best of all would be the Sohn filmstrip material *Come to Your Senses*.[3] After allowing them time to study a particular picture, the teacher should ask several students to describe for their classmates what is happening in it. Thus private impressions become public. *I* tell *you* what *I* see in this picture. I do it by selecting and organizing my words into a statement that I hope conveys the impression adequately.

In this exchange, students will note the different words each one uses as they share verbalized (private) impressions of the same phenomenon. They see the

---

[1] Hart Day Leavitt and David A. Sohn, *Stop, Look, and Write; Effective Writing Through Pictures* (New York: Bantam Books, 1964).

[2] Stephen Dunning, Edward Lueders, and Hugh Smith, *Reflections on a Gift of Watermelon Pickle . . . and Other Modern Verse* (Glenview, Ill.: Scott, Foresman and Company, 1966).

[3] David A. Sohn, *Come to Your Senses: A Program in Writing Awareness*, box of visuals and filmstrips (New York: Scholastic Book Services, 1970).

same picture for the same length of time, but it may *mean* different things to different people, and the language they choose is their means of relating these impressions, whether similar or dissimilar. It will also become evident that when differing impressions are voiced, the listeners will have a chance to question the speaker *on the spot* regarding the particular words he has used to convey his impressions to them.

Affording the listeners and the speaker an opportunity to question each other on the *ways* in which they expressed their internalized reactions is a crucial step in the teaching of composition. Note that a listener, in a face-to-face situation, has the opportunity to question the speaker. He can ask the speaker, in essence, to reorganize his statement to make it more comprehensible *to him*. At that point, if he is honestly trying to communicate publicly, the speaker will rephrase, use more examples, become more concrete, simplify his syntax, substitute key words, and so forth. He does these things because he has discovered at *first hand* that his communication wasn't at that point public enough, that he had to give it a different *composition*. In any speaking-listening situation, the speaker has an almost infinite set of opportunities to revise his composition in order to make his private communication comprehensible.

At this point the advantages of oral communication for making private notions public can be logically presented. The teacher can help the students raise to a conscious level some facts that will then become self-evident: first, when people communicate with each other orally, they don't do it just with words. They do it with many nonverbal symbols. This is true both of speaker and listener. They make faces, shrug their shoulders, make clucking noises with their tongues, roll their eyes, wrinkle their noses, yawn, scratch their heads, touch each other, and do a great number of things *other than using words* to make themselves understood. They also use many vocal inflections and speeds to clarify themselves. And (at the risk of being redundant) they do these things both simultaneously and in response, thus providing their fellow communicators immediate feedback on how their composition is affecting them at the moment. The whole significance of both *kinesics* and *haptics* (conveying meaning through gesturing and touching) should be generalized upon and emphasized during this phase of composition instruction. Much demonstration, preferably histrionic, should be used to reinforce the realization that face-to-face communication is achieved by more than words alone.

A second example of the possibilities of using vocal communication in teaching composition is a three-step procedure with a piece of writing, literary or otherwise. First, the teacher passes out a selection (or asks the students to turn to a page in their books). In this instance, Robert Browning's poem "My Last Duchess" will serve as an example. When the students have the selection in hand, they are asked to read it through once. They are then asked to think about their impressions of what happens in the poem. Shortly after this, the teacher plays for them a recording or tape of someone reading the poem aloud, enunciating and phrasing clearly but speaking in a rather dispassionate tone.

Again, at the conclusion of the recording, he asks them to consider their impressions.

Next, the teacher selects a person from the class to act as the listener to the dramatic monologue in the poem. After seating this listener in front of the class, the reader recites the monologue to him, using all appropriate vocal inflections, facial expressions, gestures, body English, and haptics. Once again he asks the students to consider what they understand about the situation from the preceding experience. It will become evident that of the three stimuli, the third one communicated most effectively, and it is then up to the teacher to lead the students to see why this was so. Once the obvious advantages of speech (oral communication) over written communication have been reviewed, the question can then be raised: "If the speaking-listening method of composition is so superior to writing, why write at all?" Again proceeding inductively, the teacher can lead the students to the realization that there are times when we need to communicate with others but just don't have the opportunity to do so orally. Examples of this should be relatively easy to come by. For instance:

1. You are a classmate of mine and I want you to know something *right now.* But we can't talk in class. *So I write you a note.*
2. You and I are friends but now we live far apart. I want you to know about something, but I can't afford a long distance call. *So I write you a letter.*
3. I am living in a big city where I see something that upsets me. I want lots of people to share my feelings. *So I write a letter to the editor* of a newspaper.
4. I am having a great time on my vacation. I want to remember somehow the great times I'm having right now and I want to preserve the memories. *So I write something each night in a diary.*
5. I am a football captain, and I have been asked to make a speech about our success to the Rotary Club at their monthly luncheon meeting. I don't want to stumble around during the twenty minutes they have given me. *So I write out my speech word for word.*

Note that, while in items one through four, writing becomes the only substitute for speaking, in item five it is a means of becoming more *careful* and *deliberate* in expressing ourselves. Thereby, we say more exactly what we mean.

Seeking reasonable and practical incentives for writing is a crucial enterprise. Once again, if activities can be student-directed, the real involvement of class members must inevitably be enhanced. Instead of the teacher posing his own interests as reasons for writing, then, he should elicit natural interest from the students by challenging them to create situations from their own experiences. This may be difficult to do, but any teacher who hasn't gradually established some degree of rapport with his students will be in trouble in evoking meaningful composition from them. Such an activity can begin with a question like, "When was the last time you remember seeing something happen or hearing about something that really made you mad (happy, frightened, etc.)

and you couldn't *tell* anybody about it? What did you do? Once a discussion has begun, the teacher often needs to be no more than a concerned listener, a catalyst, and possibly a summarizer.

Writing, then, should be seen as a substitute for speaking—and, at times, an inadequate substitute. There are times when it is the only way to convey what we need to communicate. At other times it is the most economical way, in terms of both money and time. Consider how long it would take if each student in a thirty-member class had to tell a teacher what he knew or how he felt about a given subject. When all of them write, they do it simultaneously. The teacher can then read the papers *on his own time*, thereby saving class time for other activities. There are many instances, therefore, in terms of time and space, in which writing becomes the best way of communicating.

We stated earlier that writing is at times an inadequate means of composing ideas and feelings in order to communicate. With no vocal inflections, facial expressions, or gestures, the writer must seek ways of compensating for them. He must also face the task of communicating with an audience that he can't see. It is impossible to deny the importance of the problems caused by not being face to face with the person or persons one is addressing. If, for instance, they don't understand or like what you say in a verbal opening statement, they can let you know this on the spot with both verbal and nonverbal symbols. You can then change your approach as you go along, revising, expanding, and eliminating material in response to their expressed demands. In writing, you can't do this.

A third exercise with which you might well experiment, would be to ask students to prepare an expository or persuasive verbal statement and prime the class (or certain members of it) to question or disagree with the statement throughout the presentation. One provocative statement that has been used productively by some teachers is: "Since young people have more automobile accidents, shouldn't drivers' licenses be granted only after the twenty-first birthday?" As the demand for ongoing revision becomes necessary, the speaker should see dramatically the need for altering his initially prepared statement.

A critique of an exercise such as this can point up several of the inadequacies of written composition and suggest ways of compensating for them. Before getting into the particulars, however, the point should be clearly made that when we talk about compromise and compensation in developing written composition, we are really searching for conventions in writing upon which the writer and reader mutually agree before the communication takes place. We can therefore see that the word "formal" really is relevant to written composition; the forms in which written communication is to take place need to be decided on in advance if effective communication is to take place without a face-to-face situation.

While the relation of form to content will be discussed later in this section, you may well want to allude to some of the more obvious needs for compensating in writing as you move students closer to perceiving some of the appropriate contexts for written composition. For instance, when we speak in groups of words (and we almost always do, even in the most casual or intimate conversation), we create pauses and inflections to denote that, *for reasons we choose*, certain words belong together. To symbolize them in writing, we use marks of punctuation and capital letters. When we aren't sure whether our slang or idiomatic expressions will convey what we want them to, we resort to other expressions, those that we *presume* the reader will more likely comprehend. This is what we call both *diction* (choice of words) and *usage*. Usage is a deliberate choice of one form of expression over another. In written composition, usage becomes a choice of forms we select in order to communicate our ideas to the greatest number of members of our audience. When we make a generalization and then offer a concrete example immediately following it, we are anticipating the need for qualification by our readers.

We could go on illustrating various ways of compensating and symbolizing in written discourse, but we choose merely to emphasize that any means of treating or organizing the groups of words we use is in the interest of making our purpose in composition more evident to our audience. Furthermore, written composition is almost invariably a *monologue*. It is a one-way statement that doesn't anticipate responses or interruptions. In writing, we speak continually from start to finish, and thus must make *all* our decisions about the form and direction of our statement in advance. We are usually not there to answer any questions our readers may raise as they "go through" our written statement. As teachers, one of our highest priorities should be to find ways of cultivating our students' awareness of the differences between speaking and writing.

Since writing is a substitute for speaking, and since it involves anticipating what our audience does and does not understand, one strategy that seems appropriate to encourage early in the composition process is called the "speaking voice approach." In teaching this concept, one can help the student make anticipatory decisions about who he is to be, to whom he is to address himself, and what and how much he is to say about his subject. These decisions relate to the three vital components known as *voice*, *tone*, and *attitude*.

VOICE

Even though we choose to discuss the voice component first, you will need to keep reminding students that all three components appear implicitly in every written communication, and that even if they are developed separately in class, any written composition necessarily contains all three at once. Earlier in our discussion, we considered the significance of the *face* in communication. By smiling, frowning, staring, raising the eyebrows, pursing the lips, or whatever, we can indicate the particular *mood* in which we are saying something. We also can do all kinds of things with our vocal cords. In writing, we obviously cannot do such things, so we must search for means of compensation. We must, in effect, substitute a *voice* for a *face*.

While it is impossible to reproduce the immediate effects of the face in a written composition, there are several things that can be done. A decision must be made by the writer on what kind of "speaker" he is to be. He can be friendly, folksy, sarcastic, authoritative, argumentative, among other things. The choice of his "voice" will influence his entire presentation. For instance, if he starts by using a Socratic voice, the speaker at the outset will be saying, in one way or another, "Look! I really don't know much about this problem (idea, situation). But I do know something, and I'd like to figure out some more. Let's start with what I do know and go from there." By using this voice, the writer indicates where he'll start and why, and where he's going. His total statement develops from what kind of person he is and how he will go about developing his understanding.

More concretely, the choice of a voice will necessarily influence many of the formal aspects of the written statement. An authoritative person will employ different patterns of usage than will, say, a naive person. These patterns include such matters as length of sentences, choice of words, avoidance of certain words (especially long and technical ones), the underlining of words and phrases, the use of humorous anecdotes, the matter of defining or not defining key words, the use of dashes to separate certain groups of words from the rest of the text, and the use of exclamation marks. The use of quotation marks around certain words and phrases related to dialogue provides an excellent example of a formal choice in creating a voice. The writer is asking his reader to look at certain normally accepted words *in a certain way*, to suit a particular purpose.

It would probably be worthwhile to institute some voice activities in class in order to develop the speaking voice notion. The teacher can first pose a question such as, "Let's say that I want my readers to see me as just a plain, folksy guy. What devices might I use?" He can then suggest several: lots of personal pronouns, generally simple and compound sentences, several contractions, frequent localisms and slang terms, reliance on clichés, denouncement of the complex in life, frequent appeal to sentiment and tradition, and the avoidance of big words. Instead of listing these devices, however, you might pass out a written selection that you had made up or found, which contains several of them. Once the students read it, they can, under your guidance, identify and label them as particular kinds of devices. Then, obviously, the students can (and should) engage in some writing activities in which they are assigned or choose a particular voice and *develop* it. Listing several of these voice devices on the board, opaque projector, or overhead transparency can lead to analysis and discussion by the students themselves.

An important point needs to be made to students during the development of the voice concept. The voice that a writer chooses and develops in writing is his to make. It may represent his actual feelings about a given concern, or it may be an imitation of another speaker entirely. In other words, a writer can "be himself" or he can speak through a mask, employing a voice which is not his at all. For instance, he may choose a naive mask when, in reality, he is very knowledgeable and sophisticated about the subject in question. He chooses this mask, or *persona*, to fit the purpose of his writing. To illustrate this, one has only to look at many literary selections, especially those written in the first person. The first paragraph of E. A. Poe's "Cask of Amontillado," for example, gives a good impression of the feelings of the narrator of the story. Editorialists, newspaper columnists, and writers of letters to the editor also provide excellent illustrations. Students can be asked to bring some of these materials and discuss them in terms of the mask being worn. By using short selections of this nature and asking "What kind of person?" types of questions afterward, the teacher can provide instances of a variety of masks being worn by the writer and can also strongly imply that the author isn't being himself in a given instance but is wearing a mask; i.e., Poe himself *isn't* the vengeance-bound narrator in the story cited.

The ability to shift masks (or voices) becomes a potent weapon in establishing particular purposes in writing. If a writer wishes to create a certain impression on his readers, he chooses a particular mask. It should be emphasized, though, that it is important to maintain *consistency* of voice once it has been established. One can't start out as a naive speaker and wind up as an authoritative one. Thus a writer, in order to present the voice he desires, must check his devices throughout the composition to ensure that he is the same person, whoever that may be, at the end of the composition that he was at the beginning. Practice in this habit will lead to increasingly *longer* written assignments in order for the students to develop and increase their skill at checking on whether or not they are *sustaining* the voices they have chosen.

TONE

Once the notion of establishing a voice has been established, it seems logical to move to a consideration of one's audience. A mask, after all, is designed to be worn *for somebody*. You are presenting, as T. S. Eliot so aptly put it, "a face to meet the faces that you meet." In other words, a particular voice is never chosen in isolation but in the light of the person or persons who will discern it. This we call *tone*. This component, just as a mask, is chosen in advance and maintained; we write our statement for a particular, anticipated audience, and we must keep that audience in mind throughout.

It might be helpful at this point to contrast speech with writing once again. In writing, one can't see his audience and thus has no idea how he is "going over" with them. He can, however, anticipate those with whom he would like to communicate and "read" them in advance.

The concept of audience analysis is nothing new to secondary school students, and they should be reminded of this. They are constantly making analyses about their teachers, coaches, parents, and other closely related people and figuring out ways to deal with them verbally in light of these analyses. Such statements as, "I know how to play him" or, "Just give him back his notes in the test and you get an 'A'" are representative of this awareness and of the resulting strategies, as is Holden Caulfield's treatment of his old history teacher in the first chapter of *Catcher in the Rye:*

> Well, you could see he really felt pretty lousy about flunking me. So I shot the bull for a while. I told him I was a real moron, and all that stuff. I told him how I would've done exactly the same thing if I'd been in his place, and how most people didn't appreciate how tough it is being a teacher. That kind of stuff. The old bull.
>
> The funny thing is, though, I was sort of thinking of something else while I shot the bull. I live in New York, and I was thinking about the lagoon in Central Park, down near Central Park South. I was wondering if it would be frozen over when I got home, and if it was, where did the ducks go. I was wondering where the ducks went when the lagoon got all icy and frozen over. I wondered if some guy came in a truck and took them away to a zoo or something. Or if they just flew away.
>
> I'm lucky, though. I mean I could shoot the old bull to old Spencer and think about those ducks at the same time. It's funny. You don't have to think too hard when you talk to a teacher.

The above passage from this Salinger novel provides a good example of the fact that, just as with the voice concept, literature can frequently serve as a means of introducing ways of analyzing one's audience. A look at Marc Antony's famous funeral oration in *Julius Caesar* can demonstrate vividly a situation in which a talented speaker uses audience appeal of various kinds. In fact, one of the really valuable features of literary selections as models for the speaking voice approach is that, while they frequently portray speaker-audience relationships, they are all in written form for the student reader to analyze.

There are at least two specific aspects of the tone concept that the teacher should be sure his students understand *well.* First, the audiences to whom speakers address themselves vary greatly *every day:* it makes a difference whether they are addressing individuals or groups, and the nature of the audiences varies—from peers to parents, to teachers, to upperclassmen, to underclassmen, to girl (or boy) friends, and so on. The prospective attitudes (that is, the ones perceived or anticipated) as well as the status of the audiences also change. They may be friendly, hostile, indifferent, uninformed, expert, and so on. Thus all students prepare themselves to relate to a variety of audiences virtually on a minute-by-minute basis. The need for flexibility in relating to various audiences, in writing as well as in speaking, then becomes paramount.

Another and more intricate set of relationships can be seen when one considers the distance in both time and space that a writer perceives between himself, his audience, and his chosen subject. In one instance, a writer may be describing an "incident" to an audience who is (or was) present at the event. He may be reporting what is happening to people who have also seen the goings on. His role then, either as speaker or writer, is to record faithfully what is happening to an audience who also have the ability to draw inferences and make judgments about their first-hand perceptions. In classroom situations, improvisations can be highly useful.

In a second instance, a writer can be reporting something that has happened recently to an audience who didn't see the event take place. Again, he knows his audience, and realizes that they may already have some input into the situation. But the writer was there and saw the actual event, so he was aware of his role as reporter. He then has more license to describe the incident in his *own* terms, with less concern than in the first situation. More important, he has greater latitude in stating these judgments about the situation that seem most crucial *to him* without too much fear of skeptical response from the audience. Thus, in this situation he can choose and emphasize his details more selectively, and he can make judgments to a greater extent.

In a third situation, the writer can be describing something that happened a relatively long time ago—again, to a known, specific audience who wasn't there. This situation, because of time and personal observation, allows him to take further license in selecting detail, placing emphasis, drawing conclusions, and asserting judgment.

In the fourth and final instance to be described (although, as we can see, many permutations and combinations can be developed), the writer is describing an incident that only he saw, a long while ago, to a general, unknown audience. At this point his selection of detail and conclusions, in light of a *predicted* audience, interest, and response, are of vital importance. This situation almost reverses the emphasis demanded by the first situation. The movement from objective to subjective treatment has placed the writer in a variety of possible stances in relation to his audience. It has also placed some ethical responsibilities on him. How much of the true situation *need* he report in each instance, and how much *should* he report? Questions such as this should lead to some animated classroom discussions. Needless to say, the *possibilities* for in-class writing activities for later discussion purposes would seem evident.

The potential value of tone exercises, both oral and written, should be great in aiding a young writer to establish purpose and to find his stance in a written composition situation. These exercises can be assigned in class, worked on there, read aloud, discussed, and analyzed. In the discussions, writing products can be seen as things to be *used* for subsequent, related activities—which was assuredly *not* the case with the assignment described in the opening pages of this chapter. Some examples of such activities (the teacher should obviously tailor his assignments to his groups) are as follows:

1. You are a _____ grade student who has just been kicked out of your English class for lack of attention and failure to turn in proper assignments. Explain *your* side of the story to:
   a. the principal
   b. your mother
   c. your best friend
   d. the English teacher herself
2. You have been playing draw poker for years and like the game. Explain the fundamentals of the game to a friend who has never played and whom you'd like to interest in it.
3. You are captain of a junior high athletic team (or president of a civic group in the same school). Explain its importance to the school and your role in it to:
   a. a new teacher in your school
   b. a student (athlete) leader in the senior high school you'll attend next year
   c. a seventh grader just entering your school
   d. a neighborhood friend who is home for the holidays
4. You have just invited a girl (boy) you really admire to a big party and have been turned down. Describe your feelings to:
   a. your best friend of the same sex as you
   b. your father, who you suspect heard at least part of the telephone conversation
   c. the girl herself (boy himself)
5. You are Shylock and you have just heard the judge's (Portia's) verdict. Describe your reaction to:
   a. those present in court at the time
   b. your closest Jewish associates upon your arrival home.

Note several things about these assignments. First, they are related to experiences that can be found in the immediate life of the writer, or in the case of Number Five, from his *reading*. Note further that assignments can be structured to give a writer his *choice* of audiences to whom he may address himself in a given situation. In the case of Number Two, by contrast, he is limited to one audience. Note that in all cases the assignment spells out varying degrees of *status* of speakers and audience as well as their relative *proximity* in terms of time and distance.

As previously stated, time exercises can assist a writer to develop his discourse in a great variety of roles, all dependent on whom he is addressing. They also provide for the writer's *involvement* in several degrees of intimacy. He can be himself or he can wear a mask, depending on his assessment of a particular audience and/or on his particular motives in the situation at hand. Finally, the products of the assignments can be used for further class activity that is both meaningful and related. In pursuing Number One, for instance, the teacher can ask a student to read his completed statement aloud to the class. He can then ask the class to identify the audience for whom *they* think the statement was intended. He can further ask them why (or more accurately, from what details) they came to this conclusion. Ultimately he can ask the writer himself for which audience he intended his composition and by specifically what means this should be most evident. Besides the utility of such activities, we feel that they have potential value in raising the act of composition from drudgery to an enjoyable undertaking.

ATTITUDE

At the beginning of this book, the authors expressed their basic belief that in teaching of any kind, the individual involved must consider carefully that he is teaching *something* to *someone*. In considering the third component of the speaking voice approach, that of *attitude*, the "something" in the above claim becomes the focus of attention. Once again, let us remind ourselves: attitude must always be considered in relation to voice and tone, despite the fact that here it is being treated separately. For instance, a speaker wearing a "plain folks" mask for a particular audience will probably not launch into a highly technical discussion of the objective correlative devices in T. S. Eliot's earlier poetry. Just as he chooses a *persona* in the light of a particular audience, he also chooses *deliberately* what he'll talk about (from a predictably wide range of possible topics) and *how* he will deal with this topic on this occasion. Thus *choice* and *treatment* of the subject matter are the two important considerations of attitude. Aspects of choice will be discussed at some length in the material on the rhetorical process, which is taken up in the next chapter.

Three important dimensions of attitude need to be discussed with the students and demonstrated by the teacher, both through oral-dramatic experiences and the analysis of written models. These three dimensions can each be framed as questions, of which the first one asks, "How much does the writer know (on this particular occasion) about his subject?" He may pose as having expertise on a subject that he is sure is virtually unknown to his audience. He may not know much about it in reality, but compared to their utter lack of knowledge, he may look every bit the expert. He may, on the other hand, have exhaustive knowledge. He may really know a great deal about the subject, and may proceed very cautiously so as not to "snow" or confuse the people he is addressing. (Note the pressures this places on a writer trying to communicate with a broad, unseen audience.) Or, he may know only certain aspects of his subject and will obviously highlight them, pose them as *the* important aspects, playing down or totally ignoring the others. He may be a relative novice and, in freely admitting that fact, present the feeling that relative novices like him are needed in this particular area of concern. In recent years, both

Ronald Reagan and John Glenn presented this attitude in their quests for political office. One was an actor by trade; the other, an astronaut. Yet they both contended that their very naiveté about the slimy jungles of big-time politics would be a great asset to them if elected. The writer may also take an old-timer's look at new knowledge. Having known about something in the past, he may wish to develop another perspective on the contemporary condition of this knowledge by relating it to "the way it used to be." For instance, when someone talks about the "New Math," one way of considering it may be by comparing it to the "Old Math." In any case, how much the writer knows is a matter he must deliberate carefully in advance of his presentation.

A second question to be considered in relation to attitude would be, "What is the nature of the writer's knowledge?" Each kind of experience carries with it certain particular approaches. Firsthand experience with a given matter is one kind. Eric Hoffer is a philosopher who is greatly respected throughout the world. But, unlike the stereotype of the "ivory tower" pedant, he has spent much more time *living* his life of a longshoreman, than abstracting from it. When, in college, Jack London was criticized for injecting too much brutality into a description of a barroom brawl, the writer replied, "I saw it happen in a joint in Singapore." Firsthand experience gives a writer a credibility that is particularly impressive to audiences. To illustrate this point, the teacher can reuse the time-distance exercises described in the discussion of tone. In each of these exercises, the writer's perception of his subject, especially in relation to that of his audiences, becomes a changing but always crucial issue.

Beyond that firsthand experience, the writer may have worked with or been associated with experts on a given subject. A writer may be stating significant credentials when he claims, "When I worked with Carl Rogers" or, "During the time I was Chomsky's graduate assistant at MIT. . . ." The implication, for many readers, is that being close to an acknowledged leader has had a particularly powerful effect, and it often has.

Obviously, wide reading on a subject is an important source of knowledge. While this may be considered secondhand knowledge by some, it is in fact a highly valuable source and oftentimes more accessible than firsthand experience. Frequently, when someone asks, "Have you read _____?" he is really saying, "I have and you haven't, therefore I know more about this than you do." To certain audiences, knowledge gained largely through reading would put the writer at a great disadvantage, while to others it becomes an impeccable credential. Thus, as always, the writer must decide what and how much reading background to include in terms of its anticipated impact on his audience.

Another important type of knowledge is that gained through inspiration. While many may scoff at this statement, it is all too common that the inspired speaker or writer really "gets to" his audience. The evangelical, "I just know it's true . . ." approach can have a powerful impact, but inspirational messages delivered orally are obviously much more effective, most of the time, than those put in writing. On the other hand, history shows us that many listeners and readers don't care about substantial evidence carefully ordered; they accept THE WORD and follow the giver of it, in some cases fanatically.

A third question to be asked in regard to attitude is, "What and how much does the writer feel he needs to reveal about his subject?" This is a matter of judgment that the teacher should have no trouble interesting his students in. For years, many of them have been asking the same question of their teachers, "How long does it have to be?," when confronted with a writing assignment. In using the speaking voice approach, this question can be related to strategy rather than sheer volume. In this light the answer to the students' question is, "Who are you, who are they, and what and how much do you think they need?" Thus the writer himself makes certain key decisions. It is he who decides whether to use representative aspects, or to outline an entire topic, or to include a great deal of detail on one or more components, or to zero in on one or two striking illustrations, or to document through comparison, or to employ any other approach. Once he has made his choice, then the volume (the gross number of words) falls into line, as an afterthought.

Two words that are often found in freshman composition handbooks take on new significance in regard to this question of length. These words are *emphasis* and *limitation*. When a writer who uses the speaking voice approach considers the problem of emphasis, he is asking himself, "What particular aspects of *this* subject will be most likely to persuade or clarify for this audience if I use them?" Depending on whether his goal is to please, persuade, or explain, he chooses the things to emphasize and the ways of emphasizing them in that light.

In terms of limitation, the writer can stop being a word counter and ask himself, "How much can I say about this in order to get the job done, but at the same time avoid boring my readers?" He must then consider such matters as when and where to condense, to amplify, to state conclusions, to allow inferences to be drawn, to repeat, and to be consciously terse or ambiguous. *But the choice is made in terms of communicating, not simply filling up a blank page.* Thus the term "how much" becomes a dimension of strategy, not an inquiry about required quantity. Proceed, then, as you have in teaching the other two components of the speaking voice approach—use in-class writing exercises, followed by oral reading and reaction to them. In describing attitude, we have raised several questions for a writer to consider as he begins his task. Most of these questions can be answered through educated guesswork. Animated, unequivocal class reaction to orally read materials should, among other things, provide the writer with some insights into the degree of accuracy of his guesses. Completed writing assignments, then, should be considered as potentially valuable media for feedback. Interaction situations develop more easily in classes when the teacher is continually considering the "to whom" as well as the "what" questions about teaching.

Throughout the description of the speaking voice approach, classroom activities have been suggested. By way of summary, it should be reiterated that the bulk of time spent by the teacher should be in involving the students in the act of writing, with concern placed on the aspects of writing and on the use of student-written materials in class. Lectures should be brief and relatively infrequent. Writing models should be short and should be used for class discussion. Students should be both assigned and encouraged to bring in their own illustrations of various concepts, and these illustrations should be shared with the class as a whole. Small group activity, dealing with such topics as the written development of a particular voice, tone, or attitude, could well be utilized. The teacher should make every effort to develop a classroom atmosphere in which students feel comfortable in reading their compositions to small groups or to the entire class, and in which they also feel free to react honestly to the materials read aloud or shown to them. Much time could well be devoted to interaction sessions such as the small group "cross teaching" techniques described by James Moffett.[4] We also feel very strongly that *most* writing done by students, especially in the early stages of instruction, should be ungraded. Students should be encouraged to ask, "What's it about?" or, "Does it do the required job?" rather than, "What did I get on it?" The more the threatening aspects of evaluating composition can be removed, the better. The same can be said for using writing as "busy work" and as a punitive measure. Writing should become an ongoing means of sharing ideas, perspectives, and feelings about pertinent matters. Your use of the speaking voice approach should help students identify their positions in these regards.

Once the *concepts* of voice, tone, and attitude, and their relationships to each other have been carefully introduced, the teacher can probably benefit from allowing the students to set up a few of their own speaking voice situations. It should not be difficult to encourage students to think of situations from their own personal or vicarious experience backgrounds from which speaking voice exercises could be developed. Students can be allowed to choose the masks from which they will view the action. They can describe the nature of the audience they are attempting to deal with. They can add whatever elements to the total situation they see fit. In other words, the teacher should be careful to avoid framing speaking voice situations of *his* choosing and, with increasing frequency, should encourage the class members to develop their own model and choose their stance elements. Such student-directed activity can lead to composition that is both truly pertinent to their own attitudes and convictions and highly useful in subsequent classwide concern with the products of their writing.

In the opening section of this book, much attention was given to the matter of imposing behavioral objectives on the English curriculum. During that discussion, the term "humanistic objectives" was also advanced. We feel that those who would (or who *must*) follow the behavioral pattern can do so easily in introducing speaking voice activities. The actual writing, discussing, oral

---

[4] James Moffett, *Teaching the Universe of Discourse* (Boston: Houghton Mifflin Company, 1968), pp. 188–210.

reading, and reacting situations can be made the "stimulus condition" component of the performance objective. The act of writing, of identifying components orally or by circling, underlining, or what have you, will serve ideally as "observable performances," and the teacher can set up criterion measures through her own evaluation of written and oral statements. A typical objective might be: "Given a short, persuasive selection, the student will recognize at least seven of the ten devices used to relate to a specific kind of audience." This type of objective relates directly to the instruction suggested and poses evaluation of observable activity in terms of previously specified goals.

The humanistic objectives of such instruction should be self-evident. They are implicit in questions posed to the student writer, such as "What am I?" (as a writer in this instance); "What do I want to accomplish?"; "To whom am I speaking?"; "What do I really know, or *care*, about this subject?"; or, "Am I being honest here?" Communication with other human beings through writing is, we feel, a humanistic endeavor, and a person's involvement in the act of composing to communicate can provide him with valuable insights about himself and others.

Before discussing the next set of concepts about the teaching of composition, written and otherwise, one more statement should be made about the whole matter of using the speaking voice approach. We feel that because it relates so directly and intimately to establishing *purpose* in writing, the approach should be introduced *early* in the instructional process. Secondly, we feel that, once it has been taught, subsequent composition assignments should be developed in the speaking voice manner. The actual creation of composition assignments will be considered more fully in the next chapter. We hope, however, that once the speaking voice approach is introduced, it will not be dropped and forgotten. Instead, it should become an integral part of all composition work assigned to students for as long as they are called upon to engage in composition.

Chapter 9

How to Put It Together

COMPOSITION AND THE RHETORICAL PROCESS

In the previous chapter we took a close look at ways and means of getting students personally involved in the act of composition. Next, we want you to think through another matter of major concern: the development of a working system for bringing a composition (especially a *written* one) to completion. We all recognize that between the time a composition is assigned and the time it is handed in as a finished product, *something happens*, or more accurately, some things happen. Often, however, those things are haphazard. Most students, unless instructed, probably do not have a clear-cut sense of systematic direction in their composition work. The result is often a hastily written, sketchily considered piece dashed off the night before the assignment is due, primarily (or solely) to get the "monkey" off the students' backs. Now, assuming that students can be made more readily involved in the composition act, let us describe a system we shall arbitrarily call the "rhetorical process," a system we hope students will learn well. In fact, they should learn the system so well that it becomes their *way* of approaching any assignment in composition just as a basketball player knows the moves he must make in a pattern offense.

Before describing the first step in this four-step system, let us consider another old favorite of a composition assignment, the book report. In American secondary schools, it is no exaggeration to claim that students have been writing book reports for many decades as a major activity in their English courses. Few students escape this work, and those who write more reports than required are almost invariably accorded added rewards or "extra credit."

Think for a moment about the assignment: "Write a book report. It is due (the *first* one, that is) on October 10." Not an atypical assignment by any means, and notice the things it *doesn't* say. It doesn't tell the student which book to read, or why. It doesn't tell him to whom he is making his report— is it to the teacher only, and if so, has he or has he not read the book? It doesn't tell him what aspects of the book to treat, and there could be a large number of aspects indeed. It doesn't tell him how critical he can be or what points he may emphasize. It doesn't suggest that he compare his insights with reviews already published. It doesn't tell him how to relate the book to anything, and there are several things to which it could be related: the course, its own era, present-day life, its genre, its author, its mode (comic, ironic, etc.), his own life, and so on. Most of all, the assignment doesn't give him any *direction* in com- posing his report, except of course, that he should probably read the book first before writing down whatever he chooses to say about it. In other words, it really doesn't begin to tell him *how* he is to accomplish his task. It makes reading and thinking about the book another isolated experience, in the sense that the activity does not call for any systematized procedure at all. In no way are we suggesting that students no longer be asked to compose written responses to their reading. We would offer, instead, a *way* of moving from the moment of assignment to the completion of the written report that will hopefully be simple, clear, and reasonable to a person who must write a composition but who has not developed on his own a systematic way of doing so.

INVENTION: A BIG STEP

The first of these steps, which we will label "invention" or "prewriting," is of extreme importance. It covers the activity between the initial statement of composition assignment and the putting of appropriate materials in order. Earlier we stated that writing should be the culmination of activity. In intro- ducing the invention step, the teacher gives the students an opportunity to move gradually and carefully toward the act of composition and also assists them in establishing a purpose that they can find both clear and sensible.

In beginning the invention phase, lead the students to consider a topic that *may* eventually be one on which they will write. You may either raise the topic yourself or ask for one from the students. The topic is discussed in class at whatever length you and your students agree is needed. The topic may be considered by the entire class, it may turn into several topics in which groups of students take an interest, or each student may choose a topic of his own. Obviously, class discussion techniques will vary according to conditions.

The sources of topics are many and varied. One general characteristic they should all share, however, is that they be chosen from *related* experience; that is, that they emanate from some concern in which the students have been involved or in which they show interest. When a topic is too *remote* or *abstract* for those who will eventually write about it, the completed product is often *inane*, overly general, and ultimately meaningless, both to the teacher and the student. The assignment described at the beginning of the previous chapter, on the advantages of living in a given community, is a good example.

The problem of finding topics from related experience cannot be over-emphasized. The plight of the "disadvantaged" provides an excellent case in point. Young people with limited socioeconomic backgrounds don't have too many of the experiences that teachers feel appropriate for them to develop into thematic form. The topics that do relate to their experience are often repugnant to teachers with largely middle-class orientations. Because of this, teachers more often than not ask the students to enter a totally unfamiliar world with the topics they assign.

Because of the cruciality of related experience as topical material, the teacher needs to remind himself constantly that any experiences sought must be *student* experiences, ones the youngsters have actually had and verbalized, not experiences that the teacher would like them to have had or supposes they have had. Thus an early phase of invention activities could well be a concerted effort on the part of the teacher to draw the students out in terms of the nature of their experiences and their manner of *perceiving* those experiences. When such student-centered oral interaction takes place, the experiences to be used in writing are genuine ones, not trumped up ones in which the students have no real involvement and ones that they discuss or write about only to satisfy the teacher and to meet course requirements. In initiating a search for student-related experiences, the teacher must be open to a wide spectrum of possible concerns and needs to be especially careful not to inject his own personal value judgments. He can encourage, ask for clarifications, and reflect ideas to other class members, but the essence of related experience in preparing for student writing will be most worthwhile when it is really *student* experience, when the students *know* that's what it is, and when they have had a chance to share and deliberate it without "outside" interference.

The possibilities for topics from related experience are many. They can come from the immediate environment of the school, from some aspect of the community, from prominent regional, national, or international issues. Com-mercial television may supply several possibilities. TV shows such as "All in the Family" are of great interest and could make excellent topics for many English classes. Films, both Hollywood-style and artistic ones, are also available. The whole "youth culture" issue presents several more possibilities. A variety of audiovisual selections—montages, collages, phonograph recordings, tapes, and the like, based on a variety of topics—can provide the initial stimulus for composition. Dramatic activities provide still another source. The use of improvised drama and informal role playing, described in detail earlier, also have potential. In fact, the improvised dramatic presentation is a key example of the structure of an invention exercise. The situation is chosen, roles are assigned to students, the situation may be rehearsed, the drama is presented and then discussed by the players, the audience, and the teacher. From this sequence, the class can move toward composition.

Other student-developed materials, as suggested earlier, can provide topics for consideration in the invention phase. Student-produced art objects and musical scores could be used. Obviously, the reading of various materials offers an immense source. Teachers should consider reading broadly, in terms of consideration of topics. A comic strip, *Mad* magazine, or the sports section of a newspaper could be considered equally with the "Great Books of the Western World."

We see, then, that the sources for topics for eventual composition are many, varied, and accessible. The actual consideration of them—the process of accepting, choosing, and eliminating—should be done in as democratic a manner as possible. You should be sensitive to any reactions that indicate that the students really don't want to write on a given topic, and reject it with them. The rejection, however, should be done only after critical judgment and not done offhand. The teacher needs to provide leadership in deciding *why* a topic should be eliminated. This is also the period when more than one topic may emerge for composition.

Once initial consideration of topics has been completed, the next stage of invention is the gathering of information about the chosen topic. This can be done both in and out of class, but class time needs to be provided for the gathering and sorting of available material. The important lesson of this activity is that, once a topic has been chosen, some time and effort must be spent in finding out more about it. A person who is to *compose*, that is, to put together something about a topic, must go beyond preliminary consideration. He must *know more* than has been revealed in his initial experience and choice. Obviously, the teacher's main responsibilities here are as a helper in the search (coordinating with the library, media center, etc.) and as a consultant for students as they seek out and put together relevant materials.

The third step in invention may often be taking place during the gathering period. It is one of *analyzing* the material gathered. This activity calls for (among other things) a *closer look* by the student at what he has available. It may include relistening, rereading, reviewing, and engaging in more discussion with groups, individuals, or the entire class. It may call for interviewing people who have the needed information and for focusing on key aspects of their statements. In the main, it is a process of focusing on some elements of gathered material and rejecting others. It is also a process of ranking material in order of relevance. The teacher's role here is that of critical questioner, and he should get as many students as possible to participate in this analysis. When the analysis has been completed, students should have what they need for the task of composing their statements, and thus will have given those statements a lot of thought.

The next stage of invention is a crucial one. Having made an initial decision on a topic, having gathered and analyzed whatever supporting material is available, the student must now face the task of deciding what he will say about it. He must move from recognizing the topic to adopting and stating the perspective—the *angle* from which he will view it. We encourage the teacher to make this an extended classroom activity, once the gathering and analysis have been completed. He might ask the students to write a statement, usually one or two sentences in length, in which they express the particular approach they will take to the chosen topic. One possible means of introducing this phase is to set up some small groups, give them each a topic, and ask them to discuss, agree upon, and formulate a written statement of perspective. This statement is called by some rhetoricians the *subject* of the discourse. It will reveal the personal commitment of the writer to this topic. In the group activity, the teacher can ask each group to have a spokesman first read the topic aloud to the rest of the class and then read aloud the statement of subject agreed upon. Reaction by the class and teacher may follow. The teacher can then ask the groups to take the same topic and come up with another, different subject statement, largely to demonstrate to them that a given topic can be viewed from several perspectives.

Here is an example:

Topic: Student radicalism on today's college campuses.
Subject: The use of oppressive tactics by college administrators can create radical attitudes among college students.

or

Subject: The news media have led many college students to adopt radical attitudes.

or

Subject: Student radicalism on college campuses is not new but has a long history.

The point should be clear that each of the above subjects is *about* the topic but each establishes a particular perspective from which the topic will be viewed in the ensuing composition.

It is our contention that thorough development of the topic-subject transition is one of the most vital phases in the teaching of composition. It should be made clearly evident that one can, and must, develop a *personal* context for the topic he has chosen, and that the search for and statement of it are critical stages in the composition process. One is not ready to write until he has worked through this stage. Some other important characteristics of this stage should be carefully noted:

1. It is a reconciliation of topic and personal contexts.
2. The concept of limiting the composed statement is implicit in the act.
3. The *clarity* of the statement is an important factor; the student can be helped in problems of word choice and syntactic arrangement by both his peers and his teacher.
4. This step becomes a miniature, *but ungraded*, test of writing. The ability to express a main idea is at issue here. The statement, once private, must become public and communicable to others.

5. In forming and expressing his subject statement, the student is actually developing his own composition assignment. He, in cooperation with his teacher and classmates, is deciding what he will say. The major responsibility for adapting a perspective falls primarily to *him* and is not ultimately foisted on him by an outside authority.
6. This is a pivotal activity, in that it either leads to rejection or broad re-organization of the original topic, or else it leads to the next major step in the rhetorical process: that of *arrangement*. If the student cannot write a subject statement, he may well go back and find, or gather, a new topic about which he *can* develop a personal context.

As we suggested earlier, whenever the topic-subject transition can be executed with effectiveness, the students should be given the initiative in the activity. Students, for example, can be asked to write their own topics and then be asked to bring in, on their own, a series of possible statements of subjects on those topics. *Or*, they can be asked to bring in a topic and then have the class consider and present *their* statements of subjects. (This obviously could be another writing assignment, with the student who offers the topic asking the rest of the class to write out their own statements of subject.) *Or*, the assignment could be presented extemporaneously: the teacher could unexpectedly ask certain students to "take over" the class and offer some possible topics for which the class would then supply statements of subject. When students are given the responsibility for choosing a series of topics and assuming the leadership of their peers in developing the personal contexts for those topics, then the topic-subject transition can clearly become more intimately significant. Any means of assisting the student in establishing a *personal* perspective on a given topic should be worth the effort. Student-directed activities seem a natural alternative.

It should be easy to infer that the invention step, if followed as suggested, would be a time-consuming process. A great variety of classroom activities has been suggested: reading, listening, viewing, group work, discussion, library involvement, and oral presentations, besides writing under various conditions. The central place of media in this activity should be equally clear. There are also numerous *composition* activities that do not involve writing. When a student develops a collage, for instance, he is composing as surely as if he were writing a paper. The same holds true for the development of a speech essay or a slide-tape presentation (all three of these items are described in detail in the media section of this book). The point is that in invention, compositions such as those mentioned lead to further composing and bring the student closer to *written* composition.

As we see, then, the student-directed possibilities in the invention stage are numerous. Some of these have already been described or alluded to. One or two others are also worth specific description. First of these is the use of student initiative in the observation-reflection invention activity. Students can be asked, within a given period of time (a day, a few days, a week), to observe and record a human experience they feel is of particular significance.

As they observe the experience, they obviously don't know its contextual dimensions; they only know that it is of interest to them. When they record it and bring it to class, it becomes a *topic* for the class to consider and to develop a contextual statement about; i.e., what they *imagine* might be the circumstances surrounding the event. Once that statement of subject has been made, the framing of a composition has begun, which is the primary intent of the invention step. And even more importantly, once that statement has been made, one or more can be selected (by the teacher or the students) as situations for improvised dramatic activities (described in Chapter 14). These improvised dramas, once presented, can themselves comprise the substance of material for composition development.

Controversial issues, argued orally, can be another source of student-directed transition from topic to subject. The teacher can ask the class to provide any number of topics, off the tops of their heads, which they feel are of serious concern. Anything from "Should students at _____ High have a dress code?" to "The ecology-energy showdown" may be offered. In any case, it is self-evident that any issue, by its very nature, has at least two sides and is, therefore, the potential focus for argument or debate. When controversial topics are offered by students, the next logical step is to ask for subject statements. Since such statements are, by definition, of a personal nature, the range of possible responses is infinite. Thus a debate, hopefully of a highly informal nature, could easily be the outcome of this type of topic-subject transitional activity, and the total activity could easily be student-directed. Once again the teacher has to be careful to play the role of guidance person or facilitator during the entire activity. When students are given the initiative and the topic is of sufficient importance to *them*, the teacher is clearly placed in the role of an interested and occasionally involved bystander. The summarizing functions can be shared but should never be dominated by the teacher.

During the class activities in invention, you should be prepared to spend as much time as possible working with individuals. You should guide the students during the prewriting procedures. The workshop atmosphere needed for this kind of activity must be established early and perpetuated. You must also work hard at being a catalyst for student interaction about their own writing. When students can talk to each other easily and without fear, they will be more ready to compose, and you will have gained some valuable assistants for your instruction.

Before leaving invention to go on with the next step in the rhetorical process, another instructional suggestion can be made. The use of *tagmemic games*, both oral and written, can be of value, especially in the topic-subject phase. While there is not time and space here to launch into a lengthy discussion of tagmemic theory (the essays of Kenneth Pike[1,2] and others can provide

---

[1] Kenneth L. Pike, "A Linguistic Contribution to Composition," *Tagmemics: The Study of Units Beyond the Sentence* (Urbana, Ill.: National Council of Teachers of English, 1964).
[2] ——, "Beyond the Sentence," in *ibid.*

adequate background), the application of this particle, wave, field theory to prewriting may be an attractive one to many teachers. Simply stated, the tagmemic concept is that any entity has three positions: unto itself, as it directly relates to other entities, and as it relates to its universe. In prewriting, the concept becomes a question of how many aspects or relationships the students can identify for a given thing. An obvious example would be this:

Teacher: Let's think of a common object, say a penny. How many things do we know about a penny, and what are they?"

Student A: Well, a penny is made of copper, and copper is found in _____, etc.

Student B: A penny is part of the American currency system. There are also nickels, dimes, etc.

Student C: Pennies have not always been part of the money system. They were brought in in the year _____, etc.

Student D: A penny has a picture of Abraham Lincoln. He was _____.

Student E: Pennies have printed symbols on them. These are both verbal and numerical. The verbal ones are in two languages, Latin and English, etc.

For class involvement the tagmemic game can be both enjoyable and revealing. *Many* students can contribute and, during the process, they will come to realize how much there really *is* to say about some seemingly common, uninteresting topics. The use of competitive group contests with tagmemics can add further variety. Above all, the students will be able to see vividly how things relate to each other. They can also see just how complex seemingly *simple* things are, and thus can realize the need for careful, organized explanation.

The possibilities for student-centered activity in tagmemics should be obvious. Students can bring in topics for tagmemic development and then ask classmates for possible uses. Or, if the classroom activities are conducive to competition, they can be encouraged to bring in topics and develop on their own as many *reasonable* subjects as possible. Some really exciting competitive classroom situations could well grow out of such an assignment. In any case, tagmemic activity as an invention step could easily become the genesis of some highly exciting student-centered approaches.

ARRANGEMENT

The second step in the rhetorical process, *arrangement*, takes its point of departure from the completion of the topic-subject transition. Once the student has established *his* perspective on the topic to be developed, he should gain some insights into the *limits* and *direction* of his composition. By working through activities in arrangement, he should begin to see the total organization of his statement more clearly and extensively. Again the term "formal" can be related to the arrangement step because when it is completed, the student should have a fairly lucid picture of the overall *form* of the statement he is to write.

Arrangement has to do with the sequence and manner in which the components of the composition are to be placed. By working on arrangement activities in class, the student should be able to answer some significant questions as to his proposed written statement. The first of these is where to *start* in the composition. If, for instance, the statement is to center on chronological organization, at what point in time will it begin? Furthermore, will it begin *in medias res* and then flash back, or will it actually start at the beginning? Will it be *deductive*, starting with a more or less formal thesis statement and relating subsequent details to this statement, or will it start with one anecdote, move to another, and finally to an inductively organized conclusion? If a *comparison* or *contrast*, which of the two entities to be compared or contrasted will be introduced first? The beginning of a composition often frustrates young, inexperienced writers. In dealing with this question in the arrangement step, the writer can be asked to consider *how* and *where* he will begin, *without having to put this beginning in the actual diction of an opening statement*. The choosing of words to fit the introductory component will be dealt with in the next step in the process. Here, the student need ponder his introductory device only in general terms.

The next question to be answered during the process of arrangement is twofold: What evidence have I got, and where should I place it? Obviously, evidence has been gathered and analyzed during invention. Now the student has a chance to look at it as a *totality* and then to put it into an order that makes most sense to *him*. It will also be possible for him to eliminate once again here, because he has now developed his own statement of subject that demands certain kinds of evidence and does not demand other kinds. In terms of ordering, the student also has a chance to decide where his most conclusive material belongs. Once he has decided where to start, he should be developing a fundamental notion as to where the relevant details of his argument, explanation, and other elements should be placed. In the arrangement step, he will make a series of more accurate, clear-cut decisions as to how much he needs and in what place those elements will go.

The arrangement step is closely related to the third step, which is *style*. Thus, a further aspect of the question has to do with the *variety* of placement of evidence. Does the writer continue to order his material in the same manner? Eventually, the major subdivisions of his completed statement will probably be written in paragraph form. Does it look as if the writer is going to make each paragraph look pretty much like the others? In making initial judgments about ordering details, the student may well begin to gain some early insights into the appearance of his statement to the reader.

A third question, closely related to the second, is: What kinds of appeals will the writer decide to use, and where will they go? If he is relying on *authoritative* statements or quotes to develop his position, which ones should he select, how long should they be, and where should they be placed in terms of *relevance* to the generalizations, claims, or conclusions they are intended to support? More broadly, does he need to quote directly and then comment, or can he merely paraphrase, *adapting* what someone else has said to his statement? Again the ethical considerations of such a choice need to be considered in class: to what degree can we borrow material when and if we choose to do so, and how do we acknowledge this borrowing?

As has been suggested earlier, *length* of statement is an issue that has frustrated student writers for a long time. A most important question, then, to be confronted in the arrangement step is: "How long?" The answer should ultimately be supplied by the writer himself. His decisions in terms of voice, tone, and attitude have already had implications for the length of his statement. His gathering and analyzing of materials have had still more. His movement from topic to subject, still more. As he selects amounts of supporting detail, as he chooses the *nature* of the material (authoritative statements, historical allusion, statistics), as he decides where they all belong, it should become increasingly clear to him that the length of his statement is a judgment to be made by *him* and not by someone outside. Once again we see the reversal of time-honored procedure. To many English teachers, the imposition of a word limit at the outset is conceived of as part of the *discipline* of writing. In the approach we are proposing, the writer selects his stance first, and as he gradually develops his statement in light of this stance, the quantitative dimension will emerge on its own, relating to the particular person the writer is trying to be, who he considers is his audience, and how much of his subject he needs to reveal to them. Thus, the *attitudinal* background, built during the speaking voice and invention activities, should come into play during arrangement in the self-imposed and pragmatic answers the writer presents in regard to length. Before he even asks the question "How long?" he has asked the more vital (in terms of communication) questions like "Who am I?" and "What am I doing?" The answers to these questions point to the need for *relative* length and make the actual word count of decidedly secondary importance.

One further question to be answered during arrangement is, "How do I wind this thing up?" The nature and function of concluding statements now become matters of concern. The relation of final statements to introductory ones, the avoidance of overt redundancy, the relative advantage of implicit over explicit concluding statements, all can be initially considered here, although the actual formulation into words is to be done in the next step. Once again, the selections made in speaking voice and invention activities should help to clarify these decisions. The "what" and "how much" aspects of the windup, however, can be directly considered during the arrangement process.

While a good ideal of the actual class work can be done *orally*, with the teacher and students exchanging ideas on the notion of how to put things together, one traditional component of formal (in the old sense) composition that will almost inevitably be treated here is the *written outline*. Two questions usually come up in regard to outlining, and they relate to the need for and nature of the medium. It is our conviction that, until the "need for" question is honestly discussed, any further work in outlining—especially the imposing of a requirement that all themes be accompanied by outlines—is inconsistent with the *teaching* of composition.

One of the most difficult messages teachers of past years have attempted to communicate to students is the value of developing a written outline *before* they work on their fully developed composition. The typical strategy of students, when faced with this requirement, is to write their paper first and then dub in the outline as an afterthought.

An outline should never *add to* the burden of a person who is learning to compose, especially in writing. Thus you will need to conduct some frank, unequivocal discussions with your students on the advantages of outlining as a written procedure. It may well be that many students can perform arrangement processes, that is, work through their answers to questions, without committing anything to paper. If they can do this, all well and good. By setting up some model arrangement activities for the class *as part of the* process, however, the teacher may well be able to convince the students of the real value of outlining.

Before presenting a positive argument for teachers to consider and use during arrangement instruction, we should like to offer one with somewhat negative overtones. Some of the lack of efficiency in teaching the use of the outline may lie in the fact that formality has long characterized outline form. Guided by one of several well-known handbooks or grammar texts, well-meaning teachers have presented a rigidly structured, elaborately organized superstructure as one to be first memorized by students, then applied to all compositions they are assigned to produce. The complexity, the singularity of approach, and the rigidity often frustrate students, especially those to whom honest attempts at composition represent an individual, *personal* effort. The detailed memorizing of the "proper" (heavy quotes here) ordering of Roman numerals, capital letters, arabics, small letters and numbers, surrounded by various kinds of brackets, parentheses, and what have you, becomes a momentous task in itself, thus removing the student (at least temporarily) from the act of composing. The student may well become so hung up in memorizing the *intricacies* of the form and then fitting *his* composition into *its* mold, that he may wind up rejecting the task entirely. Thus our caution: If outlining is to be required at all, *reduce its formality and complexity to a minimum*. Avoid placing the student in situations in which he must conform to a complicated, prescribed ordering of what he is supposed to be saying as an individual. The rule of thumb should be: If an outline works for *him*, if it helps *him* to order *his* ideas and arrange them more appropriately in terms of *his* stated purposes, then it's OK. If not, it becomes an added burden and, in fact, a deterrent to the process of composition. As such, it should be avoided.

The real value in any outlining process seems to be that it helps the student *separate* Step Two from Step Three in the rhetorical process. That is, it separates broader elements of arrangement from the more precise ones indicated in the stylistic operation. As a student is considering where *in general* to start, what and how evidence is to be used, and where to place it, *he should not have to be bothered* by matters of word choice and syntactic arrangement. Since thinking occurs much more rapidly than writing, a person literally "racing" to transmit ideas about broad organizational matters will be badly impeded and possibly confused if he is forced to make more exacting decisions of style. The value of the outline is that it prevents the writer from trying to do two things at once, to be in more than one place intellectually and creatively, at the same time. If this reasoning can be made acceptable to the students, then the *use* of outlining will seem more worthwhile to them. In teaching the four steps of the rhetorical process, with representative classroom activities predominating, the outlining step may be made a logical part of a system that is *broadly* useful and clearly *leads* somewhere.

As stated earlier, practice in outlining should be done as a means of moving toward actual composition. There should be an insistence upon simplicity and individuality in its makeup. We pose the outline as a *personal* means of broadly arranging a personal composition, one whose topic has been chosen and whose statement of purpose has been made by the writer himself. To be consistent, then, the outline may not necessarily "make any sense" to anyone but the writer (including the teacher). It may well be *replete* with such things as observations, nonverbal symbols, arrows, terms that to all but the writer may appear to be nonsense syllables, and crossed-out structures. It may be as brief or as elaborate as the writer believes necessary. Some practice in moving from outline to written statement may have value as a classroom exercise, in that it demonstrates to the writer whether his cryptic, hastily transcribed symbols do in fact convey adequately what he means when he puts them down hurriedly. In fact, an exercise in which the students are asked to write an outline under time pressure, leave it for a day or so, and then return to it, attempting to compose a statement from it, could do much to demonstrate to the writer the relative communicability of a set of hastily written symbols of his own devising.

In any event, an attempt to make outlining a meaningful part of the arrangement process should be part of the instruction. When the broader aspects of organizing elements in regard to previously decided *purposes* have been completed, then the teacher can move to the next step in the rhetorical process: the handling of style.

DEVELOPING A STYLE

In approaching the stylistic step in composition, let us first make some cautionary notes. So much has been said about style, and the statements are often so wide-ranging and philosophical, that some delimiting is in order. By *style* we mean simply a step in the process. Our suggestions will not deal with the metaphysics of developing an individual's style of writing, nor will they become eloquent, exhortative pleas. Instead, we suggest that you, the teacher, experiment with them if you feel them to be of potential value. You may well agree with us that once broader aspects of organization have been treated and a composition framework has been erected, some of the more precise aspects of written communication can be considered. These aspects, we feel, should be dealt with largely through nongraded, informal classroom procedures.

One more word of caution: the detailed activities that might be highly useful in the style step will be described later, in the final pages of this section. At present, let us deal with only a series of representative activities for introducing the notion of style.

In the narrow concept of style, then, the student can be introduced to a variety of micromodels—parts of sentences, sentences themselves, groups of sentences, paragraphs, and larger structures—in which certain specific, recognizable devices are at work. A good deal of this illustrative work will probably have been done in the language instruction students have received (at least, if teachers follow the persuasion of *this* book), but even so, some worthwhile review could well be done here in light of the place of style in the process.

We would suggest that the *diction element* in style needs to be either introduced or reviewed. One of the most distinctive ways a *writer* has of uniting the factors of voice, tone, and attitude in his presentation is by choosing certain words, placing them deliberately in particular contexts, repeating them in new and varied contexts and, at the same time, refraining from using other words that might under other circumstances be used as substitutes. Here the teacher must be especially vigilant not to impose *his* notion of what key words (both *abstract* and *emotional* ones) mean. If ever any phase of the composition process demanded the use of classroom interaction techniques, particularly those in which members of the class are able to ask questions and offer possible meanings, it is this phase. Basically, in his word choice, a writer is presuming that his audience will grasp his intended meaning—and most of us can cite a large number of illustrative cases in which this just isn't so. In speaking, the immediate feedback possibilities aid in clearing up initial misunderstandings; in writing a person is making an "educated guess." The teacher should try very hard to impress the class with the vital place word choice occupies in giving pleasure, persuading, or explaining; that what a writer means by a given word may not be the meaning understood by his readers (therein lies the rub). Oral reading of student-written passages, as well as of other models, should be done frequently to illustrate the arbitrary and sometimes presumptuous dimensions of word choice. In fact, student-written models are probably preferable because, with them, the writers are physically present to explain *why* they chose a given word whereas writers of published prose (or poetry) predictably would not be present. The consideration of reasons for choice of "big" words instead of more common ones, of loaded words rather than euphemistic ones, are concrete instances in which classroom interaction, guided *but not controlled* by the teacher, is far preferable to doing exercises in a vocabulary drill book. Obviously, an inter-twined series of brief reminders of the speaking voice approach should help to put such discussions into proper perspective.

Semantic choices, especially in precision and appropriateness of diction, are of vital importance in the teaching of style. So too are *syntactic* choices, the arrangements of individual words as well as word groups within sentences, and the arrangement of syntax in relation to broader elements. Much needs to be done with practice in manipulating sentences, as will be discussed later. We feel that the essential ingredient, however, is material that comes from the students' writing, not from drill book examples. Youngsters should see, for instance, that a compound sentence (in the old sense of the term) represents a cause-and-effect relationship that can be gained three ways (through a comma plus connective word (and, but, or), through a semicolon and no connective, and through a period followed by a capital letter). The emphasis of concern lies in the cause-and-effect relationship of the structure and also in the *various* ways in which structures can be joined.

Similarly, the possibility of maneuvering dependent or subordinate ele-ments in a complex syntactic structure can be emphasized. For instance, let us try to manipulate this sentence (a model here, but similar ones can be found in student-written prose): "When he was twelve years old, the wealthy man left home."

1. The wealthy man left home when he was twelve years old.
or
2. The wealthy man, when he was twelve years old, left home.

Again, the point is that the writer has the obligation toward his audience, in terms of clarity, of relating the dependent structures to the independent ones, but he also has the flexibility to move the dependent structures around to different positions, so that all his sentences don't look the same. Thus, *control* of sentences, in terms of intended meaning, can be illustrated at the same time as manipulation, for the sake of variety.

The effective use of *metaphor* is another aspect of style that can also be reviewed here. Since practical problems and principles in using metaphor have been discussed in the language section of this book, little more than introduction will be done here. In relating metaphor to writing style, however, the teacher had best remind the students of the public-private meaning of *any* metaphorical expression, as well as the background that the user of a metaphor assumes his audience has.

Another matter touched on earlier should be at least alluded to during style discussion. The matter of *usage choice*, for predetermined effects, needs to be emphasized by the teacher. Such artificial notions as right-wrong, frozen levels of usage, speaking usage versus writing usage, and other limited stances have all been discussed carefully in the language section and, as in the case of semantics, will not be elaborated upon here. If there is any area, however, where the conflict between traditional concepts of "formal" composition and the notion of *why* in teaching composition is evident, it is in this area. The use of slang or localism obviously illustrates choices of form, choices often supplemented by quotation marks—these and other, similar *deliberate* choices need to be seen not as breaches of etiquette but as aspects of a writer's intention as he tries to portray himself in a certain light, in regard to a certain subject, to a particular audience. As stated earlier, the words "purpose" and "strategy" need to be substituted for "correctness" and "errors" in relating usage concepts to writing style. The question that the writer should be asked by his teacher and classmates, or more accurately, the question that he should ask himself in the making of such choices, is: "Is this the way I want to perform this task?" Much meaningful interaction and insight may well emanate from such a question.

It may also be said that style is almost always *implied* (but never mutually understood by teacher and student) in the wording of a composition assignment. Thus, if the teacher creates situations in invention in which the student works his way through the topic-subject transition, it will be the student himself who sets the fundamental criteria for his usage choices. The teacher and the other students should be able to question him more easily on choice in light of the total task he has set for himself.

The teacher, for several reasons, may wish to have his students practice several styles in which they will hopefully gain some flexibility in making specific semantic and syntactic choices for various required writing situations. In these situations certain stylistic limitations (such as no incomplete sentences, certain restrictions in usage choice, use of synonymous words rather than repeated ones) may be imposed, but it is our hope that the teacher will make these limitations painfully clear *in advance*, along with the pragmatic reasons for them. Also, in regard to establishing stylistic criteria, the teacher should ask himself these questions before stating them to his students:

1. What are the stylistic particulars by which the piece of writing will be judged?
2. On what basis have these particulars been developed?
3. When and where might you (the student) need to use these particular devices?
4. Can a person be flexible in using or not using these devices and still communicate; i.e., which stylistic devices are vital to communication, and which are primarily dimensions of a certain fashion?
5. Do other teachers who will judge your writing understand and/or use these criteria; i.e., are there other English teacher audiences to contend with in your use of these devices?

It would seem evident that once the criteria are understood by the students, and more important, that once the rationale for imposing them is made clear, a series of performance-based objectives can be written by the teacher, and student-written products can be judged according to those objectives. Certainly the students' ability to use or refrain from using certain agreed upon stylistic devices offers a viable set of observable performances based on mutually understood criteria.

In the style step of this process, the student can do his actual writing of the composition. He can self-consciously make those exact choices he feels he needs to meet his own purposes and to round out the broad structure he started on in the arrangement step. In the early phases of *teaching* the composition process, we feel that a good deal of time should be spent in developing the various components through a workshop environment. That environment must be characterized by individual teacher guidance as well as by frequent inter-action sessions involving the student writer and his peers.

REVISION: THE LAST STEP

If the teacher has a tough selling job with outlining as a worthwhile part of the rhetorical process, revision, the final step, is hardly an easier one. Most students, particularly when their written compositions are completed in haste and under great pressure, are loath to change a word of what they have written. The feeling that an experienced teacher often senses is, "Look, I got the darn thing done, didn't I? Now just grade it, and let it stay the way it is!" A partial cause of this attitude may well be the consistent placing of composition writing far too early in the instructional sequence, a problem discussed earlier. Another probable reason is that students (and indeed *all* people who write) can easily become quite sensitive about their own "golden prose." Once completed, a written product is *ours;* not beautiful maybe, but an egg that *we* laid. There-fore, criticisms and calls for revision of this intensive, energy-consuming process are often met with indifference and even hostility.

Throughout this section terms such as "class interaction," "peer reaction," "teacher guidance," and "cross-teaching" have appeared consistently. If you make considerable effort during composition instruction to build in these essen-tially counseling situations, and if they become increasingly comfortable ones in which the students can function, then the revision step can well become an accepted part of ongoing activity, not some unwanted anticlimactic chore whose sole purpose seems to be to torment students one more time. If, during the working through of the process, as well as in the speaking voice activity, students become used to reading parts of their compositions aloud, if they become willing to listen to peer criticism and to do something about the suggestions made, then any work done in the final step of the process will merely be an extension of an already familiar activity. And when finished composition products continue to be *used* after they are finished, the students should see some value in reworking certain parts of them.

In a sense, the revision step can be viewed as an opportunity to see if the whole statement, rounded out during the style stage, does what the writer hoped it would do. Its major characteristics will be reviewed *in the light of commitments made earlier in the process by the writer himself.* Has he, for instance, stayed with his chosen voice during the course of the entire paper? Is he still speaking to the same audience? Has he been consistent with the demands of the perspective he placed on himself when he moved from topic to subject? In other words, have the *parts* of the composition, when seen together, performed the functions assigned them during the prewriting activity? A close check of arrangement can serve as an example for the possibilities of relating and reviewing earlier work to that done more recently during revision.

As a writer reconsiders his arrangement in the light of possible revision, he may wish to make some changes. He may wish to add evidence, eliminate superfluous material, or put certain supporting details in different positions. He may also wish to change the wording of key statements in his introduction so that they can relate more closely to his conclusion, or vice versa. In the light of a closer look at the wordings, he may find a redundancy that calls for elimination of certain parts for the purpose of relating them more meaningfully and economically. Since, in his actual writing, he was working on only one part at a time, he might have forgotten the way he stated and organized earlier components as he worked on later ones. Revision gives him a chance to recall and to correct his writing if he feels it to be necessary.

A brief statement needs to be made at this point about the assigning of grades in relation to revision. We are unwilling to condone the "carrots and clubs" approach sometimes used to provide incentive for this activity. Some teachers say, "If you do some of the revising I've suggested, I'll change your grade." This seems to us to be resurrecting the primacy of the grade as an outcome of composition, an attitude we have opposed consistently in this book. As understanding of the composition process increases through classroom activity, revision should become an activity a student involves himself in because he sees the need for change. The teacher should not become the ultimate judge when a student has decided that his composition is finished. Although the teacher has a perfect right to make evaluations, nevertheless, if revision is to become an integral part of the system we are proposing, he should be wary lest grades and authoritarian comments get in the way. He may need to struggle with colleagues, administrators, and syllabus requirements to keep them out of the way.

Some practice at revision may help the student involve himself in the process more easily and may even help him to enjoy an often dreary activity. One activity we propose can be called "bug the teacher." In it, the teacher passes out copies of a model composition to each student. He explains the context in which the paper was written and claims that he (the teacher) wrote it for certain clearly established reasons. The paper contains obvious flaws of several kinds (hopefully both in content *and* form), and the teacher asks his students to play the role of evaluator while *he* plays the role of student writer, requesting that they tell him what their evaluation of the paper is *at this stage*, i.e., what he should revise.

The "bugging" of the teacher can be done either individually or in groups. If groups are formed, the teacher can move about, responding to each set of suggestions, then allow the groups to summarize *their* suggested revisions for the entire class. Or he can ask a member of each group to play *his* role as writer and accept the criticisms in his place while he observes several group discussions. In either case, the class should be provided with an opportunity to confront the writer with some major questions about what he has written.

First among these questions might be those that ask him to explain his speaking voice, audience analysis, and treatment of his subject. He should be prepared to identify specific places in the text where he has made certain commitments, and he should promise to revise those passages and others where more consistency is desirable. The students should also be able (and in fact, encouraged) to ask the teacher for his statement of subject, and he should have one prepared. They should then be encouraged to tell him whether, in their judgment, he followed it.

Comments on total arrangement as well as on semantic and syntactic choices should also be entertained, and the teacher should be eager to do *on-the-spot* revising as suggested by the students. Stylistic considerations should not dominate these "bugging" sessions; rather, the main concern should be relating written statement to purpose. Nevertheless, the teacher should probably include some obvious examples, as well as some more subtle ones, of inflated language, wordiness, irrelevant details, redundancy, poor word choice, and the like. These will always bring reaction from students who patently enjoy catching teachers in boo-boos. We would urge, however, that this "bugging" procedure not be overdone, and especially that no attempt be made to introduce a large number of obvious errors in spelling and punctuation. Revision, we feel, should *not* be limited to these matters, and using papers loaded with such errors would be counterproductive in attempting to dramatize the real value of revision. In punctuation and usage, however, the teacher might deliberately include a couple of questionable choices and then, in the course of the ensuing cross-examination, defend with some animation what he was trying to achieve through those choices. This could help to emphasize the personal aspect of choices in diction, usage, and punctuation.

The teacher can write these model papers himself or he can find them. There should be a statement of subject, real or bogus, which he himself will probably have to write. In any event, he needs to be ready to "ham up" certain aspects of the confrontation; but more importantly, he should keep the discussion of revision confined to the major phases of composition instead of some of the less important concerns.

Another possible exercise for use in undergirding the value of the revision step can be called the "write-revise" exercise. Here, the teacher passes out another model theme, either as a whole or in parts at a time, and asks the students to judge it. Their judgment, however, is to be limited to *one aspect* of the paper each time. Probably the best approach would be to present the whole theme first and touch on nothing but aspects of speaking voice, one aspect at a time. Then, when suggestions for changes are made by the class, the teacher can ask them to attack—on separate classroom occasions—other components such as arrangement and style. When stylistic problems become the consideration, the teacher can ask the students to deal with such matters as word choice, usage, syntactic arrangement, and appropriate metaphor, thereby showing them the several aspects of a composition that need attention and pointing out how truly complex a product written to please, persuade, or explain really is.

As a come-on, word choice almost always provides an obvious and frequently humorous vehicle. The excerpt presented below is from a student paper written many years ago for one of the authors of this book while teaching a (*mea culpa*) summer school course for largely senior high school students, called "Better Writing." The paper was passed in at the end of the five-week course as a "culminating activity," and its opening passages run exactly like this:

ARTUR RUBINSTEIN

I intend in the following to somehow emit the meticulously reprehensible life of Artur Rubinstein.

My chronicle begins back in the nineteenth century when Ignace Rubinstein and Felicia Heyman had their nuptials blessed in an august house of God. They indeed loved each other for from them was burgeoned seven scions, the seventh of which was Artur, himself.

From the very beginning, which was in Lodz, Poland, the ostensibly versatile scion esteemed the unique impetus and amiable serenity of music. Offered a violin he demolished it. The imperious mecca which defied him contemplated the jubilant mind of the versatile Artur. Music was his prime aspiration.

Within the next three years, he enthralled two audiences into an ostensibly reprehensible ovation.

Next, Artur pervaded the Polish capital where he succinctly sapped the competence of his instructor. In this same burg, he emitted some of his resonant tones for the noteable Joseph Joachim who thereafter accentuated to him the subjects such as harmony, theory and composition by stimulating his interest in going to Heinrich Barth.

At eleven, Artur expanded his laudable reprehensibility by capitulating his audience at Berlin with his formal debut. His amiable friend Joachim conducted the Berlin Symphony Orchestra while they played Mozart's A mj. concerto. Joachim thereafter became the scion's protector.

Joachim knew Artur very well and sensed that the virtuoso was becoming nervous; therefore he sent the boy to his friend's summer domicile in Switzerland. When Artur arrived he was jubilant for the new friend was none other than the notable, unique, amiable, reprehensible and versatile Paderewski.

Artur became ostensibly embarrassed when he was cajoled to play, for he performed the Brahms Variations on a theme by Paganini adiously meager. However, the epic Paderewski disseminated the ignominious plight Artur was in and

defied him by giving him a walking stick. When Artur returned, he found a suc-
cinct epistle written him by his new friend, "Put on your best clothes, I'm having
people in." Again Artur tried to perform and much to his surprise he enunciated
an enthralling resonant poignancy of tones. There verily had been numerous
unanticipated, capricious renovations made. There was a jubilant vestige of
ovation for when Artur finished, Paderewski kissed him.

Students who have had adequate backgrounds in semantics and style, as
suggested in this book, should have a field day working with the word choice
aspect of this passage.

Beginning with such obvious problems as those found, the paper can be
analyzed each time from a different viewpoint. Some problems will undoubtedly
be more subtle in appearance, and careful classroom discussion will be needed.

A write-revise exercise can become boring whenever students are asked to
reread the same paper again and again in order to examine different problems.
Papers should therefore be chosen on the bases of brevity, potential interest
(especially humor), and variety, the latter component exhibiting both obvious
and subtle problems. If the teacher is worried about too much reading of the
same material he could choose to focus attention on the problems found in
sections on one occasion, then switch to other sections on other occasions.
The rationale, however, remains the same: to offer students a chance to isolate
one or more shortcomings in an outline statement, revise the statement, and
proceed to another aspect.

Revising models should *not*, in our opinion, constitute the bulk of classroom time spent on this final phase of the rhetorical process. Models are
meant to be used only to arouse interest and give practice in certain revision
procedures. Student compositions in the process of creation should be the
main material used. Lastly, revision should never be looked on as a *final*
activity; instead, it is one in which a composed statement is refined for use in
future, meaningful communication situations.

PUTTING IT TOGETHER

No one system will work uniformly with all of your students. The one we
propose has been tried, modified, and expanded by teaching in many places and
at several grade and ability levels. We don't claim any miracles for it. What
we *do* claim is that, once you've gotten your students involved, you probably
need to provide them with a system for putting their material together. The
process must be relatively free from complexity and should *not* be accompanied
by a bevy of technical terms. Most of all, the composition process is *not* a set
of steps to be memorized like lines in a great poetic work. To be of value,

it needs to become part of the student's working approach when he faces the need to compose orally or in writing; i.e., it needs to become an almost instinctive tool for him to use. In light of this, remember to provide lots of concrete examples for each step and to allow your students to practice each phase over and over again—in class, and without the pressure of grades. Generally, people who have a system for doing something *at their fingertips* are happier and are more successful in accomplishing their goals.

Chapter 10

Building Components of Communication

WHERE IS FORM AT?

Throughout our discussion of composition in communication we have tried to emphasize a new approach to the teaching of *form*. We have suggested that form be posed as an *adjunct* of content, as a series of maneuvers that help clarify the questions an audience might ask of a written statement. Thus the word "formal" does not connote a point on a vertical judgment scale. It is a term that identifies those components mutually agreed on by human beings who try to use written language in order to make their messages more intelligible. In this chapter, then, some attention will be paid to assisting students to develop techniques of manipulating words, groups of words, sentences, groups of sentences, as well as other factors (spelling, capitalization, and punctuation), all in the service of *clarifying* their written messages to an often broad, always unseen audience.

It should be evident by now that we place a great deal of importance on establishing purpose and introducing a system. If your students can see a reason for writing (the *why* in our basic question about teaching English) and if they have a viable means of doing it, composition won't be so likely to turn them off. But these same students must eventually face the fact that, if they are to communicate effectively, if they want to make their private ideas and feelings public, they must *learn* to observe some of the conventions. When human beings don't *share* certain formal conventions, then mutual intelligibility is impossible. Messages, to be understood by any given audience, must sometimes be clarified. Otherwise, there will inevitably be a lot of wheel-spinning in the act of communication.

THE COMPOSITION PROCESS: CLARIFYING THE MESSAGE

To begin with, students must become aware of the fact that in many cases it is far easier to sense what is wrong with a given structure than to revise it so as to make it say what it "should" (heavy quotes) say. The sentences that follow were extrapolated from actual letters written to the Department of Welfare of a here-to-be-unnamed state. Beyond the human pathos revealed in these fragments of discourse lies another, more relevant problem: that of effectiveness of communication. As the reader reads each of these sentences, he should ask himself: a) What is the writer of this statement trying to say, and b) What actually comes across?

1. "I am forwarding my marriage certificate and six children. I have seven but one died which was baptized on a half sheet of paper."
2. "I am writing the Welfare Department to say that my baby was born two years old. When do I get my money?"
3. "Mrs. Jones has not had any clothes for a year and has been visited regular by the clergy."
4. "I cannot get sick pay. I have six children. Can you tell me why?"
5. "I am glad to report that my husband who is missing is dead."
6. "In answer to your letter, I have given birth to a boy weighing 10 lb. I hope this is satisfactory."
7. "I am forwarding my marriage certificate and my three children; one of which is a mistake as you can see."
8. "In accordance with your instructions, I have given birth to twins in the enclosed envelope."

Once the guffaws have subsided, you can ask the students to rewrite the sentences, adding and subtracting as they wish, to present more accurately the ideas *they assume* are behind the statements. As they write their revisions, you can encourage them to read them aloud and ask for comments from their classmates. At least two things will probably emanate from the ensuing discussion: a) Several students will disagree as to what was actually intended, and b) The actual statement is much more difficult to write than it may have originally seemed. The various semantic and structural problems to be found in these examples can point to some conclusions about writing sentences and groups of sentences that express communicable ideas:

1. It is not easy to develop syntactic writing ability through *analysis* of someone else's writing. We really don't know what they intended to say. Maybe it is better to start with *our own* ideas, express them in sentence form, and then discuss them with our peers and the teacher.

2. When we write a sentence, we are usually trying to express to someone a series of entities seen *in relation to each other*. When we put those entities together, we have to choose the combinations of words appropriate to our purpose and our audience. Sometimes the number of things we are putting together (who, what, where, when, how, and why) is rather extensive. If we feel we have to include *several* of them in the same structure, arrangement becomes even more complicated, but still important.

3. It is perfectly natural to want to put several ideas that seem related into one structure. As people progress in school, they tend to add more and more ideas to their written work. But these elements need to be put together in such a way as to clarify the writer's ideas for the reader, not to confuse him. This is the *control* factor that must be kept in mind.

4. As they progress in school, most people not only make sentences longer by adding more things to them, but they tend to include in them different styles or combinations. This means a considerable variety in the way components can be related to each other and to a main idea. This variety *appears* in sentences, and a reader must be aware of it and be prepared to deal with it.

5. It is usually appropriate to begin by having students practice with smaller structures and then build larger ones by adding and combining. This is better than starting with long, complicated ones that someone else has written and trying to analyze and rewrite them.

6. Since compositions are made up not of individual sentences, but of groups of sentences, practice work should probably take the form of groups of sentences that relate to some meaningful idea, preferably an idea of the writer's choosing.

A variety of practice-type exercises focusing on structural forms is available to teachers of English. In the hands of a versatile and enthusiastic teacher, these exercises may encourage students to write varied yet controlled sentences according to the teaching procedures described in the style step of the rhetorical process. We will now identify several of these exercises, describe them briefly, and highlight one recently developed exercise that seems to have particular promise. Let one thing be understood before we do so, however: more time in the teaching of composition should be spent in establishing purpose and developing process activities, than in doing these kinds of exercises. Exercises should be seen as adjuncts to the more meaningful concerns of purpose and process.

J. N. Hook proposed long ago, in a chapter of his book *The Teaching Of High School English*,[1] a basic plan for aiding students to build syntactic struc-

---

[1] J. N. Hook, "How to Grow Sentences," *The Teaching of High School English* Copyright 1950, The Ronald Press Company, New York.

tures. In "How to Form Sentences," he proposed that the teacher start with a common noun; i.e., "the pilot," "the farmer," "the surgeon," "the messenger," and ask the student to supply several verbs for each one. For example:

$$
\text{surgeon} \quad
\begin{array}{l}
\text{cuts} \\
\text{worries} \\
\text{checks} \\
\text{scrubs, etc.}
\end{array}
$$

This basic two-word pattern can show the student that two words can create an idea, that a given noun is capable of taking an infinite number of verbs (or vice versa) and still make a sentence, and that tense is something to consider in choosing and placing verbs with nouns. A refinement of the Hook technique would have the teacher, in giving the class a series of nouns to couple with verbs, provide a sequence of related nouns such as:

1. Birds_____   2. Hunter_____
3. Dogs_____   4. Farmer_____

In this exercise, the verbs are chosen to develop the *situation* as well as to show basic conceptual relationships.

Hook would then ask students to take a basic noun-verb combination such as they had just constructed, and add several possible *complements* (key words; they could be direct objects or adverbial modifiers). For example:

$$
\text{man kicks} \quad
\begin{array}{l}
\underline{\hspace{1cm}} \\
\underline{\hspace{1cm}} \\
\underline{\hspace{1cm}} \\
\underline{\hspace{1cm}} \\
\underline{\hspace{1cm}}
\end{array}
$$

Again, once several isolated combinations have been worked on, some related ones could be established.

A third and vital step to Hook was the posing of three-word structures such as:

singer   sang   song

Hook suggests that the teacher can really manipulate this kind of structure in his existing exercises. He can have the students modify any one word, or all three basic words, with several modifiers, either single words or word groups. The *kinds* of modification would be up to the student, and awareness of purposeful placement as well as semantic relationships should come more readily.

Once again, cause-and-effect patterns could follow isolated ones.

Hook then poses both phrases and clauses to the students:

As he headed for home
Twirling the baton
Underneath the arches
Confused by the sign
Far from the madding crowd

and has them create structures around them to provide them with fuller and more recognizable meaning. Throughout these exercises, Hook is essentially asking students to take fragments of verbal pictures and complete them with their own words to make coherent ones. His approach has been called naive by some critics and artificial by others, but it may offer teachers a place to *start* students in the habit of developing both basic and expanded ideas with written words. We offer it as such.

Francis Christensen presents a more complex and formulaic notion of developing paragraphs and sentences in his two well-known articles, "A Generative Rhetoric of the Sentence," and "A Generative Rhetoric of the Paragraph."[2,3] Those who wish to consider the linguistic and philosophical backgrounds for these approaches can read the articles. The idea proposed by Christensen that applies most directly to *this* discussion is that of the cumulative sentence. Basically, Christensen claims that to teach students to write well-formed sentences, one must develop in them an awareness of *addition* in sentence structure. The fundamental relationships in a sentence (*who* did *what* to *whom*) are established early:

The man bit the dog.

The successful writer then adds components to that beginning, each of which makes the nature of the situation more specific and vivid:

The man bit the dog which had been following him for blocks during that frightening morning of his first day out of the psycho ward.

The words that follow "dog" create a more concise picture of the conditions surrounding the action, each subordinate structure helping to complete the total awareness like pieces in a puzzle. This sentence is an obviously oversimplified representation of the Christensen theory. His fully developed approach is outlined in the articles footnoted, and is carefully set down in an impressive programmed publication.[4]

---

[2] Francis Christensen, "A Generative Rhetoric of the Sentence," *College Composition and Communication* XIV, No. 3 (Oct. 1963): 155–161.

[3] ———, "A Generative Rhetoric of the Paragraph," *College Composition and Communication* XVII, No. 1 (Feb. 1966): 2–11.

[4] ———, *The Christensen Rhetoric Program*: "The Sentence and the Paragraph" (New York: Harper & Row, 1968).

David Conlin proposes some interesting syntactic possibilities for class-room manipulation with headline structure. He offers the headline as a structure that is necessarily terse and from which the reader must draw a variety of inferences; he must, in fact, fill in a number of missing words *himself* in order to derive meaning from it. Since headlines are found in publications that reach a broad, general audience, Conlin contends that they employ units of language (abbreviations, words, phrases, and nonverbal symbols) that are *timely* as well as comprehensible to wide populations. For example:

N Viets Fudge in Peace Talks
or
Title on Line Tonight
or
Gotham Mobs Mourn Satchmo Passing

The students' task here is to write in the words that they mentally perceive in order to make the headline intelligible. Composing these interpolated words will give those students a chance to draw inferences and perspectives on the barest of syntactic structures, and also an opportunity to develop their own sentences and groups of related sentences around a given core. The *time* and *place* implications of headlines also offer possibilities for speculation about writer-audience relationships (i.e., *what* title is on *what* line *where?*) as the students recognize the implicit agreements about such matters as ideas, people, situations, nicknames, idioms, and issues.

For a fuller description of the Conlin technique, the teacher can read the appropriate chapters in *A Modern Approach to the Teaching of English*.[5,6] His suggestions about manipulating headlines to produce a variety of *awarenesses* in words and syntactic structures will be of definite value to many teachers.

Stephen Dunning has indirectly made some interesting suggestions about syntactic manipulation approaches in his writing about the teaching of poetry to adolescents. Dunning's basic premise is that most people like to fool around with words to form amusing, different, provocative ideas, and the classroom can be a place where such word games are promoted, and the results scrutinized and generalized upon.[7]

While Dunning's ultimate goal is to lead adolescents to an awareness of their own poetic sensibilities, the implications of his ideas for developing

---

[5] David A. Conlin, *A Modern Approach to the Teaching of English* (New York: Van Nostrand Reinhold Company, 1968), Chapters 7 and 8.

[6] ———, "Can Traditional Grammar Be Modified?," *English Journal* XLVII, No. 4 (April 1958): 189–193.

[7] Stephen Dunning, *Teaching Literature to Adolescents: Poetry* (Chicago: Scott, Foresman and Company, 1966).

syntactic structures should be virtually self-evident. His classroom approach is somewhat as follows:

1. Write a sentence on a subject that is important to you. Use exactly twenty words.
2. Now eliminate exactly five words. You can move words around in the sentence or change any of the original twenty words in the process. But come out with exactly fifteen words.
3. Now look at these forms. They represent numbers of words per line.

<pre>
          — — — — —
          — — —
          — — — — —
          — —

             and

          — — — —
          — — — —
          — — — —
          — — —

             and

          — — —
          — — — —
          — — —
          — — — — —

             and

          — — — —
          — —
          — — — — —
          — — — —
</pre>

There are obviously other combinations possible, but the fundamental object is for the student to manipulate his thought first into a given *number* of words and then into a given *pattern* of words. The possibilities of this kind of exercise for promoting both interest and versatility in word choice and sentence arrangement should be clear.

A student-directed game could be used as a supplement or replacement for the Dunning activity. This can be labeled "The Telegraph Approach," and can be done with or without some ritualistic "behavior mod" techniques. With behavior modification, the students can be given a number of coupons, each of which is worth a given amount of money. They are then presented a dramatic situation in which they must become personally involved. For example:

> You are in an armed service and you have just been informed that you are being shipped immediately to a foreign country. The telephone booths are full, with long lines. You have no transportation. A telegraph booth is nearby, and you decide to use it.
>
> *or*
>
> You are supposed to meet someone at an airport tomorrow; but your flight has been postponed indefinitely because of weather. You can get there by bus,

but it will be almost a day later and at a different meeting place. The phone booths are crowded, and you must leave for the bus station. A telegraph booth is nearby and you decide to use it.

or

You have heard on the radio that a close relative has been killed in an automobile accident. You want to get a message home quickly, but the phones are tied up. A telegraph booth is nearby and you decide to use it.

In each case (and in any other you might choose to invent), the word limit for the telegram is *fifteen*. You then ask the students to write their messages in such a way as to relay the gist of what they want to say to their correspondents. For a change of pace, you can ask the students to develop situations of their own in which a message must be transmitted, but in any case, the premium is on economy of words and possibly revision of syntax, in order that the essential elements of the writer's intent be preserved.

Possibly the most useful approach in the syntactic manipulation field is that offered by Frank O'Hare in his doctoral work.[8] O'Hare developed a series of sentence-combining procedures that is both simple and enjoyable to work through. His system employs some of the concepts used by John Mellon in his research on syntactic development, but it does not require the students to study any grammar, transformational or traditional. Work in the O'Hare approach to sentence-combining can begin at relatively early grade levels, with oral practice emphasized at the outset. His overall suggestions for sequence are as follows:

1. In elementary school, simple adjective and relative clause insertions and repeated subject and verb deletions could be practiced, perhaps as early as the second grade.
2. Written exercises could start in the fourth grade.
3. The present signal system could easily be expanded to incorporate a wider range of syntactic structures, which could be practiced in grades seven through twelve and beyond.
4. Sentence-combining games could be developed.
5. Students exposed to sentence-building techniques could use these syntactic manipulative skills at the prewriting or rewriting stages of composition. They would thereby be better able to "unchop" choppy sentences and eliminate run-ons.

It is not within the purview of this book to explain the O'Hare approach in detail. His study is now in publication as an NCTE Research Monograph,[9]

---

[8] Frank O'Hare, "The Effect of Sentence-Combining Practice Not Dependent on Formal Knowledge of a Grammar on the Writing of Seventh Graders" (unpublished Doctoral dissertation, Florida State University, 1971).

[9] ———, *Sentence Combining: Improving Student Writing Without Formal Grammar Instruction* (Urbana, Ill.: NCTE Research Monograph No. 15, 1973).

and a complete workbook in his methods of sentence-combining will be published shortly. What follows is a brief description, in O'Hare's words, of some representative exercises taken from his experimental text; it should give the reader some idea of the procedures involved:

The first part of the sentence-combining text gave students practice in writing out simple sentences by matching separated subjects and predicates. It is important to remember that although these procedures are being described for the reader in grammatical terms, these terms were *never* used in the lessons. Then the students were given practice with the addition of adverbial phrases to sentences. This was followed by a series of short lessons giving students practice in converting sentences to negatives, questions, and passives. Here are a few examples which instructed the students to use a variety of the combining signals they had learned. Where appropriate the desired answer is written out and underlined below.

1. The rattler (*HOW*) slithered (*WHERE*), bit the sleeping baby (*WHERE*), and (*HOW*) disappeared.
2. *Instructions:* In the following exercise write out as many sentences as you can, using *all* of the information in *each* sentence you write.
   My car broke down.
   My car broke down during the winter.
   My car broke down every Monday morning.
   My car broke down at five o'clock.
3. Some telephones are nearby. (THERE-INS. + NEG. + QUES.)
   <u>Aren't there any telephones nearby?</u>
4. Those dirty marks will fade away for some reason.
   (NEG. + WHY QUES.)

Part two of the sentence-combining text required students to master single-embedding problems. For example:
Peter noticed SOMETHING.
There were nine golf balls in the river. (THAT)
<u>Peter noticed that there were nine golf balls in the river.</u>

These were followed by multiple-embedding problems:
SOMETHING should tell you SOMETHING.
John has not called in five days. (THE FACT THAT)
You are not going steady anymore. (THAT)
<u>The fact that John has not called in five days should tell you that you are not</u>
<u>going steady anymore.</u>

Lesson Thirteen presented a particularly difficult problem for this researcher. How could he devise a combining signal that would, in non-grammatical terms, enable students to convert an adverb to an adjective and change its position in the transformed sentence? He came up with over fifty unsatisfactory or partially successful "solutions" before stumbling on the right one. For example, how to get students to change "The child shivered violently" to either

"The child's violent shivering . . ."
   or
"The violent shivering of the child . . ."

so that either can be inserted in another sentence? The solution was so obvious that it eluded this researcher for a long time. Almost every adverb when changed to an adjective drops "ly." Therefore, the parenthetical command (⧸L⧹Y) is called "LY with the cross through it" in the lessons. The student follows the (⧸L⧹Y) command and positions the new word according to where it appears in parentheses. For example:

The child shivered violently ('S + ING + ⧸L⧹Y)
    becomes
The child's violent shivering . . .

   and

The child shivered violently (⧸L⧹Y + ING + OF)
    becomes
The violent shivering of the child . . .

The single-embedding problems were followed by multiple-embedding problems that required the students to transform and embed two, three, four, or more kernel sentences into a single sentence.[10]

The O'Hare system, while not posed here as *the* answer to aiding students to write well-developed structures, has certain highly attractive features:

1. It employs synthesis rather than analysis, an approach favored by most English educators and language learning specialists.
2. It is simple and can be taught in relatively early stages of a student's written language acquisition period.
3. It is cumulative. Exercises in substituting and embedding move from relatively simple operations to increasingly complex ones.
4. It can be (and was in the experiment) most enjoyable and leads easily to a games approach in which students are offered opportunities to play with the written form of their language.
5. It does not take the form of a right-wrong, only-one-alternative type of drill activity. Students can create material with their own words and ideas without fear of penalty.
6. It utilizes neither abstract grammatical concepts nor technical grammatical terminology, which, most authorities contend, tends to "snow" or confuse students.

The immediate future in this area of English construction could well give rise to approaches similar to the O'Hare system as well as to attempts to refine and expand it. Teachers should be on the lookout for both possibilities.

A brief comment about the teaching of suprasegmental features: if the reader is looking for some intricate and supposedly foolproof techniques in teaching spelling, capitalization, and punctuation in these pages, he is doomed to disappointment. One approach to punctuation that should at least be

---

[10] *Ibid.*, pp. 78–81.

mentioned, however, is that of *logic*. If writing (as we have contended earlier) is a substitute for speaking, then punctuation marks are a set of conventions agreed upon by writer and reader, that substitute for pauses and inflections in the language and influence meaning. We agree, for instance, that the presence of a question mark at the end of "I'm going to fail this course?" calls for a rising inflection and changes the nature of the communication, in this case, from a statement of fact to a question. Marks of punctuation represent definite kinds of pauses and inflections, some more distinctive than others. For instance, a period indicates the need for a relatively long pause, and as such is relatively easy to learn to use in one's discourse. Its presence also indicates the need for another convention, a capital letter, to lead off the next segment. The period, then, is an indication of both an obvious pause and a terminal one.

A *comma*, on the other hand, indicates a shorter pause, a less pronounced change in voice inflection, and is found only in the interior of a sentence. Because of these three characteristics, it is harder to detect and harder to teach. The ear must be more sharply attuned to commas than to periods, and students tend to make more errors in the placing of commas than they do in the placing of periods. Some fairly simple orally-stated structure, replete with various kinds of pauses and inflections and played on a tape recorder in class, can be most helpful in illustrating the several ways of substituting through punctuation. It is also desirable, as we see it, to ask the student during cross-teaching sessions— which feature oral reacting to completed material—*why* he used certain marks of punctuation rather than others. In this way, punctuation can become part of a writer's personal strategy rather than a set of fixed rules that assume him incapable of producing written communication.

In this chapter, we have attempted to treat writing in a more human, intimate manner than has been done in the past. We trust that this approach to the usually more mechanical aspects of teaching will reflect the overall mood of the entire book.

Part V

How Do We Use Media in Communication?

Chapter 11

Introducing Media Productions by Students

Media in the English classroom are nothing new, but the way they are being utilized is new and exciting. The proliferation of books, articles, and professional conferences about media-study and media-making as an integral part of English instruction can be overwhelming and frustrating to the classroom teacher.

Media have been promoted by commercial distributors as the way to motivate and involve the students in creative, relevant activities. Short films have been produced that are stimulating as well as informative. Pick a subject, a mood, an abstraction, and someone somewhere has a film about it. In contrast, previous educational films were bland presentations of lectures about Shakespeare, or letter-writing, or punctuation. Often they were poorly made. The teacher felt he could do just as well without having to hassle with the red tape of ordering the film, waiting for its arrival (usually weeks after the planned showing), contending with the technical difficulties of threading it or fixing it when attempting to show it. As a result, teachers became convinced that films weren't worth the effort.

Tapes and records of poets reading their own poetry or of actors performing a play have been in the English classroom for decades. The mechanics of using these materials were not so difficult, and many teachers found them a reprieve from listening to inept student renditions.

Overhead projectors have been substituted for chalkboard writing by some teachers. Other instructors have been more creative in the preparation and use of transparencies. At times, they have relied on commercial distributors to design and package a set of transparencies to be used as instructional materials.

Media, in the past, have been used primarily as an instructional aid made or used exclusively by the teacher. The new emphasis—as in all areas of the curriculum—has shifted from the teacher to the student. Student film-making, tape-recording, and picture-taking are commonplace in some schools. However, these activities meet a great deal of resistance from many English teachers. They reject them as "frills," as "expensive time-wasters," in view of all the other skills and knowledge that students "must master" in literature, composition, and language. So the students have made a film—so what? What have they learned? Why should class time be spent viewing Hollywood productions that the students will probably see on their own? These are the types of questions usually raised by the "anti-media" forces.

Media study should not be rejected or accepted wholesale. Media-making should not be cast aside as a "frill," for it can be a vital means of teaching the skills of writing, listening, and speaking. These are basic skills that you are trying to teach anyway, and media-making is a *haptic* approach that totally engages the students while they are learning. Film study should not be accepted *only* to make English relevant and exciting, or as a panacea, or as a replacement of other teaching and learning activities, for it is a serious and important art form that deserves special consideration in order to help students develop aesthetic and critical awarenesses and abilities—often termed "visual literacy."

The focus in this chapter, therefore, will be on student-made media projects as adjuncts to literature, composition, and language study. In the next chapter, we will discuss various aspects of film study and film-making in the English classroom.

To illustrate how media projects can be used in a literature class to help students develop skills and concepts, the following poetry unit is offered. As you know, most students, especially boys, hate poetry. Next to grammar, it is probably the least liked aspect of the whole school curriculum. There are several reasons for this distaste, but two reasons seem fundamental. One is the way poetry has been taught. The second is that students don't know how to *read* poetry aloud, that is, to interpret it. Even advanced students who can analyze poetry, describe its elements in technical vocabulary, and discuss the various levels of meanings, often cannot give a proper oral interpretation. If this is true, then the teaching of "prespeaking" skills is as important to the reading of poetry as the teaching of "prewriting" skills is to composition. To test this notion, a teacher taught the following poetry unit to seventh-grade students of varying abilities.

A UNIT ON POETRY

The unit began with the question: "What is a poem?" Following some class discussion, students were asked to turn to any page in their textbook that had a poem on it and to compare that page with a page of prose. They were asked to explain the difference between the two pieces of writing. Usually the students answered that the pages "looked" different, noting that the prose material ran to the margin and that the poem did not. This led to a discussion of why the two types of material looked different, which revealed to the students that the poet is more limited in terms of space and/or form. To further illustrate this point, the students turned to a poem written in iambic pentameter, and they were asked to take any line and count the number of syllables in that line. (Obviously, they came up with ten.) It was briefly explained that this type of verse is called *iambic pentameter*, which means that there are five beats to a line and that there are two kinds of beats, accented and unaccented. This explains why the poem doesn't use up as much space across the page. The poet is restricted because he is writing in this particular style. When he uses up ten syllables, what does he do? (He goes to the next line.)

Following this discussion, the fundamentals of oral interpretation were explained. Since the poet has to move to another line when he has run out of beats, he doesn't necessarily end his statement at the end of each line; so when someone is reading his poem, the poet doesn't expect the reader to stop at the end of each line or to read the line accenting each beat. Instead, the poet tells the reader when to stop, usually by means of some kind of punctuation signal. The teacher then demonstrated how it sounds to read a poem in a sing-song fashion, stopping at the end of each line. Then he read it for "sense," letting the important words receive the emphasis and stopping at the punctuation signals. He then noted that this is one of the "rules" in reading poetry—read for sense, and the sound will take care of itself. Various rules for oral interpretation were given and demonstrated.

The first assignment was for each student to pick any poem that he liked to read aloud to the class. The poem had to be at least ten lines in length but no longer than thirty lines. This limit was placed on the students so they would have enough material to work with, but not so much that an entire class period would be taken up by one student's reading. They were asked to bring two copies of the poem—one for themselves and one for the teacher. They were instructed to mark their poem as a script (an essential ingredient for later media projects). It was explained that double slashes are used for long pauses and single slashes for short pauses. They were told to look up all of the allusions in the poem and to know the meanings of all the words, for the important words are usually the thought-carrying words. These thought-carrying words should be underlined. Finally, they were asked to read the poem *aloud* at home at least three times to prepare for their presentation in class.

The next day the students began reading their poems to the class. When they made errors, they were stopped. (Don't let them run through the entire poem and then point out all of the mistakes at one time. For example, if they stop at the end of a line where there is no signal, stop them. Ask them why they stopped. Have them begin again and read through to the indicated or "natural" stop. If they are reading too fast or are not enunciating properly, stop them. Tell them to slow down, that you can't understand them, and ask them to begin again.) This may seem like a terribly slow process that can humiliate the student, but several interesting things happened. First, when the student finally sat down, he had done a good job of orally *interpreting* the poem. He had succeeded, and he knew the difference between how it sounded the first time he read it and how it sounded in his final rendition. This experience was also cumulative. Other students began to make constructive critical remarks—"Why did you stop?" "You aren't enunciating," and so forth. The last students to read their poems tended to do so better and with less effort.

At first, this activity progressed slowly. (If you don't get through more than five readings in a period, that's okay. Don't rush your students. You must realize that you are teaching *interpretation*—a very important *reading skill*. Once taught well, it will be used again and again, not only in the reading of poetry, but also in the reading of drama.)

The next assignment was a mini-media project that took the students a month's time outside class. The project was the construction of a poetry notebook. A list of twenty or thirty themes or topics, such as "nature," "animals," "friendship," "war," "eerie" or "ethereal," "love," "death," and "family," was given to the students. They were told to select a poem they liked for each topic and to select one illustration for each poem. They could draw the illustrations themselves, or take their own photographs, or use magazine pictures. Instructions and hints were given on how to make a poetry notebook ("If you don't, you will have slipshod productions"). The instructions included how to select pictures, how to "edit" them, how to crop them, how to mount them, and possible ways to arrange them—all of these aspects deal directly with similar concepts in writing because picture editing is a visual form of word editing, and the students can understand the concepts much more graphically with pictures than they can with writing.

It was explained that they would have to look at a number of pictures before finding the one that seems to go with the poem. Sometimes they might find a photograph first and then search for a poem to go with it. Sometimes they will find advertising in the picture, which is extraneous material, so they will have to cut it out (edit it). Sometimes they will want to use only a portion of a picture, so they'll have to crop it.

Once they had found the pictures and selected the poems, they were ready to mount them and arrange them. Instructions on mounting procedures were given. (For example: "Don't use paste or Elmer's glue because these elements crinkle and ruin the pictures. Use rubber cement. If extra rubber cement spills or spreads, you can rub it off with your finger. In mounting, good sense tells you that the pictures should face the poems, but imagination should be used. It's a good idea to shift pictures and poems around on the page for variety —like a variety of sentence structures. If every page looks or is arranged like every other one, it is not as interesting.")

It was suggested that they could put their poems and illustrations in ready-made scrapbooks, or they could make their own scrapbooks out of construction paper. If they intended to write their poems in white ink on black pages or colored pages, they were warned to let the ink dry thoroughly so that it wouldn't come off on the facing pages. (Don't assume that students know these things. Specificity in the assignment and demonstration of techniques leads to good finished products—the same as in writing.)

The students were given a month to construct their notebooks. To get them started, a week of library time was given them to search for poems, and poetry books and magazines were brought into the classroom. Then the students were asked to bring a variety of magazines to class to look through and begin to select pictures. The enthusiasm began to generate.

Class time for the next two or three weeks was spent in reading and discussing poems. When the poetry notebooks were due, they were checked in by the teacher and the students selected a notebook other than their own to look at. When they were finished with one, they took another. (You may want to spend class time on this phase of the activity the rest of the day and the following day, depending on the amount of interest your students show.)

Now that they had been taught and had practiced the fundamentals of oral interpretation and of picture selection, editing, and arrangement, the next project was a slide/tape presentation of a poem. For this project, students worked in small groups or individually. They selected a poem to be read or interpreted on tape, combining any music or sound effects they wished to use to supplement the reading, and made a series of slides (using an Ektagraphic Visualmaker) to be shown with the tape. This again involved a great deal of sorting, selecting, arranging, editing, coordinating, timing, and work. The sounds the youngsters chose to supplement the reading, they were told, should be appropriate to the tone and mood of the poem, or they could juxtapose dissimilar sounds for contrast. The pictures became literally *images* of the poem's imagery. The poem itself became the script, which had to be studied, planned, marked, and used as the basis of their presentation. When working with a poem this closely, the students learned not only the words of the poem, but also how sounds, images, and form are integral parts of meaning.

THE USE OF TAPES

Tapes, in the form of speech essays and slide/tape presentations, can also be used in a variety of ways in composition classes. The techniques used in selecting, arranging, and editing sound and pictures demonstrate all of the verbalizing English teachers do about the composing process. Instead of getting back a composition covered with red marks, the students will see their shortcomings or hear them in their tapes and pictures. They seem to be more willing to erase a tape and revise it or edit it than they are to erase words and edit themes. One of the reasons for this is that they know other students will be seeing and experiencing their media productions, while only the teacher will read their themes. The force of peer acceptance or criticism seems to mean more to them when they are literally "on display."

In planning a speech essay, the students go through the same processes that were discussed in the composition section of this book. They must decide their purpose, voice, tone, and attitude. Once these matters are decided, they must do a great deal of planning and writing (in the form of a script) in order to decide how the sounds will be arranged and what types will be stylistically effective to accomplish their purpose, using a particular voice for a particular audience.

In the poetry unit just described, the poem was the basic script; in composition classes, the students will write the script, which will include both the narration and the sound correlations. You must insist that before any taping is done, the students prepare and submit a script. (This is true for all media productions because good productions are based on good planning, which is evidenced in well-prepared scripts.)

To demonstrate what a speech essay sounds like, play for them the record "What the World Needs Now Is Love," by Tom Clay, and produced by MOWEST (Motown Recording Corporation) (MW 5002F). After playing the record, analyze the techniques used. How does it begin? How does it end? (It begins with live interviews with children asking them what such words as "segregation" and "prejudice" mean. It ends with the same sequence. In writing, this is called "full-circle.") What holds the "essay" together? (Throughout the six-minute recording, the song "What the World Needs Now Is Love" fades in and out—that's the main theme.) How is the theme illustrated? What are the details or incidents used to demonstrate that the world needs love? (Excerpts from actual news bulletins and broadcasts of John Kennedy's, Martin Luther King's, and Robert Kennedy's assassinations and excerpts from their speeches are juxtaposed with the theme song and other sounds of violence.) This juxtaposition of dissimilar sounds *shows* that the world needs love. So in speech essays, as in effective written communication, vivid details help to develop the thesis or generalizations. Again, this is a basic notion stressed in composition textbooks and by composition teachers that students can't seem to relate to very effectively in their own writing. However, *hearing* an actual recording makes a powerful impression on them, and making a tape recording so that they can hear themselves makes an even greater impression.

How Do You Make a Speech Essay?

1. *Basic Equipment*
   Tape recorder (preferably stereophonic)
   Record player (radio or television set)

Every school has tape recorders and record players, so the availability of equipment should not pose a problem. It is easier to use a stereophonic tape recorder because you can record the narration on one track and the music or other sounds on the other track, editing each track as needed without erasing the other. However, you can also do an efficient job with a mono tape recorder or even a cassette tape recorder. If you are limited to the latter, it only means that the planning and timing will have to be precise and that while one student is reading the narration, others will have to fade in or out with the music or other sounds simultaneously. Or, students can record the narration on one tape recorder, and the other sounds on a second machine, and then play both machines simultaneously so as to record the whole presentation on a third tape recorder. As a teacher, don't worry about the procedure. The students will figure out a proper way, and their patience and ingenuity will probably amaze you.

To help the youngsters assemble a variety of sounds or music, check with your media center. Many media centers and libraries have on hand a variety of sound effects records, as well as recordings of poets reading poetry, excerpts from historical speeches, and so forth. The sources are limitless. The use of "live interviews" can also be quite effective. To make them effective, though, you must stress to the students that they have to prepare a variety of good questions that will elicit more than "yes" or "no" answers from the interviewees. This in itself is a good prewriting activity, for the students will be forced to think about their subject in a variety of ways in order to ask the proper questions. Kenneth Burke's Pentad could be taught here as a means of "brainstorming" about the subject.[1]

After the students have decided on a series of questions and have conducted their interviews, they will find that they probably won't want to use all of the answers, but only parts of them. The editing process becomes vital. This again demonstrates the need to "cut out" extraneous material, not only to make an effective speech essay but also to make effective written communication.

2. *Basic Techniques*
   a) Plan—write the script.
   b) Develop questions if using a "live interview."
   c) Record "live interview" on one track or one tape.
   d) If not using live interviews, then record speech content on one track or one tape.
   e) Edit speech content according to your script.
   f) Record sound correlations/readings/music/miscellaneous sounds on second track or tape, according to the script.
   g) Do further editing as required.
   h) Juxtaposition of sounds (often dissimilar moods) is central to the technique of speech essays.

---

[1] For a clear explanation of Burke's Pentad and how to use it, see William F. Irmscher, *The Holt Guide to English* (New York: Holt, Rinehart & Winston, Inc., 1972), pp. 28–38.

    i) A great deal of thought must go into the editing of the original speech and the selection of any material to be added, in order for the production to be effective.

3. *Technical Information*
   a) How to operate the tape recorder

     Since there are a variety of tape recorders, no one set of instructions will be accurate for all makes. You should talk to the person in charge of the equipment at your school and have him instruct you how to use it properly. After you have become familiar with the equipment, teach your students how to use it and check out each student's performance before letting him go off on his own. Again, specificity in instruction and demonstration of techniques helps assure better results from your students and brings fewer complications and misunderstandings.

   b) How to splice tape

     1. Cut the tape at a sixty-degree angle with an overlap, so that the ends will line up. Cutting the tape in this way will eliminate detection of the splice on the recording (the "click" sounds).

     2. Align both ends of the tape, with the uncoated side up (shiny side on plastic, gray on paper).

     3. Cover the aligned ends with *Scotch splicing tape* (not regular Scotch tape) evenly and securely.

     4. Trim off any excess splicing tape. Cut into the recording tape backing very slightly, in order to eliminate a "sticky" splice.

How Do You Make a Slide/Tape Presentation?

1. *Basic Equipment*
   a) Index cards
   b) Ektagraph Visualmaker, Instamatic camera, or 35-mm camera
   c) Slide projector (preferably Carousel)
   d) Tape recorder

    Most schools have all of the equipment listed above, with the possible exceptions of an Ektagraphic Visualmaker or Instamatic cameras. Many students will have these inexpensive cameras, which are capable of taking slides. The Visualmaker is handy to have, for it allows you to take slides of magazine pictures, small objects, or pages from books. It comes in a briefcase and includes two copy stands, one for 8 × 11 material and one for smaller pictures (3 × 3) that you might want to photograph. It also includes an Instamatic camera. Write to Eastman Kodak Company for prices and other information.[2]

    The index cards are used for planning the photographs. These are "idea cards" on which scenes are sketched or outlined in order to plan the slides that

---

[2] Motion Picture and Education Markets Division, Eastman Kodak Company, Rochester, N.Y. 14650.

will make up the presentation. Most professional photographers do not go out and shoot pictures willy-nilly. They usually know exactly what they want to photograph, plan it, then find it. This is especially true if they are shooting pictures for a specific purpose for someone else. The person requesting the pictures must give the photographer specific information as to the type of subject matter and the angle of the shot (whether a close-up or a wide-angle shot). Students must learn to plan their photographs as carefully as they plan their narration.

2. *Basic Techniques*
   a) *Plan your work* using the same techniques as outlined in the composition process. Decide on your purpose, voice, tone, and attitude. As in any good communication situation, you must analyze your audience's background and interest and relate them to your purpose.
   b) *Gather ideas*—"brainstorm," use various methods of prewriting such as questions developed on the basis of Burke's Pentad or the "particle-wave-field" approach to analyze your subject. Jot down ideas and notes. Write down your ideas on cards and then organize the cards, arranging them in a logical sequence or by groups. The editing process can begin here by changing the order of some of the cards within a group or by changing the position of entire groups. The organized cards function as an outline that will guide you in planning both your pictures and your narration.
   c) *Plan the pictures*—usually, in a slide/tape presentation, pictures carry the bulk of the communication task, so the pictures you choose must be interrelated and show continuity, just as words or sentences and paragraphs must be related in writing. Look over your idea cards and decide what type of pictures should go with the narration by trying to sketch what you have in mind. Remember that you want a variety of picture angles, just as you want sentence variety to lend interest to your "style" of presentation. You won't want to use all close-ups, or all long or medium shots. (The work done on picture editing and cropping for the poetry notebook should give practice in helping students make these decisions.)
   d) *Take the pictures*—it is better to shoot too many pictures than too few, just as it is better to write too much, so that you can edit and select the best from what you have in order to get your point across. You must also keep in mind that an audience will get bored if one picture is kept on the screen for too long a time. Usually it takes only three seconds for an audience to see and be able to "read" a slide. So if you are going to present a three-minute tape, you should make between fifty and eighty slides. Obviously, some slides will need to be projected for a longer time than others. This will depend on the picture and the narration that goes with it. If you are using the Ektagraph Visualmaker, collect the magazine pictures and other objects you want to photograph and arrange them in the order you want to use them. In this way, you can photograph eighty or ninety pictures in a matter of minutes. At times, some of the pictures or objects you are photographing will be smaller than the area

of the copy stand. Mat them with construction paper so that the table top on which you are photographing will not show, and so that the slides will contain only the content of the pictures you want to show. Remember that careful planning in all respects will pay off in a better-looking/sounding production.

e) *Prepare the narration*—make notes for each picture. Then use your notes to practice narrating with the slides, in order to acquire a proper sense of pace for your production. Your narration should tie the pictures together. A good narration should be simple, brief, and to the point, and it should not call attention to itself. Don't explain obvious things. For example, if you are showing a slide of a man reading a newspaper, don't say: "Here is a man reading a newspaper." The slides should illustrate whatever generalizations you make, or a series of slides may serve as examples of the point you wish to emphasize. After you have run through your slides and have practiced narrating them several times, record and play back your presentation. When the words and pictures seem to work together nicely, write your working script. If a poem is your script, then you should mark the poem for stresses and pauses, as discussed in the oral interpretation portion of the poetry unit. Your final script will contain narration for each slide, cue marks for slide changes, and cue marks indicating where background music or other sound effects will be used. Be sure that all cue marks are carefully and accurately marked in your script. When you have a number of pictures to run through in three minutes or so, it is easy to forget just exactly when each picture should be projected. Furthermore, you want to know what is going on at all times, and it is easy to forget just exactly when to push the button. *Do not rely on memory!* And bear in mind that there is a slight time lag from the time you push the button until the slide is projected; therefore, you must be sure to time your cues so that each picture appears when you want it.

e) *Prepare the tape*—use the same techniques in preparing the tape portion of your presentation as you did when preparing a speech essay.

g) *Synchronize sound and slides*—the simplest way of doing this is for the projectionist to change slides by following the cues in the script while listening to the tape. Using sound cues such as "beeps" is distracting and is not recommended.

The teacher should attempt to make a slide/tape presentation himself, just as he should attempt to write some of the themes he assigns to the students. *You* can learn by doing, too. And the more you learn by doing these activities yourself, the more you will be convinced that they are not frills, but are valuable projects that take time and skill. Furthermore, you will acquire a working knowledge of the step-by-step procedures, thus enabling you to help students when they encounter problems or ask for recommendations.

Chapter 12

Films: What They Are and How They Are Made

FISH

Lady: That doesn't look like a fish.

Picasso: It's not a fish, it's a painting.

Substitute:

> "critic" for
> "lady"
> "novel" for
> "fish"
> "director" for
> "Picasso"
> "film" for
> "painting."[1]

Before you decide what to do about film study in your classes, you must remember that a film is not a fish, not a painting, not a novel—but a film. Furthermore, if you select films for study in your classes, they should not be considered as "visual aids" or "means to an end," but unique art forms that are ends unto themselves. Once you have made these necessary distinctions, the next thing you must decide is whether or not *you* are convinced that film study should hold an important place in the English curriculum. To be convinced, you must believe that a film can offer insights into the human experience,

---

[1] Clark McKowen and William Sparke, *It's Only a Movie* (Englewood Cliffs, N.J.: Prentice-Hall, Inc., 1972), p. 48.

that a film can offer a stimulus for critical thinking, writing, and speaking, that a film can help one to develop aesthetic awareness, and that a film can be a potent and significant means of communication that warrants careful scrutiny. Next, to fully appreciate the film as an important and serious art form, *you* must become a "reader" of films, just as you are a reader of literature. Experiencing films of all kinds is essential in order for you to gain insights into how films do what they alone can do and to provide you means of interpreting the language films use to express their messages. In other words, to be visually literate, you have to undergo a learning process that has little to do with learning facts. It is a process that necessitates a creative response, an aesthetic awareness, and an emotional as well as an intellectual involvement.

Although you yourself may be convinced that film study is a worthwhile endeavor, it may be difficult to convince administrators. Among their concerns will be the expense, the justification, and the scheduling problems. You will have little control over the financial aspect of the problem; however, the problem is not unsolvable. Many district and county media centers are purchasing more and more of the short films useful in a film study course, which your school may use free of charge. The larger state universities have media centers that can furnish such films for relatively low rental fees. Furthermore, student lab fees can help defray the costs, since film study courses are usually electives and students can be charged. It is possible to rent as many as twenty short films for $100.00. These films wouldn't be enough for a full semester's course, but they would make a significant start for a six- or nine-week unit.

The justification problem is one that you alone can alleviate to a great degree if you are willing to approach it; however, you will not convince anyone, especially administrators, if you don't have something concrete to support your claims. A simple explanation that film is relevant is not enough. The response might be that kids get enough of film on television and at theaters, and most of what they "get" is trash. The "trash" complaint has been leveled against English teachers for a long time in their attempts to bring contemporary and adolescent literature into the classroom, but contemporary and adolescent literature *are* there because the teachers have rebutted that kids need to have some critical insights into literature and some means of determining what's "good" and what's "bad." Students can only gain these insights if you can get them to *read*. To get students to read often requires that you use materials that are relevant to them, leading them into open discussion that, in turn, can lead to other "significant" books. In other words, just because students can read print, they can't necessarily read literature critically. Similarly, just because students have spent hundreds of hours in front of a television set or in a theater, they don't necessarily know how to "read" films critically. One of our aims as English teachers is to help students develop aesthetic awareness in literature. Film is a vital part of this literature. Stating this, however, still may not be enough. You must be able to demonstrate how you would conduct a film study course, or show how it has been done in other schools. The Willowbrook Cinema Study Project is a good example.

The Willowbrook Project was a two-semester, junior-senior elective course in the study, analysis, and appreciation of the film as an art form. The course included the showing of a variety of feature, short, and documentary films, grouped into ten units. The first unit was a cross-media study of film and literature for the purpose of analyzing the similarities and differences in technique and idea that a film-maker employs when he adapts a short story or novel. The films and readings used included *An Occurrence at Owl Creek Bridge*; *Silent Snow, Secret Snow*; and *The Informer*. In Unit Two, the students were trained to become aware of the form, technique, and tools of film language used to reveal mood, idea, and content so that they could acquire some criteria to use in evaluating film. Other units were developed around topics (comedy, war, the western), while still others were presented to illustrate other concerns and techniques of film (documentaries, the director, and the actor). The final unit was a presentation of student projects in the form of a film festival. Throughout the course, students did more than just "watch flicks." They were involved in writing critical reviews, scripts, scenarios, and research reports. They took part in large and small discussion groups and presented reports and lectures on specialized topics. They were required to do a great deal of reading in supplementary books and periodicals. In other words, they were involved in all kinds of activities usually found in an English classroom—and more—but the basic content was film.[2]

The third problem, that of scheduling, should be no problem at all with the advent of flexible scheduling. Even if your school is not on flexible scheduling and you are restricted to 50- or 55-minute periods, you can show feature films in two or more installments and most short films once, sometimes twice, in a single class period.

KINDS OF FILMS

There are various kinds of films available for study, just as there are various kinds of literature. Basically, there are two kinds that can be used as the basis for a film study course. The first kind is the *feature film*. These films are usually an hour or more in length and are comparable to novels or plays. Many of them are considered classics in their own right; e.g., *Citizen Kane, Battleship Potemkin*, and *La Strada*. These and hundreds of others are available in 16 mm from many film distributors. Rental fees vary, but they usually range from $50.00 to $300.00. The average cost is around $100.00.

The second type of film is the *short film*. These films run from three to forty-five minutes in length. They range in type from short documentaries to

---

[2] The complete curriculum is available from Geo. A. Pflaum, Publisher, in the booklet *Willowbrook Cinema Study Project*, by Ralph J. Amelio *et al*. The booklet also contains an excellent annotated bibliography of film books, periodicals, and films that were viewed in preparation for the course.

visual poems, short stories, humor, satire, fantasy—the complete spectrum of film art. An entire film study course could be based on these short films because of the variety of types available. Many of these films, too, are considered classics; e.g., *The Chairy Tale*, *Dream of the Wild Horses*, *Neighbors*, *Night and Fog*, and *An Occurrence at Owl Creek Bridge*. These are available in 16 mm from film distributors, universities, and local media centers. (Before you place any orders, check with your librarian for the local listings. You will find that the media center is a new and growing entity in both large and small communities. They may have more materials available than you think they do.) Rental fees range from $3.00 to $30.00, depending primarily on the length of the film.

Both feature and short films can be used in many ways in the English classroom. As in the Willowbrook Project, film alone can be the content of a year's course, or film courses can be designed for a semester, quarter, quinmester, or even six-week period. The full-fledged film course usually focuses on themes, topics, directors, or actors, in much the same way as literature courses. Or, films can be used as part of a literature course in which they are considered as another artist's statement about a theme, and thus they can be compared with poems, short stories, and novels. Films that are adaptations of other genres can also be studied to analyze how the film-maker's version is different and why. Films about writers can add depth to one's understanding about those writers and their works. Films that have no dialogue, such as *Glass* or *Leaf*, can be used to stimulate student writing. For more suggestions about films and how to use them, see especially: *Themes: Short Films for Discussion, Exploring the Film*, and *Film: The Creative Eye*, all published by Geo. A. Pflaum; *Film Study and the English Teacher*, by David Sohn (Indiana University Audio-Visual Center); *The Motion Picture and the Teaching of English*, by Sheridan *et al.* (Appleton-Century-Crofts); *Film and Literature: Contrasts in Media*, by Fred H. Marcus (Chandler Publishing Company); *The Uses of Film in the Teaching of English*, Curriculum Series No. 8 (The Ontario Institute for Studies in Education); *It's Only a Movie*, by McKowen and Sparke (Prentice-Hall, Inc.); and the monthly periodical *Media & Methods*.

HOW DO YOU MAKE MOTION PICTURES?

Once students become interested in films, they will probably want to make some themselves. Perhaps the best way to learn about film art is to dabble in it. If your students have worked with speech essays and slide/tape presentations, they should have become familiar with script writing and its importance, with editing, with the necessity of planning pictures, and with the basic skills of putting it all together. Working with motion pictures, however, is not the same as working with still photography. We recommend that you move through a series of types of films with them, going from simple films to complex ones, so that your students will be better able to understand and appreciate the differences between still photography and motion picture photography.

There will be three limitations under which students will have to learn to work: time, money, and equipment. The time element can be controlled to a certain extent if they don't attempt to make elaborate productions and if they plan their work carefully. Money is always a limiting factor, especially when working with media, because film and equipment are expensive. Many teachers collect a dollar per student as a lab fee, but you can't do much with thirty or thirty-five dollars, so you must stress to them that they have to be careful with their budget—*make every foot of film count.* Equipment may seem to be the major limitation. However, all you need is one Super 8-mm camera and one projector. The school may have these items. If not, one of your students may. Super 8-mm cameras are relatively inexpensive, so you might be able to get the school to purchase one.

When working under these limitations, it should be made clear to the students that not everyone can be the cameraman or the star of the show. In putting together a movie, many people are needed: set designers and builders, make-up artists, costumers, prop gatherers, script writers, film editors, directors, and so forth. Each student will have a job, and each job, whatever its nature, is vital if they are going to make a successful movie. The media projects discussed in the previous chapter involved individuals and small groups; film-making can be a class project in which everyone can realize his sense of worth by making his own contribution.

You can begin with a simple project that doesn't cost anything. This is *film painting* or *film scratching.* Though there aren't any basic "English skills" to be stressed, film painting will get the students used to thinking in terms of "motion picture time." More importantly, it's fun and it gives the teacher an easy way to introduce film-making.

1. *Basic Equipment for Film Painting*
   a) Old or exposed 16-mm film
   b) Paints, inks, brushes, pens, felt-tip markers, stylus

You can get exposed 16-mm film from local television stations free of charge. They throw away reels of film weekly. We have found *water*-based paint used in painting model airplanes to be a good medium because it is inexpensive, comes in a variety of colors, and dries quickly. Another good medium is the markers used on transparencies. Felt-tip pens are not good because the colors are not vibrant and project poorly.

2. *Basic Techniques*
   a) Take an old 16-mm film and wash off the emulsion by placing it in undiluted bleach. This will leave the film clear. Be sure to wear rubber gloves and an apron, in order to protect your hands and clothing.

b) Line up a row of tables so as to make a long, continuous work surface, and fasten the filmstrip to the tables with masking tape. Everyone gets a certain number of feet of film to paint on. Or, cut off so many feet of film for each student. If you cut the film, it is easier to clean and paint it. Once everyone has painted his strip, you simply splice the whole film back together using 16-mm splice tapes. Paint along the strip with solid colors, stripes, diagonal strokes, or whatever. Some students may want to "hold" an image on the screen by repeating the image across several frames. This is how the concept of "film time" can be introduced. Since 16-mm film goes through the projector at a rate of twenty-four frames per second, they will have to repeat the image twenty-four times in order to hold it on the screen for one second. Count the sprocket holes to give you some indication of how long a particular image will show on the screen.

c) To scratch an image on a film, paint the strip a solid color and use a stylus, which can be any sharp-pointed instrument, such as a hatpin or a compass point. To add more color, fill in the scratched design with felt-tip markers. You can also get unusual effects by pricking holes through the film with the stylus.

d) Select a lively piece of music as your "sound track" (play a record or tape), and project the film. An example of a professionally made film painting is "Begone Dull Care," produced by the Canadian Film Board.

Another type of film project can be *kinestasis*. *American Time Capsule* is probably the best-known example of this technique. It was first shown on the Smothers Brothers Television Show and is used in many schools throughout the country. Kinestasis is basically filming still pictures on motion picture film. If the students have done any slide/tape presentations, this will be an easy, natural next step.

1. *Basic Equipment for Kinestasis*
   a) Super 8-mm camera with single frame release
   b) Tape recorder
   c) Super 8-mm projector
   d) Tripod
   e) Music stand or easel
   f) Two photo floodlights
2. *Basic Techniques*
   a) *Plan*—pick a subject that can be developed with many paintings or photographs from books, magazines, and other sources. Pick your photographs, deciding which ones you want to emphasize or possibly repeat. Arrange the pictures in the order you want to shoot them.
   b) Pick a sound track that has a distinct musical beat. Attempt to time the beats. Make a shooting script matching the number of beats with the picture or pictures to be shown with them. This is where knowledge of "film time" is of utmost importance. A silent 8-mm film runs through the projector at eighteen frames per second. In kinestasis, you will not want an image on the screen for less than three frames (one-sixth of a second).

Most of the images you use will probably run from ten to twelve frames. The length of time you will want each image to appear depends on the sound track you select and what you want to emphasize. You are not only working with sound rhythm but also with visual rhythm. You will have to listen to the sound track many times, decide what to do with your images, and write your shooting script accordingly. If you want an image to appear for half a second, simply push the single-frame release button nine times. If your camera doesn't have a single-frame release, you will have to experiment with the camera trigger to determine how light or long a touch you should apply. If matters don't work out exactly right using this technique, you can then edit your film, cutting out the excess number of frames.

c) *Shoot the film*—set the camera on a tripod in front of the easel, with the lights aimed on the pictures so as not to create a glare. Shoot the pictures in sequence for the length of time marked on your script

d) *Synchronize the sound*—after your developed film returns, project it along with your tape. Note any editing that needs to be done. Do the editing. You should now have an exciting film if you have been careful with timing.[3]

One way this technique was used by a class of high school seniors was to make a "kinestasis yearbook." Using their annual publication as the source, and inserting additional pictures that students had taken throughout the year, they prepared a movie about their senior class and its last year in high school. Their production was so well done and so fascinating that it was shown several times to the entire student body (at its request), to the PTA, and to other high schools in the area. The school has decided to make this sort of production an annual project.

Another introductory project can be a film about a *topic*. In preparing to do such a film, students will be learning the techniques of writing a film treatment and a shooting script for a motion picture. In preparing these materials, the composition processes again come into focus. The particle-wave-field theory, mentioned in the composition section of the book as a means of determining various aspects of the subject, can be used effectively here. This method of prewriting is an extension of the field theory used in physics. In a magnetic field (equivalent to the context in writing), there are numerous particles of metal filings (words or subjects within a context). If a magnet is passed over the field, the particles cling together in patterns or waves (just as in writing, some ideas, images, or aspects of the topics "cling" together). In using this approach as a means of prewriting, a series of questions can be formulated about the subject (the particle), what it is, and what it isn't within a particular context (the field).

---

[3] For more information on how to make sophisticated kinestasis films, see Charles Braverman's article "How to Make Your Own Complete Color Sound Movie About Anything for Less Than $50.00," *Media and Methods* (Nov. 1969).

For example, if a teacher assigns students to write a theme or to make a film about the topic "shoes," most students will find it difficult to write or film anything interesting. "Shoes" seems like such a limited topic. However, by using the particle-wave-field technique of questioning, they will "discover" a great deal of information about shoes. In the particle component, the basic question is, "What is a shoe *not* in the context of clothing?" A shoe is not a hat, for it is worn on a different part of the body and serves a different purpose. Even though worn on the foot, a shoe is not a sock, and so forth. In the wave component, the basic question is, "How can you change a shoe, what variations can you have, and still have a shoe?" What are the styles of shoes? What are the various purposes of shoes? Do different culture groups wear different kinds of foot apparel? Why are they different? Do different occupations require special shoes? What are some of the varieties? Do different sports require different kinds of shoes? Why? What are they? What are the various materials that are used in making shoes? The questions in this component are numerous, and any one of them can become the "subject" of a theme or a film. The final component, the field, asks, "How do shoes fit into the matrix of clothing?"

Suppose, then, that the topic of a film project is going to be shoes and that the purpose of the film is to show how shoes are related to personality. It is decided that nothing will be filmed except feet, in footwear from sandals to boots, from bare feet to work shoes. Each shot will tell a story. We will ask the audience to try to imagine what the owner looks like by the shoe he or she wears, what you can tell about a culture group by their footwear, from Christ's sandals to a knight's armoured foot covering. Not only can you tell the personality or the culture of a shoe-wearer, but you can tell what kind of work he does or what kind of sports he plays. After we have looked at different situations, we will flash back to the first shoe, pan up to the person wearing them, and identify what he looked like, then cut to a quick cover to see what he was doing and end the film with a pretty young girl's foot writing "The End" in wet sand. A pair of men's boots appears on the scene and straddles the foot and the words.

The previous paragraph is a rough overview of the film. From this, a sequence of scenes can be listed—much like an outline. This is the process of writing a "film treatment":

8-mm COLOR FILM
10 minutes
   1. OPEN . . . CREDITS AND LEGEND . . .
   2. SPORTS . . . FROM SKYJUMP TO GOLF
   3. INDOOR . . . FROM BEDROOM SLIPPERS TO JAPANESE HOUSE SHOES
   4. WORK . . . FROM CONSTRUCTION TO COWBOY
   5. CRIMINAL . . . FROM SNEAKERS TO PRISON SHOES
   6. GOVERNMENT . . . FROM FIREBOOTS TO SAILORS

7. ENTERTAINMENT ... FROM GO-GO BOOTS TO CLOWN'S SHOES
8. SCHOOL TYPE ... FROM SANDALS TO BOOTS
9. FASHION ... FROM MODELS TO PLAYBOYS
10. PLAY ... FROM CLIMBING TREES TO BEACH (BARE FEET)
11. CLOSE

From this first sketch, each scene will be outlined in more detail. For example:

SCENE 1

OPEN ... WE WILL OPEN ON A PHOTO OF ARMSTRONG'S FOOT AS IT REACHES FOR THE MOON ... SLOWLY PULL OUT AS WE ROLL OUR LEGEND ...
SUPER LEGEND OVER PHOTO ...
"SHOES AND PERSONALITIES ARE USUALLY IN HARMONY. FOR THOUSANDS OF YEARS MAN HAS WORN SHOES FOR MORE THAN PROTECTION. IF YOU'RE GOING TO WALK ON THE MOON, YOU CAN'T AFFORD TO WORRY ABOUT STYLE ... BUT FEW MEN HAVE HAD THAT WORRY.... OUR FILM DEALS IN THE IDENTITY OF PEOPLE BY THE THINGS THEY PUT ON THEIR FEET. SEE IF YOU CAN TELL WHAT THE CHARACTERS IN THE FILM LOOK LIKE ... WHAT THEY ARE DOING ... AND WHERE THEY ARE BY THEIR FOOTWEAR.... YOU'LL SEE PEOPLE FROM SPORTSMEN TO CRIMINALS ... AND FROM COWBOYS TO PLAYBOYS.... AS THE OLD SAYING GOES, "IF THE SHOE FITS, WEAR IT," AND THAT'S WHAT THEY'RE DOING...."
CUT TO SHOT OF FEET WALKING TOWARD WATER WITH FLIPPERS ON ...

SCENE 2

SPORTS SHOES (OUTLINE)
THIS SCENE WILL COVER THE AREA OF SPORTSWEAR.... WE WILL NOT ONLY SHOW THE MANY DIFFERENT TYPES OF FOOT-WEAR USED IN SPORTS, BUT WE WILL ATTEMPT TO TIE IN A PERSON-ALITY OR CHARACTER TYPE THAT MIGHT BE FOUND WEARING A SPECIFIC SHOE SUCH AS A BOXER WITH A BROKEN NOSE ... OR A FISHERMAN WITH A HAT OF LURES.... ON OCCASION, WE WILL THROW IN A RINGER, SOMETHING COMPLETELY IN-CONGRUOUS SUCH AS ARMY BOOTS JOGGING IN THE SAND.... WE DISCOVER THEY ARE BEING WORN BY A MATRONLY LADY IN AN OLD-FASHIONED BATHING SUIT. (*This helps pace the film, but should be used very sparingly.*) WE WILL TIE OUR LAST SPORTS SHOE INTO THE NEXT SCENE ON INDOOR SHOES TO MAKE A SMOOTH TRANSITION....

After completing the more detailed outline, the shooting script will be written. The shooting script is very detailed in that it describes the sequence of shots, the camera angle and/or action, and the action of the people in the scenes. For example, the sports shoes scene just outlined would employ the following sequence of shots with some camera notes:

SCENE 2 (SEQUENCE OF SHOTS)

1. FEET IN FLIPPERS . . . SKIN DIVER IN COMPLETE WET SUIT
2. HUNTERS' BOOTS . . . COVER OF HUNTER SHOOTING AT BIRDS
3. BOOTS ON BIKE . . . BOY AND GIRL ON A BIG CHOPPER . . . THEY PULL OFF
4. BASKETBALL SHOES . . . FEET RUN BACK AND FORTH THROUGH THE FRAME . . . THEY STOP IN FRONT OF THE CAMERA . . . CAMERA PANS UP VERY SLOWLY TO TALL PLAYER FROM A LOW ANGLE . . .
5. OLD JUMP BOOTS . . . OLD LADY JOGGING ON BEACH
6. ICE SKATE BOOTS . . . YOUNG GIRL ON SKATES
7. BASEBALL SHOES . . . PRO PLAYER IN ACTION
8. GOLF SHOES . . . MIDDLE-AGED MAN WITH FEET ON OUTDOOR TABLE, DRINK IN HAND . . .
9. FOOTBALL SHOES . . . PAN UP TO SHOW QUARTERBACK WIPING HANDS ON TOWEL . . . TOWEL IS TUCKED INTO CENTER'S WAIST IN BACK . . . ZOOM INTO HANDS AS THEY USE TOWEL . . . CUT TO BEGINNING OF NEXT SCENE . . .
   (START SCENE THREE WITH GIRL DRYING FEET WITH TOWEL AND SLIPPING FEET INTO SHOWER SHOES.)[4]

In order to make the film, you should be familiar with the following basic techniques:

1. *Basic Equipment in Film-Making*
   a) 8-mm camera
   b) Photoflood lights
   c) 8-mm projector
   d) 8-mm editor with viewer

2. *Basic Techniques*
   a) *Shooting techniques*—a motion picture consists of numerous indicated scenes. Good continuity in sequence employs a series of related scenes placed in a logical manner. A sequence entails three basics: a long shot, a medium shot, and a close-up shot. LS (used in script writing for "long shot") establishes the area around the subject. MS ("bridge" or "medium shot") is a transition from LS to CU. A CU ("close-up") is the most important one—it examines closely for detail. The shock of moving directly from an LS to a CU is too great for the audience. Eyes can recover quickly, but the camera cannot. An audience cannot orient itself outside the boundaries of the screen, so an MS is employed.

---

[4] Developed by Robert E. Gilbert, St. Petersburg, Fla.

You must *always keep the audience in mind* when filming. An extreme long shot (ELS) gives the overall setting for a motion picture story and usually introduces the story. A close-up (CU) is more dramatic and focuses on details. Camera angles play a vital role in using LS, MS, or CU.

b) *Uses of angles*—camera angles act as pointers to direct the audience's attention to the most important parts of the picture. Angles can make movement seem slower or faster than it actually is, or they can make objects seem immense or insignificant. They help to supply the psychological effect. There are five basic camera angles:

1. *Eye Level*—approximates normal angle of vision.
2. *High Angle*—gives comprehensive view of subject. Reduces apparent height and emphasizes pattern and compositional lines.
3. *Low Angle*—increases apparent height, adds to importance of subject, suggests movement, speed, and action.
4. $\frac{3}{4}$ *Front Angle*—gives good depth, adds interest.
5. *Flat Angle*—is usually uninteresting, gives only one side of subject and lacks depth.

Good angle shots make the audience unaware of them. The camera's duty is to transmit ideas to the audience, while never calling attention to itself. Camera angles change with each scene. Have students pay attention to the use of angles and the use of LSs, MSs, and CUs while watching television. Have them note what the camera emphasizes and how.

c) *Development of story*—the techniques helpful in presenting an interesting story are as follows:

1. Good continuity must be developed.
2. Emphasis on certain parts is required. This is accomplished by the use of CU, unusual angles, and a compositional arrangement that features a definite center of interest.
3. The tempo of the picture is established and controlled by the length of the scene and the action rate of the subject. The scene should appear on the screen long enough to orient the audience.
4. The complete *treatment* and *script* should be prepared before starting a motion picture, and they should include:
   a. Purpose to be achieved
   b. Type of audience for which motion picture is intended
   c. Material to be included
   d. Method of presentation
   e. Approval.

In order to achieve continuity in filming, a complete shot breakdown should be worked out from the picture sequences. This is called the "shooting script." It includes:

   a. Scene number
   b. Type of shot

c. Specific effects and transitions
d. Description of material to be presented
e. List of props
f. Data pertinent to film.

Most stories are broken into three components: 1) introduction—locale—characters and action established; 2) build-up—plot develops—characters or subject in relationship; 3) climax—questions or situations resolved.

It is advantageous and desirable to shoot the film in the sequence intended as the final version, for it facilitates the planning of shots and camera angles and makes it easier for the editor to organize and follow the continuity. However, a lot of time can be lost moving the camera from scene to scene and making the actors change costumes, among other things. The other way to shoot films is "out of sequence," by grouping shots according to various locations. It is then the editor's job to put the shots in the right sequence according to the script. Again, this is why a complete and specific script that lists the exact sequence of scenes is so very important.

To maintain good continuity, action from one scene to another must be smooth and uninterrupted. This is accomplished by *overlap*. Overlap is reshooting of action that has taken place on the tail end of the previous scene. Despite the fact that the angle and image size have changed the flow of action, it will be smooth and continuous when the film is cut and edited.

d) *Editing motion picture film*—there are two kinds of editing: "in camera" and "bench" editing. You edit "in camera" by following the shooting script precisely and by shooting each sequence in the order as written. Even when you do this carefully, you may find that you want to cut out certain segments of the film after it has been developed. Then you must "bench" edit.

You also "bench" edit when you have shot the film out of sequence and want to rearrange the order of scenes according to the script. You need an 8-mm editor, which usually includes a splicer and a viewer. There are certain rules that should be closely followed in editing:

1. Avoid long scenes from one camera angle only. Use shots from different angles. Follow the LS, MS, and CU techniques.
2. Avoid abrupt angle changes. Don't let the audience feel they are jumping from one place to another.
3. Avoid the use of two or more short scenes together. They require a second or two for comprehension. When placed together, they may confuse the audience.
4. Scene cuts should be smooth and natural and should not call attention to themselves. The editor sets the tempo of the film by controlling the scene lengths. Short scenes increase the tempo; long scenes slow it down.
5. Match the action as to the center of interest and continuity.

6. Retain "screen direction"; that is, the direction of movement on the screen as seen by the audience. This is referred to as "screen right," "left," "up," and "down"—as in stage directions. To change screen direction, first prepare the audience for the change, then 1) have the subject change direction, or 2) gradually work around the subject, or 3) divert the audience. The first method is the most effective, since the audience sees the change on the screen. In the third method, the audience seldom remembers more than one scene back, so you can divert their attention for more than one scene—but don't overdo this.

Though students may prefer a dramatization of some sort, it can be seen that films about topics can be interesting and that they require planning, writing, and imagination. Yet they are simple enough to be completed successfully even when working under the limitations of time, money, and equipment. Then, too, by beginning with this type of film, students learn how to prepare film treatments and shoot scripts, and learn the various functions of the camera. With this experience as a background, you can at last give them the opportunity to make a dramatic motion picture.

From our own experience, we have found that students have the most success and fun when dealing with stereotyped plots and characters. Charles W. Curran, in his book *Screen Writing and Production Techniques* (Hastings House, 1958), includes a section on thirty-six basic plots and the principal elements employed in developing them. He also includes a formula for story-writing by listing all of the different kinds of characters whose backgrounds would make entertaining stories because of their social statuses or occupations, physical characteristics, wealth, education or lack of it, and so forth. Next, he lists interesting places in which a story might take place. Then, by using the lists of the thirty-six basic plots, characters, and locales, along with the suggestions for developing the plot, anyone could write an interesting story or make an interesting film, even though it be a stereotype. There is a treasure house of ideas in Curran's book that could keep young film-makers busy for years.

Thus, in making a movie and participating in other media projects, students will be utilizing the skills of writing, speaking, and listening, and they will be practicing creative dramatics by trying to apply all these skills at once in a very demanding, yet exciting, communication experience.

Part VI

Where Is the Teacher in All of This?

Chapter 13

Style: Strategy in Classroom Leadership

GETTING TO WHO YOU ARE

In this chapter we want to confront more fully and directly the question of how you function in a classroom with live adolescents. It involves such issues as who you are, how you "come on" as a teacher, and what choices you make in arranging your content. Obviously, the ways in which teachers communicate with adolescents about English are woven throughout the fabric of this book. We have already cited a large number of situations in which your approach to a given issue or type of material is a vital factor. Moreover, we have voiced our contention that the question of "how" could only be asked in light of the answers to "what," "to whom," and "why." In this section, however, we will face directly and intimately the factors involved in who the teacher is in the classroom and what strategies he may choose to employ in bringing English to people.

An important dichotomy to note at the outset is that of *style* and *method*. We will again define style as the way the teacher presents himself as a human being to other human beings—in this case, his students—and develops ways to communicate with them effectively. The term "persona," utilized in the Composition section, applies here. Style has to do with the purposeful mask a teacher wears in a particular teaching-learning situation. It has to do with the way he projects himself to others in order to direct them, their attention, and their activity. Generally, teaching style can relate to *any* content area. It involves ways of maneuvering people into circumstances wherein learning is largely unencumbered and relatively enjoyable.

Method, on the other hand, refers to the ways in which a particular content, such as English, can be manipulated in order to make it clear, interesting, and coherent to students as well as relevant to their perceptions of reality. It has to do with the formulation of objectives for the teaching of a given aspect or component of the content and the resultant patterns of organization devised to fulfill those objectives. It also has to do with the ways in which teachers evaluate the relative impact that their instruction has made on the students once that instruction has been completed.

STYLE IN ENGLISH CLASSROOMS

We need to voice one major caution in our consideration of teaching style. In a very real sense, this style is an extension of the personality of the individual doing the teaching, e.g., *you*. We should not refer to the teacher here; we probably should adopt the Emersonian concept of non-teaching as found in *The American Scholar*. That is to say, it is impossible (at least for us) to divorce an individual's personality from the way he teaches. Thus, much of teaching style cannot be learned, at least not through conventional, law-of-effect means. One cannot deliberately choose to become someone he really isn't in order to create a more electric learning atmosphere. Because of this, the suggestion made by many experienced teacher-supervisors to students and inexperienced teachers that they not imitate another teacher, is probably sound advice. This reservation also has relevance to the discussion to come: suggestions made about style should be perceived as tentative ones, which will apply in varying degrees to different people. Remember: there are not many teachers who ever become dynamic and perceptive just by *reading a book*. For the most part, the roles of book readers, like the roles of students, are *personal* ones. Most of your initial choices and refinements in teaching style will necessarily be made as your teaching is going on and immediately afterward, when some *reflecting* can be done. Hence, the suggestions we offer are abstract ones, necessarily apart from flesh-and-blood classroom situations, and should not be construed as hidebound mandates without which teaching success is impossible. On the other hand, we have been involved in discussions with enough high school students and prospective teachers who said they remembered English (for better or worse) *because of the teacher*, to lead us to consider, at least tentatively, your actual role as a teacher and how you can improve it. In other words, use what seems appropriate for you as a person, and *adapt* your technique as frequently as necessary for your own situation.

YOU IN THE CLASSROOM

Let's start with a hypothetical classroom situation. It's Friday, last period, in mid-October, in a senior high classroom. The "Homecoming" football game is tonight. You are in the midst of some instruction involving the reading of a literary work, instruction that began several days ago. The bell rings. The kids are loud and unruly. What to do?

First of all, you might well consider the atmosphere in which your instruction is being carried on. Students at any age don't live in a vacuum but are involved in a variety of ongoing experiences (most of them nonacademic) that preoccupy them constantly. You can't overcome this condition; you can only deal with it and not allow initial noise and confusion, especially when generated by upcoming events, to frustrate you in terms of *your* goals. First of all, consider your introduction. It is probably better *not* to jump immediately into the content or learning activity you have planned. Better to wait a few moments to see if the noise will subside. Then, when you finally project yourself, do so in as strong a voice (without shouting) as you can muster. Be simple and direct at the outset. Repeat yourself. Look at the students. Gauge their responses before going on.

Another important factor in these opening moments is *what* you talk about. The beginning of a classroom session generally involves an administrative phase. This may involve taking attendance, passing out materials, assigning pages to be read, setting up equipment, or organizing for group work; in any case, the administrative moves really provide two vital functions: they aid in establishing the atmosphere you need for carrying out your objectives of the day, and they help to focus attention on *you*, since you are going to be the one to put things in motion. Most important, there isn't any *English* being taught during this period. The students are being maneuvered into a position in which they will be ready to receive instruction. One of our instructor-friends used to begin his seventh-grade classes each day by walking into the room brandishing a chalkboard eraser. He would then wait a few moments, then toss it at someone in the class (each day a different student). After a few days, the students began to recognize when the class was to begin: when someone got hit with the eraser. Although obviously a gimmick, it did provide a means of focusing attention on when the day's action was to begin. By following this course of action, you can substantially reduce the incidence of students' interrupting you with questions of a "what are we supposed to do" nature once your teaching has begun.

Let's assume that now you have set up the atmosphere for class involvement. What next? In most cases, it's a good idea to remind the group of where they are, in this instruction, at the moment; i.e., where they *were* at the end of the previous session. It must be remembered that things have happened to your students since you last met with them. They have *lived* during this interim, and they may well have allowed these interpolated experiences to reduce or crowd out their concern with what they were doing in "good old English" last time, even though you have been thinking about it a great deal. Thus a short, pointed review is often quite helpful. It gets the students more attentive to what's going to happen next, and also provides a context that they may have forgotten or didn't previously understand.

You begin the class, and move through a particular phase of your teaching plan. The students are involved in listening to you, when a latecomer arrives. This creates some disturbance and causes the class to be diverted from the concern at hand. What do you do?

In general, it is wise to react to disturbances. Seldom are schools situated in environments so isolated that they are noise-free. Several schools in large cities, for instance, are situated on the approaches to large airports. While the big jets are going over, nothing much can be communicated—and this happens frequently when the traffic is heavy. All teachers need to be ready to reconcile disturbances with classroom activities. It is best to stop what is going on, wait for the disturbance to subside, remind the group where they were before the disturbance took place, and then go on. This applies to student speakers and to media presentations, as well as to you.

The case of the latecomer is a special one. As well as being an interrupter, he is a member of the class, ostensibly part of the activity of the day. Thus, in order to accommodate the situation *and* him, it is desirable to *stop* the activity upon his entrance, get him seated, orient him as to what is going on, answer his questions if any, and *then* proceed with the instruction. If latecomers and other interruptions aren't noticed, classroom experiences can become confused. The attention of students isn't always easy to maintain. In many cases they need reminding of the task at hand once it has been interrupted. The late-comer provides a matter of special concern because if he isn't properly oriented, he may well decide to "tune out" the activity, a decision that often generates *control* problems.

The class continues. You are giving a reasonably large amount of instruction on a given topic, when it becomes evident that student attentiveness is decreasing. There is restlessness, bored expressions can be noted, and stealthy whispering sessions begin to crop up. Again, what do you do?

One vital role in organizing for classroom instruction, especially in light of a situation such as the last period before "Homecoming," is to build in a *variety* of activities throughout the unit, the week, and the day. There is no "golden" number of minutes or portions of periods to spend in a particular endeavor: that depends on the nature of the activity. It is important, however, to consider the attention spans of the students, and these are to a large degree the products of the "to whom" discussions presented in the opening section of this book. When it seems clear that attention may well be divided in a given class period, more than one *kind* of activity should be planned if possible. For instance, once you've talked awhile, get some reaction to what you have said by asking questions. Plan to *show* things relevant to your verbal descriptions.

Interrupt reading sessions to ask pertinent questions, after which the reading can be resumed. Comment and solicit comments from students after a group presentation or an audiovisual performance. Assign short, in-class writing sessions after various stimuli have been presented. As a rule, the attention spans of teen-age students must be reckoned with as specific classroom activities are being planned. You will learn a lot about the attention spans of students in your classes as you get to know them.

In the case of students "tuning out" your one-way presentation, the assigning of *listening responsibilities* may help to sustain attention. The students should be aware of the answers to a series of questions as they *listen* to you, another person (such as a guest speaker, student participant, or panel), or a recorded statement.

1. What should I remember from this? (Main ideas, details, points of view)
2. Should I be taking notes or not?
3. If taking notes, how much and what do I need to transcribe?
4. Can and/or should I react to this *during* this particular presentation?*
5. Can and/or should I react *after* the presentation?

These questions need to be considered *early in the year*, and specific responsibilities, plus the rationale for them, should be reiterated and emphasized at appropriate intervals. In the composition section of this book we laid great stress on the need for making use of what was composed by the students, especially in terms of oral class interaction. Unless students understand clearly their responsibilities while someone else is performing, such interaction will probably be difficult to promote.

Another kind of activity that may help you through this Friday session is the assigning of individual work to be done at the students' desks. This can involve reading, writing, reviewing materials studied, analyzing visuals, meeting demands of a learning contract, finding and using reference material, viewing individual media (if laboratory or card facilities are available), and the like. The important dimension of this kind of activity, however, is the teacher's involvement. This is *not* the time to sit behind the desk and correct papers. It affords the teacher one of the few opportunities he has to venture into the classroom and work with individual students. During this period, one can help students with various problems in their writing, point out matters in reading material they might have missed, ask them about their progress in a given task, or answer questions that they are willing to ask on a one-to-one basis but not as a member of the group. A number of kinds of personal communication can be conducted during these individual work-study activities, and the teacher ought to be ready to make full use of them. This kind of tutorial activity does aid with class control. When you're out there in the class working with students, it is a sign that you want them to stay with the task and not use time for less productive pursuits. When, during your work with these individuals, you sense that

---

* Note how difficult this is to do if the listening is to be recorded through note-taking.

certain concepts or procedures are being misconstrued or overlooked by *several* students, you have this opportunity to stop the individualized silent activity and review what you had presumed was clear. In this sense, the individual work period gives you an opportunity to check up on what you haven't reinforced fully enough.

There is yet another aspect of that Friday class that you might take into consideration. Let's say that your class that day involves a read-and-discuss sequence, wherein time is allotted for the students to read one or more selections and then engage in some oral interaction on those selections. At some point in time, then, you the teacher must decide to end the reading and begin the discussion. This means a *transition* in classroom activities and as such introduces some potential problems. For instance, what if you begin the discussion before several students have finished their reading? What if others want to think about it for awhile before expressing themselves? What if others want to jot down a few notes to aid them before beginning the discussion? In other words, what if the students aren't ready to begin the discussion when you are? In all probability, confusion will reign instead of the orderly discussion you had hoped for.

Any transition in class activity, such as moving from the silent, individual act of reading to the shared, overt act of talking, needs to be conducted smoothly and forcefully. And it is *you* who must lead this transition because *you're* the one who decided on the nature and variety of activities for this particular session. Therefore, in order to ensure that all students understand each activity and have an equal opportunity to participate, you should habitually remember to *summarize* the previous activity and *introduce* the following one with care and decisiveness. Keeping your eye on the class, responding to nonverbal cues, and asking questions of individuals you suspect of being unready for what's coming up—all these acts will help to smooth the transition. The value of this type of approach for maintaining class control should be obvious. Plans for ending one activity and beginning another within a class period don't need to be elaborate or written out in lesson plans. Instead, take care to inform students of the order of classroom activities and to encourage *their* ideas and help each time a transition is made. Remember: all of you should begin on the same foot.

You must always maintain certain rules of classroom behavior. There should be specific rules about such matters as talking without recognition, interrupting others who are speaking, and working on the activity *assigned* during individual periods. You have to establish these rules with your class early in the year. For example, you must make it clear to everyone:

1. What happens when work assigned is not turned in
2. What happens when work assigned is turned in late
3. What happens when tests are missed
4. How make-up periods for missed tests are established
5. What standards of classroom atmosphere should be observed, and when.

You must occasionally remind your students of these rules throughout the year, and ask them periodically if they are aware of the contingencies of certain classroom requirements. But today, some students refuse to live by the rules, and are manifestly uninvolved in the work at hand. What do you do about this?

HANDLING "DISCIPLINE" IN YOUR CLASSROOM

There are no cookbook solutions for handling "discipline problems," and no pat answers can be suggested. Worries about "handling" unruly students, however, continue to appear high on the lists of student and inexperienced teachers, so some *tentative* suggestions should be made. A strong voice, movement away from the desk or rostrum and into the class, lots of eye contact—procedures all mentioned earlier—can be of help in many cases. Knowing all of your students as well as possible can also be of assistance. Take time to consider the "to whom" factor discussed in the opening section of this book. Know the regulations of your school and fashion a classroom code that complies with them. Early in the year, discuss with your class the rationale for rules that seemingly limit individual freedom. When classroom disturbances occur, especially in individualized work, vocal reminders of classroom conduct to the entire class might also help.

In dealing with *your* problem, however, there is a delicate balance to be achieved. Shrill reprimands seldom do the job. Although they may treat the immediate symptom and thus create silence for the moment, they seldom effect a lasting cure. The use of sarcastic or humiliating statements is also a questionable means of solving a problem. On the other hand, pretending that obvious disturbances aren't occurring seldom proves effective either. If one student transgresses and is successful in being noticed by his peers but not by the teacher, another student may try the same behavior.

Therefore, identifying classroom problems *early* in the school year, without engaging in excessive anger or vindictiveness, is probably the ideal "middle ground." One worthwhile approach, at least with first offenders, is to ask them *quietly* to see you after class. At that time, a discussion of *their* perception of the class situation, especially in terms of *their* involvement, may bring about some mutual understanding. What do they expect from the course? What, in their opinion, are the ways in which they can attain their course objectives successfully? What would *their* reaction be to classroom happenings were they in the teacher's place? The object of such a conversation is neither to intimidate nor to "save" the student in question. It is to clarify the situation for him, especially with regard to the teacher's stance. Then the decision as to what direction to take is *his*, and the consequences are *his* as well. Reasonable appraisal of student conduct, with alternatives clearly and unequivocally stated, may reach many recalcitrant students. Some youngsters may be indifferent or hostile, however, and when the teacher has exhausted all reasonable approaches, a referral of some kind may be the only way to solve the problem.

As stated previously, there are no clear-cut solutions to some discipline problems. This is especially vexing in English, where communication about the human situation is so central to our purposes. Clearly established goals, avoidance of ridicule or condescension, and face-to-face consideration of decisions and consequences—with the possiblity for recruiting outside counsel and assistance—are the best procedures we can offer at this time.

But the clock is moving, and the classroom period is coming to a close. You have not progressed quite as far as you had hoped with your plans today, but there are still a few minutes left in the period. Of course, the kids are getting a little fidgety, but maybe if you just become forceful and enthusiastic enough, you can cover the next point in your outline. Good idea?

Just as timing is important at the beginning of a class, so is it at the end if you want your instruction to be effective. At the end of a period, particularly one like that described, attention spans can be badly strained. The students know that the period is almost over—and so do you. As a general rule, very little substantive material is ever well received during the last few minutes of class, and new ideas, directions, or procedures are better left until next time. It is probably better to use the final few minutes of class for certain clearly diminished activities such as:

1. Summarizing the material covered during the class, with some emphasis on the students' contributions
2. Asking questions that will help the students and the teacher know where they've been and where they're going
3. Answering any questions the students raise about relevant and future matters (these questions should be solicited, encouraged, and answered fully)
4. Pointing ahead to what is to take place in the immediate and, if appropriate, long-range future relative to the present (this should obviously include a reminder of upcoming student responsibilities)
5. Socializing—when the other four steps are successful, there is no real need to prolong consideration of the "Great Truths" of tenth-grade English (what *you* think about the "Homecoming" scene might be of interest).

Although these proposals may not sit well with certain civic mastodons, especially those who think of accountability with a huge "A," the authors see no great need for "teaching through to the bell"—especially when no one is listening or thinking.

What we have attempted to do in our description of the Friday classroom situation, is to illustrate some *representative* issues and show how teaching style can be adapted to them. Our suggestions have been deliberately broad in scope and general in nature. Let us now deal with a more specific aspect of teaching style: promoting verbal interaction in an English class.

There are two general kinds of teaching style: *direct* and *indirect* teaching.

In the direct approach, communication is largely one way. The teacher *tells* the students what to do, he *explains* concepts, he *gives* information, he *directs* activity, he *assigns* tasks, and he *supervises* their completion. This is an economical, forthright, and in many instances, valuable approach. Sometimes, however, the teacher would do better to use an indirect approach, in which he recruits the students' interest, imagination, and background in a search for goals, concepts, and needed information. In this type of approach, the teacher and students work *together* toward identifying what is important to learn in a given area. When cooperative decisions have been reached, the teacher and students plan ways of moving toward the established goals. This approach can be related to McLuhan's concept of "cool media," in which the viewer perceives a vast array of stimuli and puts together what is relevant to him, *in any order he feels appropriate*, to meet his needs in a given situation. Thus the learner, like McLuhan's viewer, isn't *told* what to learn; he is asked to choose what he needs to know more about from the stimuli available, and is then asked to assimilate ways of learning it.

Obviously, the teacher who uses the indirect approach must be highly skilled at asking questions. We would like to make some suggestions about the proper technique for asking questions, and to describe one *system* that can give a certain direction to discussion.

Let us again visualize a classroom in a secondary school; this time, *you* choose the grade level. The students have either been provided with a stimulus by the teacher—a printed selection, a media presentation, a topic from their immediate experience—or they have chosen one themselves. Your goal is to explore the students' background, perspective, interest, and awareness of several dimensions of this stimulus. How do you go about it?

First, consider the arrangement of the room. In the first half of this century, the chairs in most rooms were bolted to the floor. Moving them was impossible. Almost all modern classrooms, however, are provided with movable chairs and/or desks. This provides you with the opportunity to arrange the seating in virtually any way you wish. The traditional arrangement of rows is not a particularly effective setup for interaction sessions. Students who are going to communicate with each other will be better off facing each other, not staring at the back of someone's head. A circular arrangement, or some variation of it, will greatly facilitate interaction. It also takes *you* out of your position at the head of the class, so that you can more easily become a contributor and less of a director. Make your judgment about appropriate seating arrangements before class begins, and arrange the room quickly once you've made your decision.

Next, you need to observe the suggestions made earlier about *beginning* the class. Be careful not to begin things too abruptly, and allow all students to be aware of what is to be discussed and, if necessary, in what manner. Beginning a discussion period in a general state of confusion can cause problems that may not be cleared up for a long time. When confusion remains or grows, control problems can easily emerge, and no discussion can progress.

The first question the teacher asks his students is a crucial one. It must be brief, simple, and leading. It can come directly from the teacher, or it can take the form of: "Well, what is the first thing we should look at in _____?", thus allowing the students to choose their own point of departure. In any case, the teacher needs to watch carefully the *diction* of his question. The word choice in any question needs to be free of *any* element that might confuse. This is where student teachers and inexperienced teachers often get into difficulty. They *presume* awareness of the meaning of abstract and technical terms on the part of their class, and use them with considerable abandon. In committing this error in a first question, a teacher can create enough doubt and confusion in his students to set a negative tone for the entire discussion. For this reason, we suggest that teachers write out their questions, especially their opening ones, analyze them for vocabulary and syntax, and revise them if necessary. *Reviewing* opening questions before voicing them may help because a teacher needs to look at his students while questioning them in order to observe their facial expressions (the *kines*) and reactions.

If you allow the class to frame the opening question, you must be prepared to begin at a starting point you would not necessarily have chosen yourself. If you don't like that possibility, you shouldn't use this approach. Once committed to it, any arm-twisting or manipulating that you do may well cause you to look insincere and dictatorial in the eyes of your students. If you are willing to start where they desire to start, however, you need to keep at least two things in mind. First, be patient. Wait for the students to frame what they want to investigate in their own words. Don't register irritation or lack of agreement. Secondly, help (tactfully) with the wording of the question, so that the oral expression of an individual contributor can be shared by all the class. Whether the opening question is provided by teacher or student, it must be broadly understood in order for any discussion to get off the ground.

The teacher should also remember that most students need *time* to think about a question, particularly one which demands that they perceive relationships among several entities or relate something to their own experience. One potential way to promote response is to pause between asking the question and calling on a student by name. It is probably wise to pause even when students' hands shoot up immediately after the question has been posed. The teacher who does not do this may seem to be impatient, and this can lead to students' inferring that he is waiting for *his* answer rather than theirs. Or, they may infer that the question, in the eyes of the teacher, is an *easy* one, one they should answer quickly. Neither inference promotes a relaxed, natural classroom atmosphere. The teacher needs to be especially aware of the needs of students who are less articulate or who grasp relationships more slowly. These youngsters need more time to consider their response. If a discussion is to be something more than a track meet or a "session you get through," it is the teacher who, largely through timing, must create this atmosphere.

In beginning the discussion, you must insist that students who contribute speak up so that all the class can hear them. "Discussions" are all too often perceived as a two-way process between teacher and student, with all others "tuned out." This is *not* what most of us want. We want ideas and information to be shared by *all*. *They can't be if people can't hear each other.*

Once again, tact is necessary. An overbearing, repetitive "I can't hear you!" or "Did you get that, class?" will both cow and antagonize many potential contributors. One possible way to combat the problem is to solicit response to a muted contribution. That is, when your tiny-voiced contributor has presented his statement, ask someone who is situated far from him, and possibly in rather histrionic tones, "Do *you* agree with that, George?" More than likely, George will respond with, "What?" to which you reply, "With what Sue said"; again, the probable comeback will be, "I didn't hear it." And then you can come back with (surprised look, arched brows), "Oh! You didn't? Sue, will you please repeat what you said? How about getting George's impression of it?"

An approach like this will hopefully put the soft speakers on notice that part of their responsibility in your course is to communicate loudly enough to be heard by all. In addition to being done tactfully, *it must be begun early in the year*. Discussions can be very helpful in the opening days of the school year, as part of the "feeling out" process by which you and the students get to know each other. This is the ideal time to begin promoting adequate vocal projection. Keep in mind that there may not be many classes in which indirect teaching and truly *open* discussion are common practices. For this reason, many students may be unfamiliar with this approach and therefore a bit hesitant to try it. Furthermore, you must be *persistent*. If you don't succeed in getting a student to speak up the first time, come back to him later. Let him know, without directly stating so, that he is expected to speak loud enough for others to hear him. Procuring oral reactions that can be heard can only be accomplished by establishing them as a habit. In order to establish classroom habits, you must start early and you must be persistent.

Another issue that must be faced is that of who will speak. Let us consider the hypothetical situation: A teacher begins a series of questions about a given topic with his opener. A student whom the teacher recognizes (from past experience) as a perpetual volunteer, raises his hand. The teacher accepts the answer and subsequently goes on to Question Two. Again, the same student's hand. Again, the acceptance of the answer, and so it goes.

Simply asking the student to quiet down is probably not the best approach; one thing the teacher really needs to think about is: what are the other thirty-plus students doing while their colleague is talking? Chances are, they're pretty well accustomed to his role as leader of the discussion. This being true, *if the teacher accepts this situation*, the others won't become too involved in the discussion and probably won't try very hard to participate. If they are not prepared to be active participants, there is a good chance they are not going to follow the discussion too avidly, and thus they will gain little from it. Instead, they may seek other means of whiling away their time in class—and that's one way classroom disruptions begin.

Securing widespread contribution should be a goal in any discussion situation. Convincing kids to speak up isn't easy, but by starting early and by being persistent, good habits can usually be established. One decision that a teacher must make is whether to solicit volunteers or to call on students by name. While we advocate a combination of both approaches, we suggest calling on students by name at the outset. When the year begins, the teacher usually doesn't know the students, and vice versa. During this time, the teacher can try hard to convince his students of two attitudes regarding discussion sessions. First, he wants everyone involved in the discussions, so he will call on as many as possible during a given lesson. Because of this, he expects people to be *prepared* to respond. Second, he will *never* react sarcastically or "put down" any sincere attempt at response.

So, early in the year, the teacher should make a mental or written note of who did contribute and who didn't, and call on the nonparticipants the next time. By doing this, he can put *all* students on notice that they are potential contributors every time discussions are held and that he welcomes whatever attempts they make.

If you are not able to recall specifically who contributed, the use of a seating chart may help. In the early discussion periods, you can keep the chart in front of you and merely make marks in the appropriate block when a student responds. Later, you can use pluses or minuses to indicate the *quality* of the response. By doing this, the teacher will have a concise summary of who contributed in a given discussion and who didn't.

There are some aspects of this problem of striving for widespread response that merit attention. First, it is not a good idea to shut out your hypervocal student completely. His enthusiasm should not be squelched, but in order for the rest of the class members to feel comfortable, it needs to be *channeled.* Once several other people have been called on by name, he should be allowed to have his say. He should continue to be recognized at intervals, and the teacher needs to be careful not to react sarcastically to the number of times he wants to speak, or to what he says when he gets the chance. When the teacher calls on other people by name *while his hand is waving*, however, it puts both him and the rest of the class on notice that he wants to hear from others as well as him—in fact, from as many as possible.

Once the discussion becomes a habitual mixture of volunteering and being called on by name (generally more students will start volunteering once contribution becomes more widespread), other matters can be dealt with. One is the reluctant contributor. There are many excellent students in American secondary schools who don't say much. They are superior and interested readers, they write good compositions, they do the assigned work, they show up well on both teacher-made and standardized tests, they like school, but they have little desire to participate in classroom oral activities. Given a specific speaking assignment, they will probably complete it and do quite well, but they don't desire to participate in less structured oral situations. Then, there are other students who, for a variety of reasons, feel that they are inadequate verbally, that they have neither sound, relevant ideas, nor the wherewithal to express those ideas that seem significant to them. These students may be interested, even intensely so, in what they read, see, or hear being discussed. But they are determined *not* to participate, at least not voluntarily. Both groups can be called, for our purposes, reluctant contributors.

We offer three suggestions concerning the handling of reluctant participants. First, let them alone if they betray much reluctance. Don't cajole or push them if they back off. Shyness or reticence is seldom changed by teacher aggressiveness. If they manifest a desire to be uninvolved in early discussions, back off gracefully and without making threats. But keep them in mind; don't give up on them yet! Second, remember to *reward* contributors consistently. We don't advocate such hokum as, "Well, Linda, your answer is totally screwed up, but you look great in that sweater." Overacceptance has distinct shortcomings, but be ever ready to congratulate the person who has made a good try, and do so in terms that are unequivocal and forthright. Conversely, be careful of consistent negativism. One of the authors once observed a bright, aggressive student teacher discussing some modern American poetry with an accelerated eleventh-grade class. She asked six questions and received six voluntary, enthusiastically voiced responses. She accorded each response some form of negativism: "Well, don't you think _____?" "Yes, but what about _____?" "Well, I don't agree with _____." Then, in each case, she proceeded to supply *her* answer to the questions she had originally raised. By the time she got to the seventh question, she received no response at all. The students had probably decided that their ideas weren't too important to that young teacher, that she was just going through the motions of asking the questions, and that she herself was going to give them the "right answer" eventually anyway. Giving rewards for responses and avoiding consistently negative reactions would seem like obviously sound approaches, but in some cases teachers, in their enthusiastic desire to "get somewhere" in a discussion, forget to reward and simply negate.

When reluctant contributors perceive consistent rewarding and do not find negation in the teacher's handling of responses, they may be more willing to contribute to future discussions. Third, we encourage the teacher to keep an eye out for erstwhile reluctant contributors and to welcome their attempts at contribution whenever it is possible to do so. This is one more instance when eye contact with the whole class can pay off. The teacher will catch the hand furtively raised and the facial expression that indicates a desire to contribute. Remembering to reward these halting, initial contributions can pay rich dividends.

Another problem a teacher faces when seeking to make his discussions classwide is the "I don't know" answer. As in any aspect of classroom interaction, what to do about "I don't know" depends largely on the relationship the teacher assumes he has established with the student in question. Here are a few suggestions about directions in which to move once that type of response has been offered.

For the most part, the "I don't know" answer occurs for two reasons: the student hasn't attempted to prepare for the discussion at hand, or, if he has, he hasn't clearly understood one or more aspects of the topic under discussion. In most cases, the teacher should pursue this response. Once the student feels that his reaction will be accepted and not pursued further, he may decide that he can get away with this sort of thing in future discussions and thus opt out. In attempting to lead the student to reflect on the *reasons* for his answer, the teacher is, among other things, putting him on notice that this kind of "cop-out" won't work. The teacher's response to "I don't know" might be, "*What* don't you know?" This means that the teacher feels his question may not be clear. He is asking the student to explore it with him in order to make it eventually comprehensible. Once the question is restructured, the student may have an easier time in making *some* sort of response.

The teacher's use of "*What* don't you know?" may also lead to a realization that the question called for too much abstract thinking or perception of too many relationships in one question. In other words, by pursuing the "I don't know" answer, the teacher may find that he needs to ask one or more specific, concrete questions before the student is capable of giving a satisfactory response. Here is an illustration:

Teacher: What kind of a person was Montresor (the narrator-protagonist in Poe's story "The Cask of Amontillado")?

Student: I don't know.

Teacher: Well, Charley, when do we first meet him in the story?

Student: Right away in the story.

Teacher: That's right. As a matter of fact, isn't Montresor the person who is speaking in the very first paragraph? Let's all turn to it.

Student: Yeah, he's talking about some guy named Fortunato.

Teacher: Does Montresor seem to like Fortunato in that paragraph, Charley?

Student: No, he sounds pretty mad at him.

Teacher: Show me the lines in the paragraph that give you that idea, Charley.

As the discussion progresses, the teacher, realizing that Charley can't generalize about the character at this point, leads him back to the initial treatment of the character in the first paragraph, thus going from the general (total text) and abstract to the specific and concrete. Note also that the teacher involves the entire class in the search for evidence (Let's all turn to it . . .") and that he insists that Charley *use the text* ("Show me the lines . . .") to verify his initial impression.

Among other things, this type of approach can be helpful in that the student can be made to see (through the teacher's guidance) that he *does* know something about the topic at hand; he just needs to reconsider what he had perceived somewhat casually the first time around. A series of inductively organized questions may show Charley quite dramatically that he does in fact "know" a good deal, and this awareness can breed confidence for future participation.

When the "I don't know" reflects a negative attitude on the student's part, a very different problem exists. We suggest that the teacher still pursue the response until he and the student know where they stand. At this point an individual, private conference with the student might well be in order. During this session, the teacher can attempt to find out what the student's attitude is toward the topic, discussion sessions, the English course, and other factors relative to his attitude. Once again the student is the person faced with the decision. Once he is made aware that his teacher considers participation in discussions a vital part of the course, he can choose his future action in that light.

We would next place much emphasis on the importance of what happens *after* a question is asked and a response readied. A crucial issue in promoting interaction lies in what a teacher *does* with a student response once it is given. If teachers are to convey to students that the main reason they introduce discussion is to share ideas, information, and perspectives openly and honestly, rather than simply to "get through" a prepared list of questions, their handling of student responses will vividly illustrate that reason. Therefore, avoid consistent use of questions to which the most logical response would be "yes" or "no." Once such a response is given and accepted, there is seldom much more to do than go on to the next question. The questioning then becomes little more than a cataloguing of items of information, mostly concrete, and mostly unrelated. It would often help if the teacher would look at his questions. Having written them out, check carefully on those that would obviously lead to a "yes" or "no" response, and consider the possibility of adding some form of a "why" to them. Without this kind of addition, such questions lead typically to rote responses and seldom to any kind of self-expression.

Once a response represents an attempt at developing an idea or attitude, the teacher should be prepared to pass it on to other members of the class. We have already discussed the need for adequate projection; without it, discussions can devolve into two-way communication between teacher and respondent with the rest of the class "tuned out." In promoting more widespread interaction, the teacher can ask other members of the class to reply to the initial response. Ask questions such as:

"Do you agree with that, Charley? Why, or why not?"
or
"Would that have been your answer, Charlene? What else might be said?"
or
"Jerry, yesterday you said _____. How does Ray's comment jibe with that?"

In using such a technique, the teacher must *listen closely* to what his students say or have said. If he is too closely committed to his lesson plan and desires simply to get to his next question, good listening will be hard to do. An effective discussion should include a good deal of class time in which the students talk to and question each other. This is generally an indication of overt interest in the topic at hand. It also indicates that the students are concerned with developing an idea or defending a position, not merely verbalizing responses to please the teacher.

During sessions in which students are communicating with each other on an issue, the teacher has a highly important but subtle role to play. He must, more than anything else, be both a *guide* and a *catalyst* in the discussion. As guide, he needs to be ready to keep the discussion on the right track, and this must be done with real finesse. "No, you're all wet," is *not* the way to deal with irrelevant or superfluous information. Try to reward the contribution in some way, but ask the class to consider the elements that pertain to the main issue. When a response is really wide of the mark, a comment such as, "That may well be true, Jake, but weren't we looking at . . . ?" may be of service. At any rate, a teacher needs to be sensitive to where a largely student-directed discussion is going and, by his own careful editing, keep it from meandering. In ideal situations, wherein the students are both able and willing to direct their own discussions, the teacher is best advised to play the role of *listener*, but when obvious irrelevancies follow one upon the other, he should be prepared to assist in reestablishing proper direction.

Another technique a teacher can use is to *rephrase, restate,* or *reflect* the comments of students to the class as a whole. In rephrasing, the question raised is: are there elements in the students' response that may not be clear or may be ambiguous to the others? Sometimes, supplying a synonym for a key term or phrase, *always by asking the respondent if this is what he means,* will help make responses more generally communicable. A restatement is a more comprehensive teacher reaction. Such leads as, "Do I get you right, Jane, when I say _____" are in essence attempts by the teacher to restructure a whole response into clearer, more organized language. Either rephrasing or restating should take the form of a question to the respondent, rather than a teacher pronouncement of what he has said. Tact is the obvious key in using such a technique.

Reflecting on what a contributor has said is another means by which the teacher can both clarify responses and give direction to the discussion. After accepting a response, rewarding the contributor, and rephrasing what has been said, the teacher might ask a member of the class, or the group as a whole, a question based on the response. For instance, he might say, "That's a good point, Max. He seems to feel that _____," or, "What arguments might he get on that?"

In handling all responses, it is a good idea to relate them to personal experiences and/or expressed attitudes of the class members wherever possible. Asking people to relate generalized notions to their own experiential background remains a consistently viable means of making abstract matters concrete. The more members of the class who are asked to make this relationship, the more potential contributors there will be.

One final point should be made about the use of responses to stimulate interaction. The question often arises, "Where does the teacher's opinion, background, or information pertain to a given discussion?" To say that it does *not* seems both naive and extreme. For the most part, the teacher is well-informed about topics of classroom discussion, and his contribution can be of real value. It is in the *timing* of his contribution that the potential problems exist. It is our conviction that the earlier the teacher makes his contribution, especially when he seems to make it in the form of a *pronouncement*, the more difficult it is both to initiate and to sustain meaningful interaction. We suggest, therefore, that the teacher refrain as best he can at the outset of the discussion, that he be very careful to classify his opinions *as such* and not as THE TRUTH, that he respond more to students' requests for his expertise rather than volunteering it, and that he identify his sources of information whenever appropriate. When the teacher interjects himself too often as "giver of the word," he can turn many erstwhile active participants into passive ones. After all, the students will conclude: why strain oneself to synthesize an idea and explain it when the teacher is going to give us the answer anyway?

SYSTEMATIC QUESTIONING

One further consideration in the use of indirect teaching would be that of establishing a *direction* for discussion through the use of a particular system of questions. Of the many systems described in professional literature, the one described by the psychologist J. P. Guilford seems to be a relatively simple one to explain and demonstrate and yet one that also specifies a clearly recognizable sequence of question types. Guilford provides a set of four categories of questions: cognitive memory, convergent, divergent, and evaluative.[1] Let us describe these categories briefly, place them in what seems to be a logical sequence, and illustrate them through an activity that might take place in a secondary English class.

Cognitive memory questions are those that ask "who," "what," "where," and "when." They seek to establish the most concrete features of the topic under consideration. They demand of the respondent that he recall facts, items, details, and elements of a given concern in *isolation*. They do not demand that he relate these matters in any fashion, nor do they call for any interpretation of knowledge. They demand only thinking, and do not relate to attitudes. They are closely related to behavioral analysis: either you *know*, or you *don't* know. They can often be used as the beginning phase of exploration of an

[1] J. P. Guilford, "The Structure of Intellect," *Psychological Bulletin* 53, No. 4 (July 1956): 267–293.

issue or concept. Seldom are they an end in themselves; they usually lead to generalized information. They are of most value as building blocks of information. Without being aware of their actual presence, the learners will be hard-pressed to find more searching kinds of questions.

For example:

1. *Where* do you find the main verb in this sentence?
2. *Who* is telling the story in *Moby Dick?*
3. *What* is the topic in the first sentence of this paragraph?
4. *When* did Achilles kill Hector?

Convergent questions typically ask "how" or "why." They ask one to put items of information together and draw a conclusion from them. The answers depend on facts or details, but the respondent must put them together and draw his own conclusion as to what they mean *taken as a whole.* Thus one of the important factors in framing the answers to such questions is how the respondent perceives order and what elements predominate for him in such an order. Clear perception of what is *there* in the topic is obviously important here but so is the individual's notion of *how* the pieces fit in.

In answering convergent questions, the respondent can follow a deductive or an inductive approach. But whenever the main part of his response appears, either at the beginning or the end, he has put pieces together to form it in order to solve the problem. For him, then, there is probably one "right" answer to such a question. Note their dependence on answers to questions of cognitive memory.

For example:

1. *How* did Macbeth get himself into his final predicament?
2. *In what ways* does standard dialect differ from nonstandard dialect?
3. *Why* did Brutus decide to aid in the assassination of Caesar?
4. *Explain* how the great vowel shift in the English language took place.

A *divergent* question asks the respondent to suppose that certain hypotheses were true. It asks such questions as: "What if _____"; "Consider what might _____"; "If such were true _____," or, "Suppose that _____". It asks the student to produce a variety of possible ideas and answers to a given question. In doing so his task is to relate what he knows and/or has concluded (through convergence) about a given topic to his own experience and to imagine what conclusions could be drawn if certain things were true. Such answers call for creative thinking, use of the imagination, uncommon ideas, or new approaches to material being stated. As such, there are no necessarily "right" or "wrong" answers in the usual sense of those terms. Since the respondent is relating his awareness of the topic to his particular perception of reality relevant to it, we must allow him to *work out* his answer and can only ask him to explain *how* he established that answer. Most important, it demands that the respondent *use* what he understands about a topic to relate to whatever notions he has about *his own* world of experience. While he obviously needs the products of cognitive memory and convergent thinking, his main task is to relate these products to what he has already established or is in the process of establishing.

For example:

1. *Suppose* that you had to teach an English-speaking child about his language. Where would you start?
2. *What if* Ole Anderson had asked Nick Adams for help in escaping the killers?
3. *If* your audience is obviously hostile to your way of thinking on this subject, what approaches might you use to win them over?
4. Consider what might have happened if Scrooge hadn't met the Ghost of Christmas Future.

The other type of question is the *evaluative* one. In essence, it asks the respondent, "so what?"; it asks that he assess or formulate an opinion, or place the topic on some scale of value. He may be asked, in regard to certain topics, to express a moral judgment. The main question here is: "Of what worth (good, relevance) is the topic as I perceive it, *or* as it is compared to an accepted scale of value?" In answering such a question, the emphasis rests heavily on the respondent's experience and resulting value system. He has either established his own criteria for judgment, or he has accepted someone else's. Again, as in divergent questioning, it is difficult to judge such responses as "right" or "wrong." The emphases lie in: 1) the clear presentation of criteria used, 2) the clarity of perception of the topic being evaluated, and 3) the coherence and clarity of the evaluative statement.

For example:

1. *Which* makes the stronger case against Southern racial injustice: Chapter Three of this Sociology Text, or Erskine Caldwell's story "Kneel to the Rising Sun"?
2. What does close textual analysis of a poem tell us that we need to know?
3. *Why* should a teacher explain the social and psychological factors involved in English usage before presenting "right" and "wrong" choices?
4. *In what ways* is Arthur Dimmesdale more to be pitied than blamed?

These examples touch on a variety of topics relevant to the English curriculum. In the following hypothetical situation, a teacher has asked his senior high school class to read a poem, "Richard Cory," by Edward Arlington Robinson, individually and silently. Then comes a series of questions he could ask about the poem questions that reflect the Guilford categories in a sequence we feel can lead the class to some meaningful insights about the poem and its significance.

Richard Cory

Whenever Richard Cory went downtown,
  We people on the pavement looked at him:
He was a gentleman from sole to crown,
  Clean-favored, and imperially slim.

And he was always quietly arrayed,
  And he was always human when he talked:
But still he fluttered pulses when he said,
  "Good morning," and he glittered when he walked.

And he was rich—yes, richer than a king—
  And admirably schooled in every grace:
In fine, we thought that he was everything
  To make us wish that we were in his place.

So on we worked, and waited for the light,
  And went without the meat, and cursed the bread;
And Richard Cory, one calm summer night,
  Went home and put a bullet through his head.[2]

QUESTIONS

1. Who is speaking in this poem? Where do you find this out?
2. Was Richard Cory rich or poor? Friendly or unfriendly? Smooth or a clod?
3. What did Richard Cory do at the end of the poem? When?
4. What kind of people are telling this story?
5. How did other people look on Richard Cory? Why?
6. Did the people telling the story know Richard very well?
7. Suppose Richard himself had spoken in the poem. What might he have said?
8. If the people telling this story asked you why Richard did what he did to himself, what would your answer be?
9. What might we conclude about rich people and happiness, having read "Richard Cory?"
10. What details might the author have added, if any, to make this a better poem?

In this sequence, we move from the concrete, factual nature of the poem to what some of these details, considered together, could mean, to an interjection of what might have been, and finally to what the *poem might* be saying about the human situation as well as how well its points have been made. This sequence is not sacrosanct. One might wish to begin deductively, using con-

---

[2] "Richard Cory" is reprinted by permission of Charles Scribner's Sons from *The Children of the Night* by Edwin Arlington Robinson.

vergent questions first—or, for that matter, evaluative ones—then using cognitive memory items to verify generalizations or judgments. He might also start with divergent questions, in order to provoke interest, and then move to other types. The point is that the organization of questions is a *purposeful* one. It allows the questions to move from one specific aspect of the topic to another in a coherent manner. It also allows the individual considering the topic to place himself in certain perspectives with respect to the topic and to make some judgments about it, in which he combines his awareness of what *is* with ways in which it relates to *him* as a participant and judge of human experience.

Before leaving this topic of teaching style, one final contrast might well be made between direct and indirect teaching, in the spirit of the "if-then" consideration discussed in the first section of this book. If a teacher is concerned with direct, concise, immediate transfer of ideas and information to his students, the *direct* approach is obviously preferable. In this approach, the teacher can provide information and then respond to questions from those class members who may have missed some aspect of the information, or who may not have fully understood it or the rationale for their involvement in it. The direct approach is also economical. Instead of striving toward generalizations, you can present *what* you want to present, and in the manner and amount of detail you choose. That way, you save time for other classroom activities. Also, as part of the direct approach, you can assign both reading and writing activities to be done outside of class, and use class time for considering the results of these activities. Thus, the direct approach can be very economical in terms of time and effort.

The *indirect* approach, on the other hand, offers an opportunity for student involvement not provided by direct teaching. By using indirect means you can allow students to select their own topics, set their own goals, and interact with each other as well as with the teacher in search of new insights, conclusions, and awareness. By listening to what is said during interaction and commenting on it selectively, you can guide class involvement in desired directions. Unquestionably, the indirect approach is more time-consuming than the direct. It can also be more frustrating: even with the most skillful teacher, interaction sessions can become rudderless or move determinedly in directions not appropriate to the Grand Design. Unquestionably, however, the indirect approach allows more of an active learning experience on the part of the student than does the direct. This fact is a highly imposing one. We suggest that you consider both types of approach and that you don't use one at the expense of the other.

As you become more experienced in the classroom, you should try to move more and more toward the institution of student-centered activities. It is probably necessary for largely inexperienced teachers to rely heavily on teacher-centered approaches. As you become more accustomed to dealing with groups of teen-agers at various grade or maturity levels, you will undoubtedly become more comfortable with letting students set their own goals and guide their own classroom activities. This approach is sometimes risky;

it relies heavily on outstanding support between teacher and class, as well as on sincere student motivation.   Ultimately, however, it is the ideal approach, since it demands total student involvement in the learning tasks they have set for themselves.

In moving toward student-centered activity, you must change your method from one of talk-assign-judge to one of listen-diagnose-guide.   You must learn to listen for and diagnose the *content* of what students offer verbally and in writing.   This content can reveal interests that lead to more sincere involvement in literature study and more meaningful production in written composition.   You should also pay close attention to the *style* of these student-initiated offerings.   This will lead to a more relevant series of language analyses in your classroom, such as those described and illustrated in Chapters 6 and 7.   Above all, you must be constantly alert for expressions of student interest so that you can capitalize on them and turn them into sessions in which students examine the content and style of what *they* have said and written.

Several years ago, one of the writers of this book was teaching an "average" twelfth-grade class in a Tallahassee, Florida, senior high school.   There were twenty-three boys and four girls in the class, and the group was informally labelled "non-college bound" by the administration.   The class met during the last period of the day.   At the beginning of the year, the entire school population had been told by the principal that the environment of the school would be "open": that there would be no rules on dress, off-campus activity, attendance at classes (unless stipulated by individual instructors).   That was in September. One day in early February (a rainy Friday), the principal called the entire senior class into the auditorium and scolded them profusely for their appearance, their attendance, and their attitude.   He told them that the morale of the entire school had been eroded by their lack of leadership.   Then the principal instituted some distinctly rigid rules, to be enforced immediately.

When the seniors were dismissed, one group proceeded to their assigned last period class, English, taught by the author.   That unlucky individual could sense, when the first two or three students entered the classroom, that something was radically wrong.   So the unit of instruction currently underway (believe it or not—"The Essay") was suspended, and the class was asked what was wrong. For most of the period the students voiced their reactions to the meeting in the auditorium: their bitterness at the rebuke, their humiliation at having been blamed for the low school morale, and their sense of the unfairness of having a set of rules changed so abruptly and autocratically.

The instructor listened for most of the period and, when the initial surge of anger seemed to have abated somewhat, challenged them with the question, "What do you want to do about it?"   After some of the more violent suggestions were dismissed, the class decided to list their grievances on the board.   The next decision, again made by the class, was to draft a letter to the principal expressing these grievances and inviting him to their English class to discuss the problem.

During the following class period (the next Monday), the class worked on a draft of the letter. It was revised on Tuesday and delivered by an elected representative before school Wednesday morning. The principal appeared at the Wednesday class meeting, and a truly open discussion of school morale problems was held. Although the author's previously cordial relationship with the principal changed rather abruptly at that point, the class had satisfied its desires and a problem had been dealt with.

This anecdote serves to illustrate the need for you to be alert to students' immediate concerns. If you aren't, they will give you only divided attention, and if you are, you can often turn the situation into a language analysis session characterized by high student motivation. The author still considers this one of the most meaningful composition activities he has ever been involved in. And—believe it or not—he had no idea it would come about in this manner.

Student-centered instruction is worthwhile because it allows use to be made of student concerns about various aspects of their environment. Once these concerns have been revealed, the classroom becomes a laboratory for the examination of their content and the style in which they are expressed. It is difficult, if not impossible, to *plan* for such activities. But teachers who are not alert and who don't capitalize on such opportunities are missing the mark. The question you must ask yourself is, "Is it more important to cover ground (*my* lesson plan) or deal with matters that are of immediate significance to my students?" We hope you will opt for the latter.

The ability to build student-centered activities in an English course is the mark of an increasingly sensitive and creative teacher. Be a bit cautious in the early stages but, as you gain classroom experience and rapport with your students, take chances more and more frequently. Having students actively involved in the learning process and at least partially responsible for the direction of their activities—these are keys to truly effective instruction in any subject and at any level.

Chapter 14

Organizing What We Are to Teach

Needless to say, teaching style is not something you learn by reading a book. You can, however, continue to reflect on how you come across in classroom situations. Let's now turn to method, which to us involves the conscious manipulation on the part of a teacher of the content he is to reach. The strategies we have suggested relative to teaching style could, almost without exception, be applied to any content area. In method, the focus is narrower: a description of ways of shaping the various components of English to make them more clearly perceivable and relevant to adolescents, both early and late, both gifted and limited, both affluent and impoverished. Throughout the following discussion, the answers to the questions "what," "to whom", and "why" should be kept firmly in mind. Our approach will be largely based on our answers to those questions.

One problem a teacher with little experience faces quite early in his career is that of *imitation*. This was touched on in Chapter Thirteen but from another perspective. When considering methods for classroom use, the new teacher frequently tends to rely on the techniques used *on him* by his most recent teachers (almost invariably college professors).

Because of this influence, it is not unusual for beginning teachers to rely heavily on lectures, to assign large reading assignments in relatively difficult material to be done outside of class, to demand long, meticulously written papers on fairly esoteric topics, and to punctuate the course at one or two points with "challenging" examinations. It is customary to be quite restrictive in the *range* of material they present and assign. Like the teachers they so recently served, they adopt a kind of "academic canon" of materials to be used and seldom stray from the prescribed limits.

It should be evident that the authors of this book hope for a broader conception of method than this. Such an approach is both limited and inappropriate because it presumes both academic background and motivation on the part of students who are less mature, less knowledgeable, less intellectually self-directed, and less willing to worship at "the shrine of academics" than they may seem. It also demands an attention span that many of them simply do not have. Furthermore, it fails to take into account the *selling* job an English teacher must do with students before any of the "Great Truths" can become meaningful to them. It must be remembered that English is still *required* in most American public school curricula, and there is considerable evidence to indicate that its popularity remains somewhat low among adolescent students. Your method(s) can help you overcome this problem of motivation when you encounter it.

In our attempt to persuade teachers of the potential value of breadth of method, a pertinent point can be made. Whereas most college students, for a long time, have had considerable latitude in the courses they take, the hours they take them, the relaxation time they have between classes, the instructors who teach their courses, the right not to attend classes, and the right to retain or drop certain courses, the high school student has almost none of these privileges. On the contrary, he generally faces a six-or seven-period day, five days a week. He has little choice in courses, probably none in instructors, is penalized for missing classes, and has little leverage in dropping or adding courses. Thus, as he plows his way through a series of back-to-back curricular experiences, this person may become understandably bored or irked by rigid, lockstep procedures *within* his classes, along with the lockstep sequence in which they are provided him. This situation is particularly frustrating when the student has little or nothing to say about the system in which he finds himself. The social upheaval we have all been witnessing in recent years indicates that many people are becoming more overt in their resistance to such rigidity and monotony. The elective system is one attempt to give students a voice in what they study.

Consider the following two touchstones to development and improvement of method in order to avoid some clearly unpopular teaching situations. They illustrate a *variety* of approaches to a given instructional unit and provide for active student involvement in the various learning situations. Although we have found these suggestions to be valuable, you will undoubtedly be able to think of many additional ideas as you work with your classes.

Our description of methodological approaches will be a relatively brief one. Several specific methods, related to various components of English, have been described and illustrated earlier in this book. Here, we propose a series of strategies for organizing instruction in secondary school English.

We begin with a fairly simple one: consider carefully and realistically the the place of "The Text" in your course of study. Postman and Weingartner offer some significant insights into the group obsolescence of the one-book approach to organizing instruction in *Teaching As a Subversive Activity*. There is so much experience today that is directly relevant to the English classroom that can't be found in a book, that only the most myopic of teachers can stand by "The One Book Method" as the way of dispensing information and ideas. This is hardly an original revelation. In 1958, in the first edition of *Literature Study in the High School*, Dwight L. Burton contended:

> Organizing the literature program according to an anthology may seem too obvious to list, but any honest analysis of classroom practice must place this method of organization first in frequency. In many English classrooms, the literature anthology *is* the program in literature. It would be easy to grow cynical about this, and to place blame for impressive results in the high school literature program on unimaginative plodding through the anthologies. Some blame may be justified. There are those teachers who use the anthology as a convenient excuse for not doing any of their own planning or organizing. Yet in some schools the crowded curriculum in English and the excessive teacher loads make any other course of action virtually impossible. Quite possibly, too, the teacher who "teaches" an anthology well may be achieving much more important results than the teacher whose program is completely haphazard, or permits only on Fridays periods of "free reading" or unguided browsing in the library.[1]

Properly considered, the one-text approach has little to do with any of the first three questions posed about teaching English in the opening pages of this book. Those teachers who firmly believe in such an approach really don't need to bother with this discussion. They already have their curriculum clearly mapped out, and it will change only as revised editions of their favorite books are published.

It is our feeling that a text is only one resource among many. Various other materials exist, many of them quite reasonably priced, most of them easily available, and many in nonprinted form. Materials should be chosen in the light of instructional goals and the nature of your students. When one allows his text to become his sole course of study, he has allowed someone else to frame a definition of his content for him as well as to structure the way in which it will be offered. Again, considering the three questions posed at the outset, it would seem more effective if systems, schools, and teachers, both individually and in groups, took major responsibility for designing curricula in the light of *their* answers to these questions, and then chose both sequences of activities and materials based on those answers.

The problems of developing lesson plans for effective methods are a bit more subtle than those involved in choosing and using a text. For most teachers there is real need for *some* kind of written plan. In fact, one of the ways in which thoughtful but inexperienced teachers compensate for lack of background is to plan a great deal of activity, realizing that they may well not do everything they had planned. It takes a highly knowledgeable, extremely sensitive person to teach effectively without any written preparation at all. Most effective,

---

[1] Dwight L. Burton, *Literature Study in the High School* (New York: Holt, Rinehart and Winston, Inc., 1959), p. 258.

experienced teachers have thought through their objectives, styles, and methods carefully even though they may not make detailed written plans.

Lesson plans of some kind, then, are important to almost all teachers. Many school systems require plans to be prepared and submitted to administrators in advance (sometimes *well* in advance) of their use in the classroom. The critical question lies in the degree to which a plan, once formulated, becomes a straitjacket for its user. The plan can be of great aid but, when it becomes seemingly necessary to follow it exactly and exclusively, the *vitality* of the class may suffer considerably; i.e., the lesson plan, like the text, should not become an end in itself. This is particularly true when the teacher, in developing the plan, includes strict time components for each stated activity. While there are sometimes unavoidable administrative reasons for time inclusions, the teacher needs to face realistically the ways in which strict adherence to "The Plan" relates to the "to whom" question we posed earlier. Certainly, those teachers who see the value in indirect teaching (and indirect teaching is a most obviously appropriate way to provide for student *involvement*) need to do a lot of thinking about ways of reconciling such teaching with strictures in the plan. For instance, what happens when your plan calls for "twenty minutes of discussion" on a given topic and your students show both the wish and the need to pursue the topic beyond that limit. Since most lesson plans are inevitably written apart from the students and in advance of the teaching act, it is virtually impossible to predict how much time will be needed for any activity that calls for active student participation. When the twenty minutes are up, the teacher has a critical decision to make: is it more important to "cover ground" vis-à-vis the lesson plan, or to continue to consider and reinforce ideas under consideration at the moment? Obviously, there is no conclusive or mutually acceptable answer to this question, but the more rigid the lesson plan and the more determined the teacher is to pursue it to the letter, the more difficult the task of encouraging honest student involvement. Getting through the daily or weekly material on time and without interruption as an end in itself can easily make any teaching pretty sterile in nature. One of the main concerns of the British educators at the Anglo-American seminar at Dartmouth (1966) was that they were confronted with so many sequential and cumulative plans for English devised by the Americans for children that no one apparently had ever seen and whose abilities, backgrounds, and interests could only be presumed.

Lesson plans need to be developed and utilized with considerable flexibility. We maintain that if the study of English is to have any meaningful connection with the needs of adolescents, at least four kinds of operations need to be interjected frequently by teachers:

1. *introduce* for consideration significant, often many-faceted issues of human experience;
2. *involve* students (rather than pontificate) in open consideration of them;
3. *interact* with those in search of possible solutions;
4. *reinforce* important generalizations, insights, and commitments that emanate from the students.

In order to ensure that *any* of these operations are introduced into *your* classroom, you will need to consider the time dimensions and prescribed sequences of your lesson plans.

One representative classroom activity, observed by one of the authors, can illustrate some problems and dilemmas you will face in incorporating these operations in your lesson plans. A student teacher was working with a bright, interested tenth-grade group on a project in imaginative writing. In this specific phase of instruction the teacher wanted his students to develop a "shocker" ending to a short fictional piece they were writing. To illustrate this, he had assigned for homework the reading of Shirley Jackson's "The Lottery" the night before the class in question. His lesson plan called for a "short discussion" of the story followed by a more lengthy (thirty to thirty-five minutes) writing session in which the students would work on their own endings for it. The problem was that most of the students had done the reading, and most of them were powerfully affected by the story. Thus when he attempted to move the "short discussion" along, he met with considerable resistance. Questions were constantly being raised such as, "Did those people *really* stone that lady to death?", "Why would anybody go along with such a custom?", "Where were the police that day?", and "Why didn't her family defend her?"

By these and other such questions, the teacher became increasingly irritated. Sure, the story was a good one, he conceded, and worth talking about, but he wanted to do what his lesson plan called for: presenting the ending as a model *and then getting on to the writing* [italics mine]. When he couldn't do this smoothly, he became more obviously irritated, and never did get substantially into the writing phase.

It seemed evident that the teacher's problem was not being either able or willing to reconcile his plans with the impact the story had visibly made on his students. To them the impact of the ending had become a gripping matter and not, at least for the moment, the writing model their teacher had hoped it would be. They were therefore not *ready* to see it in the desired perspective because they wanted to examine it as an entity unto itself. It was clear that the teacher hadn't anticipated this type of response, and for better or worse, he did little to adjust to it.

The simple fact that we need to keep reminding ourselves of is that texts, curriculum guides, master plans, and daily lesson plans are made so that we can more easily and coherently teach people about something, and that their real test lies in their relative impact on those people. Thus, if they are not flexible to some degree, we can only hope that the people will all fit into the grooves we created for them when we wrote the plans. Arranging to meet with groups of our fellow teachers and/or inviting students to participate in the planning process can sometimes help to anticipate some of the flesh-and-blood effects of The Plan.

A willingness to go beyond the text and the lesson plan, then, is an important condition for providing variety in classroom activities. The lecture—a one-way communication approach—needs to be minimized, to be used sparingly, and then only for short periods of time. In-class reading, both silent and oral, should be considered as an activity of potential value.

It is always dangerous to assign a great deal of required reading for students to complete outside of class. Many of them simply won't do it. And when those who have trouble with silent reading have questions about the assignments, there is often no one to help them. Thus the in-class reading of assigned material provides all students with an opportunity to read and also affords the teacher a chance to observe his students in the act of reading and to answer any questions they may want to raise as they read.

ORGANIZING IN-CLASS READING

Silent classroom reading can be organized in several ways, in terms of *kinds* of responses desired. One way is to assign questions to be considered *before* the reading begins. This has both the advantages and disadvantages of limiting the reader's perspective on his material. It can also give clear direction to whatever reaction activity follows the reading period.

For a more individualized approach, response requirements can be provided each student as he finishes the material in question. When the student finishes his reading, the teacher can provide reaction assignments best fitted to his ability. This approach allows the teacher to discuss with each student the nature of whatever responsibilities he is assigned. For the teacher who is aware of the reading abilities of his students and who has prepared a wide variety of questions aimed at varying levels of reading achievement, this approach can pay rich dividends.

Reading can be assigned with no reaction requirements at the outset. Once the reading has been completed, questions of various kinds can be asked. This strategy allows each student to consider a variety of matters pertaining to the material he has just read. When conducting any subsequent reaction sessions, the teacher must be careful to allow individual impressions to be voiced. Tactful guidance of the reaction period is an important dimension of assigning reading without asking for specific responses. The discussion can be structured or unstructured.

Variety in in-class reading activity can also be achieved by developing materials to be read by the students. The teacher can assign all students the same text, or he can assign different texts to different groups, or he can assign individual texts to individual students. The procedure can also be varied by asking various individuals to approach their reading with different purposes in mind.

We see, then, that silent reading activities have much potential for diversification. In-class reading can help the teacher and student to work together more closely on ideas found in the material assigned, and a good deal of variety can be injected into the assignments.

ORAL READING

Oral reading activities can provide further variety to in-class reading. The reading can be done by individuals or by groups, and can involve selections of all genres and of various lengths. Whole works or special excerpts can be used. Reading selections can be assigned by the teacher or chosen by the students, based on previously established criteria. Critical listening groups can be assigned for the oral readers, with specifically delegated responsibilities for reaction. The taping and replaying of oral reading done by students can also add to the value of this activity.

Whatever the organization or purpose of oral reading sessions, we do offer one basic suggestion to the teacher. Unless he has an exceptionally able and enthusiastic group of oral readers, the teacher should consider the wisdom of providing *preparation* time before any oral reading takes place. Most oral reading is designed to reinforce understandings gained from silent reading. In order to provide sound reinforcement, the oral reading should be fluent and expressive. In our experience, most adolescents have trouble being fluent or expressive when engaging in unprepared oral reading. By allowing students some time for preparation, either in class or at home, the teacher can ensure more effective performance.

There is another reason for allowing for adequate student preparation. Few adolescents enjoy appearing inept or clumsy in front of their peers. If they are not provided with a chance to look over the material they are to read, they may be placed in a gauche posture, which can lead to resentment toward the teacher.

WRITING

Writing activities can also be greatly varied. Writing can take the form of contributions to personal journals, involving a highly individualized series of composition activities, as described earlier. Both in and out of class, written work can be done in answer to questions posed about topics, selections, or films. The work can be completed during the class period and turned in. Sometimes it can be retained by the students in their notebooks, to be checked occasionally by the teacher. Writing can be a type of response to a hypothetical life situation as posed by the teacher or agreed upon by the class. It can take the form of partial or abbreviated scripts used in an improvised dramatic activity.

Writing activities can be structured or "open." They can be used as responses to tightly phrased questions on material read, heard, or viewed. They can, on the other hand, emanate from the *students'* interests, questions, or perceptions, as described in the invention phase of composition in Section IV. Writing can also take the form of a mere mechanical activity, such as in note-taking from oral statements, reading, summarizing, outlining of various kinds, and copying specific, key content from resource materials. Again, *varying* the writing situation is a key to effective strategy, and providing class time for teacher guidance and response should be included frequently.

SPEAKING

Speaking activities can also be used frequently in the classroom. Informality should generally be the rule; students should be freed from rigid rules and the fear of negative teacher pronouncements regarding *form* as often as possible. Too many perception situations should probably be avoided and the discussion technique, described earlier, could be frequently utilized.

Students can speak as voluntary respondents to questions posed by teachers and peers. They can raise their own questions and offer solutions to a variety of issues. They can be assigned specific topics to cover in an oral presentation, or they can be given a range of topics from which to choose. Informal debates, panel discussions, and other group activities also afford ideal speaking situations, and they can take on a variety of structures. A more elaborate set of suggestions for group work will appear later, but group speaking activities often become a most effective means of introducing or reacting to a topic, issue, or selection.

Student participation in speaking situations can come from prepared statements, paraphrases, or totally extemporaneous material. Students can speak from notes, read from texts, or rely completely on their inner perceptions, imaginations, or memories. When using collages, montages, slide/tape presentations, and speech essays, speaking can be combined with visual and written presentations. The student-made film is yet another speech situation.

LISTENING AND VIEWING

Listening and viewing activities add to the variety of possible classroom endeavors. In developing an effective teaching style, you will need to consider the potential value of clearly establishing listening responsibilities in a variety of situations. Whenever you or someone else is speaking to the group, the students should be aware of what and how much they will be expected to retain. Thus, the need for taking notes, following along in a text, recalling details, identifying main ideas, drawing inferences, or making judgments should be restated often, especially when dealing with less mature or less motivated groups. Practice exercises using taped presentations can aid the teacher in diagnosing student problems, both of skill and attitude. The teacher can observe how the students approach the task, how long their attention span is sustained, and by asking questions, determine what they have *retained*.

Another approach to listening work is to assign critical listeners to the speaker(s). One, two, or any number of students can be asked, as their special responsibility, to paraphrase, summarize, or interpret a given oral statement immediately after it is made or more subsequently. In any case, speaking and viewing activities need built-in listening activities that are understood in advance by the students. They make it much easier for the teacher to follow these activities with ones featuring *responses* of various kinds from the class.

VISUAL LITERACY IN ENGLISH

Since viewing activities are dealt with extensively in other sections of this book, they will be only briefly considered here. It should be evident to all teachers that the opportunity for providing visual stimuli in learning situations has increased tremendously in recent years and can affect profoundly and positively both the *relevance* and *variety* of virtually any unit of instruction. Refinement of young peoples' abilities to perceive and respond to their visual world is unquestionably part of the English teacher's responsibility today. The potential for the use of several media in increasing understanding, developing skill, and affecting attitudes needs to be investigated, and experiences need to be planned at all levels. The relation of the visual to the verbal is an ability that teachers have worked on from the beginning levels of schooling. Further activity in this area is a necessary ingredient of secondary school English curricula. You must develop your own skills in this aspect of English, since many teachers have had little preparation in it.

The constructing of graphs, time lines, charts, models, and the like are also activities the teacher may wish to pursue. These activities are valuable for several reasons:

1. They help students understand better by *constructing* the material or *viewing* it once it is constructed.
2. They allow students with artistic and/or manual talents to participate more fully in a print-oriented activity.
3. They allow students, whether creators or viewers, to relate visual and verbal media in understanding.
4. They can provide stimuli for classroom response situations, both written and oral.
5. They often help to make abstract concepts more concrete.
6. They allow students who do not possess advanced verbal skills to express their own interpretations.
7. They help individualize classroom activity in a given area of study.
8. They often demand that the artist or maker draw on a variety of reference materials to complete his project.

These activities are in no way "Mickey Mouse" but, when related to a matter of concern, can provide excellent reinforcement. The use of the old Globe Theater model can serve as an excellent example here. Since drama is written not to be *read silently* but to be *played* and *viewed*, a look at what the Shakespearean actors had to function in should be of considerable assistance to those who must visualize the often complex action at the same time they are attempting to understand the speeches.

The whole activity of finding and using reference material may well become part of a teacher's method. Using classroom sources of information can be a unit of instruction in itself. Work with the particular problems of finding information in dictionaries, encyclopedias, manuals, and other sources needs to be introduced and reviewed as an integral part of instruction. Most of this work is probably best done on an individual instructional basis with grades minimized or excluded. The problem-solving approach, as an active means of acquiring skill, is usually preferable to lecture/recitation. The use of the library and its resources can be included in this phase of planned classroom activity. Content-oriented units can easily go aground when teachers presume that students have the special locational, reviewing, and other study skills needed to utilize resources and identify their whereabouts. Before resource materials can become a means to an end, they must be demonstrated to the students in terms of location, format, and use.

In the foregoing discussion, the breadth of activities available to any teacher has been indicated. Most of them have been described only briefly. We wish to elaborate somewhat on group work at this point, however, because this method of instruction is quite popular but poses problems for many teachers.

IMPROVISED DRAMATIC ACTIVITIES

One classroom technique that has broad application is improvised drama. Briefly stated, this is an activity in which members of the class consider some problem, issue, event, or situation as a dramatic activity. On this basis, roles of possible character participants are identified and assigned. The setting is described and then the situation is acted out by the characters as they perceive their roles.

An improvised drama has numerous characteristics, many of which can be applied flexibly. The situation can be agreed on by the participants and can be spelled out in fairly rough terms; no elaborately contrived situation is necessary. Very few, if any, props, costumes, set decorations, or the like are needed. The "stage," which is the classroom, comprises the entire set. Most details can be ad-libbed or pantomimed by the actors.

There are no scripts in improvised drama. While *some* preparation may be involved, it does not consist of writing out prepared parts for each actor. Preparation time can vary. For some presentations, the situation and setting may be established, parts assigned, and the drama begun immediately. In other cases, some preparation time, ranging from a few to several minutes, may be allowed. The actors get together to discuss their roles, the sequence of activities, and the location of the various dramatic situations. Seldom, however, will whole class periods or homework be devoted to preparation.

One possibly effective approach to this activity, in terms of preparation, can involve the establishing of the dramatic situation near the end of a given class period. The actors can use the last few minutes of class for preparation time. Then, if they so desire, they can get together on their own to make further preparations for the dramatic presentation. On the strength of that preparation, the drama is presented early in the ensuing class period. One of the flexible aspects of the improvised dramatic technique, however, lies in the fact that preparation time is usually quite brief, so that the beginning of the dramatic activity can be quickly approached, occurring almost any time during the class period.

Once the basic situation and setting have been decided and the roles identified, each participant is on his own in creating and developing his role. *He then plays it in relation to the other characters.* Instead of memorizing and repeating a set of lines as he would in formal stage drama, he creates his own lines, generally on the spot, and thenceforth speaks and acts in relation and reaction to what the other actors say and do. He cannot develop careful, preconceived speeches because he does not know what the other actors are going to say or how they are going to react verbally or kinesically to what he says. Thus he must truly *improvise*, fitting his dramatic activity most relevantly to the total situation. As long as he is a character in the drama, he must think on his feet.

Obviously, in this approach the genesis must be clearly established. *What* the situation is, *where* and *when* it is taking place, and especially *who* is involved— all these factors must be well understood by all the participants. It is probable that the geneses need to be greater in number and more emphatically defined for early adolescents than for older students. In any case, the total activity is task- or problem-centered. The situation represents an issue or problem to whose solution the actors make appropriate contributions. The solution will develop as the group interacts dramatically on the problem.

The origins of situations for dramatic improvisation are many. Before identifying specific ones, however, a basic dichotomy should probably be established between *loose* and *tight* dramatic situations. When the situation originates purely within the class—that is, from individual experience, real or imagined, of class members—we have a basically loose drama. The genesis can be invented, changed, or added at will because the originating force is the imagination of the individual. When the origin is of an established nature, however, as in the case of a work of literature read by the entire class, the situation is a tight one. The genesis has been established and is recognized by the entire group as well as by the teacher. In identifying this dichotomy, we are not suggesting one type over the other. The instructional situation will largely dictate the degree of looseness or tightness of the dramatic presentation.

More specifically, several stimuli for dramatic improvisations are possible:

1. Individual experience—a teacher can ask each class member to recount some recent experience that he has observed or in which he has participated and to identify its dramatic ingredients. The student will describe the action and its setting and identify the participants. Once all or most of the class have had a chance to speak, the students can choose one episode for presentation, clarify and expand on it, and establish the role players. This is by far the most flexible and loosest means of establishing a particular dramatic improvisation. It also provides for student origination and choice. We recommend its frequent use.
2. Literary selections—all literary selections that involve human interaction are in essence *dramatic*. Thus all novels, short stories, biographies, and plays— and many poems—are excellent sources of improvised dramas.
3. Shared student experience—a school or community experience of which all class members are aware can provide for dramatic enactment. These can evolve naturally from the immediate, shared environment, or the teacher can *contrive* them by several means.
4. Still visuals—photographs, paintings, drawings, transparencies, slides, cartoons —any still picture that displays a dramatic human situation—can be the origin of an improvised drama. Filmstrips can establish a related *sequence* of dramatic situations.
5. Motion pictures—any motion picture based on human experience provides a ready origin. This is particularly true of the great number of recently produced short artistic films, both with and without words, which are described in Section V of this book.

6. Television—a great variety of television shows provide obvious stimuli. This medium has particular potential in that there are so many TV shows that are eminently popular with young people.
7. Small group discussion—groups of students, organized in the class through one of several ways, can evolve a dramatic situation from shared experience or from imagination. The teacher may sometimes wish to contribute to the development of the group-evolved situation.

In relation to the major, traditional components of English—language, composition, and literature—dramatic improvisation can provide a wide range of relevant activities. There is a great variety of language situations in which drama is possible, and which can be enacted during classtime.[2] The language of advertising, politics, business, or military service, among other things, contains a variety of components (usage, dialects, semantics, syntax) that can serve as stimuli for a variety of dramatic presentations in the classroom. A tape or video recorder for instant or delayed replay can prove a helpful adjunct.

Dramatic improvisations can offer a number of stimuli for written compositions. A dramatic presentation, for instance, can provide the beginning of a narrative sequence. The students in the class can be assigned the written composition of the next installment.

The dramatic improvisation can illustrate a theme, issue, or conflict. The students can discuss it if they wish and then write a critical analysis of it. They can also develop written arguments supporting either one side of an issue or the other. They can be asked to describe in writing the physical or emotional situations they have viewed. They can compose comparative and/or contrasting situations. These suggestions are barely representative of the writing possibilities inherent in improvised drama.

In considering strategies for the teaching of literature, we stressed the significance of *readiness* and *reinforcement*. Dramatic improvisations can foster both of these concepts. Before a class is asked to read a particular work, the teacher can propose a dramatic situation that contains whatever setting, situation, and character mix he wishes to relate to it. Once the situation is established, the students can improvise and their dramatization can be discussed. Thus, before the reading begins, the class can consider the situation, the people involved, and the thematic concerns they will find in the work itself. Improvisation can thereby provide reading readiness.

Once a class has read a literary work, the most common means of soliciting response are written and oral. Students write interpretive papers, answer thought questions, compose character sketches, or become involved in discussions or oral reports on various aspects of the work. Improvised drama provides still another kind of response activity. The class has read the work and is thus familiar with its basic elements. The teacher can then pose a hypothetical situation that could occur subsequent to the author's conclusion, or

---

[2] Neil Postman, "Linguistics and the Pursuit of Relevance," *English Journal* 56, No. 8 (Nov. 1967): 1160–1165.

he can suggest an alternate course of events to those that actually transpired. He could say, for instance, "Let's say that Nick and George are sitting in the diner as they were at the end of Hemingway's story. Nick decides to reject George's suggestion that he simply forget about Ole Anderson's plight. Just then the door opens and Ole enters, begging for help." A group with any imagination can take it from there.

In the above example, dramatic improvisation offers another kind of re-inforcement technique for literary consideration, one in which the student is directly involved rather than viewing the work in an abstract manner. He is asked to relate his own thoughts, actions, and feelings intimately to those of the characters in the work he has just read.

Throughout the dramatic improvisational experience, the teacher is, more than anything else, a catalyst of class activity. His job is to assist the group in finding and choosing dramatic situations that are worthy, *in their eyes*, of enact-ment. Once they are committed to a particular situation, it is then his vital responsibility to clarify and expand their perception of the dramatic experiences in which they are about to become involved. Through questions rather than mandates, he can help them become fully aware of all the *givens* of other situa-tions. Once a segment of the drama has been played, he can probe them with questions about the nature of the interaction and its possible impact. But he needs to keep a low profile throughout. Don't take over. If your students were heavily involved in the choice of the situation and the identification of the characters, be consistent. Let *them* carry the burden. And don't forget: once an improvised drama begins, the lines are those of the *students themselves*. Therefore, you correct and editorialize only at your peril. When you can incisively move the action and help to clarify matters through *indirect* tech-niques, do so. *But don't run the show!* The potential of improvised drama for student direction is one of its main strengths.

There are several potential problems in using this technique, and some of them are probably obvious. While younger children are usually more willing to get involved in such activities, senior high students, because of their self-consciousness, may balk to some degree. Thus, we suggest the use of improvised dramatic activities early in the course of study and early in the school year. Early involvement may well help to break down some of the barriers of inhibi-tion. Also, during early sessions, don't be afraid to take part yourself. When your students see you enthusiastically lending yourself to the spirit of the activity, they may become more willing to participate.

With all students, but especially with older ones, clear purposes need to be established. The "why" needs to be established early. If not, the students may well perceive the whole activity as a lark or a waste of class time. It may be well to prepare and present some demonstrations with the aid of dependable students early in the game.

Faulty introductions and inadequate establishment of the setting and situa-tion can cause students real trouble in "feeling" their roles. *You* must clarify these elements at the outset or, through questions, lead your students to do so.

Lack of audience involvement can result in a presentation that has no impact. At the other extreme, damage can obviously result if participants become too personally involved in their roles. Remember: you are *not* a drama specialist, nor are you a therapist. Dramatic improvisation isn't psychodrama. So keep your eye on the *degree* of individual involvement.

Despite its possible problems, improvised drama has lots of possibilities for the English classroom. Several of these have been identified already, but we would now like to emphasize two major ones, both of which we alluded to previously. They are student involvement and flexibility.

Improvised dramatization can be set up with or without an audience. Several classroom groups can be organized, each representing a separate dramatic situation and each offering each of its members a role. The dramas can then be enacted simultaneously, without an audience.

If the teacher or the class decides that the improvisations should be carried out before an audience, then all the students can still be involved through one of several devices:

1. Role players can be interchanged during the playing of a given situation.
2. The teacher or the groups can create a new character, whose role can be played by a student who was up to that point a member of the audience.
3. Once a scene has been played, a subsequent, causally related one can be created. In this next scene, all or part of the cast can be changed.
4. All casting can be either voluntary or assigned.

Another dimension of flexibility and involvement can be introduced when promoting discussions by the audience once a presentation has been completed. In these discussions, any student who so desires can describe a particular role as *he* would have played it, thereby adding to the multifaceted nature of the drama and providing more individual involvement.

Entire books have been written about classroom uses of dramatic improvisation. We have presented only the briefest of summaries of possible techniques, with emphasis on their practical application. Improvisation has lots of potential, largely because it can get all of your students into the act.

GROUP ACTIVITIES IN ENGLISH

Group activities can be used for several purposes, probably the most prominent of which are to develop an idea and then present it to the whole class or to react to an assignment, again through preparation and presentation. While some group activities culminate in the production of a *written* statement and others terminate with discussion within the group itself, we will focus on the group situation in which an oral presentation follows a period of preparation.

Group work needs to be carefully thought out and organized by the teacher. The overt art of introducing the activity, establishing goals, and maneuvering students into groups can become very confusing. As a rule of thumb, we suggest that at least one class period be devoted to organization. If the teacher has never attempted group activity before, a set of procedural notes might prove helpful.

A major consideration in the organization phase is the makeup of each group. While makeup will vary with the purpose of the activity, heterogeneous groupings are often worthwhile in that students with various backgrounds, interests, and abilities can then *share* ideas and perspectives. In addition, it is usually important to choose group leaders at the outset and to orient them as carefully and as early as possible to the goals of the group, the direction in which preparation and presentation should probably move, and then assign the appropriate responsibilities. If several group activities are to be introduced during the year, various groupings would probably be advisable, and several different individuals should be offered the opportunity to serve as group leaders. When the leadership responsibilities are clearly defined by the teacher, there is less need for academically talented students to be the only ones to fill this role.

Whenever groups have common responsibilities, those responsibilities should be made clear at the outset. For instance, if each group has a certain aspect of a stimulus to consider (a book, a film, a speech, a school tradition, or what have you), the fact should be emphasized that the topic is common but the perspectives will differ from group to group. Groups should not be formed and begin to function until these general goals, together with matters of procedure, have been ironed out. Once the teacher releases these groups to function as separate units, he must realize that he has "x" number of miniclasses functioning simultaneously rather than the original one; therefore, each unit should have a clear concept of what its task is.

Assignments to group members are generally more meaningful when they are individualized. Individualizing can be done in several ways. In a unit called "Metropolitan America," for instance, the teacher can build reading lists of literary selections each based on a prominent American city. Each group can be assigned a city and provided with a reading list. Each student can then choose one or more selections, *which he will investigate on his own*. When the investigations have been completed, the various perspectives can be discussed within the group and statements can be prepared for presentation to the class.

A topic can have several dimensions, and the study of these dimensions can be meted out to the individual groups. A film such as *Bridge on the River Kwai* contains the following dimensions:

1. Characterization by actors
2. Following and deviating from the Boulle text
3. Techniques of filming

4. Development of suspense and climax
5. Relation to history
6. Matters of symbolic representation.

This, of course, is only a partial list. Other factors can also be identified and considered. The essential activity, however, is subdividing each of the dimensions so that each member of the group has a special problem to consider as he views the film. For example, each member of the group considering "characterization by actors" can be asked to choose one of the actors in the film and discuss his impression of the way that actor interprets his role. Each member of the group considering "development of suspense and climax" can be asked to select one incident in the film and explain in adequate detail what *it* illustrates. Each of the other aspects of the film can be subdivided in like manner.

Another means of employing individualization is to assign each group one source material on a given theme, issue, or topic, and ask each group member to examine one or more aspects of the source *as it relates to the theme.* In a unit on the heroic concept, for example, each group can be assigned a different, long, histrionic or biographical text in which a hero is described or created. Each member of the group can then be asked to take a close look at one or more aspects of the heroic concept *as seen in the group's text.* A unit entitled "The Literary Hero" provides illustrative questions used in such an assignment.[3]

ESSAY QUESTIONS FOR HERO UNIT

1. Explain how the five characteristics of the epic (already identified) apply to the work you have read. Does the work differ from them in any way? If so, how?
2. Describe in detail the surroundings and/or atmosphere into which the hero enters. Why are they appropriate ones for the heroic poem?
3. Describe the importance of the supernatural in your story. What is the apparent relationship between man and supernatural beings here?
4. What factors in modern (twentieth century) society would make it impossible for this story to have happened today? Discuss factors of *attitude* as well as concrete ways of life.
5. In what two or three important ways does this man appear to be a great hero?
6. Describe the praise given the hero by himself and/or other members of the story and explain why this kind of praise is vitally important in heroic literature.
7. Are this man's great deeds more significant than his inner moral qualities, or vice versa? Explain.

---

[3] Stanley B. Kegler and John S. Simmons, "Images of the Hero: Two Teaching Units," *English Journal* 49, No. 6 (Sept. 1960): 409–417.

8. To be truly great, a hero needs a worthy opponent to conquer. Describe the nature of the opponent or opponents, real or supernatural, with whom your hero must contend. Discuss also those flaws that cause the opponent's downfall.
9. What seems to be the reward that your hero ultimately receives for his noble deed? Describe.

When each member of a group has an individual concern with which to preoccupy himself, more balanced work should come from the total group, and there will be greater opportunity for active involvement by *all* members.

The assignment breakdowns need to be worked out in careful detail by the teacher. He needs to make them clear to the class as a whole, and he needs to assist the group leader in the assigning of responsibilities once the groups have been set in motion. During the ongoing preparation period (as long as the teacher feels necessary), the teacher needs to spend as much time with each group as possible. As in the workshop approach to teaching written composition, he needs to be away from his desk and into the classroom, raising issues with each group, clarifying individual and group goals, suggesting sources of information, considering the order of oral presentation, and dealing with other such matters. Periodic meetings with the group leaders to assess progress, consider difficulties, and point out new directions may also prove helpful. This is taxing work, but we feel that teacher involvement in the preparation phase of group work is vital to its success.

When the group presentations are made, care should be taken to avoid monotony. One way this can be done is for the groups to question each other once a presentation is made. For instance, Group A may be asked to act as critical listeners to Group B, as well as to make its own presentation. Group B may react to Group C, and so forth. Or, the class as a whole can be asked to react. Group reports can, in some situations, be broken up and related to each other, allowing certain aspects of one group's presentation to be followed immediately with similar aspects of the presentation of another group. The teacher can also act as a reactor, both during and after a group presentation.

This description of group presentation procedures also illustrates another desirable trait of this type of activity: that *use* be made of that which the group presents. The goal of a group report should be to share information and ideas with others interested in a matter of common concern, not merely to "get through" a report. It is an important responsibility of the teacher to keep the issue of relevance before the class.

Group work can be highly valuable *if* there are clear goals, active individual involvement, perceivable directions of preparation activity, and truly informative presentations. Without them, it can be chaotic, repetitive, and a flagrant waste of time. Only a teacher who can manage a diverse learning situation should attempt to set one in motion.

Now that various individual activities have been described, some mention should be made regarding *sequences* in which they can be performed. One sure characteristic of a healthy learning situation is one in which an activity grows naturally out of another, in which it relates to what preceded and to what follows in a causal manner. Several obvious combinations of relatable activities in English instruction can be briefly identified:

1. Students *read* a given selection; then they
2. *write* a reaction to that selection; then they
3. *speak* in relation to it, based on what they have written.

or

1. Students *view* a film of an experience that represents a given human issue; then they
2. *read* a selection that also focuses on the issue; then they
3. *compare*, in *speech* or *writing*, the treatment of the issue in each medium.

or

1. Students *listen* to a presentation in common; then they
2. *consider* various assigned aspects of the presentation in groups; then they
3. present *orally* their feelings about those aspects they were asked to consider.

Each activity represents a particular aspect of language arts instruction but instead of existing autonomously, there is an organic relationship among them. A more elaborate and specific illustration of sequential activity would be as follows:

1. A group of students are asked how they feel about one or more given life situations. They discuss them at some length, and consider and respond to classmates' points of view. This opening discussion is guided, catalyzed, and summarized by the teacher.
2. *Then* the students work on certain reading skills that they will need to be proficient in when they read a certain literary selection silently.
3. *Then* the students read the literary selection assigned by the teacher. It illustrates the life situations that the students discussed earlier. It also contains the reading problems in which they have just had some directed practice.
4. *Then* they listen to a record of a professional actor (or to a teacher-made tape) reading the selection they have just finished.
5. *Then* they view slides, photographs, or drawings of scenes from the selection and relate them to the appropriate passages in the text. They compare these visual materials to the mental images *they* had drawn during their reading.
6. *Then* they prepare and present some brief, improvised dramatic scenes based on divergent questions that relate to the text in several ways:
   a) what the situations or events that occurred *before* the time of the selection read might have been like;
   b) what the situations or events that occurred *after* the time of the selection read might have been like;
   c) what might have happened if certain situations or events *in* the selection read had been changed.

7. *Then* they choose a character from the selection and write a statement presenting their impression of what kind of person he was and how he contributed to the situations and events in the selection.
8. *Then* certain selected members of the class (as time allows) read their characterizations aloud to the class. The class is encouraged to react to each characterization.

In this sequence of activities, we observe a variety of language situations illustrated and practiced by the class. Students are involved in reading, both written and oral. They work with their own language as well as that of others. They discuss human experience both before and after reading about it. They practice reading skills and then immediately apply them in their work. They view and listen to excerpts from a literary selection they have read silently. They speak and write about what they have read, heard, and viewed. Most important, they participate actively in a related series of classroom activities built around a literary selection that is seen to be relevant to their own lives and about which they are able to organize, express, and reflect upon their own ideas and those of their classmates. When classroom activities deal with matters of concern to students and relate to each other in meaningful ways, the study of English will have a greater impact on those who participate in it.

Both style and method are vital dimensions of the way an English teacher purveys his content to his students. Each aspect can be studied and practiced, but each one is rooted in the nature of the individual who would teach. The thoughtful consideration of both style and method is needed to promote genuine student concern and interest in what can become either a subject of vital importance or a real "bomb."

In the last two chapters we have made a lot of suggestions about placing yourself in the role of English teacher. Bear in mind, though: we are not trying to *be you*. From the moment you begin thinking about teaching, through the moment you make your debut in front of a class, until the moment you begin thinking about what you did, you will realize that you *are* the teacher and do what you do because you're *you*. The essential style of teaching is *yours*, and that is the way it must be. Our goal has been to provide suggestions for alternatives, tactics, and reinforcement strategies to make your task a little easier and more cohesive.

There need be no elaborate or eloquent summary to this book. Throughout these pages, we have tried to express our conviction that teaching, especially English teaching, is a human act filled with inconsistencies, irregularities, and false starts. We have not tried to offer you a manual of directions. We have, instead, posed some representative situations, asked you to consider them, and frequently offered some possible approaches. We have done so largely in the light of *our* experiences. We wish you well as you move into your own experiences as a teacher. If they are in any way similar to ours, they will afford you a varied, absorbing, and ultimately self-fulfilling way of life.

Index

Abbreviations, 163–168
Abstractions, study of, 60, 139–146
Accountability, 4, 20, 24–25
Acronyms, 164
"Adolescent Literature, Adolescent
    Reading and the English
    Class" (Donelson), 98–99
Adolescents, 41–45 (*see also* Junior
    literature):
  early, 51–71
  older, 72–106
Advertising, language of, 146–162
Ahdoolo! (Miller), 95
Alienation, as course theme, 76
America (Wolfe), 139
American Scholar, The (Emerson), 262
American Time Capsule, 250
Among the Valiant (Morin), 95
And Now Miguel (Krumgold), 92–93
Angel Loves Nobody (Miles), 93
Angles, camera, 255
Animation, 150
Anthologies:
  multiethnic literature in, 90–91
  use of, 285–286
Appeals, choice of, 210
Appearance vs. reality, as course
    theme, 77

Appreciation, literary, 50–51, 98
Appropriate Placement for
    Excellence (APEX), 26–30
Arnez, Nancy L., 96–97
Arnold, Elliot, 94
Arrangement:
  of a classroom, 269
  of a composition, 208–212
"Artur Rubinstein," 219–220
"As a Matter of Fact," 146
Assessment of students, 37–45
Atmosphere, classroom, 56, 199,
    263–267, 269
Attention span, 62–63
Attitude, student, 54, 275
  toward composition, 181–182,
    196–198, 199
  toward literature, 14–16, 61–63
Auden, W. H., 59–60, 86
Audience analysis, 175–176, 192–196
Authors:
  backgrounds of, 57–58, 102, 197
  voice of, 191–192

"Basic Issues in the Teaching of
    English, The" (Stone), 8–9
Beauneu, Mary, 7
"Begone Dull Care," 250

Behavioral objectives, 5, 20–25,
    199–200, 215–216
Bernstein, Basil, 114–116
Billy Lightfoot (Erno), 94
Biloquialism, 116–117
Biography, study of, 95, 101–102
Birmingham, John, 42–43
Black, Max, 112
Black experience, as course theme, 77
Black literature, 91–92, 96–97
Blood Brother (Arnold), 94
Bonham, Frank, 93
Bontemps, A., 90
Book reports, 201–202
Books (*see* Literature; Textbooks)
Booth, Wayne C., 54
Borland, Hal, 94
Born to Play Ball (Mays and
    Einstein), 95
Bridge on the River Kwai, 299–300
British primary schools, 34–36
Britton, James, 54
Brooks, Charlotte K., 91
Brothers Under the Skin
    (McWilliams), 96
Brown, Claude, 95
Brown, Dee, 95
Brown, George Isaac, 57
Browning, Robert, 187
"Bug the teacher" exercise, 217–218
Burdett, Silver, 65
Burke, Kenneth, 241
Burns, Richard W., 22–23
Burton, Dwight L., 15, 98, 286
Bury My Heart at Wounded Knee
    (Brown), 95

Caesar Chavez (Franchere), 93
Candita's Choice (Lewiton), 93
"Cask of Amontillado" (Poe), 192
Catcher in the Rye (Salinger), 193
Censorship, 74, 92
Character development, study of,
    101–102
Chicano (Vasquez), 93
Chicano literature, 92–94, 95
Child development, 39–40, 43–44

Christensen, Francis, 226
"Christmas Carol, A" (Dickens),
    13–14, 53
Chronology:
    organization by, 74–75
    study of, 70
Ciardi, John, 54
Classics, study of, 16–17, 61
Classroom atmosphere, 56, 199,
    263–267, 269
Clay, Tom, 240
Cleaver, Eldridge, 88
"College Survival Kit," 31
Colman, Hilda, 94
Come to Your Senses (Sohn), 186
Commas, use of, 232
Communication, purposes of,
    184–188
"Communications" (Fabun), 133
Composition:
    activities in, 290–291
    assignment of, 181–182
    form in, 222–232
    length of, 198, 210
    nonwriting, 183, 206
    preparation for, 183–189
    purpose of, 184–190
    student attitude toward, 181–182
    writing of, 201, 202–221
Comprehension, reinforcement of,
    67–70
Conclusion:
    of a class, 268
    of a composition, 210
Conferences, private, 267–268, 275
Cognitive memory questions,
    277–278
Conlin, David, 227
Conquering Hero, 94
Controversial issues, 207
Convergent questions, 278
Corle, Edwin, 96
Corporate campaign, 151
Counterculture, 28–29, 41–44, 100
Crabbe, John K., 30–31
Creative and Mental Growth
    (Lowenfeld), 114
Creativity, development of, 101–102

Creativity in English (Summerfield), 101

Critical reading, teaching of, 54, 62, 70–71

Criticism, 137, 216–220, 273, 276

Crones, Kathryn, 93

Cummings, E. E., 84–85

Cumulative program, 9–11

Cumulative sentence, 226

Curran, Charles W., 257

Curriculum:
development of, 28–29, 35
nongraded, 27–28

Custer Died for Your Sins (DeLoria), 95

"Dead Boy" (Ransom), 87

Death of a Salesman (Miller), 60, 82

Debating, 88

DeLoria, Vine, Jr., 95

Demian (Hesse), 100

Democracy, participative, 42, 43

DeMott, Benjamin, 15

Deschooling Society (Illich), 34

Dickens, Charles, 13–14, 53

Diction, 190, 213–214, 270

Direct teaching, 268–269, 281

Disadvantaged, teaching of, 203

Discipline problems, 267–268

Discussions, 269–277

Disturbances, classroom, 264

Divergent questions, 278–279

Dixon, John, 36

Dizenzo, Patricia, 92

Dodds, Barbara, 91

Donelson, Kenneth L., 98–99

Down These Mean Streets (Thomas), 95

Drama (*see also* Role playing):
improvised, 203–204, 294–298
teaching of, 81–83

Dunning, Stephen, 186, 227–228

Early, Margaret, 50, 62

Editing of film, 256–257

Einstein, Charles, 95

Electives, 25–34, 91, 99

Eliot, T. S., 86, 192

Ellison, Ralph, 98

Ely, Donald, 21, 22

Emerson, Ralph Waldo, 262

Emphasis, in composition, 198

Encyclopedia of Educational Research, 119–120

Ends and Issues—1965–66, 10

English courses:
models of, 8–17
value of, 6–8

Environment (*see* Atmosphere, classroom)

Erno, Richard, 94

Ethnic literature, 89–97

Evaluation, 217–218 (*see also* Grading; Testing)

Evaluative questions, 279

Exercises:
in composition revision, 217–220
progressive, 64
in syntax, 224–231
in understanding literature, 64–71

Experiences, 66, 203–204

Exploring the Film, 248

Expressive language, 130–131, 136–139

Eye contact, 273

Eyerly, Jeanette, 92

Fabun, Don, 133

Facts vs. inferences, 145–146

Fader, Daniel, 62

False claims, in advertising, 152

Feature films, 247

Federal funding of research, 9–11, 24, 26

Felsen, Henry, 92

Fig Tree John (Corle), 94–95, 96

Film: The Creative Eye, 248

Film and Literature (Marcus), 248

Film Study and the English Teacher (Sohn), 248

Films:
as instructional aids, 78, 235
making of, 248–257
study of, 245–248, 299–300

Florida State University Curriculum Study Center, 130

Forgotten People (Sanchez), 95
Form:
  importance of, 222
  teaching of, 223–232
Forster, E. M., 80
Fox, Mary Carroll, 31
Foxfire Book, The, 102
Franchere, Ruth, 93
Frazier, Alexander, 10
Free schools, 34–36
Friedenberg, Edgar Z., 40–41, 44
Fuller, Lola, 94
Funding of research, 9–11, 24, 26
Future, as course theme, 77
Future Shock (Toffler), 19

Galarza, Ernesto, 95
Games:
  reading-study, 33–34
  tagmemic, 207–208
  to teach syntax, 228–229
Gateway anthologies, 90–91
Generation gap, as course theme, 77
"Generative Rhetoric of the
    Paragraph, A" (Christensen),
    226
"Generative Rhetoric of the
    Sentence, A" (Christensen),
    226
Generative-transformational
    grammar, 118–119
Genre:
  organization by, 75
  teaching of, 78–89
Gerlach, Vernon S., 21, 22
Giles, Janice H., 94
Girl from Puerto Rico, The (Colman),
    94
Girl Like Me, A (Eyerly), 92
Glenn, John, 197
Go Ask Alice, 58
"God is dead," as course theme, 77
Grading, 26, 55, 199, 217
Grammar, 111, 118–119, 120–121
Greer, Mary, 57
Grouping, 117–118, 298–301
Growth Through English (Dixon), 36

Guilford, J. P., 277
Guth, Hans, 23–24

Haptics, 114–118, 187, 188
Hayakawa, S. I., 54, 86, 112, 130,
    132, 136, 138–139
Headlines, in syntactic exercises, 22
Heider, Fritz, 39, 43
Hemingway, Ernest, 57, 80
Hinton, S. E., 57–58
Hoffer, Eric, 197
Hook, J. N., 13–14, 224–226
Hooked on Books (Fader and McNeil)
    62
Hosic, James, 119
House Made of Dawn (Momaday), 9⊾
How Does a Poem Mean? (Ciardi), 5⊾
Human Teaching for Learning
    (Brown), 57
Humanistic objectives, 5, 23–25,
    199–200
Humanities, objectives for, 23–25
Hunter, Kristin, 96
Hypervocal students, 271, 272

"I don't know" answers, 273–275
Idea-bound words, 135, 145
Illich, Ivan, 34
Imagination, 15, 70–71, 136–139
Imitation of teaching styles, 262, 284
Impact textbooks, 91
Improvised drama, 203–204, 294–298
    (*see also* Role playing)
"In a Station of the Metro" (Pound),
    83
Indian literature, 93–95
Indirect teaching, 268–283
Individualism, as course theme, 77
Individualization, 34–36, 61,
    265–266, 299
  in reading, 99–100, 289
Inferences, 145–146, 151
Informal schooling, 34–36
Information, gathering of, 204, 293
Initiation, as course theme, 77
Interviews, 241
Invention, stage of, 202–208

Invisible Man (Ellison), 98
"Is She Skinny, Thin, or Svelte?" 130
It's Only a Movie (McKowen and Sparke), 248

Jackson, Shirley, 64–71
Johnny Osage (Giles), 94
Joyce, James, 57
Julie's Heritage (Marshall), 92
Julius Caesar (Shakespeare), 193
Jungk, Robert, 19
Junior literature, 98–99 (*see also* Literature)
  ethnic, 90–96
  list of, 102–105
  novels as, 79
  plays as, 82–83
  on pregnancy, 92
  short stories as, 79–80

Kaiser Aluminum News Bulletin, 133, 134, 135, 144, 145
Katz, Michael, 110
"Killers, The" (Hemingway), 80
Kinesics, 187
Kinestasis, 250–251
Krumgold, Joseph, 92–93

Labyrinth of Language, The (Black), 112
LaFarge, Oliver, 94–95
Laird, Charlton, 110
Language:
  of advertising, 146–162
  defined, 111–113, 121
  development of, 12–13, 38–40
  functions of, 130–131, 136–139
  of military, 162–175
  nature of, 131–139
  origin of, 132
  social implications of, 114–120
  and symbols, 124–130
  teaching of, 117–118, 121–123
Language (Sapir), 111
Language in Thought and Action (Hayakawa), 54, 112

Languaging model, 12–13
LaRaza (Steiner), 95
Latecomers, dealing with, 265
Laughing Boy (LaFarge), 94
Learning, process of, 35
Learning outcomes, 22–23
Leavitt, Hart Day, 186
Lectures, 288
Lehner, Andreas, 28–29
Lesson plans, 286–288
Lewis, Sinclair, 140
Lewiton, Mina, 93
Light in the Forest, A (Richter), 94
Limitation, in composition, 198
Linguistics, 11–13, 110–111, 114–115
Lions in the Way (Rodman), 91
Listening responsibilities, 265, 290, 292
Literary appreciation, 50–51, 98
Literary experience model, 13–17
"Literary Hero, The," study of, 300–301
Literature (*see also* Junior literature):
  behavioral objectives for, 23–25
  ethnic, 89–97
  teaching of, 13–17, 49–106
  types of, 78–97
  value of, 98, 100
Literature as Exploration (Rosenblatt), 15, 98
Literature Study in the High School (Burton), 286
Loban, Walter, 54, 100, 119, 120
Logo, 151
London, Jack, 197
Loon Feather, The (Fuller), 94
Loose drama, 295
"Lottery, The" (Jackson), 64–71
"Love Song of J. Alfred Prufrock, The" (Eliot), 86
Lowenfeld, Victor, 114
Lueders, Edward, 186

McCrimmon, James, 102
McKowen, Clark, 248
MacLeish, Archibald, 55
McLuhan, Marshall, 110, 269

McNeil, Elton B., 62
McWilliams, Carey, 95, 96
Main idea, writing of, 205–208
Main Street (Lewis), 139–141
Man and nature, as course theme, 77
Manchild in the Promised Land (Brown), 95
Marcus, Fred, 248
Marshall, Catherine, 92
Materials, for sample course, 32–33
Mays, Willie, 95
Meaning, problem of, 139–146
Media, as instructional aids, 67–70, 78, 235–236, 292–293 (*see also* Films; Tapes, use of)
Media centers, 241, 248
Mellon, John, 229
Metaphor, 64–65, 86, 136, 214
Method:
  defined, 262
  types of, 284–303
Mexican Americans (Steiner), 95
Mexican Americans in the Southwest (Galarza), 95
Mighty Hard Road (Tarzian and Crones), 93
Miles, Richard, 93
Military, language of, 162–175
Miller, Floyd, 95
Miller, Helen M., 95
Miller, Walter James, 94
Milton, John, 112, 113
Models of English courses, 8–17
Modern Approach to the Teaching of English, A (Conlin), 227
Moffet, James, 199
Momaday, N. Scott, 94
Mood, of composition, 190–192
Morin, Raul, 95
Motion Picture and the Teaching of English, The (Sheridan), 248
Motivation of students, 39–40, 52
"Musée des Beaux Arts" (Auden), 59–60, 86
My Darling, My Hamburger (Zindel), 92
"My Last Duchess" (Browning), 187

Naive psychology, 39, 40, 43
National Consortium on Educational Alternatives, 36
National Council of Teachers of English, 8–11, 24–25, 90, 118–119
Negativism, 273
Negro Literature for High School Students (Dodds), 91–92
New Indian, The (Steiner), 95
Newspapers:
  games with, 33
  underground, 42–43, 44
Nonfiction, teaching of, 87–89
Nongraded programs, 26–30
Non-teaching, 262
North from Mexico (McWilliams), 95
Norvell, George, 61, 98
Notebook, poetry, 238–239
Novel, teaching of, 78–79

Objectives (*see also* Behavioral objectives; Humanistic objectives):
  of elective course, 32
  of teaching English, 4–5
O'Hare, Frank, 229–231
Old Ones, The (Silverberg), 95
"One-Book Method," 285–286
Open classrooms, 34–36
Ordeal of Running Standing, The (Tall), 94
Ordering, in composition, 209
Organization:
  of an English course, 74–78
  of information, 126–130
  for instruction, 117–118, 285–303
  of questions, 281
Our Time Is Now (Birmingham), 42–43
Outcomes, learning, 22–23
Outline:
  of an elective course, 32
  of a film, 252–253
  teaching of, 211–212
Outnumbered, The (Brooks), 91
Outsiders, The (Hinton), 58
Overlap, in shooting film, 256

Painting of film, 249–250
"Parable of the Blind Men and the Elephant, The," 135–136
Paredes, Americo, 95
Participative democracy, 42, 43
Particle-wave-field theory, 208, 251–252
Patterns of symbols, 126–130
Peanuts (Schultz), 145
Pearl, The (Steinbeck), 96
Pentad, 241
Perception types, 114–118
Period, use of, 232
Perspective, selection of, 205–208
Phasing, 26–30
Philosophy of teaching English, 3–4
Phoebe (Dizenzo), 92
Piaget, Jean, 35, 50
Picasso, Pablo, 245
Pictures, selection of, 238–239
Pike, Kenneth, 207–208
Plays (*see* Drama)
Pocho (Villarreal), 93
Poe, Edgar Allen, 192
Poems to Solve (Swenson), 101
Poetry:
  asking questions about, 279–281
  background for, 58–60
  a multimedia unit on, 236–239
  teaching of, 83–87
Point of view, 140–141
Pooley, Robert, 120
Postman, Neil, 74, 112, 285–286
Pound, Ezra, 83
Pregnancy, literature about, 92
Prewriting:
  of a composition, 202–208
  of a film, 251
"Progressive Exercise," 64
Proximity of audience, 194–195
Psychology of Interpersonal Relations (Heider), 39
Puffed-up advertisements, 151
Punctuation, teaching of, 231–232
Purves, Alan C., 21–22

Question mark, use of, 232

Questioning:
  to promote discussion, 271–277
  systematic, 277–281

Ransom, John Crowe, 87
Readiness activities, 63, 64–66
Reading:
  basic teaching of, 53–54
  critical, 54, 62, 70–71
  oral, 237–238, 290
  silent, 289–290
Reagan, Ronald, 197
Referential language, 130–131, 136–139
Reflections on a Gift of Watermelon Pickle (Dunning et al.), 186
Reinforcement, 64–71, 81–82, 273, 276
Reluctant contributors, 272–273
Rephrasing, 276
Research, professional, 9–11, 50
Resource persons, 157–158
Restating, 276
Restricted code, 114–118
Revision, 216–220
Revolutionaries, 41–43
Rewards (*see* Reinforcement)
Rhetoric of Fiction, The (Booth), 54
Rhetorical process:
  defined, 201
  described, 202–221
"Richard Cory" (Robinson), 279–280
Richter, Conrad, 94
Riemer, Everett, 34
Robinson, Edward Arlington, 279–280
Robinson, Jackie, 90
Rodman, Bella, 91
Role playing, 70–71, 73, 184–185, 195 (*see also* Improvised drama)
Rosenblatt, Louise M., 15, 98
Roszak, Theodore, 41–42
Rubinstein, Bonnie, 57
Rules, classroom, 266–267

"Sailing to Byzantium" (Yeats), 85
Sanchez, George, 95

Sapir, Edwin, 111
Saturation, 150
School Is Dead (Riemer), 34
School Reform (Katz), 110
Science fiction, writing of, 58
Scrapbooks, poetry, 238–239
Scratching of film, 249–250
Screen direction, 257
Screen Writing and Production Techniques (Curran), 257
Script, shooting, 254–256
Self-identification, 40–41, 44, 91
  as literary theme, 76
Sentences, writing of, 223–231
Sequence:
  in composition, 209
  in shooting film, 256
  study of, 70
  in teaching, 301–303
Sequential programs, 9–11
Shapiro, Milton, 90
Sherburne, Zoa, 92
Sheridan, Marion C., 248
Shoes, as film topic, 252–254
Shooting script, 254–256
Short films, 247–248
Short stories, 79–81
Silverberg, Robert, 95
Skimming games, 33–34
Sledd, James, 116–117
Slide/tape presentation, 158–161, 239, 242–244
Smiley, Marjorie, 90
Smith, Hugh, 186
Smith, Jack E., 29
"Social Structure, Language, and Learning" (Bernstein), 114–115
Socrates, 100
Sohn, David A., 186, 248
Soul Brothers and Sister Lou, The (Hunter), 96
Soul on Ice (Cleaver), 88
Sound effects, 241
Sparke, William, 248
Speaking activities, types of, 291
Speaking voice approach, 190–200
Speech essay, 240–242

Spelling, 135
Splicing tape, 242
Steinbeck, John, 96
Steiner, Stan, 95
Stereotyped film topics, 257
Stone, George W., 9
Stop, Look, and Write (Leavitt and Sohn), 186
Students:
  assessment of, 37–45
  attitudes of, 14–16, 37, 54, 61–63, 98, 181–182, 275
  background of, 52–53, 56, 58–60, 62, 73, 75–76, 85–86
  criticism of, 137, 216–218
  and curriculum development, 28–29, 43
  grouping of, 117–118, 298–301
  motivation of, 39–40, 52
  variations among, 39, 45, 72–73, 113–118
Style:
  teaching, 261–283
  writing, 213–216
Subject statements, 205–208
Success in Reading, Book One (Burdett), 64
Summerfield, Geoffrey, 101
"Surveying the textbook" game, 34
Swenson, May, 101
Symbols, 124–130, 134–135
Syntax, 214, 223–231
Systems approaches, 19–25, 34

Tagmemic games, 207–208
Talbot, Charlene Joy, 93
Tall, Thomas, 94
Tapes, use of, 158–161, 239–244
Tarzian, James J., 93
Teachers:
  background of, 51–52, 62, 100
  education of, 38–39
  inadequacies of, 18–19
  role of, 37, 183, 189
  style of, 261–283
Teaching as a Subversive Activity (Postman and Weingartner), 112, 285–286

Teaching of High School English, The (Hook), 224–226
Technocracy, 41
"Telegraph Approach, The," 228–229
Testimonial, 151–152
Testing, 17, 29–30, 158, 173
Textbooks (*see also* Junior literature; Literature)
　games with, 34
　types of, 90–91, 285–286
That Bad Carlos (Lewiton), 93
Thematic organization, 75–78
Themes: Short Films for Discussion, 248
"Theories of Language Origin," 132
Thomas, Perri, 95
Thunder Rolling (Miller), 95
Tight drama, 295
Timing, 263, 268, 270, 287
Toffler, Alvin, 19
Tomas Takes Charge (Talbot), 93
Tone, in composition, 192–196, 199
Too Bad About the Haines Girl (Sherburne), 92
Topics:
　composition, 202–204
　film, 251–257
Tracking, effects of, 26
Transitions in classroom activities, 266
Tripod model, 8–11
"Trouble with Is, Is Is, The," 146
Two and the Town (Felsen), 92

Underground newspapers, 42–43, 44
Unique selling proposition, 152
United States Office of Education, 21, 24
Usage, 162–175, 190, 214–215
Uses of Film in the Teaching of English, The, 248

Vague reference, 151
Vanishing Adolescent, The (Friedenberg), 91

Variety, importance of, 264–265
Vasquez, Richard, 93
Viewing activities, 292–293
Villarreal, Jose Antonio, 93
Visual literacy, 236, 292–293
Visualmaker, 242
Visual persons, 114–118
Viva Chicano (Bonham), 93
Vocabulary games, 33
Voice:
　in composition, 190–192, 199
　projection of, 271

Walker, Jerry, 50
War, as course theme, 77
We Have Tomorrow (Bontemps), 90
Weingartner, Charles, 18–19, 74, 112, 113, 285–286
Weise, Donald F., 26–28
"What the World Needs Now Is Love" (Clay), 240
"When serpents bargain for the right to squirm" (Cummings), 84–85
When the Legends Die (Borland), 94
Whyte, William H., 51–52
Wilkinson, Andrew, 12–13
Willowbrook Cinema Study Project, 246–247
Will the Real Teacher Please Stand Up? (Greer and Rubinstein), 57
With a Pistol in His Hand (Paredes), 95
Wolfe, Thomas, 139
Word attack, 53, 64–66
Word choice, 190, 213–214, 270
Words, idea-bound, 135, 145
"Write-revise" exercise, 218–220
Writing (*see* Composition)

Yearbook, kinestasis, 251
Yeats, William Butler, 85

Zindel, Paul, 92